Educational Administration in Canada

Fifth Edition

T.E. Giles
A.J. Proudfoot

Detselig Enterprises Ltd.
Calgary, Alberta

T.E. Giles
A.J. Proudfoot

The University of Calgary

Canadian Cataloguing in Publication Data

Giles, T.E. (Thomas Edward)
    Educational administration in Canada

    Includes bibliographical references and index.
    ISBN 1-55059-086-3

    1. Education – Canada.   2. School management and
organization – Canada.   3. Teaching – Vocational guidance.   I.
Proudfoot, A.J. (Alexander James).   II. Title.
LB2890.G54   1994   370'.971   C94-910372-1

© 1994 by Detselig Enterprises Ltd.
210, 1220 Kensington Road N.W.
Calgary, Alberta T2N 3P5

Printed in Canada   SAN 115-0324   ISBN 1-55059-086-3

Preface

Educational Administration in Canada has touched many of the new teachers of the decades of the seventies, eighties and nineties. The decade of the seventies grew out of the changing social climate of the 1960s. Growth was vigorous. Times were good. Educational innovation was the thing. The 1980s was a time when we in Canada patriated our constitution and codified the rights and freedoms which were to be enjoyed by all Canadians. Educationally, we followed U.S. President Ronald Regan's advice, *we stayed the course,* even in the face of economic down times and increasing government deficits. Employment and trade dominated the thoughts of most politicians and many Canadians. In the decade of the nineties, as we move toward the 21st century, we are faced with restructuring of the system, downsizing of staffs and thus educational offerings, and entrenchment.

During this time the purpose of our text has remained constant, to freely admit that the central role of the teacher is to teach, but to call to the attention of the beginning teacher that there exists a very important supportive role to be performed, the administrative role of the teacher.

Educational Administration in Canada is directed to those education students who will soon be entering the classrooms of the nation as newly certified teachers. As with previous editions, the purpose of this edition is to examine the role of the teacher within the historical, legal, structural, and administrative settings as provided by the neighborhood, municipal, provincial, federal and professional communities.

Effective teaching requires considerable effort in planning and in the thoughtful execution of the many and varied responsibilities of competent practice.

The teacher has many publics to serve – the students, professional colleagues, central office staff, department of education officials, and parents, to name but a few. The teacher has many roles to play – instructor, counsellor, confidant, friend, colleague, and administrator. The teacher lives and works educationally in a number of communities – the neighborhood and its school; the various levels of municipal government, especially the school board and central office staff; the department of education and the various activities, services, laws and regulations to be found at that level; the national scene including the aspirations and desires of the Canadian people; and the community of professional teachers, all of which formulates a set of expectations upon the classroom teacher. It is not possible for the teacher to disregard these forces. However, by understanding the structure within which one operates, the teacher will be better able to cope – or at least, be better able to avoid some of the sanctions which can be brought to bear by different referent groups. By understanding the full range of responsibilities the teacher should be more able to perform as a fully professional employee.

Part One, Development of the Canadian Design for Education, provides first of all a brief description of the historical threads which come together to produce Canada's unique design for delivering education – a design which was formalized in the Canadian Constitution of 1867 (*British North America Act*); and second, because all major pieces of legislation must endure court challenges in order to establish the true meaning intended by the legislators who enacted the law. This proved to be especially true with respect to those sections which dealt with provincial control of education and the rights awarded to certain religious minorities, and linguistic groups.

Third, because of the central role played by Canadian provincial governments in the delivery of schooling, a chapter was devoted to describing the main features of the structure of a department of education. As the Canadian design for the governance of education was developed, school boards, the representatives of the local community, assumed an important role. Their role could not be overlooked in a text on educational administration. Someone said that "money makes the world go round"; true or not, it is well beyond dispute that the nature and level of educational financing is important in providing for the professional capabilities needed to educate children. Finally, Part One concludes with a short chapter on the involvement of the federal level of government.

Part Two of the book contains four chapters devoted to some of the legal concerns associated with the role of the teacher. One chapter is devoted to legal literacy, a second to the teacher's legal liability, a third to selected aspects of family law (child welfare legislation and the *Young Offender's Act*) and a concluding chapter on the topic of copyright violations. In this section we attempt to explain, in not too legal language, a number of issues central to the day-by-day responsibilities of being a Canadian teacher.

Part Three contains four chapters directed toward explaining the nature of the teacher's workplace as an organization; the authority and role of those school administrators most directly and closely associated with the classroom teacher, as well as describing a number of basic administrative and organizational concepts such as leadership, decision making, and school climate. Also included in this section are descriptions of effective schools and some of the supervisory processes and skills which make them so.

Current thinking on longitudinal and cross-sectional organization of the student body and a description of many of the administrative and clerical duties of the teacher make up Part Four which is entitled "Organizing the Schools." Teacher responsibilities regarding student attendance, detentions, suspensions, and expulsions and topics such as student control, student progress records, administration of student evaluation programs, report cards, and the problems of defamation (libel and slander) as it applies to the teachers. Communications and several other current topics have been included in Chapter 17, the longest chapter in the text. Administration of education from the teacher's perspective means doing all of these things, and more.

The final part of the book is devoted to topics associated with teaching as a profession. Included is a discussion as to whether teaching is indeed a professional calling, and of several important concepts associated with the quality of the teacher's work life, and a final chapter on that ever important topic – the teacher's pay cheque.

It is our hope that by using the table of contents, the index, and the side titles, the reader will be able to move efficiently through the textual materials to the issues which are of most pressing concern.

Thank you, and we wish you every success in a long and fruitful professional career in one of the more significant roles in Canadian society.

T.E.G. and A.J.P.

Contents

Detselig Enterprises Ltd. appreciates the financial assistance for its 1994 publishing program from the Department of Communications, Canada Council, and The Alberta Foundation for the Arts, a beneficiary of the Lottery Fund of the Government of Alberta.

Part One

Development of the Canadian
Design for Education

Education in Early Canada

In a land where the people are king, it is essential to educate the sovereign.
David Tyack, *Turning Points in American Educational History*

> Section 93, Canadian Constitution, 1867
>
> Education in New France
>
> The British Conquest
>
> Beginning of Separate Schools
>
> Early Education in Lower Canada
>
> Early Education in Upper Canada
>
> Influence of the United Empire Loyalists

Introduction

The passage by the British Parliament of the *British North America Act, 1867, (Constitution Act, 1867),* which brought Canada to the point of nationhood, and particularly Section 93 of that Act, which deals specifically with education, provides the teacher with a very convenient and useful division of Canadian educational history, especially in relation to the administrative structures which have evolved. The change in name of the 1867 Act was a product of the passage of the 1982 Constitution when our first Constitution (*British North America Act,* 1867 was patriated, modified by Canadian legislators and enlarged to include the *Canadian Charter of Rights and Freedoms,* a document of immense importance to teachers in their professional roles as school teachers, as well as in their position as Canadian citizens. The *Constitution Act,* 1982, was proclaimed on April 17, 1982. Section 15 of the *Charter of Rights and Freedoms,* (equality rights) however, did not come into force until April 17, 1985. Equality rights (before and under law) are the subject of a considerable portion of the latter part of this text, but for the purposes of this chapter attention is drawn to another important part of the 1982 Act.

patriation

Section 93 of the *British North America Act, 1867,* granted the provinces sovereign power over education and guaranteed, by force of the Parliament of Canada, that certain specified citizens would enjoy denominational rights respecting their schools. However, because the *B.N.A. Act,* 1867, was an act of the British Parliament, pre-patriation activities had to ensure that these rights were maintained in our new constitution. The *Canada Act,* 1982, also an act of the British Parliament, granted Canada sovereignty over her own constitution. It then became the responsibility of the Canadian Parliament to pass the

sovereign power

British North
America Act

Canadian constitutions, to ensure that the Canadian design for education, the federal-provincial division of powers and other matters, which had been hammered out by pre-Confederation negotiation, remained intact. The *British North America Act* was renamed the *Constitution Act,* 1867, and *Article 29* of the *Constitution Act,* 1982 was drafted to read:

> Nothing in this Charter abrogates or derogates from any rights or privileges guaranteed by or under the Constitution of Canada in respect of denominational, separate or dissentient schools.

Without getting into details, and before describing the historical development of Canadian education as it exists today, it is interesting to note that both Canada and the United States, as they carved nationhood out of the New World, experimented with the federal system of government. Federalism was not a system from the old world, transplanted into the new world. New ideas were being implemented as new nations were being developed out of a vast North American wilderness. Although we accepted many United States practices, especially those relating to local control of schools and curriculum design, we approached the division of federal-provincial (state) powers, especially those respecting education and the inclusion of religion within schools, quite differently.

residual
powers

The Constitution of the United States specifies the powers of the Federal Government. Those powers not specifically mentioned are termed "residual powers" and are thus powers which fall to the several states. Control over education is not specified in the United States Constitution, thus it falls within the power of the state governments. However, in the first Canadian constitution (1867) education was specified as an exclusive right of the provincial governments. "In and for each Province the legislature may exclusively make laws in relation to Education, subject, and according to the following provisions." This was done for good and calculated reasons – in short, to ensure that schools remained in the control of provincial governments, especially the government of the Province of Quebec.

church
and state

As the subsequent subsections of Section 93 (which follows) are studied, it is noted that certain classes of persons (Roman Catholics and Protestants), provided they are the religious minority in the community, enjoy the right to separate schools. The United States constitution, however, specifies there be a strict separation between church and state, thus the provision of our type of separate schools would be clearly unconstitutional south of the border. The United States permits a system of parochial (religious private schools) to satisfy the religious/educational needs of religious minorities. The principle of the separation of church and state has been affirmed by the American courts in numerous judgments over the past two hundred years.

The sections which follow will attempt to tell our story; a story which in many ways is very different from the American story. The clear delineation of the provinces' sovereign power over education came early in Canadian history. Section 93 of the *Constitution Act,* states:

In and for each Province the Legislature may exclusively make Laws in relation to Education, subject and according to the following provisions:

1. Nothing in any such law shall prejudicially affect any Right or Privilege with respect to Denominational Schools which any Class of Persons have by Law in the Province at the Union:

2. All the Powers and Privileges, and Duties at the Union by Law conferred and imposed in Upper Canada on the Separate Schools and School Trustees of the Queen's Roman Catholic Subjects shall be and the same are hereby extended to the Dissentient Schools of the Queen's Protestant and Roman Catholic Subjects in Quebec:

3. Where in any Province a System of Separate or Dissentient Schools exists by law at the Union or is thereafter established by the Legislature of the Province, an Appeal shall lie to the Governor-General-in-Council from any Act or Decision of any Provincial Authority affecting any Right or Privilege of the Protestant or Roman Catholic Minority of the Queen's Subjects in relation to Education:

4. In case any such Provincial Law as from Time to Time seems to the Governor-General-in-Council requisite for the due Execution of the Provisions of this Section is not made, or in case any Decision of the Governor-General-in-Council on any Appeal under this Section is not duly executed by the proper Provincial Authority in that Behalf, then and in every such case, and as far only as the Circumstances of each Case require, the Parliament of Canada may make remedial Laws for the due Execution of the Provisions of this Section and of any Decision of the Governor-General-in-Council under this Section.

The limitations imposed upon the exercise of provincial educational authority as listed in Section 93 were designed to protect the existence of denominational or separate schools which had been legally established by the two religious minorities prior to Confederation. Historical records and later judicial actions substantiate that the intention of the provisos appended to the lead sentence of Section 93, subsections 1 to 4, was to protect the religious, rather than the language rights, which have become the focus of recent controversy.

denominational schools

The division of responsibility for education in Canada at the senior levels of government is unique at least among the older nations which contributed to Canadian cultural heritage. The following pages explores this further.

The purpose of this chapter is to review briefly the events which lead to the enunciation of Section 93. Events which followed passage of the *Constitution Act, 1867*, and which gave substance to, and further defined the intent of the Canadian nation with respect to the legal structure of education, will be reviewed in the next chapter.

If personal time permits, the Canadian teacher is encouraged to devote a few hours to studying, in depth, a most fascinating history – the history of education in Canada. This activity is not only entertaining but also provides a useful backdrop against which to consider current educational events and structures which impinge upon the administrative role.

fabric
of society

Trite but true, a country's educational system is inescapably part of its social, political, and economic substance. No less so, the history of a nation's educational institutions is interwoven in the fabric of its early social, political and economic life. For Canada, the constitutional provisions as set forward in Section 93 were in large measure the adoption of a pattern which had been established many years previously through the interchange of the old and the new worlds in a unique geographic and cultural setting.

parish schools

grammar
schools

Our early schools were modeled upon the parish schools of pre-revolutionary France and the petty and grammar schools of 18th and 19th century Britain. These institutions sought to perpetuate the social and cultural backgrounds of the early Canadian settlers. However, the cultural traditions which they sought to perpetuate were indigenous to Europe and the products of hundreds of years of the social conditions characteristic of Europe. The North American wilderness presented conditions to the early settlers which were quite foreign and in many instances very harsh. The Old World was, for the most part, built upon a class structure consisting of an educated and privileged elite and a semi-literate lower class of artisans and peasants. With few exceptions, this structure was simply not operative in the American wilderness, and further it was not in tune with the emerging social democracy of the New World setting. Educational systems built upon foreign social and economic structures cannot maintain their viability for long. They must give way to changing circumstances, and so the early history of education in Canada is a description of how the inhabitants adjusted their schooling system to these new and changing circumstances. This was not easy, since one clings to what one understands and values. People cling to their heritage, even in the face of harsh circumstances. People strive to model their schools upon the familiar, but this is not always possible.

Social, political and economic events and circumstances, in Upper and Lower Canada are of particular importance in shaping the education provisions of the *Constitution Act,* 1867.

Education in New France

New France, for the purposes of the story of the development of Canadian education, is designated as those areas of French settlement along the shore of the St. Lawrence River and in Acadia. The purposes for establishing the colony

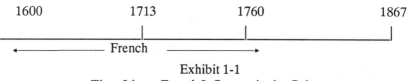

Exhibit 1-1
Time Line – French Influence in the Colony

fur trade

were threefold: first, for profit to the French merchants hoping to gain through the fur trade; second, for the development of agriculture through the granting of free land; and third, to further the burgeoning missionary spirit of the Roman

Catholic Counter-Reformation. The fur traders and habitants were accompanied by men and women "of the cloth" desirous of spreading Christianity among the natives. Current events often question this practice, but at that time it was considered the right and proper thing to do, in the name of The Church. In particular, the Jesuits made heroic efforts to bring their faith to these people. The newly-arrived habitants were French. Education was under the control and sponsorship of the church in collaboration with the parents. This design was not unusual, indeed, it was very natural, since in France, education, hospitals, and social welfare activities, services which we today consider to be the responsibility of civic authorities, were under the control and sponsorship of *The Church*. In this respect the church functioned as the civil service.

Jesuits

New France followed a known and established pattern. There was but one authority in religious and educational matters, the Bishop. He made all decisions of any consequence. Settlements were, for the most part, based upon a parochial structure with civic, educational, and social activities centring around the church and under the watchful guidance of the parish priest and his senior, the Bishop. There were no secular laws governing the operation of schools in New France prior to the British conquest. The Bishop's control and financial support of the schools had the complete support of the civil authorities of the day. Thus, the parish priests kept a careful watch over the education of their young parishioners and carried out the educational decisions of their Bishop. Simple, straight-forward, understood and accepted by the people, best describe the administrative procedures of the early days of the new colony.

the Bishop

parochial structure

The educational efforts of the Church in New France bore a striking resemblance to its efforts in France. In 1685 there were 36 established parishes in New France. By 1756, just prior to the British conquest, this number had grown to 88 (one-half of which were financially self-supporting); there were 16 parishes served by neighboring churches, and 19 places "in need" of a church. Thus, by the middle of the 18th century the parish structure of school governance was well established and flourishing in the colony.

The parish school, frequently indistinguishable physically from the parish church, offered a rudimentary basic education consisting of catechism, reading, writing, arithmetic, a little grammar, no geography, and for the gifted, the rudiments of Latin. By the standards of the times, the quality of education offered in New France compared favorably with that offered in France itself. This was due in large measure to the untiring efforts of the priests and sisters, many of whom possessed an excellent general and pedagogical education provided by the seminaries and convents of their mother country. The Jesuits, Ursulines, Recollets, Sulpicians, Frères Charon, and the sisters of the Congregation of Notre Dame carried the major burden of providing schooling. The Ursuline sisters concentrated their efforts on providing education to the daughters of the wealthy but with some primary instruction being offered to the daughters of the poor. On the other hand, the Jesuit fathers were heavily involved in evangelizing the native population and, in the instances where they

pedagogical education

Collège
Laval

classical
education

Ursuline
Sisters

land grants

elitist
dominated

entered into serious educational endeavors, they followed the pattern of their European order by providing for advanced instruction. As a consequence, Canada's first college and seminary was established in Quebec in 1635, an institution which later became Laval University, and as Canadian historians are quick to point out, an institution of higher learning which predated Harvard College by two years. It is also important to note that the Jesuit College was modelled upon similar Jesuit colleges in France and thus it introduced the tradition of a classical education into the new colony. (This tradition remained strong in Quebec education.) The work of the orders based in Europe was assisted by Canadian orders such as the Brothers Hospitallers of the Cross and the sisters of the Congregation of Notre Dame. The efforts of the religious orders were augmented somewhat by the work of devoted lay teachers.

In almost all instances schools were operating with the solid support of the parents. The education of young ladies as provided for by the Ursuline and Notre-Dame Sisters, for example, was regarded by most authorities as being exceptionally fine. The quality of education for young men was not, however, of a comparable level. This was not due to any lack of effort or skill on the part of the Jesuit priests and those involved with male education, but was probably more a factor of the times, the need for young men to engage in the industries of the parish.

There was no direct public support, in the form of taxes, for education during the French Regime, but The Church did receive large land grants in support of education. Further, the King of France made direct cash grants to the Bishop in support of education in the colony and, thus, the reader is urged to recognize that government support was, even at this early date, being made available to schools. The Bishop was generous in his financial support. Religious orders sacrificed themselves to provide elementary education and the few lay teachers who were available were not less devoted. The colonists gave freely whenever the church needed money for education.

Most authorities agree that the educational system operated well and thus it had made the necessary adjustments to New World conditions found in the French settlements. This is surprisingly so since during the early years of the French settlement there had been no attempts to establish a permanent settlement. However, the early settlers had persevered. There existed episcopal, monastic and also charitable schools for the orphans, and an elitist-denominated secondary education, provided mostly by the Jesuits. The quality and extensiveness of schooling was not high by today's standards but the parish schools appeared to meet the requirements of the parents and the church.

A brief chronology:

1608 – Population of Quebec City, 28 persons.

1616 – First school established in Trois Rivières, with Brother Pacifique Duplessis as teacher.

1633 – Recorded that Jesuit priests were teaching Indian boys.

– Jesuits establish first elementary school in Quebec.

– Collège de Quebec opened; the only secondary school in Canada prior to 1760. By 1661, the college was providing an education preparatory to a religious life. The site is now occupied by Quebec's City Hall.

1641 – Population of New France recorded as 500. This is compared to the 40 000 living in other European colonies in North America.

1655 – The Jesuits extended the instruction of the elementary school which they had established in Quebec, to include the secondary level.

1665 – The Seminary of Laval was established. This later became Canada's first university.

1666 – The population of New France was 3 418 persons – one-half of whom lived in Trois Rivières, Quebec, and Montreal.

1689 – The population of New France was approximately 12 000.

1700 – The Fourth Synod of Quebec spelled out the priests' responsibility to supervise those who operated the schools..

1760 – Population of New France was almost 85 000. The parish school system was operating satisfactorily. Changes were imminent.

In summary, education in New France was a product of the Old World institutions modelled closely upon French society (where educational institutions were strictly controlled by the church) and the needs of New World colony sitting on the edge of a wilderness frontier. "The Canadiens appreciated education only to the extent that it proved useful in this practical sense, and the church schools, while never abandoning their classical/liberal foundations, responded by offering 'useful' knowledge and skills as well." (Titley & Miller, 1982, p. 14). In summary, as Henchey and Burgess (1987, p. 22) state:

church
initiatives

> In spite of church initiatives, general conditions in the young colony did not encourage much interest in education and schooling. The early preoccupation with the fur trade, the harsh environment and the lack of significant numbers of settlers caused the Catholic colony of New France to grow far more slowly than the Protestant Colonies of New England to the south.

The British Conquest of Canada

Exhibit 1-2
Time Line – English Influence in the Colony

Seven
Years' War

The French were numerically inferior to the British and were thus unable to defend the large tract of land which they had claimed in North America. This fact plus other European events lead to a French defeat in the Seven Years' War.

In 1760 the British had conquered Canada. This period of our educational history is frequently referred to as the British Regime (1760-1867). The conquest had profound social, political and educational consequences for the residents of New France. It introduced a new religion, and a new political and social life. What influence did this have? In a word, considerable. There were strong indications that France relinquished her colony (acres of snow in Voltaire's terms) with no particular regrets. Civic officials and many clergy returned to France. No new clergy, the backbone of the colony's educational

abandoned

system, were sent out, and those who elected to remain seemed abandoned by the French authorities. Perhaps this statement is overly harsh, but certainly they did not receive the encouragement and support to which they had become accustomed.

The residents of new France had become very dependent upon the mother country for government, educational structures, commerce, and cultural leadership. They now felt abandoned so, even more than before, they turned to the Catholic church. The Church continued to assume a predominant role in the lives of the French-speaking population. The acceptance of the Roman Catholic church as a major cultural support to the people of New France, in the face of their conquerors, provides the historical roots for the "religion" provision of the 1867 Constitution. Historically, the French inhabitants believed the *The Church*, through its teaching and dogma, was the "carrier" of their French culture. Current events now point toward the French language as the accepted major "carrier" of the French culture in Canada. The Catholic Church was being

Anglicans

challenged however by the Anglican religion of the British conquerors, thus setting the stage for the denominational division of the school system into Roman Catholic and Protestant tracks.

The educational system was neglected, and the system of parish schools deteriorated. Very little monetary support was available for education and certainly the British were not prepared to provide government funds for education. They did not provide state funds to support education at home, so why would they provide funding for the newly acquired colony?

A brief chronology:

1713 – Britain acquired Nova Scotia (the former French colony of Acadia) by the *Treaty of Utrecht*.

1758 – The first representative assembly, the Nova Scotia Assembly, met in October.

– Britain captured Louisburg (Cape Breton).

1763 – *Treaty of Paris* ended the Seven Years' War between Britain and France (Quebec City had been captured by the British in September 1759, and Montreal in September, 1760).

 – French law was abolished by Royal Proclamation.

1766 – British civil agencies protested the practice of trying to administer justice in Canada in the French language and without the benefit of local usages and customs.

1769 – Prince Edward Island was separated from Nova Scotia and established as a separate political entity with an elected assembly.

1774 – The *Quebec Act* restored French civil law to the "Province of Quebec," but required that English criminal law remain in place. (Full Roman Catholic freedom of religion, tithe collection, and property rights were confirmed.)

1784 – New Brunswick was separated from Nova Scotia and established as a separate entity with an elected assembly.

1791 – The *Constitutional Act* repealed large parts of the *Quebec Act*. Of special significance, it divided "The Province of Quebec" into Upper and Lower Canada, each with its own legislative assembly as had been done in Prince Edward Island, and New Brunswick.

1840 – The *Act of Union* united Upper and Lower Canada into the "The Province of Canada." "Canada" had one Legislative Assembly and one Legislative Council with equal representation for English and French. Later this changed as the English population exceeded the French in numbers.

1848 – Nova Scotia and the Province of Canada were granted the powers of responsible government.

1864 – The Charlottetown and Quebec Conferences laid the foundations for confederation.

1865 – The seventy-two resolutions drafted at Charlottetown and Quebec City were adopted. Section 43(6) became Section 93 of the *British North America Act, (Constitution Act,* 1867).

1866 – The London, England conference, a prelude to the passing of the *British North America Act,* was held.

1867 – February 21, 1867, the *British North America Act* was ratified by the British Parliament. Canada commenced the drive to true nationhood which it finally achieved in 1982.

Following the British conquest, an economic recession struck the Canadian colony. The *state* was attempting to play a new role by supplanting the church as governing authority in educational matters. Coordination and centralization of education, as well as in other governmental matters, were considered necessary. These factors resulted in a decided deterioration in the quality and quantity of education available to the inhabitants. This picture is not pretty, but accurate.

Treaty
of Paris

The period following the *Treaty of Paris* (1763) saw the two races in confrontation, wherein the English felt that understanding and acceptance would be found in assimilation while the French were attempting to preserve their religious and civic laws. Periods of confrontation and compromise ensued and perhaps we have not as yet emerged from those times. In any case, a major area of confrontation and compromise was education. This is the story of the *Constitution Act*, 1867 and particularly Section 93. However, there are many factors and events which intervened before Canada achieved nationhood, the major ones of which will be related at this time.

The Beginning of Separate (Dissentient) Schools

Treaty
of Utrecht

By the terms of the *Treaty of Utrecht* in 1713 and through which France restored to Britain the territories around Hudson Bay and the Island of Newfoundland, the French habitants were permitted one year to return to France. If they did not elect to return, they were guaranteed, among other things, free exercise of their religion (Roman Catholicism). This item in the *Treaty of Utrecht* provided sufficient precedent for a similar guarantee in the *Treaty of Paris* (1763), which ended the Seven Years' War and through which the British gained the territories which are referred to as New France. Historians appear to agree that the British showed no particular hostility toward the French language or the Roman Catholic religion at that time. The motives for this apparent tolerance are sometimes obscured, but they probably relate more to fear of colonial uprisings than to any feelings of either animosity or genuine understanding.

Treaty
of Paris

As later events unfold, it becomes apparent that the actions of the British in guaranteeing free exercise of religion to the French inhabitants was sufficient in itself to set the basis for the establishment and nurturing of the separate and denominational school systems of Canada.

The Beginning of English Education in the Newly Acquired Colony

British parents'
petition

By 1768, there were sufficient English speaking residents to cause the parents to petition the British governor for a teacher. Five years later, in 1773, the Governor received a petition requesting a Protestant school in Quebec City. That same year, the English residents of Montreal secured a school master, and by 1789, they requested governmental assistance to finance their school. Thus, historically, the initiative for separate schools came from the British, not the French.

Quebec Act

Backing up in the sequence of events, due to a number of circumstances, the British deemed it advisable to soften their earlier stance with respect to the French; so, in 1774, the *Quebec Act* was passed. Besides the civil consequences of restoring the French legal system as being better suited to the traditions of the people, and modifying the land holding system in favor of the French seigniorial system, the educational consequences abounded in that the British once again guaranteed free exercise of religion to the adherents of the Church of Rome, and affirmed the government's right to give recognition of and support to the Protestant religion. The short-range consequence of the *Quebec Act* was the anger of the English merchants, however, and the French Canadians, who were scarcely affected by politics and the commerce of the day, appear to have devoted themselves to clearing the land and raising their families. Most paid little attention to either the new act or to the British.

The British continued their efforts to establish a strong centralized civic and educational system under the control of the Governor and small ruling class. In 1789 a Committee of Council recommended the establishment of a free parish or village school in each community and a superior school in each central town of a county, plus a non-denominational college for the liberal arts and sciences to serve the colony. This educational system was to be governed by the judges, Roman Catholic and Protestant Bishops, and ten laypersons. Religious opposition, founded upon fears of complete central control of education by the government and undue Protestant influence, made this plan unacceptable. The stalemate, however, did not end at this point.

superior
schools

The Committee's recommendations became law under an 1801 act. The migration of the United Empire Loyalists to the Maritimes, Upper St. Lawrence Valley and Niagara Peninsula introduced a third factor, the tradition of local self-government and common schools. The British authorities were now faced with the problem of designing a constitution for Canada which would accommodate three potent influences, the French Catholic, the British Protestant and the United Empire Loyalist. The *Constitutional Act* of 1791 was the result of their efforts. It divided Canada into Upper Canada (predominantly British and Anglican) and lower Canada (predominantly French and Roman Catholic). As later events illustrate, this did little to ease passage into nationhood – the "great compromise" as confederation is frequently called. Divisions remained strong.

United Empire
Loyalists

Constitution
Act

Developments in Lower Canada

The recommendations of the 1789 Committee of Council did not remain dormant. In 1801, its recommendations were modified somewhat in an attempt to make them more acceptable to the inhabitants and were then enacted under *"An Act for the Establishment of Free Schools and the Advancement of Learning in this Province."* The 1801 Act established a non-sectarian school in each parish and a superior school in central towns (the first public schools in Quebec). Instruction was to be given in the mother tongue and religious instruction could be offered by the local priests or ministers.

1801 Act

The establishment of the non-sectarian parish (official or royal) school was to be made by a free decision of the parish through a petition whenever a majority of the citizens indicated their desire for one, and their willingness to pay for it. Further, provisions were made to exempt all schools operated by religious orders, and those private schools existing prior to 1801. And further, it was recognized that schools established under this Act in Catholic parishes would be Catholic; those established in Protestant parishes would be Protestant.

royal schools

As a consequence, two types of schools were recognized – official or Royal and separate or private. Under the law, a seventeen member board called the Royal Institute was to be established to administer these new schools. This proved to be a daring attempt to organize a public educational system. However, fears of a single central authority made the plan inoperative.

Finally, in the year 1818, the Royal Institute for the Advancement of Learning, although it had been established in the 1801 Act to serve as the Ministry of Education, came into being through the nomination of members to the board. The Royal Institute met with considerable opposition, mainly from the Roman Catholic priests. This should not have come as any surprise to the legislators since 13 of the 17 board members were Protestants and the Chairman was the Anglican Bishop. School regulations were published in 1820 and in 1823, but few royal or official schools were established and those that were, were short-lived. Only schools of the Royal Institute could receive government support, and only Protestants (Anglicans) could teach in them. Many of the French people believed that the purpose of this structure was not to provide schooling. They believed the educational benefits were the last thing being considered; proselytizing to one belief seemed to be the more important goal. While the Anglicans seemed to be in almost complete control, it proved to be a losing battle because their numbers were so few, so the *Fabric Act* of 1824 was passed. It permitted individual parishes to establish schools under the control of the church vestry. By 1826, Governor Dalhousie, in an attempt to overcome the difficulties experienced by the Royal Institute, suggested two systems – Roman Catholic and Protestant – each to have management rights over its own schools. This suggestion was later modified to propose two committees be established with the Royal Institute, a suggestion which came to fruition. (This action provided the framework for the current educational structure in the Province of Quebec.)

By an act passed in 1829, the *Legislative Assembly Schools Act* (*Sundics Act*), the Legislature of Lower Canada was given supreme authority over schools. A permanent committee on education and schools, called the Committee of the Assembly on Education, was established. The Act also provided for annual grants for teachers, buildings, and poor students. Further, provisions were made to permit a community to form a local school authority and elect school trustees where there were twenty or more students. This action initiated the practice of placing schools under the control of a locally elected school board rather than a church body. No mention was made of denominational schools although, in fact, that is what they were. The right to establish secular common schools had been legitimized. This, in turn, eventually led to two distinct denominational school systems for the Province of Quebec. As we entered Confederation the wording of Section 93(1) became:

> 1. Nothing in any such law shall prejudicially affect any Rights or Privileges with respect to Denominational Schools which any Class of Persons have by law in the Province at the Union.

Marginal notes:
- Royal Institute
- Anglican control
- Fabric Act
- Sundics Act
- elected trusttees
- secular common schools

The *Legislative Assembly Schools Act* was successful in encouraging the establishment of a large number of schools in Lower Canada in the ensuing years. By the mid-1830s there were in excess of 1 200 schools in operation. The majority were public schools managed by elected trustees. A few were Royal schools, some were parish corporation (fabrique) schools, others were private religious schools.

private religious schools

What had been established through the years was the knowledge that any successful system of education for Quebec would have to be built upon the co-existence of the French Catholics and the English Protestants.

Developments in Upper Canada

Upper Canada was created in 1791 by provisions of the *Constitutional Act* whereby this part of the colony, basically present-day Ontario, was separated from Lower Canada, basically present-day Quebec. Each part was provided with its own legislative assembly.

Constitutional Act

Seven years after the province of Upper Canada had been created, the first land grants were awarded in support of grammar schools and a university. In 1807 an act, entitled *Act to Establish Public Schools in Each and Every District of This Province*, was passed. It made provisions for the establishment of eight school districts, each managed by an appointed board of five trustees. Further, each district was to receive £100 to support the hiring of a teacher, thereby introducing the concept of direct government grants to cover operating expenses. The term "public school," as used in the 1807 Act, referred to public school education in the English tradition, i.e., what we would currently in Canada call private schools. Much of this movement was headed by John Strachan, a Scot who converted and eventually became the Anglican Bishop of Toronto. As early as 1791 there had been pressure and by 1807 the *District Public School Act* had authorized the establishing of eight schools which were known to cater to the children of the middle and especially the upper classes. The curriculum was British.

1807 Act

Strachan

District Public School Act

The United Empire Loyalists

United Empire Loyalists

Exhibit 1-3
Time Line – United Empire Loyalists Influence

The *Common School Act* of 1816 moved the province of Upper Canada quickly toward the concept of public school education in the American tradi-

local option

tion. There had developed a considerable negative reaction to Strachan's schools (in the British mold) so by 1816 pressure for the establishment of common schools was mounting. Both types of schools (British and common) received state funding but by 1840 the distribution of government support had become so distorted that the "British" schools were receiving approximately nine times the support per student as was being received by the newly established common schools. The influence of the United Empire Loyalists, those independent people who, although loyal to the British cause, enjoyed the freedoms and traditions of local self-government to which they had grown accustomed in the American states, had a considerable impact upon our educational structure. The *Common School Act* 1816 also made provisions for what was called a local option, that is, when a community had grown to a size where it had twenty-five or more school-age children it was permitted to elect three trustees whose responsibility it was to provide a schoolhouse, nominate a teacher, recommend textbooks, and make other regulations for the governance of the schools. As a consequence, a system of state-supported education (common schools) became established in Upper Canada. By the year 1838 the Upper Canada school system had 651 schools, with an estimated total enrollment of 14 700 students.

Act of Union

The *Act of Union* passed by the British Parliament in 1840, and proclaimed in Montreal in February 1841, united Upper and Lower Canada under a single Representative Assembly with equal representation from the two provinces. At this point the history of the development of education in English Canada became inextricably tied to developments in French Canada. In earlier legislation, the *School Act* of 1841, the Assembly had created the position of Superintendent of Education with two assistants – one from Upper Canada and one from Lower Canada. This Act also granted the municipal districts that had been created in 1840, the responsibility of receiving money for school purposes and raising additional funds by school taxes. Prior to the union of Upper and Lower Canada, Upper Canada has been largely rural and self-sufficient. By mid-century, growth in population and industrialization, especially in Toronto, changed the way of life of the inhabitants and thus the need for, and the direction to be taken by, education.

Ryerson

Egerton Ryerson, a person of immense influence in public education in Ontario and Western Canada, was appointed Chief Superintendent of Education in 1846. Ryerson was among a number of educational leaders in Europe and North America (Horace Mann of Massachusetts being another) who believed that widespread social and technical advances and increased urbanization dictated that changes must be made in schooling. He had travelled extensively to review schools, especially in Europe, before accepting the appointment. Ryerson looked to the schools to inculcate loyalty and patriotism and to foster social cohesion, self-reliance, and social change. He had a strong belief in free public education.

> One of the most formidable obstacles to the universal diffusion of education and knowledge is class isolation and class exclusiveness – where the highest

grades of society are wholly severed from the lower in responsibility, obligation, and sympathy . . . and where the mean of liberal education regard the
education of the masses as an encroachment upon their own domains, or beneath
their care or notice. The feeble and most needy, as also the most numerous
classes, are thus rendered still feebler by neglect, while the educated and more
wealthy are rendered still stronger by monopoly. (Egerton Ryerson 1851 –
Annual Report for 1850 as found in Alison Prentice *The School Promoters*).

He was also intent upon diminishing the Anglican control over schooling.
He believed that education should be involved in moral socialization, but he
also believed that it should be secular in design. In 1845, 1846, 1849 and 1851,
four distinct acts were passed with respect to education in Canada. These acts,
among other things, charged school trustees independent from municipal
councils with the responsibility of administering the common schools. They
defined the duties of teachers; defined the roles of superintendents; set forward
the methods for appraisal of property for taxation purposes; created examining
boards for inspecting teachers, and established normal schools for training
teachers. These were ideas associated with Egerton Ryerson.

four education acts

Other actions which further determined the Canadian design were the
establishment of the position of French Superintendent of Schools in 1845, and
the provision for denominational school systems in Montreal and Quebec City
in 1846. Prior to this date Protestant and Roman Catholic districts had existed,
but they were not so clearly defined as the labelling Montreal Catholic, or
Montreal Protestant now provided for. In 1864, funding was provided to the
Protestant Association of Teachers in Quebec. Backing up a moment to pick
up the separate school question again, in 1841 an act respecting religious
minorities was applied to Upper Canada. It stated that those professing a
religious faith different from the majority in a township or parish would be
permitted to dissent collectively from the common schools; to signify their
desire to establish a separate school; to elect trustees to govern their school, and
to receive public support in proportion to the number of students enrolled. This
act stressed, however, that separate schools and separate trustees would be
governed by the same regulations as those governing the majority (common)
schools.

French superintendent

association of teachers

An 1845 act respecting religious minorities in Lower Canada (Canada East)
provided similar provisions as the 1841 Act had for Upper Canada (Canada
West). However, it extended the terms of the 1841 Act to make provisions for
trustees of separate schools to levy taxes on their own supporters. A similar
adjustment was extended to Upper Canada in 1863 through provisions of the
Separate School Act, which also provided that separate schools could share in
municipal as well as provincial grants. Further, it became possible to establish
separate schools (Roman Catholic schools were being addressed) in rural areas.
But the separate schools so established were required to accept provincial
school inspectors, provincial control of the curriculum and textbooks, and
government control over teacher education. This act became the basis of
Ontario's separate school system and a model for all parts of western Canada.

separate school trustees

In summary, in the quarter century between 1841 and 1867, two provincial systems became firmly established. In Upper Canada (Canada West) a solid municipally based structure was established in which the administration of the common schools became an important part, but with provisions for dissentient schools. In Lower Canada (Canada East), the parish divisions were retained and the confessional (Roman Catholic and Protestant) character of both common and dissentient schools were encouraged by differences in curriculum, textbooks, and the qualifications and training of teachers.

Although Upper and Lower Canada differed in many details, principally those noted above, a common basic Canadian pattern had been established with regard to the structuring of responsibility for education. In general terms, a shared responsibility between the provincial level which assumed responsibility for the educational system including such matters as the curriculum, training and certification of teachers, and the local level which had responsibility for the actual operation of the schools through their powers to employ teachers, construct and maintain school buildings, and raise and expend money for day-to-day operations. Shared responsibility extended also to the financing of education. Schooling was supported by a combination of government grants and local tax levies. Chapter Five provides the reader with an overview of educational funding.

shared
responsility

> A school house is no longer a matter of choice but of necessity. It is now fairly generally understood that if a community desires its youth to keep pace with the march of events going on almost everywhere, it must educate them; to neglect to do this would be to make them pariahs in society – hewers of wood and drawers of water for their better educated neighbors. *The Stratford Examiner*, in 1869 (found in Alison Prentice *The School Promoters*).

The setting in which the various education acts of the middle 1800s were drafted included the following beliefs. First, that all children should have the benefits of some elementary schooling. Second, that the management of schools should be taken out of private hands and that the state should be the central agency in the control of schooling. Third, that within the framework of central control, the parents should have some choices as to which school system their children would attend (mainly church related schooling with the aid of tax support). Fourth, a pervasive view held that responsible government is the best kind of government, but that the elected trustees in small local school districts did not care to see beyond their own boundaries and did not understand how what happened educationally in their jurisdiction affected the whole country. These local folks did not understand (the view of some cabinet ministers and senior civil servants) that their narrow view of schooling and their attempts to run schools as cheaply as possible ultimately affected the life chances of individual students.

1800s education
beliefs

The *Constitution Act* of 1867 brought Canada to nationhood. Spurred by a desire to keep Canada British in the face of the threat from the United States, influential statesmen performed a number of political maneuvers and reached a number of compromises which laid the framework for Confederation.

Because schools were essentially local in nature and because the education of the young is so closely related to matters of language, religion, customs, and values, fears of centralization at the federal level and the consequent loss of local autonomy ran high prior to the drafting of the *Consitution Act.* Education became a major area of compromise as the Fathers of Confederation set about the task of drafting a framework for the new nation.

fear of centralization

minority rights

The solution, although difficult to arrive at, was very simple. Education was retained as a provincial responsibility, that is, it became the prerogative of the provincial governments to make laws respecting education. This pattern had become well-established by the colonists. It became simply a matter of recognizing it formally in Section 93 of the *Constitution Act*, 1867. Secondly, the colonists had established provisions whereby minority religious groups could dissent from the common schools. These rights were protected through subsections one to three of Section 93, with a further provision through subsection four for remedial action in the instances where the rights of the minority were disregarded.

The reader will note that this brief summary concentrated upon educational developments in two areas, first New France, French Canada, Lower Canada, Canada East which became the Province of Quebec, and second English Canada, Upper Canada, Canada West which became the Province of Ontario. These two areas were selected to illustrate the influence of the French, the British, and the Americans upon Canada's unique design. Much could have been written about matters such as classical education, social reconstruction through schooling, technical education, or pedagogical training, but the central features of the Canadian design seem to us to be central control of decision making, provincial control of education, the central place of the common schools (with provisions for private schools and other alternatives), locally elected school boards, shared local and central financing, and the presence of denominational religious education through separate schools (the provision for dissent in the Protestant/Catholic tug-of-war over schooling).

The Provinces of Canada

Chapter Two provides a number of illustrations as to how political action and inaction, and the decrees of the courts defined and refined what was intended in 1867. A brief section on the effects of the Charter of Rights and Freedoms is included. A fuller discussion on the Charter's possible legal impacts has been included in Part Two, Chapter Seven.

Province	Notes		Date Admitted to Confederation
New Brunswick			1867
Nova Scotia		The original	1867
Ontario (Upper Canada before 1840)	The "Province of Canada"	four provinces signing the B.N.A. Act in 1867	1867
Quebec (Lower Canada before 1840)	between 1840 and 1867		1867
Manitoba			1870
British Columbia			1871
Prince Edward Island			1873
Alberta	Provisional district until 1882		1905
Saskatchewan	Provisional district until 1882		1905
Newfoundland			1949
"The Canada North"			....

Exhibit 1-4

Date Admitted to Confederation

It must be noted that when reference is made to the Canadian constitution, it is to *The Canada Act,* 1982 which is made up of five sections:

1. The *Constitution Act,* 1867;

2. The acts of British Columbia, Manitoba, Prince Edward Island, Alberta, Saskatchewan, and Newfoundland, which brought these provinces into Confederation;

3. *The Statute of Westminster,* 1931;

4. Amendments to the Constitution of 1867 (*B.N.A. Act*); and

5. *The Constitution Act,* 1982.

2

Interpretations of the
Canadian Constitutions, 1867 and 1982

December 6, 1866 Macdonald and Cartier drew up Section 93, the famous
educational clause of the B.N.A. Act.

Wilson, Stamp, Audet, *Canadian Education: A History*

Section 93

New Brunswick School Question

Manitoba School Question

Provincial versus Federal Rights

Minority Rights

Non-Roman Catholic, Non-Protestant

Effects of the Charter

Introduction

Education was not a matter of much discussion at the Charlottetown and
Quebec conferences; in fact it was originally listed as one of the general powers
of the Federal Government. At the Quebec Conference there was an equally
general reference to the federal powers to protect minority rights. But when the
seventy-two resolutions which were to form the basis for the B.N.A. Act
(*Constitution Act*, 1867) were finally drafted, Section 43(6) gave control of
education to the provincial legislatures with a provision that the rights and   control,
privileges, regarding denominational schools, of Protestant and Roman Cath-   of education
olic minorities in both Canadas (Ontario and Quebec) be protected when the
Union came into effect. D'Arcy McGee (leader of the Irish Catholics in Canada
East), who sponsored the resolution, had made no reference to minority rights
as *existing in law*, which became the wording of Section 93, but talked generally
of guaranteeing a religious minority all its educational rights and privileges.

Section 93 states: Constitution Act

> In and for each Province the Legislature may exclusively make Laws in relation   B.N.A. Act
> to Education; subject and according to the following provisions:
>
> 1. Nothing in any such law shall prejudicially affect any Right or Privilege with
>   respect to Denominational Schools which any class of Persons have by Law
>   in the Province at the Union;

21

2. All the Powers and Privileges, and Duties at the Union by Law conferred and imposed in Upper Canada on the Separate Schools and School Trustees of the Queen's Roman Catholic Subjects shall be and the same are hereby extended to the Dissentient Schools of the Queen's Protestant and Roman Catholic subjects in Quebec:

3. Where in any Province a System of Separate or Dissentient Schools exists by law at the Union or is thereafter established by the Legislature of the Province, an Appeal shall lie to the Governor-General-in-Council from any Act or Decision of any Provincial Authority affecting any Right or Privilege of the Protestant or Roman Catholic Minority of the Queen's Subjects in relation to Education:

4. In case any such Provincial Law as from Time to Time seems to the Governor-General-in-Council requisite for the due Execution of the Provisions of this Section is not made, or in case any Decision of the Governor-General-in-Council on any Appeal under this Section is not duly executed by the proper Provincial Authority in that Behalf, then and in every such case, and as far only as the Circumstances of each Case require, the Parliament of Canada may make remedial Laws for the due Execution of the Provisions of this Section and of any Decision of the Governor-General-in-Council under this Section.

provincial responsibility

Although other sections of the *Constitution Act*, 1867, would have an indirect bearing on education within the various provinces, Section 93 dealt directly, if somewhat generally, with the matter of schooling. The preamble stated very definitely that education was a provincial responsibility, subject only to the four subsections following the preamble. It should be remembered that Section 93, in 1867, referred only to the provinces of Quebec, Ontario, Nova Scotia and New Brunswick (Section 43(6), the precursor of Section 93 had referred only to Ontario and Quebec). As other provinces joined confederation (Manitoba in 1870, Prince Edward Island in 1873, British Columbia in 1871, Alberta and Saskatchewan in 1905, and Newfoundland in 1949), Section 93 applied only to the extent that the incorporating act stipulated. Section 22 of the *Manitoba Act* of 1870, for example, began:

Manitoba Act

In and for the Province, the said Legislature may exclusively make Laws in relation to education, subject and according to the following provisions:

1. Nothing in any such Law shall prejudicially affect any right or privilege with respect to the Denominational Schools which any class of persons have by Law or practice in the Province at the union.

Revisions to the wording of Subsection 1 of Section 93 as it was incorporated into the *Manitoba Act* would, as later pages will illustrate, create a problem for Manitoba's Roman Catholic minority.

British Columbia Act

The Province of British Columbia brought Section 93 into its constitution by way of the following words:

10. The provisions of the "British North America Act," 1867, shall (except those parts by reasonable intendment may be held to be specifically applicable

to and only affect one and not the whole of the provinces comprising the dominion and except so far as the same may be varied by this minute) be applicable to British Columbia in the same way and to the like extent as they apply to the other provinces of the Dominion and as if the colony of British Columbia had been one of the provinces originally united by the said Act.

This section of the *British Columbia Act* was not as clear as it might have been because the original Section 93 referred, directly and indirectly, to three different situations – that of Quebec, of Ontario, and of Nova Scotia and New Brunswick. The application referred to the *British Columbia Act* was really the application applicable to Nova Scotia and New Brunswick, where no public separate schools existed at the time of joining confederation. Before referring to the other provinces, however, it would be profitable to consider the Section 93 provisions as they applied to the original signatories.

> 1. Nothing in any such law shall prejudicially affect any Right or Privilege with respect to Denominational Schools which any Class or Persons have by Law in the Province at the Union;

original signatories

Subsection 1 refers to denominational schools. Of the four provinces, only Quebec had denominational schools, and therefore Subsection 1 stated in fact, that in Quebec, upon entering confederation, no provincial act could affect the denominational schools that existed. The denominations were, then as now, Roman Catholic and Protestant. (Later, the province was forced to address the matter of the rights of those citizens who were neither Roman Catholic nor Protestant).

denominational schools

Section 93:

> 2. All the Powers and Privilege, and Duties at the Union by Law conferred and imposed in Upper Canada on the Separate Schools and the School Trustees of the Queen's Roman Catholic Subjects shall be and the same are hereby extended to the Dissentient Schools of the Queen's Protestant and Roman Catholic Subjects in Quebec;

To oversimplify, Subsection 2 states that whatever "rights, powers, privileges and duties" the Roman Catholics had in Ontario in regards to education, the Dissentient (minority) group in Quebec (whether Roman Catholic or Protestant) also had. Some question has been raised as to whether Quebec ever had Dissentient (Separate) schools because historically the province had operated on the basis of two educational systems (one Roman Catholic and the other Protestant) rather than as one educational system that combined the majority (public) and minority (separate) schools.

However, Section 93, Subsections 1 and 2, appears to have been interpreted to mean that any denominational and dissentient (separate) schools that were lawfully existent in Quebec, Ontario, New Brunswick, and Nova Scotia in 1867 were to have continued protection. Nova Scotia and New Brunswick (as later legal interpretations will dictate), not having separate schools by 1867, did not therefore have any protection for separate schools. However, if separate schools were established in the future, they would then enjoy the same protection as if they had been in existence in 1867.

dissentient schools

Subsections 3 and 4 provide for appeal to the Governor-General and the right of the Federal Government to make any necessary remedial laws to enforce compliance with Subsections 1 and 2.

Section 93:

remedial laws

3. Where in any Province a System of Separate or Dissentient Schools exists by law at the Union or is thereafter established by the Legislature of the Province, an appeal shall lie to the Governor-General-in-Council from any Act or Decision of any Provincial Authority affecting any Right or Privilege of the Protestant or Roman Catholic Minority of the Queen's Subjects in relation to Education;

4. In case any such Provincial Law as from time to time seems to the Governor-General-in-Council requisite for the due Execution of the Provisions of this Section is not made, or in case any Decision of the Governor-General-in-Council on any Appeal under this Section is not duly executed by the proper Provincial Authority in that Behalf, then and in every such case, and as far only as the Circumstances of each Case require, the Parliament of Canada may make remedial Laws for the due Execution of the Provisions of this Section and of any Decision of the Governor-General-in-Council under this Section;

In events following Confederation and as subsequent provincial enactments were made, the provisions of Section 93 demanded further clarification. These events are often referred to by Canadian historians as the *educational crisis* or the *school question*, and indeed they were for those most closely involved.

school
question

Today our interests have become more academic and more centred in the legal outcomes rather than in the emotions of the moment as was the case in those problems which arose in the two decades immediately following passage of the Constitution. The remainder of this chapter describes some of the many

court
decisions

situations which resulted in court decisions as to what was meant by the four subsections of Section 93. Those sections remain current even though there is now a new constitution in place. The Constitution 1982 in Section 29 reinforces the rights guaranteed in Section 93 when it states:

29. Nothing in this Charter abrogates or derogates from any rights or privileges guaranteed by or under the Constitution of Canada in respect of denominational, separate or dissentient schools.

The New Brunswick Schools Question

As stated earlier, compromises between the Protestants and Roman Catholics in New Brunswick and Nova Scotia have resulted in a school system devoid

tenuous peace

of legally established separate schools similar to those in the Province of Ontario or the two denominational school systems in Quebec. This should not be interpreted as meaning that mutual satisfaction had been achieved, but rather that a tenuous peace had been struck between the two sides.

In the years prior to Confederation, schools existed which loosely, but not

denominational

legally, could be considered separate (or at least denominational) in nature. The first agitation over the guarantees provided in Section 93 arose in the Province of New Brunswick. In 1871, four years after New Brunswick entered Confederation, the New Brunswick legislature passed *The Common Schools Act* providing for the formation of school districts in the place of parish districts, the election of trustees, the sharing of school financing between provincial and local resources, and what subsequently became the offending general provision of establishing a free, tax-supported school system which was non-sectarian in nature. This was followed, in 1872, by regulations which would be unfamiliar to most young educators from across Canada. These regulations provided for the recitation of the Lord's Prayer, a reading from the Bible, and the omission of the emblems and symbols of any society, political party or religious order. The latter provision would have prevented members of religious orders from teaching.

parish districts

non-sectarian

Obviously, the minority (New Brunswick was approximately one-third Roman Catholic) were not pleased with the act and its subsequent regulations. The Premier had not consulted with the Catholic minority, nor had the substance of the law and regulations been part of the preceding election. The Catholic clergy refused to accept it. Some people withheld taxes, but the majority of the minority, believing in the justness of their cause and the strength of Section 93, petitioned the Federal Government in accordance with the provisions of Section 93(4). In Ottawa, Sir John A. Macdonald in his role as Minister of Justice, ruled that passage of the act was within the power of the New Brunswick Legislature (*intra vires*); therefore he refused to disallow it. An appeal was also made to the New Brunswick Supreme Court in the Renaud Case, 1873. The Court stated in essence that there were *no* legally established separate schools in New Brunswick at Confederation and therefore any subsequent establishment of a separate school system would rest entirely with the provincial legislature. The Court pointed out however, that at this time or at any future time, if publicly supported separate schools were established by law then the provision of Section 93 would apply. The court also held that Section 93 protected the rights to denominational schools, but not the right to religious instruction. The Maher Case, 1874, followed the findings of the Renaud case. Having exhausted all legal avenues and having discovered what they considered to be a flaw in Section 93, several of the Roman Catholics turned to violence. The Caraquet Riots was an example of this. The provincial election which followed resulted in a situation where only five of the forty-one members of the legislative assembly were separate school supporters; thus some modifications to the regulations were made but the basic tenet of the legislation – no publicly supported separate schools – continued. Within a decade of Confederation, events in New Brunswick had illustrated that Section 93 was inadequate in protecting the interests of Roman Catholics outside Ontario and Quebec, unless denominational or separate school practices had been sanctioned by law prior to the entry of the province into the Dominion. In the issue which follows (Manitoba School Question); one is able to see the implications of Section 93 upon legislation passed by a practice after the province has entered Confederation.

no consultation

John A. Macdonald

Renaud case

Maher case

Caraquet riots

The Manitoba School Question

The Setting

missionary
schools

Prior to 1870 schools were supported and operated by various religious denominations (missionary schools). In the period between 1812 and 1870 officials of the Red River Settlement and the Hudson's Bay company provided grants and land to support the schools. In the year 1818, the first Roman Catholic School (St. Boniface College) was established. The first Protestant school (St. John's School), a boarding school run by the Anglicans, opened its doors in 1820. In 1866 the Red River Academy was founded, and by 1871-1872 the University of Manitoba, the St. John's College (an affiliate of the University of Manitoba), Manitoba college (Presbyterian), and the Wesleyan Institute (Methodist) had all been established.

In 1870 the population of Manitoba (which was much smaller in area than it is today) was 10 000. Approximately one-half spoke English; the other half spoke French. A dual system of education was in place.

two school
sections

As Manitoba entered Confederation in 1870, this design was maintained and passed into law: provincial authority over education was proclaimed; the Federal power of disallowance affirmed. A Board of Education, consisting of two sections, Protestant and Roman Catholic, was formed. The Board was composed of eight ecclesiastics and four lay persons. Superintendents and secretaries were appointed for each section. Twenty-four school districts (twelve Protestant and twelve Roman Catholic) were formed. Parish schools were absorbed and operated under the Manitoba *Education Act.* the population in 1871 was approximately 12 000 consisting of roughly 1 500 whites, 6 000 mixed race (French and Indian [Native]), 4 000 mixed race (English, Scottish and Indian [Native]), and 600 Indians [Natives] who were recorded by the census.

The Cause of the Problem

boundaries
extended

Between the years 1871 and 1890, there was a heavy influx of English speaking immigrants, mostly through Ontario. The boundaries of the province had been extended to their present alignment. By 1882 the school population trend was obvious. There were (in 1883) 271 Protestant schools with a population of 10 831 and only 40 Roman Catholic schools with a population of 1 941 students. By 1890 the number of Protestant schools had grown to 629, while the Roman Catholic section operated 90 schools, a ratio of approximately 6 to 1, and much different from the situation only 20 years earlier.

population
ratio

abolished
denominational
schools

The *Public Schools Act* was passed in 1890. Through it, the legislature abolished the denominational system of public education, and enacted that the Protestant and Roman Catholic school districts should be subject to the provisions of the *Public Schools Act.* That Act provided that the public schools should be nonsectarian and free, that religious exercises should be conducted according to the regulations of an advisory board, that such religious exercises should be held just before the closing hour in the afternoon, and that they should be held entirely at the option of the school trustees of the district. Included was a "conscience clause" requiring the teacher to allow children to withdraw during these exercises upon written request by parents or guardians. A second act created the Department of Education which was to consist of the Executive Council and an Advisory Board of seven members, four to be appointed by the Department of Education, two to be elected by the public and high school teachers of the province, and a seventh to be appointed by the University Council. The Advisory Board was to make regulations regarding textbooks and courses of study, the qualifications of teachers, and the appointment of examiners, as well as the forms of religious exercises for the schools. *The Public Schools Act* declared that any school not conducted in accordance with the provisions of the act or the regulations of the Advisory Board would not be deemed a public school within the meaning of the law, and could not participate in the legislative grant.

Advisory Board

Appeals to the Courts

When the Lieutenant Governor assented to the *Public Schools Act* on March 31, 1890, there were only three recourses open to the Roman Catholics: (1) appeal to the Governor-General-in-Council to disallow the legislation; (2) appeal to the Governor-General-in-council to intervene on behalf of the minority; or (3) appeal to the courts to have the Act declared *ultra vires* (beyond their powers). The Catholic minority were forced to the third option. Two cases (Barrett and Brophy) ensued.

Catholics appeal

The Barrett Case

Proceedings were commenced in November, 1890, to test the validity of the Manitoba educational acts of 1890. Dr. Barrett, a Roman Catholic ratepayer, presented an application to quash a by-law of the city of Winnipeg fixing a rate of taxation for public school purposes and passed under the authority of the newly created statutes (*Barrett v. The City of Winnipeg* (1891) S.C.R. 19, 374-425). Action was taken under sub-section 1 of Section 22 of the *Manitoba Act*, on the grounds that the legislative acts prejudicially affected a right or privilege enjoyed by the plaintiff in respect to denominational schools; it being contended that he formed one of a *class of persons* who had, *by law or practice*, such rights at the time of the union.

by law or practice

Section 22, sub-section 1 stated "nothing in any such Law shall prejudicially affect any right or privilege with respect to Denominational Schools which any class of persons have by Law *or practice* [author's emphasis] in the Province at the Union."

Justice Killam dismissed the summons, holding that the rights and privileges referred to in the *Manitoba Act* were merely those of maintaining voluntary denominational schools, of having children educated in them, and of having inculcated in them the doctrines peculiar to the respective denominations. He regarded the prejudice affected by the imposition of a tax upon Roman Catho-

voluntary denominational schools

lics for schools to which they were conscientiously opposed as something so indirect and remote that it was not detrimental.

moral rights

An appeal was made to the Manitoba Court of Queen's Bench and judgment was given in February, 1891. Two justices held that *rights and privileges* included moral rights, and that whatever any class of persons had been doing in reference to denominational schools before the union, should continue and not be prejudicially affected by Provincial legislation, but that none of these rights and privileges had been affected by the Act of 1890. The dissenting judge held that the right or privilege existing at the time of the Union was the right of each denomination to have its denominational schools with such teaching as it might think fit, to have the privilege of not being compelled to contribute to other schools to which members of such denomination could not in conscience avail themselves. He concluded that the Acts of 1890 invaded such privilege and were consequently *ultra vires*.

ultra vires

The case went to the Supreme Court of Canada, where judgment was delivered in October, 1891. The Supreme Court unanimously reversed the decision of the Manitoba Court of Queen's Bench, holding the Acts to be *ultra vires*. Chief Justice Ritchie held that Roman Catholics could not conscientiously continue to avail themselves of the benefits of the *Public Schools Act, 1890*, when the effect of that Act was to deprive them of any further beneficial use of the system of voluntary Catholic schools which had been established before the union, and had thereafter been carried on under the provincial system introduced in 1871. In other words, the *practices* prior to the union had given a right or privilege after the union. Mr. Justice Patterson pointed out that the words "injuriously affect" in section 22, sub-section 1 of the *Manitoba (Constitutional) Act*, would include any degree of interference with the rights or privileges in question, although falling short of the extinction of such rights or privileges. He held that the impediment put in the way of obtaining contributions to voluntary Roman Catholic denominational schools (by reason of the fact that all Roman Catholics would, under the Act, be compulsorily assessed by another system of education) amounted to an injurious affecting of their rights and privileges within the meaning of the sub-section. Mr. Justice Fournier pointed out that the mere right of maintaining voluntary schools, if Catholic parents chose to pay for them, and of having their children attend such schools, could not have been the right which was intended to be reserved to Catholics or other classes of persons, by the use of the word *practice*. He held that such a right was undoubtedly enjoyed by every person or class of persons, by law. Mr. Justice Taschereau took the same view, holding that the contention of the appellants gave no effect to the word *practice* inserted in the section. The fifth presiding justice concurred, but did not render a separate judgment.

impediment
injurious

Thus for the Supreme Court of Canada, six judges decided the Act to be *ultra vires* and three decided that the *practice* before the union did not extend beyond the establishment of denominational schools by voluntary subscription and that it did not create any greater a privilege after the union.

Appeal was taken in the Barrett case from the Supreme Court of Canada to the Judicial Committee of the Privy Council (Britain, and the highest court for the Dominion of Canada).

Privy Council

Their Lordships contended that in Barrett's case, the sole question raised was whether the *Public Schools Act* of 1890 prejudicially affected any right or privilege which the Roman Catholics had by law or practice when Manitoba joined Canada in 1871. They arrived at the conclusion that this question must be answered in the negative. The only right or privilege which the Roman Catholics then possessed, either by law or in practice, was the right or privilege of establishing and maintaining (for the use of members of their own church) such schools as they pleased. It appeared to their Lordships that this right or privilege remained untouched, and therefore could not be said to be affected by the 1890 legislation. It was not doubted that the object of the first sub-section of Section 22 (Manitoba's constitution) was to afford protection to denominational schools, or that it was proper to have regard to the intent of the Legislature and the surrounding circumstances in interpreting the enactment. But the question which had to be determined by Their Lordships was the *true construction* of the language used. They noted that the function of a tribunal is limited to construing the words employed; tribunals are not justified in forcing into words a meaning they cannot reasonably bear. Further, a tribunal's duty is to interpret, not to enact.

not prejudicial

> The question is, not what may be supposed to have been intended, but what has been said. More complete effect might in some cases be given to the intentions of the Legislature, if violence were done to the language in which their legislation has taken shape; but such a course would on the whole, be quite as likely to defeat as to further the object which was in view. Whilst, however, it is necessary to resist any temptation to deviate from sound rules of construction in the hope of more completely satisfying the intention of the Legislature, it is quite legitimate where more than one construction of a statute is possible, to select that one which will best carry out what appears from the general scope of the legislation and the surrounding circumstances to have been its intention.

The Brophy Case

This case came before the Supreme Court on October 4, 1893. Judgment was rendered on February 20, 1894 (*Brophy v. Attorney General at Manitoba* (1894), in Olmstead (1954) 1:316-343).

Chief Justice Sir Henry Strong decided that the difference in expression between the *British North America Act* and *The Manitoba Act*, could refer to nothing but a deliberate intention to make some change in the operation of the respective clauses, and that every presumption must be made in favor of the constitutional right of a legislative body to repeal the laws which it had itself enacted. He held that the Legislature of Manitoba had absolute power over its own legislation, untrammeled by any appeal to Federal authority and that rights or privileges created after the union only existed until the laws creating them were repealed by the legislature that had passed them. The appeal to the

absolute power

Governor-General-in-Council applied, in his opinion, only to matters prior to the Union.

Mr. Justice Fournier took exactly the opposite view.

Mr. Justice Taschereau, after questioning the jurisdiction of the court to act at all, decided that the *British North America Act* applied to all provinces of the Dominion except Manitoba, because the words not quoted in *The Manitoba Act* were intended not to apply; that, therefore, there could not be any appeal; that legislation could not at the same time affect legal rights and not be *ultra vires*; that the *Schools Act* of 1890 had been declared *intra vires* and that the petitioners were only renewing their impeachment of the constitutionality of the legislation of 1890 upon yet another ground. "No rights or privileges had been created since the union."

intra vires

Mr. Justice Gwynne decided that the appeal in sub-section 2, and the redress given in sub-section 3 related to rights and privileges created under sub-section 1 and that, therefore, rights and privileges could not be created after the union. An appeal could only lie as to matters as they existed at the time of the union.

Mr. Justice King agreed with Mr. Justice Fournier.

Therefore, three members of the Supreme Court of Canada decided that an appeal could exist, while two held that it could not because no rights and privileges within the meaning of the sub-sections had been prejudicially affected. The case then went to the Privy Council.

remedial
order

Argument in the appeal from the Supreme Court's decision was opened before the Judicial Committee of the Privy Council in December, 1894. The Decision of the Privy Council:

> With the policy of these Acts Their Lordships are not concerned, nor with the reasons which led to their enactment. It may be that as the population of the province became in proportion more largely Protestant, it was found increasingly difficult, especially in sparsely populated districts, to work the system inaugurated in 1871, even with the modifications introduced in later years. But whether this be so or not is immaterial. The sole question to be determined is whether a right or privilege which the Roman Catholic minority previously enjoyed has been affected by the legislation of 1890. Their Lordships are unable to see how this question can receive any but an affirmative answer, but Their Lordships are of opinion that the second Subsection of Section 22 of the *Manitoba Act* is the governing enactment, and that the appeal to the Governor-General-in-Council was admissible by virtue of that enactment, on the grounds set forth in the memorials and petitions, inasmuch as the Acts of 1890 affected rights and privileges of the Roman Catholic minority in relation to education within the meaning of that sub-section. The further question is submitted whether the Governor-General-in-Council has power to make the declarations or remedial orders asked for in the memorials or petitions, or has any other jurisdiction in the premises. Their Lordships have decided that the Governor-General-in-Council has jurisdiction, and that the appeal is well founded; but the particular course to be pursued must be determined by the authorities to whom it has been committed by the statute. It is not for this tribunal to intimate

the precise steps to be taken. Their general character is sufficiently defined by the third sub-section of Section 22 of the *Manitoba Act*. It is certainly not essential that the statutes repealed by the Act of 1890 should be re-enacted, or that the precise provisions of these statutes should again be made law. The system of education embodied in the Acts of 1890 no doubt commends itself to, and adequately supplies the wants of the great majority of the inhabitants of the province. All legitimate ground of complaint would be removed if that system were supplemented by provisions which would remove the grievance upon which the appeal is founded, and were modified so far as might be necessary to give effect to these provisions. (Privy Council, Britain, 1894)

Appeals for Federal Intervention in the Manitoba School Question

Numerous appeals were made for federal intervention on behalf of the Roman Catholic minority of Manitoba. These were followed by an appeal to the electorate. After surviving three cabinet crises (in March and July, 1895, and in January, 1896) the Bowell government finally introduced a remedial bill into Parliament at a special session called for that purpose early in 1896.

cabinet crises

The Remedial Bill was modelled largely on the *Manitoba Schools Act* of 1890, and was framed on the plan of allowing the provincial government to control and operate the school system in its entirety. Only when the provincial government did not act would the dominion government do so.

The bill provided for the appointment of a Separate School Board of not more than nine members, all of whom were to be Roman Catholics. The Lieutenant-Governor-in-Council (Manitoba) was to make the appointments, but if this was not done within three months the dominion government would do so. The Bill provided for the election of separate school trustees and defined their powers. Roman Catholics who wished to support the public schools were free to do so. Those Roman Catholics who wished to support separate schools were allowed to tax themselves for the maintenance of such schools, and they would be exempted from taxes for the public schools.

Separate School Board

The Roman Catholic schools were to be subject to inspection by the provincial school inspectors; financial assistance could be withheld if they were deemed inefficient. The textbooks used by the separate schools were to be those of either the public schools of Manitoba or the Roman Catholic separate schools of Ontario. The bill also provided that the separate schools were to be given a proportionate share of the legislative grant, but did not state how these directives were to be accomplished in the event that the provincial government declined to comply. The 1896 federal election was fought in part on the Manitoba school issue and the contents of the *Remedial Bill*.

The Conservatives supported the content of the remedial legislation proposed by Manitoba. The Liberals opposed it. The hierarchy of the Roman Catholic Church were in support. But in one of those "twists" characteristic of Canadian politics, Laurier was able to use his resounding victory at the polls in Quebec, and the much smaller majority which he enjoyed in the rest of Canada to provide him with a mandate. He set to work.

Laurier victory

The Election Aftermath

With the accession of Laurier and the Liberals to power, it remained to be seen what effect the use of what Laurier termed "sunny ways" would have on the hitherto stubborn Manitoba Government.

The proposal for a commission of investigation and conciliation, which Laurier had touted during the election campaign, was quietly shelved. In the end, Laurier's "sunny ways" consisted simply of leaving the important portfolio of the Ministry of the Interior vacant while negotiations with the Manitoba leaders were carried on. Clifford Sifton, who was a prominent member of the provincial government, and who had repeatedly declared that no changes in the school legislation would be made because no injustice had been done, now evidently decided that perhaps some changes were in order. The Laurier-Greenway compromise was the result. The details were made public in November, 1896, and at the same time Sifton entered the Dominion cabinet. The necessary modifications in the school legislation were enacted in March, 1897, at the next session of the provincial legislature.

Laurier-Greenway compromise

The Laurier-Greenway Compromise – 1897

The federal cabinet's first task was to settle the Manitoba school question. It became apparent that the three points upon which concession might be made were: separate religious exercises, a teacher of the minority faith, and the use of the French language in the schools. Weeks of consideration were required to reach agreement. It was not until the middle of November that a settlement was effected.

concessions

The settlement embodied three concessions. First, religious teaching was to be carried on between half-past three and four o'clock, by any Christian clergyman or deputy, when authorized by a resolution of the local board of trustees or requested by the parents of ten children in a rural school or twenty-five children in an urban school. (The rural-urban distinction has been replaced by a school-size distinction, and not upon the number of students, but upon the number of classrooms.) Different days or different rooms might be allotted different denominations; no children were to attend unless at the parents' desire. (Today, the restrictions respecting time of day when religious instruction could be offered has been lifted but the total amount of time remains at 150 minutes per week.) Second, at least one duly certificated Roman Catholic teacher was to be employed in urban schools where the average attendance reached forty, and in village and rural schools where it reached twenty-five, if required by parents' petition; similarly, non-Roman Catholic teachers were to be employed when requested by a non-Catholic minority (this provision was dropped in 1980). Third, "when ten of the pupils in any school speak the French language or any language other than English as their native tongue, the teaching of such pupils shall be conducted in French, or such other language, and English." The provincial government also agreed that fair Catholic representation in the Advisory Council, inspectorships, and examining boards would be kept in mind in the administration of the act. In essence, the agreement left the

religious teaching

Catholic teachers

language

system of public schools intact, but secured for the minority distinct religious teaching, and where numbers warranted, teachers of their own faith and the maintenance of the French tongue. The language clause had been framed in general terms by the provincial authorities in order to make it apply to the German Mennonites as well as to the French Catholics.

The Norris Administration passed amendments in 1916 which dealt the death blow to the bilingual system of instruction. English alone became the official language in all public schools of Manitoba.

There the matter rested, basically unsettled. Rumblings from within successive governments of Manitoba indicate the matter of public support for separate schools in Manitoba will again become a live issue.

not yet settled

Provincial versus Federal Rights

Section 93 of the *Canadian Constitution*, 1867, states quite clearly that education concerns are matters for provincial governments. This point has been made many times, and Chapter Six will discuss the general matter of federal involvement in education. However, there have been direct challenges which have resulted in the courts clarifying, to a much greater degree, this basic provincial right and the legal division between provincial control and federal involvement. A few of the more interesting court cases are summarized.

challenges

Christian Brothers Case, 1876

In this infrequently reported case (*Canada Supreme Court Cases 1875-1906*, p. 1), an application had been made by the Christian Brothers (a teaching order founded in 1684) to become incorporated as a teaching company under federal authority. Upon appeal, the Supreme Court of Canada ruled in the negative on the basis that a bill to incorporate the Christian Brothers as *A Company of Teachers for the Dominion* was unconstitutional. The basis for the decision was the first sentence of Section 93 of the *Constitution Act*, 1867.

> In and for each province the Legislature may exclusively make laws in relation to education . . .

Hildebrand Case

In 1873, a time for the encouragement of immigration from Europe to fill the West, the Federal Government, by an Order-in-Council, stated to a group of immigrants that:

> The fullest privilege of exercising their religious principles is by law afforded to the Mennonites, without any kind of molestation or restriction whatever, and the same privilege extends to the education of their children in schools.

Some of the Mennonites who settled in Manitoba did so believing this Order-in-Council promised them exclusion from provincial education requirements. Hildebrand (*R. v. Hildebrand*, (1919) 3 W.W.R. 286), in contravention of Manitoba's compulsory attendance laws, refused to send his children to school. The courts ruled that the Order-in-Council, as it applied to educational

Mennonites

matters was *ultra vires* the federal powers, and thus Hildebrand was forced to have his children attend public school. This court case was held in 1919, however in 1962 in magistrate's court in Fort Vermilion, Alberta, reference was again made to the 1873 Order-in-Council as a defense against compulsory attendance. Again the same result prevailed as in the Hildebrand case. The contents of the 1873 Order-in-Council were provided once again by the Mennonite people as evidence in defense of their own special schooling arrangements for their children, and the school attendance issue unfolded in the Province of Alberta through a case known as the Holdeman Mennonite Case (*R. v Elmer Wiebe*, (1978) Oral Judgment). This group of Mennonites in Alberta had refused to send their children to the public schools, contending that public school activities violated their religious beliefs, and that, in any case, they had been exempted from required school attendance by the 1873 Federal Order-in-Council.

Defining Minority Rights

Reference is made to the Chabot Case (*Chabot v. Les Commissaires d'Écoles de Lamorandiere* (1957) Que. Q.B. 707 (C.A.)). In this example, the Chabot children were Jehovah's Witnesses, attending the only school provided in the area – a public school in a predominantly Roman Catholic community. By regulation of the Quebec council of Public Instruction, all students were compelled to attend the religious instruction classes which were considered to be part of the curriculum. Refusal to do so by the Chabot children resulted in their expulsion from school. As a result of the ensuing court case, it was established that the non-Roman Catholic children of the Chabot family had a right to attend the Roman Catholic school in the area (there being no Protestant school) and that the Chabot children did not have to attend the religious instruction part of the school curriculum. The court held that while the province has the right to make laws in regards to education, there are other rights, such as freedom of religion, which cannot be transcended by educational laws and regulations.

Jehovah's Witnesses

Refer to the Bartz Case (*McCarthy v. City of Regina and the Regina Board of Public School Trustees* (1918) 32 D.L.R. 741). In this 1917 Saskatchewan case, Bartz, a Roman Catholic living in a separate school district, wished to have his school taxes paid to the public school district. The ensuing litigation confirmed that his taxes must be paid to the separate school district. Justice Newlands stated:

destination of taxes

> Can it, then, be argued that such a district is established only by those voting in favour of it? There being no individual right to form such a district, how can it be said that the individuals voting for the formation of the district are the ones who established it? The minority voting are bound by those in the majority, if they decide not to form such a district, and are they not equally bound where the majority vote is in favour of forming the district? Otherwise what is the object of taking the vote? Surely it is to decide whether the religious minority as a class will establish a separate school district, and surely when that vote is

favorable, that the whole class is bound, as it would be bound if the vote was unfavorable.

The principle arising from the Bartz case is that when the minority ratepayers of a district have established a separate school district in Saskatchewan, all the ratepayers of the same denomination in the district are bound to contribute taxes to the support of the school, and cannot contribute to the public school district. The Renaud Case which follows appears to contradict this decision, but the Adolf Schmidt Case (the most recent) appears to affirm Bartz. In a sister case, Neida, a Protestant, wished to send his children to a separate school and be assessed for separate school support. the court ruled:

destination of students

> Not being of the religious faith of the minority which has established the separate school he cannot exercise the right guaranteed only to such minority and cannot escape the obligation of being assessed for the support of the public school (*McCarthy v. City of Regina and Regina Board of Public School Trustees* (1917) D.L.R. 32:741-755).

Reference is made to the Renaud Case (*Renaud v. Board of Trustees of R.C. Separate School Section 11 in the Township of Tilburby North* (1934) O.W.N. 218 (1933) 3 D.L.R. 172 (1933) R.R. 565). In this 1934 Ontario case, the Renauds, who were both Roman Catholics, decided to have Mr. Renaud's taxes paid to the public school district and Mrs. Renaud's taxes (on a different parcel of land) paid to the separate school district, and to have their children attend the separate school. The separate school board refused to accept the children. The assessor had incorrectly designated the residency of the mother and so the children's names did not appear on the annual enumeration roll of the separate district (required by law). The parents sought a writ of *mandamus* (court order) requiring the board to accept their children. The lower court refused to grant the mandamus and in its judgment observed:

mandamus

> It is not the ownership of property in the section by the parents' or guardianship of a child, it is not the assessment of such property and the entry of the owner as a separate school supporter, it is not the religion of the parent, guardian or child, that imposes upon the trustees the duty provided for it adequately accommodating and legally certified teachers, it is solely the name of the child on the annual enumeration that poses the duty *quoad hoc* (to this extent) for that child.

Justice Kerwin of the High Court of Justice decided, in reversing a lower court ruling, that this arrangement was legally unacceptable.

> It is admitted that Mrs. R's residence is in the same school section and that she is actually a supporter of the school under the control of the respondent Board. That being so, the error made by the assessor in stating the residence in the school section cannot deprive the applicant of any rights that she may have. The two parents of the child live together and both are Roman Catholics. There is nothing to prevent one parent, under these circumstances, being assessed as a public school supporter with respect to one parcel of land, and the other parent as a Roman Catholic Separate school supporter with respect to a different parcel

of land. The assessor has adopted the wishes of both parents in naming the mother as parent in the enumeration and what the assessor did was correct.

children
follow taxes

One may read between the lines and speculate as to what political actions the father and the trustees were attempting to take, but this case confirmed that, in Ontario at least, ratepayers could pay their taxes to whichever school system they wished (public or separate), but having made that choice, the children would have to attend the school of the same system. (See the later Adolf Schmidt case where Ontario parents move to Alberta and assume the same to hold true in the Province of Alberta.)

Ontario
different

In 1962, another case (*LeBlanc v. Board of Education for City of Hamilton* (1962) 35 D.L.R. (2d) 548) furthered the Renaud case decision by confirming that, in Ontario, a Roman Catholic can withdraw his support from the separate school.

minority
obligations

Now refer to the Schmidt Case (*Schmidt v. Calgary Board of Education and Alberta Human Rights Commission* (1975) 6 W.W.R. 279 (1975) 57 D.L.R. (3d) 746 (1976) 6 W.W.R. 717). Since earlier cases indicated that (in Saskatchewan) the formation of a separate school by the minority group obligated all members of that minority group, and that (in Ontario) where the children can attend the schools of the system to which the parents decide to pay their taxes, a more recent basis has now developed for challenging earlier court rulings. The basis has been found in the human rights legislation, the main point of argument in the Schmidt case which was commenced in Calgary in 1974.

Mr. and Mrs. Schmidt, both Roman Catholics, moved to Calgary from Willowdale, Ontario, where their taxes and children went to the public school district even though they resided in a separate school district. In Calgary (where there is both a public school district and a Roman Catholic separate school district) the Schmidts decided to send their children to the public school. Since there was sufficient accommodation, the children were accepted, but Mr. Schmidt was charged tuition fees at the rate of twenty-two dollars per month per child. Mr. Schmidt filed a complaint of discrimination with the Alberta Human Rights Commission under a section (exclusion from a public place on the basis of religion) of the 1972 *Alberta Individual Rights Protection Act*. The Commission agreed with the interpretation of Mr. Schmidt but was not able to reach an agreement with the Calgary Board of Education, the public school board. Therefore, Mr. Schmidt appealed to the Minister, who ordered a Board of Inquiry (still within the provisions of the same act). This Board ruled the *Individual Rights Protection Act* did not supersede the pertinent sections of the

schools not
public place

School Act, and further, if it did, the school was not a place of public accommodation, and therefore the pertinent sections of the *Individual Rights Protection Act* would not apply in any case.

Mr. Schmidt's subsequent appeal to the Supreme Court of Alberta was successful, with the court saying that charging tuition fees on the basis of religion was discriminatory. The Calgary Board of Education was ordered to repay the fees.

The Calgary Board of Education, upon appealing to the Appellate Division of the Alberta Supreme Court, effected a reversal of the earlier court decision. Mr. Schmidt's subsequent appeal to the Supreme Court of Canada resulted in a refusal by the court to hear the appeal, an indication that they agreed with the ruling of the Alberta Appeals Court.

This case appears to have confirmed the supremacy of the provisions in Section 93 of the *Constitution Act*, 1867 as worded in the 1905 *Alberta Act*, over subsequent Alberta human rights legislation. The *Alberta Act* states in part:

> 17. Section 93 of the *Constitution Act*, 1867 shall apply to the said Province, with the substitution of paragraph 1 of the said Section 93 of the following paragraph:;
>
> 1. Nothing in any such law shall prejudicially affect any right or privilege with respect to separate schools which any class of persons have at the date of the passing of this Act, under the terms of chapters 29 and 30 of the *Ordinances of the Northwest Territories* passed in the year 1901, or with respect to religious instruction in any public or separate school as provided for in the said Ordinances;

This case also helps establish the extent to which public schools provide public accommodation. However, many other areas of human rights legislation, as they relate to the educational scene, will require further court definition.

public accommodation

Language

Finally, refer to the Ottawa Separate School Board Case (*Ottawa Separate School Trustees v. City of Ottawa* (1917) A.C. 76, 32 D.L.R. 10, 30 D.L.R. 770, (1916) 24 D.L.R. 497). In 1915 the Ottawa Separate School Board, representing Roman Catholics who were primarily French, decided that the language of instruction in the schools under its control would be French. This action was not permitted by the Ontario Department of Education, with the result that qualified teachers were not hired by the board and the schools remained closed. As a consequence, an Order-in-Council abolishing the separate school board was passed. The trustees were to be replaced by an appointed commission. The authority for this action rested on a provincial statute passed by the Ontario Legislature that same year.

language of instruction

The question of whether a separate school board could be abolished by the province was negated by the Privy Council. They indicated that the trustees' rights, in Ontario, were protected by Section 93. Therefore the province could not abolish a separate school board through action which was based on a provincial statute. The court ruled further that even though the right to maintain a separate school board was inviolate by the province, the right did not extend to separation from the Ontario educational system as such. That is, the province was quite within its rights to pass laws and regulations governing the conduct of schools, both public and separate; only this specific action was in question. Further, the results of the Ottawa Separate School Trustees' case confirmed that under Section 93, the minority rights provisions related to religious beliefs and not to *race* or *language*.

no right to abolish

The Privy Council stated:

> ... the class of person to whom the right or privilege is reserved must ... be a class of persons determined according to religious beliefs, and not according to race or language. Roman Catholics together form within the meaning of the Section 93 a class of persons and that class cannot be subdivided into other classes by consideration of the language of the people by whom the faith is held.

The Ottawa separate schools operated as private schools until 1927. During this period no provincial grants were paid. In 1927 arrangements were made which settled the controversy and provincial grants were reinstated.

Non-Roman Catholic, Non-Protestant

Newfoundland

The provisions of Section 93 clearly recognized Protestants and Roman Catholics, the two groups which included (at least nominally) nearly every person in Canada in 1867. The *Newfoundland Act* of 1949 distinguished among Roman Catholics, United Church, Anglican Church, Salvation Army, Seventh Day Adventists and Pentecostal Assemblies. Problems have arisen in the provinces which have separate schools when determinations are needed as to which school system should be attended by the Jewish, and the other groups of children who are non-Roman Catholic and non-Protestant. While there is no doubt about their right to attend the public school, because that is the school for all those except the minority (Protestant or Roman Catholic), problems sometimes arise when the public school is primarily Roman Catholic and the separate school is Protestant. Basically, this dilemma has been solved by agreement and negotiation, usually resulting in an agreement with the Protestant public or separate schools. This problem does not arise in the provinces which do not have separate schools, namely, British Columbia, Manitoba, Prince Edward Island, Nova Scotia and New Brunswick.

definitions
Roman Catholic
Protestant

Interesting definitions have arisen out of the courts, for example: a Protestant is anyone who denies the authority of the Pope in Rome; a Roman Catholic is a Christian who accepts the authority of the Pope in Rome (*Pander v. Town of Melville* (1922 W.W.R. 1923, 3:53-58)). The rights of Protestants to establish separate school districts refers to the rights of all persons of that group, not to a single specific denomination from within the Protestant faith.

Before concluding this chapter, it is necessary for the teacher to address what has become one of the major issues in Canada's failed attempts to devise a *whole* constitution.

Thomas Berger in *Courts in the Classroom* states:

> The disputes about separate schools in New Brunswick in the 1870s, in Manitoba in the 1890s and in Ontario in the early years of our own century were not simply disputes about religion, schools, curriculum and language; they were disputes about the place of the French Canadians in the English-speaking provinces. In New Brunswick and in Manitoba the dispute was ostensibly over religion, in Ontario over language – two different carriers of culture. But in

each case the underlying issue was the same: were the French Canadians to have a distinct and inviolate place in the life of the English-speaking provinces.
. . .

Effects of the Charter

The pre-eminence of the individual over institutions is now clearly established in the *Charter of Rights and Freedoms*. As noted earlier, education is a provincial matter and provincial laws respecting education have been supreme and exclusive. The one exception, enunciated in the *Constitution Act* 1867, was the prohibition against laws which "prejudicially affect rights and privileges with respect to denominational, separate and dissentient schools." However the provinces are no longer supreme. The *Constitution Act* 1982 provides that any provincial law that is inconsistent with the provision of the Charter is of no force and effect. Thus, provincial control over education has given way to federal policies and to judicial intervention. The authority of schools and teachers may be waning in the face of court interpretations.

supremacy

The full impact of the Constitution and especially the Charter will remain unknown until Canadian courts (the final arbitrators) have fully considered issues such as minority language education rights, rights to schooling, compulsory school attendance, freedom of conscience and religion, patriotic exercises, freedom of expression, suspension and expulsion, corporal punishment, freedom of assembly, freedom of association, and legal rights of students – especially those enunciated in sections 7 to 14. The implication for the teachers of several of the issues listed will be covered in "Part Two, Legal Concerns."

several
freedoms

It is necessary to encourage the teacher to address what has become one of the major issues in Canada's attempts to find what we mean when we say *Canada*. Thomas Berger in *Courts in the Classroom* raises this issue by posing a number of questions. Why do we believe in Canada? What things are most important in our shared history? Why has Canada persisted? In response to his own question, Berger states:

> Some believe that the Canadian achievement lies in the development of our natural resources – the establishment of the fishery, the gathering of fur, the development of the grain trade, the building of an empire in timber, and now the exploration of oil and gas and minerals on our frontiers and beyond.

Berger states that he believes the distinctive Canadian contribution is not listed on the achievements above, but is to be found in "a distinctive Canadian intellectual contribution to the legal and political order, a way of enabling human rights and fundamental freedoms to prevail in a world where minority rights are constantly in danger of being extinguished. . . ." This Berger calls a *regime of tolerance*.

human rights
and freedoms

A number of legal cases respecting education have arisen as a result of the passage of the 1982 Constitution. Several centre upon minority language rights.

Minority Language Education Rights

religious
rights

mother
tongue

The reader will recall that Section 93 of the *British North America Act (Constitution* 1867) provided for the transfer of authority for public education to the provinces. The federal government's sole responsibility was to ensure that the rights of the religious minority were protected. Section 23 of the *Constitution,* 1982 provided for the federal government's further presence in public school education through the constitutional guarantee of the minority's (English or French speaking) rights to have their children educated in their *mother tongue.*

(3) The right of citizens of Canada under subsections (1) and (22) to have their children receive primary and secondary school instruction in the language of the English or French linguistic minority population of a province

a. applies wherever in the province the number of children of citizens who have such a right is sufficient to warrant that provision to them out of public funds of minority language instruction; and

b. includes, where the number of those children so warrants, the right to have them receive that instruction in minority language educational facilities provided out of public funds.

Several members of Canadian society have used legal means to ensure they enjoy the rights of Section 23.

The existence of the parent's right is not disputed, but the "where numbers warrant," the level of service required, who is to control and manage the school, and the need for a separate building have been disputed in the courts. The following section provides a brief summary of the judgments to date.

public funds

circumstances

A useful example is to be found in *Marchand v. Simcoe* (County) *Board of Education* (1986) 61 OR (2d) 651. The plaintiff in this case brought an action against the school board and the Crown (Ontario government) requiring them to fulfill Section 23 of the *Charter* by providing their children secondary school education in the French language, in French language facilities, provided for out of public funds. The level of instruction was to be equivalent to the level found in English language secondary schools. The defendant was judged to have met "the where numbers warrant" test and were thus entitled to Section 23 rights. Also, in 1990, the Manitoba government requested a review of their legislation which proposed to set the basic number required at 23 students. The court held the number 23 students could not be pre-ordained. Numbers required were to be dictated by the circumstances. In *Lavoie v. Nova Scotia* (1989) 47 DLR (4th) 586, the court held that the number of 50 students was sufficient to guarantee minority language rights, but not sufficient to require separate facilities. In *Mahe v. Alberta* (1990) 3 WWR 97, students were schooled in a French school which was directed by an English-speaking school board. There were 242 French speaking students in the school and over 3 000 French speaking children in Edmonton. The plaintiff sought the right to have their own school board to manage the school. The court granted the petition, contending that the matter of the rights to manage the school depended upon the answer to the question of numbers. In Manitoba, also in 1990, the court, in responding to a request for an interpretation of a piece of legislation, concluded that the power to control or manage did not expressly, or by implication, require the power to be exercised at the discretion of the minority. Again in 1990, the Manitoba government requested the court to test the rights to a separate building for French speaking education. The court held that a separate building was not required to satisfy Section 23 requirements. Finally, some writers have suggested that, since the *Charter* refers to *everyone* in other sections, the number for Section 23 should be one.

Many times court challenges as well as changing public opinion result in new or revised statutes. For example, the 1988 revision of the *Alberta School* Act resulted in this new insertion:

statute revision

5(1) If an individual has rights under section 23 of the Canadian Charter of Rights and Freedoms to have his children receive school instruction in French, his children are entitled to receive that instruction in accordance with those rights wherever in the Province those rights apply.

(2) The Lieutenant Governor in Council may make regulations respecting anything that may be required to give effect to subsection (1).

Summary

As the Dominion of Canada developed from the original four signatories in 1867 to the inclusion of Manitoba in 1870, British Columbia in 1871, Prince Edward Island in 1873, Alberta and Saskatchewan in 1905, and Newfoundland in 1949, and became a nation from sea to sea, the right to provincial control in education was incorporated into the Constitution of the newly-established province. These sections have remained intact.

provincial control

Depending upon the presence or absence of separate or denominational schools in the province at the time of the province joining the Dominion, the subsidiary clauses of Section 93 were included and sometimes modified, but the power of the Federal Parliament to take remedial corrective action was maintained. The Manitoba School Question (reviewed in some detail) represents the only Federal Government challenge which a province has faced.

remedial corrective action

It has become clear that separate (denominational) school supporters are bound to support their school districts where they exist, and that the method for determining residency of the child is the religion (Protestant or Roman Catholic) of the parent.

residency

Further, although provincial governments have control over education, it appears for example, that the abolition of the separate school boards is not within their powers. A Protestant, for the purpose of denominational and separate school clauses in our *Constitution*, is anyone who denies the authority of the Pope in Rome. Individual church denominations within the Protestant movement do not qualify for separate school status, only Protestants as a group hold this right.

Protestants

religious
minorities

Finally, provincial control of education (grades 1-12) and the rights of religious minorities (Protestant and Roman Catholic) appear to be set in stone – with perhaps a little erosion here and there – but these two pillars of Canadian education have stood a long time without major changes. Recent developments suggest that language (English and French) minorities have not only the right under the *mother tongue* provisions of the Constitution, 1982, to schooling in their own language, but also that they may have (at present not clearly defined) rights to administer their own schools. Some provinces have already modified their school legislation to make provision for French language school boards.

mother
tongue

Often people remember the *Constitution* of 1982 as though it consisted only of the *Canadian Charter of Rights and Freedoms*. The statute in fact consists of two schedules, Schedule A and Schedule B. Schedule A deals with procedural matters as to how we as Canadians achieved control over our constitution. Part I of Schedule B is the *Charter*. Part II addresses the rights of aboriginal people. Part III concerns provisions for equalization and for handling regional disparities within Canada. Part IV deals with constitutional conferences regarding aboriginal peoples. Part V is a lengthy part of the document, setting forward, in 12 sections, the procedures for amending the *Constitution*. Part VI sets forward amendments to the *Constitution Act* (1867) (*BNA Act*) reaffirming the Act especially with respect to Section 92A (non-renewable natural resources and forestry resources) in regards to provincial authority in these areas. Part VII declares that the Constitutions of Canada is the supreme law of Canada and that any law which is inconsistent with the Constitution has no force and effect. It also requires that all amendments to our constitution be made in accordance with the *Constitution* (Part V). This part also makes the Minister of Justice responsible for preparing the French version of the Constitution.

aboriginal
people

3

Departments of Education
and Centralized Control

Bureaucracies, good and bad . . .
Gue, An Introduction to Educational Administration in Canada

Evolution of Central Control

Departments of Education

Duties of Ministers of Education

School Legislation

Decentralization Through Regional Offices

Constitutional Relationships

French School Board

The Canadian Design

The key to the Canadian design for education lies in federal decentralization. The *Constitution Act*, 1867 (*British North America Act*, 1867) and the acts of provincial establishment, for example the *Manitoba Act*, 1870 – which is the constitution for the Province of Manitoba – provide the legal framework for government action. The origins of the legal provisions for Canadian education, however, predate Confederation. For example, legislation providing for the establishment of schools in Lower Canada was passed in 1801. The Upper Canada Board of Education (rudimentary by comparison to the complex bureaucratic structures which constitute a modern-day department or ministry of education, but similar in function and intent) was established in 1822. Provision for separate schools was part of the *Act of Union* passed in 1841.

federal
decentralization

Provincial control over education constitutes the cornerstone of the design of provincial statutes, while customs, usage, and judicial review help to broaden, or narrow, and further define the scope of provincial designs respecting their schools. The legal basis is found in federal and provincial constitutions, but the solution may be found in common (court) law. The powers vested in federal, provincial, or local governments, or in persons or bodies appointed by such authorities may clash with the interest of local authorities or individual members of the community (frequently parents). Resolution of these clashes of interest frequently requires judicial settlement.

provincial
control

Provincial authority was granted through Section 93, of the *Constitution Act*, which states, "In and for each Province the Legislature may exclusively make Laws in relation to Education, subject and according to the following provisions."

The only limitation placed upon the exercise of these powers is contained in the subsections which protect denominational and separate schools formed by the religious minority.

As was indicated in the first chapter, and elaborated upon in the second, each province is responsible for all education – pre-school, elementary, secondary and post secondary – within its borders. True, there are limitations, but these deal mainly with national security, national interest, protection of the guarantees provided to certain religious minorities, and provision of education for native peoples. Within these bounds, the provincial governments have a great deal of latitude in providing education for their constituents. This sovereignty has an advantage in that it gives the Canadian school system a flexibility which permits experimentation without risk to the educational system of the entire nation. Many extensively centralized educational systems (such as found in European countries for example) do not enjoy this luxury. The extent of provincial autonomy would lead one to expect great differences among the provinces but surprisingly, the educational structures of the provinces are more obvious for their similarities than their differences. This chapter considers provincial centralized control of education and the organizational structure of Ministries of Education.

centralized
systems

Considering the historical development of education in Canada, the local school district or the local school would be expected to be the main decision making unit, with the larger units and the provincial Department of Education being secondary in importance. The emphasis of the supremacy of the local school has been indigenous to the English school system and, considering the emigration from England to Canada in the formative years, the "local authority" principle would be expected to become established. Secondly, early education in what is now Quebec was based on the idea of the parish school – a close educational tie to the local parish church. Thirdly, the United Empire Loyalists brought into Canada from the United States a strong tradition of the supremacy of the local school district. However, in spite of these three major influences, there developed in Canada a structure in each province in which the Provincial Department of Education (or its equivalent) became the central authority, followed in power by school board control, and lastly by the community surrounding the local school. Various writers have tried to explain this phenomenon. They have suggested three main reasons. First, Egerton Ryerson, Superintendent of Education in Ontario (Upper Canada) from 1844 to 1867, was very influential in determining the direction education was to take in this fledgling country – and he was a strong advocate of centralized control. Secondly, the inability of either the Protestants or the Roman Catholics to gain complete domination over the other, in the Canadian legislature of the day, tended to push the control of education a little further away and thus on to the more neutral and less emotional ground, the central (provincial) government. Thirdly, Canada has been an agricultural nation, particularly in its formative years. The local communities did not have the population and resources upon which to develop a sound educational program.

supremacy of
local school

Evolution of Central Control

Many of the early schools were established by Christian denominations working among the natives. Pioneer settlers also began establishing schools for their children. The first colonial legislation regarding the establishment of schools was passed in 1776 by the Nova Scotia Legislature.

first
legislation

In the beginning, central colonial governments assumed minimal responsibility by providing some funds to assist local schools. A second step was to provide small incentive grants for the opening of schools. Next the receipt of grants became conditional upon the local authorities meeting specified minimal standards, based mainly upon fears that the locally elected school trustees did not, or were not able, to see the far reaching consequences of local decisions, especially those made upon the level of funding. Eventually colonial agencies, such as the Council for Public Instruction (an independent administrative board established by the *School Act* of 1850), were established to take charge of the school system. Legislation in 1874 changed the character of the board by introducing elected membership and by granting enhanced authority to prescribe provincial courses of study and the appointment of high school inspectors. In summary, the changes over time were from voluntary to compulsory schooling, from denomination to lay control, from private to public control, and from local to central control. These changes resulted in the following general patterns for the Canadian departments of education. They traditionally prescribed programs of study, qualifications of teachers, examinations on the syllabi, maintained a corp of inspectors to evaluate the teaching of the centrally designed curricula, and set forward a structure to permit some degree of local autonomy. For the above noted and other reasons, today we have a highly centralized (provincially) form of educational direction and control, followed by some area control, and lastly by limited local control.

elected
trustees

Thus, in each province the Department of Education of the government is the central educational authority, a position which none of the provincial governments appears willing to vacate. All authority is delegated to the Department of Education, through its minister and by way of various provincial legislative acts and regulations (mainly the school acts). This authority delegation can be recalled at the whim of the provincial government, subject of course to the electors at the next provincial election. That is, the various types of local or regional organizations (districts, divisions, units, counties) and their respective governing bodies exist at the pleasure of the provincial legislatures. By law, the responsibility for education in each province rests with the provincial government, a position which cannot be avoided. School districts and school boards then become creatures of the provincial government. In the event the school board neglects its responsibility, the lost authority must then be recaptured by the provincial Department (Ministry) of Education. School boards, publicly elected or appointed, can and have been, dismissed by the provincial governments.

delegated
authority

authority
recaptured

As stated, the Canadian design for education is a strong centralized authority located at the provincial government level, supplemented by elected and/or appointed school boards with limited authority, and with usually ineffective vestigial bodies associated with the local school. Provincial politicians, in response to pressure from school boards and constituents, have from time-to-time attempted to give the impression of considerable local autonomy for school boards and, to a lesser degree, individual schools. Departmental curriculum guides for individual subjects are slowly becoming less prescriptive; local advisory councils to advise school boards are becoming more fashionable; departmental inspectors and superintendents are less in evidence, school evaluations rather than teacher inspections are now becoming the Canadian way. However, these are mainly surface features – there has been very little real change in the control departments of education have over education. Inspectoral bodies are becoming advisory bodies but the monitoring functions are still there; the leadership services provided are often mantles of *suggestive* prescription.

local school boards

Often in the business world the statement is made that whoever controls the purse strings wields the greatest power. This is also true in education. The provincial governments need not dictate that a particular program be initiated or furthered, because provision of sufficient financial incentive will achieve the same purpose. Chapter five will explain how incentive grants (*carrots*) are made to work for provincial purposes, often worthy, but nonetheless provincial purposes.

financial control

This brief discussion of centralized authority is not meant either as a support for centralized authority nor as a criticism. Rather, it has focussed on the importance of education as perceived by the provincial governments and the determined efforts to fulfill their responsibilities in this regard.

The Department (Ministry) of Education

Governmental structures in the Canadian provinces are, without exception, modelled on English law and practice. The Lieutenant Governor performs certain symbolic functions. Executive powers rest with the premier and cabinet, a body representing the elected assembly. Education in Canadian provinces occupies a position similar to that held by other government services. The government department responsible for schools bears the same relationship to the cabinet as those dealing with, for example, health, municipal affairs, highways, culture, and agriculture. Differences in power and influence of the various departments depend upon provincial priorities and the capacities of individual ministers. Cabinet control and cabinet solidarity guarantee that the former is most often the case. Provincially hired educational officials are civil servants subject to the same regulations for appointment and pay as apply to all civil servants. The protection of education against undue political interference is bound up with the status of the civil service as a non-partisan, politically neutral body. Further, if one were to survey the employees of provincial departments of education it would become obvious that in virtually every

executive powers

cabinet control

position of decision making (other than in accounting and similar management functions) the incumbents are firstly, school teachers, then school teachers with specialized training, but nevertheless educators from the lowest to the most senior rank.

In each province the senior position in the Department of Education is the Minister of Education, an elected member of the Legislative Assembly, granted the portfolio of education from the Lieutenant Governor upon the recommendation of the Premier. The Minister of Education is a leader of the government side of the house who has obtained the position through politics and must, at all times, remain politically sensitive if he/she is to maintain the position. The essential skills are the ability to sense public opinion, to negotiate, and to compromise. A good public image is helpful. All other members of the Department are hired, non-elected, employees of the government. The structure and organization of the Department of Education vary from province to province. In general, however, there is a deputy minister responsible directly to the minister, and two, three or four associate or assistant deputy ministers each in charge of a particular part of the responsibilities of the department. For example, one associate deputy minister may be concerned with instruction and curriculum development, another with research and development, and another with finances, grants and taxation. The Deputy Minister and Assistants will almost invariably be former school teachers and school administrators. Their job is two-fold; first to advise the Minister on professional information that is available on policy matters, and second, to implement the policy and directions of the Minister. Much of their involvement is at the political interface. At the next lower level of operations the duties become more specific. The person in charge, normally called a Director, has much more specific areas of concern, and is leader of a staff employed to fulfill that function. They tend to work more at the professional level and are involved very little in political activities.

Minister

politics

Deputy Minister

Structure of the Department of Education

Extent of Provincial Control

Each province has by statute, assumed control and direction in the following areas:

1. Teacher education and certification. Teacher education is usually provided by universities but under the general policy directions of the Department. Teacher certification is normally granted by the Minister upon the recommendation of a specialized unit within the Department of Education set aside to perform that function, upon the advice of the universities.

2. Provision for educational and associated services, including the Program of Studies, the definition and general organization of educational services (including special education and vocational and technical education), the listing of approved teaching texts and materials, the granting of secondary school leaving certificates and diplomas, and defining the rights and duties

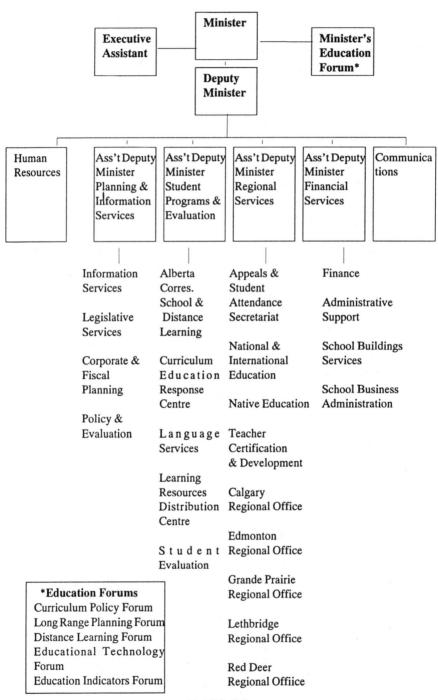

Exhibit 3-1
Organization Chart by Functions
Typical Department of Education

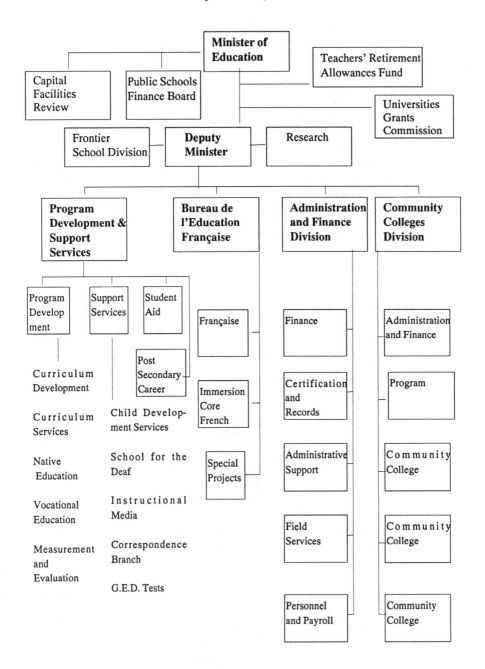

Exhibit 3-2
Organization Chart: Manitoba
Department of Education

of students and their parents regarding religious and patriotic exercises and instruction.

3. Student rights and responsibilities including access to education, language of instruction, compulsory attendance, excused absences and acceptable standards of student conduct.

4. Size and nature of local school administration units, including the duties of trustees, the operating of districts, powers of school boards, documents and reports required, oath of office, conduct of meetings, property assessment, financial cost-sharing and limitations on local taxing authority (sometimes present).

5. The employment of teachers, the qualifications of teachers and supervisory personnel, the nature of teacher contracts of employment, termination procedures, appeals to termination, and in some provinces, salary agreements.

6. The employment of non-teaching employees and officers, including secretary-treasurers and school superintendents.

7. Provision for province-wide examinations and power or bench-mark tests.

8. The length of school day and school year.

9. Private schools, home schooling, and other acceptable alternatives to attendance at a public school.

Organizational charts, at best, are illustrative of the major areas into which the work has been divided and they suggest how communications, authority, and responsibility are *expected* to flow. Chapters 11 through 14 suggest how major bureaucracies such as departments of education and larger school jurisdictions are liable to work, in practice.

post-secondary education

In addition to a Department of Education, some provinces have established separate departments responsible for post-secondary education, which frequently carry additional responsibilities such as manpower (Alberta) or Science and Technology (Quebec).

differences

The organization of the Departments of Education in Quebec and Newfoundland and New Brunswick are somewhat different from those of the other provinces mainly as a consequence of denominational religion considerations or languages. In Quebec the dual aspect (Roman Catholic and Protestant) is represented by two Associate Deputy Ministers, one Roman Catholic and the other Protestant, and through them two confessional committees of the Superior Council of Education. In Newfoundland the department organization is complicated by the existence of six denominational systems – Roman Catholic, Anglican, United Church, Salvation Army, Seventh Day Adventists and Pentecostal Assemblies. Each has an Assistant Superintendent but it is the council of Education, consisting of the Minister and Deputy Minister meeting with the Assistant Superintendents, that achieves unity in standards and curriculum, in vocational training, in teacher education, and in adult and higher education. Amalgamation of denominational schools in Newfoundland in recent years has reduced considerably the denominational emphasis which used to exist. In New Brunswick the Educational Services Division of the department has an English and a French section, while the Finance and Administration division (the other part) is bilingual in operation. No special provisions for denominational education are made in the organizational structures of the Departments of Education in Ontario, Saskatchewan and Alberta where publicly supported separate schools exist. British Columbia does not have a publicly supported separate school system, but like many other provinces, the hard line division between public and parochial education has become eroded.

Duties of the Minister of Education

The introductory paragraph to this chapter made note of the high degree of similarity among the organizational structures of the provincial departments of education. There is also a high degree of similarity among the provinces with respect to the legal duties of the Minister of Education. The sections which follow summarize the major areas of responsibility.

legal duties

The Minister of Education is in charge of the department of Education and is thus responsible to the Lieutenant-Governor-in-Council of the province for the administration of the department, of the school act (education act), and the regulations relating thereto and the appropriate parts of other statutes such as labor relations and child welfare where they impinge upon education, and the regulations accompanying them also. The reader is reminded that a regulation is a law made by the Cabinet (not the Assembly) under the authority of a statute such as the school act, labor act, or child welfare act.

School Legislation

The school acts (education acts) for each of the Canadian provinces is a unique piece of legislation (statute) developed and modified over time in order to meet the schooling requirements of the residents of the province. Although the specific sections and subsections of each act vary in intent and thus in wording there is a commonalty in the matters addressed, the structure of the enactments, and in many instances even in the intent, if not in the specific content.

Each act usually begins with a preamble (not part of the legislation) which sets forward a statement of intent – a belief statement. This is followed by a set of definitions and interpretations which usually begin with the statement, "In this Act . . ." For example, *board* means a board of trustees of a district or division, or subject to the County Act, a board of education of a county under that Act (Province of Alberta *School Act*). Frequently, the interpretations section is followed by several sections which set forward the role and authority of the Minister of Education to administer the school act and the regulations attendant thereto.

act format

School legislation is drafted in three broad classifications. Mandatory sections of the act require that something *will* be done, *shall* be done – some person or board is responsible for an action. Prohibitive sections and subsections require that something *not* be done – a person or board is prohibited from . . . . The third category, permissive legislation, is the portion of the school act which allows for local school board or teacher initiatives. These are the sections which permit local autonomy. The view of the government in power, on the question of centralized/decentralized power, is readily discerned by inspecting the ratio of must to may sections and the centre of importance of the issues enumerated in each category. Also, search out the partnership sections.

Most school legislation can be grouped into the 12 main areas indicated.

areas of
legislative
power

1. *Students.* These sections normally cover such matters as right to access to school, student duties, courses of studies, required attendance, consequences of non-attendance, right to privacy, nature and access to records, language of instruction, responsibility for damage to school property, and right to appeal either by the parents or the students on their own behalf.

2. *Parents.* Most school legislation will include provisions for parents to call for review of their child's education, especially those decisions concerning the placement of their children in a particular school program, or the suspension or expulsion of their child from school, or the provision or prohibition of religious exercises and instruction, and patriotic exercises and instruction.

3. *School Boards.* Since the school act is an act respecting the governance of schools it is to be expected that major sections of school legislation will deal with the responsibility and authority of school boards. Sections will detail the number and size of school boards, the establishment of public and separate and private school districts. Other sections will instruct the Board on the provision of educational and other services such as student transportation, tuition agreements with other jurisdictions, student maintenance allowances for those students required to be away from home, and the provision of health services. And, other sections will specify the duties of trustees and the board chairman, the requirements for meetings, reading of by-laws, keeping of records, inspection of documents, reasons for trustee disqualification, and contractual requirements.

4. *Schools.* Schools are the centre of the educational system but most school acts tend toward enunciating the provisions for education to be received outside the conventional school structure by enacting legislation respecting private schools, home schooling, and alternative programs such as distance learning centres. Much of the school and instructional "law" comes through regulations. In this grouping of clauses and sub-clauses, however, the reader will find laws regarding the length of the school day and the school year, and provisions for parental choice, or restrictions on choice regarding the school their children will attend.

5. *Program of Studies.* Statutory references to the program of studies are usually limited to requiring the school board to implement the program of studies, to make provisions for the special education student, for the development of

student placement and placement appeal policies, for early childhood services, or for alternative programs (programs of choice). The major part of the program of studies will be found in Department of Education regulations, teacher guide books, and related ministry documents.

6. *Resolution of Disputes.* Besides the provisions for resolving disputes between teacher and school board (employee and employer), most school legislation makes legal provision for appeals at the system, third party and Ministerial levels. Normally the appeal procedures relate to issues of special education placement, language of instruction (for some provinces), home schooling, suspension and expulsion of students, accuracy of student records, and payment of tuition, book rental, and other instructional fees.

7. *Teachers and Principals.* Much of the legislation concerning teachers and principals is contractual in nature in that it specifies qualifications required for employment and defines the various contracts (temporary, interim, part-time, continuing, etc.) a teacher can enter into. Legal provisions covering transfer, suspension, and termination will be included as well as termination appeal provisions to a Minister's appeal tribunal (Board of Reference).

The *School Act* for Alberta, for example, provides several instruction-related specific directions to teachers:

teacher
duties

Section 13. A teacher, while providing instruction or supervision, must:

a. provide instruction competently to students;

b. teach the course of study and education programs that are prescribed, approved and authorized pursuant to this Act;

c. promote goals and standards applicable to the provision of education adopted or approved pursuant to this Act;

d. encourage and foster learning in students;

e. regularly evaluate students and periodically report the results of the evaluation to the students, the students' parents and the board;

f. maintain, under the direction of the principal, order and discipline among the students while they are in the school or on the school grounds and while they are attending or participating in activities sponsored or approved by the board;

g. subject to any applicable collective agreement and the teacher's contract of employment, carry out these duties that are assigned to the teacher by the principal or the board. (R.S.A. 1988, s. 3.1)

Ontario legislation (R.S.O. 1980, c. 129, s. 235, *Education Act*), as another example, legally defines the teacher's duties in Section 235, in that Ontario teachers have a duty:

a. to teach diligently and faithfully the classes or subjects assigned to him by the principal;

b. to encourage the pupils in the pursuit of learning;

c. to inculcate by precept and example respect for religion and the principles of Judaeo-Christian morality and the highest regard for truth, justice, loyalty, love of country, humanity, benevolence, sobriety, industry, frugality, purity, temperance and all other virtues;

d. to assist in developing cooperation and coordination of effort among the members of the staff of the school;

e. to maintain, under the direction of the principal, proper order and discipline in his classroom and while on duty in the school and on the school ground;

f. in instruction and in all communications with the pupils in regard to discipline and the management of the school,
  i. to use the English language, except where it is impractical to do so by reason of the pupil not understanding English, and except in respect of instruction in a language other than English when such other language is being taught as one of the subjects in the course of study, or
  ii. to use the French language in schools or classes in which French is the language of instruction except where it is impractical to do so by reason of the pupil not understanding French, and except in respect of instruction in a language other than French when such other language is being taught as one of the subjects in the course of study;

g. to conduct his class in accordance with a timetable which shall be accessible to pupils and to the principal and supervisory officers;

h. to participate in professional activity days as designated by the board under the regulations;

i. to notify such person as is designated by the board if he is to be absent from school and the reason therefore;

j. to deliver the register, the school key and other school property in his possession to the board on demand, or when his agreement with the board has expired, or when for any reason his employment has ceased; and

k. to use and permit to be used as a textbook in a class that he teachers in an elementary or secondary school;
  i. in a subject area for which textbooks are approved by the Minister, only textbooks that are approved by the Minister, and
  ii. in all subject areas, only textbooks that are approved by the board.

duties of principals

School principals are presented with a set of instructions by both provinces. Each Canadian province has its own format, and sometimes the requirements appear in regulations or other official documents, but the intent in each instance is to define legally the minimum job requirements of the practitioner. They are expressions of public expectations.

Section 15 of the Province of Alberta *School Act* states that a school principal *must*:

a. provide instructional leadership in the school;

b. ensure that the instruction provided by the teachers employed in the school is consistent with the courses of study and education programs prescribed, approved or authorized pursuant to this Act;

c. evaluate or provide for the evaluation of programs offered in the school;

d. direct the management of the school;

e. maintain order and discipline in the school and on the school ground and during activities sponsored or approved by the board;

f. promote cooperation between the school and the community that it serves;

g. supervise the evaluation and advancement of students;

h. evaluate or provide for the evaluation of the teachers employed in the school;

i. subject to any applicable collective agreement and the principal's contract of employment, carry out those duties that are assigned to the principal by the board. (R.S.A. 1988, s. 3.1)

In addition to the duties of being a teacher, the Province of Ontario requires the school principal (Section 236, *Education Act*):

a. to maintain proper order and discipline in the school;

b. to develop cooperation and coordination of effort among the members of the staff of the school;

c. to register the pupils and to ensure that the attendance of pupils for every school day is recorded either in the register supplied by the Minister in accordance with the instructions contained therein or in such other manner as is approved by the Minister;

d. to establish and maintain, and to retain, transfer and dispose of, in the manner prescribed by the regulations, a record in respect of each pupil enrolled in the school;

e. to prepare a timetable, to conduct the school according to such timetable and the school year calendar or calendars applicable thereto, to make the calendar or calendars and the timetable accessible to the pupils, teachers and supervisory officers and to assign classes and subjects to the teachers.

f. to hold, subject to the approval of the appropriate supervisory officer, such examinations as he considers necessary for the promotion of pupils or for any other purpose and report as required by the board the progress of the pupil to his parent or guardian where the pupil is a minor and otherwise to the pupil;

g. subject to revisions by the appropriate supervisory officer, to promote such pupils as he considers proper and to issue to each such pupil a statement thereof;

h. to ensure that all textbooks used by pupils are those approved by the board and, in the case of subject areas for which the Minister approves textbooks, those approved by the Minister;

i. to furnish the Ministry and to the appropriate supervisory officer any information that it may be in his power to give respecting the condition of the school premises, the discipline of the school, the progress of the pupils and any other matter affecting the interests of the school, and to prepare such reports for the board as are required by the board;

j. to give assiduous attention to the health and comfort of the pupils, to the cleanliness, temperature and ventilation of the school, to the care of all teaching materials and other school property, and to the condition and appearance of the school buildings and grounds;

k. to report promptly to the board and to the municipal health officer or to the school medical officer where one has been appointed, when he has reason to suspect the existence of any infectious or contagious disease in the school, and of the unsanitary condition of any part of the school building or the school grounds;

l. to refuse admission to the school of any person whom he believes is infected or exposed to communicable diseases requiring quarantine and placarding under regulations made pursuant to the *Public Health Act* until furnished with a certificate of a medical officer of health or of a legally qualified medical practitioner approved by him that all danger from exposure to contact with such person has passed;

m. subject to an appeal to the board, to refuse to admit to the school or classroom a person whose presence in the school or classroom would in his judgment be detrimental to the physical or mental well-being of the pupils; and

n. to maintain a visitor's book in the school when so determined by the board (R.S.O. 1980, c. 129, s. 236).

8. *Cost Sharing.* Through the school act, teachers, school boards, and of course the public are informed as to how the provincial share of the cost of education will be funded and distributed. Specific regulations and dollar amounts are rarely included since they require frequent amendment, but the structure of the grants system, payment dates, default provisions, and similar matters of principle are set forward in law.

9. *Taxes.* School legislation also includes sections on the levying of taxes, the school boards' authority to borrow money, limits on the extent of borrowing, right to issue debentures, sale of property, purchasing of school sites, expropriation of land, disposal of property and other similar financial and property matters.

10. *Boundaries.* The boundaries of school jurisdictions are not a static thing, especially in urban centres, so several sections of school legislation will be devoted to stating the provisions for boundary changes, alteration of district names, adjustment of assets, annexation procedures, and the provision for public hearings on the above noted and similar matters.

11. *Public Initiatives.* Most current school legislation sets forward procedures for presenting and reacting to public petitions, including the eligibility.of signatories, legal time lines, hearing the petitioners, and provisions for school board debate and vote as are required by law. Usually school boards have the authority to conduct plebiscites on matters of special local interest.

12. *Annual Meetings and Elections.* It is difficult to describe a pattern in school legislation, but in addition to the areas noted above, most legislators, through their school act or sister acts such as municipal election legislation, make provision for annual general meetings of the public, and specific timelines

for school board elections in order to ensure local accountability of the trustees and through them, the professional staff.

Regional Offices

In an effort to decentralize the work of the departments of education, many provincial governments have established regional offices of the department, located in major cities across the province. These offices perform many of the functions for which the department, located in the capital city, is given responsibility. Teachers will note that a similar practice is followed with large urban and many large rural school jurisdictions. The main purposes of decentralization are to shorten communication lines and provide for local initiatives. For example, see column 3, Exhibit 3-1.

decentralization

Teachers work within an organizational structure which extends beyond the local school and school district to include the provincial department of education (ministry of education). Much of their role as administrators and as teachers is dictated by the nature of the structures within which they work. Many factors affect the way people act at work. The characteristics of the organization (in the case of the specifics of this chapter, the extended educational bureaucracy) are among the most important influences upon our behavior as teachers. Part Five, Teaching as a Profession, will summarize some of the research findings associated with being a professional in an centralized bureaucracy.

Summary

The purpose of this chapter was to describe in sufficient detail the operations of the ministry (department) of education and to illustrate the degree of central (provincial) control which exists in public and also separate and private schooling.

4

School Boards and District Organization

A country is as great as it is educated and intelligent.
Egerton Ryerson

> Early School Districts
>
> The School Consolidation Movement
>
> School, Municipal Amalgamations
>
> School Boards
>
> Division of Power
>
> Superintendent, Principal, Teacher
>
> Organization of a School System

Introduction

The overall responsibility for basic education lies with the province. However, the structure through which the service is provided should permit a significant amount of autonomy in decision making by local school boards, schools, professional teachers, and students.

It is the responsibility of society to set forward the broad goals of education. It is the responsibility of the provincial government to, through its agencies, translate these goals into specific objectives and to define the skills and knowledge required to achieve these purposes. The provincial education ministry should designate those objectives which are to be included in common education for all, and ensure they are incorporated into locally designed programs, but it should restrict its intense involvement in activities which can be effectively conducted locally.

goals of education

Educational planning at all levels must accommodate input from those having a vested interest in the outcomes of the planning. The *basics* in education are those learning experiences that develop and modify skills and attitudes to provide for continued learning, self fulfillment, social awareness and morality, adaptability to change, productive employment and personal well being. Local school jurisdictions, representing Canadian communities, have a vested interest.

School Districts and Early Consolidation

divisions

The basic unit or organization for the operation of schools in Canada is the school district. Sometimes the term "school division" is used to describe the basic jurisdictional unit, but most often *division* is used to describe the larger administrative units which were legislated into being in order to overcome the educational and financial shortcomings associated with the small, usually rural school unit. School jurisdictions vary in size and shape and in the organization of the controlling board, but the common element of all is that they are recipients of the delegated authority from the legislature through the Department of Education. In those provinces where legislation provides for a denominational or linguistic division of the school population two school boards, public and separate, English and French, for example, will serve the educational needs of the same geographic area.

The historical Canadian school district was organized to serve the population, usually rural, located within reasonable walking distance of a central point where the schoolhouse was located. In some parts of early Canada, the building was the local church, thus the parish school unit.

four-by-four

In response to the growth in new settlements there developed thousands of small districts (sometimes called *four-by-fours* in Western Canada because of their size, i.e., four miles by four miles.) The purpose of the school district was to provide schooling for the children of the new community and therefore each local school board built a school building, usually a one-room structure, and employed a teacher. In this small school, under the direction of a poorly paid and often inadequately trained teacher, students of many different grades and cultural backgrounds received a rudimentary education.

inadequate

Financing these schools was difficult, and the provision of an education beyond the elementary grades often became impossible. The product was inadequate to meet the needs of an expanding and growing Canada. These hardships often resulted in cooperative efforts among districts, that is, a consolidation of efforts and finances. The first consolidated school districts in Canada were formed in Prince Edward Island and Nova Scotia in 1900 and 1903, in Newfoundland in 1903, and in British Columbia in 1905, but the main

consolidated
districts

swing to consolidated school districts awaited the improvement of roads and the beginning of the motor age in the 1920s. Saving of money was supposed to

savings

occur with consolidation because there would be one building instead of several to equip and maintain, and fewer teachers would be required due to the increased student-teacher ratio which would now be possible. The anticipated cost saving, however, was rarely achieved. Costs of transportation became an added financial burden. Also, a greater range of subjects was offered at the senior levels and thus additional costs for space, teachers, and equipment were incurred. Offices for administrators were required, as well as release time from teaching for administrative tasks, further increasing the overall costs.

Instead of one board of trustees for each district, one board was required for the enlarged (consolidated) district, with one trustee representing an area which formerly was represented by a number, usually three, trustees. The purpose of the board remained the same, however. The board became the buffer between the general public and the professional staff, the policy-setting body, as well as the administrative body which hired the teachers, hired a local farmer to cut the grass on the school yard, hired someone to dig the well, and did a host of other administrative chores. The larger the consolidated school district, the more these administrative details were left to the hired staff and, more and more, the school board became a policy-making body. With the growth in size of the districts came an increased number of administrative and financial officials. Whereas in earlier times one of the elected trustees would act as recording secretary and *keeper* of the limited financial records necessary, now an employee known as secretary-treasurer would be hired. Whereas in earlier times the school board would hire the teacher and ensure the program of studies was in place, now it began to rely more heavily upon Department of Education (Ministry) inspectors, or in the larger (usually urban) districts, their own school superintendent to perform this activity.

hired staff

Larger School Jurisdictions

Roads continued to improve and increasing demands were being placed upon the educational programs of Canadian schools. In the middle 1930s another school district reorganization began – that of the enlarged local units. Timelines varied, but province after province moved toward the formation of larger administrative units, usually for those areas outside the major cities.

The reasoning paralleled that of the earlier change to consolidated school units from the individual one-room schools. There would be, the proponents of enlarged units would say, a real cost saving. This was not to occur. However, other advantages were achieved – larger centralized schools were better equipped, better staffed and more able to provide a much wider range of subject offerings, including non-academic courses such as home economics and shop. Also, specialists could be hired to travel among the schools in these larger units to teach French, band, shop, home economics, and other subjects, as well as to provide services in counseling, libraries, and student testing. The model for this expanded local unit was the school division developed in Alberta in 1936. The principle features of this were as follows.

real cost savings

expanded programs

Alberta school division

1. The district organization remained, but the duties and responsibilities of the local *divisional district* school boards were drastically reduced, in fact, their sole duty soon became to decide whether religious instruction would be given and to nominate the name of one teacher for the local school, and to do those things specifically requested by the divisional board. Usually the duties were few in number and infrequently performed.

2. Initially, school divisions consisted of rural districts only, but they were later modified to include villages and town districts in many instances. The slowness of including the village or town unit was probably due to a fear of the loss of local autonomy.

3. The school divisions were to be governed by an elected board of trustees consisting of from three to five trustees (plus elected trustees from larger towns within the division) on a three-year revolving basis. The school division was divided into wards called subdivisions with one trustee representing one subdivision.

4. There would be a central office with a full-time staff, supplemented by a provincially-appointed superintendent of schools assigned to that particular school division to act as advisor to the divisional board of trustees, and to ensure that provincial standards were maintained. Inspection of high school teachers and the approval of the high school program of studies were the prerogative of a provincially appointed staff of high school inspectors.

5. The school divisions varied in size but averaged about 75 districts per division and would cover a geographic area of perhaps 50 by 100 kilometres.

6. The school divisions (units, township units, regions, regional units) were organizational structures which resulted in the closing of many of the small schools and the consequent building and equipping of larger centralized schools.

repercussions
The formation of school administrative units and the subsequent centralization of schools were not without repercussions however. The closing of a smaller, local school was viewed as a threat to the local merchants; local school board members feared loss of authority and prestige, and students had to spend longer hours on a school bus over roads which, in many instances, had not yet been developed to satisfactory standards.

School-Municipal Amalgamation

Throughout Canadian educational history there has been, in general, a determined separation of school and municipal governance. There have been many examples of overlapping between the governing bodies, but today, the provision for the governance of education and municipal affairs tends to favor distinct entities in most Canadian provinces. The common element is, and has been, property taxation as a major source of revenue. Financing education will be discussed in greater detail elsewhere but it is an important consideration in school-municipal relations and has been known to create deep divisions in an otherwise placid community.

distinct
entities

duplication
Where school districts pre-dated municipal organization, the school districts obviously had to collect their own taxes from property owners. With the formation of municipal districts, the duplication of costs and efforts were judged to be unnecessary and costly and thus one body, the municipal district, became the collector of taxes. The feeling of elected municipal officials has frequently been that school boards were extravagant and not as responsible as the local municipal council, a position that has been abetted in some cases by provincial legislation limiting the local mill rate (a measure of taxation) permissible. Many municipal councillors, forced to collect whatever tax monies

the school boards requested, felt that if only they could control education, everything would operate much better, or at least taxes would be lower.

Another factor was the duplication of central offices, space and staff. Protagonists for amalgamation of school and municipal affairs argued that one central office could serve both purposes. Also, if there was one board, fewer meeting days and thus less mileage costs and expenses for trustees and councillors would be incurred. Municipal districts which had been quite cooperative in snowplowing school driveways and bus routes, and in the maintenance of roads felt this cooperation, plus maintenance of buildings and equipment, would be improved by one joint organization rather than two. These, and other reasons were advanced by the pro-amalgamators. Underneath, however, one of the prime justifications was for the municipal authority to gain control over education expenditures. For example, in 1950 the *County Act* was passed in Alberta permitting the formation of counties (integrated omnibus form of local government). The first attempts were to include hospital organization as well, but this idea was soon dropped as being not feasible. In 1951, the first counties were formed. Others followed through the years so that by 1969 thirty-one counties in all had been formed. One was subsequently dissolved. Therefore, approximately half of rural, settled Alberta was organized into counties and the other half into school divisions.

amalgamation

counties

The main complicating factor arises when there are towns and villages within the county which are part of the county system for educational purposes but not for municipal purposes.

complicating factor

In Alberta, the county board of education does not have the power to borrow money, collect taxes for educational purposes or pass the final budget. Other than these limitations, the board of education operates in exactly the same way as does a board of trustees for other educational jurisdictions. Trustee duties will be described later.

The amalgamation of municipal and educational services is more imaginary than real. The financial and bookkeeping aspects, for example, are kept separately for provincial accounting and funding purposes, even though housed in the same building. Provinces other than Alberta have worded their legislation differently and designed different structures, but the essence of the dispute still revolves around the deep-seated tradition of local autonomy in education matters.

local autonomy

School Boards

Because school boards are elected municipal bodies with few restrictive qualifications for membership, it is not unexpected that the role of the board is often misunderstood by those persons who expect to see more structure, more training, more order, and less politics.

Within the local school jurisdiction there are two groups of people who are centrally involved with the governance of education. They are: (1) school

ultimate power

boards who hold the ultimate power and responsibility for the operation of local schools, and (2) the executives, advisors, administrators and teachers (the professionals), whose task it is to inform and provide advice in the decision making/policy making activities of the board, and do the actual work – planning, organizing, implementing, and teaching.

Role of School Boards

accountable

School boards are a creation of the provincial governments subject to the will of the province, and are accountable to the provincial government (Minister of Education) for the implementation of the statutes and regulations which direct the educational services provided to Canadian communities, and are also accountable politically to the local populace for implementing their common wishes respecting the education of their children.

statutes

The school board operates under three distinct kinds of statutes and regulations. The first are those statutes and regulations which are prescriptive, that is, they specify what the board *must* do. The second group are prohibitions, in that they state what the board *must not* do. Thus the prescriptions and prohibitions define the board's role as an agent of the provincial government. The third group of statutes and regulations are declarations of *permission* in that they specify what the board *may* do. The latter group of statutes set the boundaries of freedom to govern. They establish the role of the school board as a local governing authority.

corporate body

The school board is a corporate body with a legally defined range of duties, which exists apart from those individuals who make up the board. This means that the board members act only as a board, not as individuals, and there can be a change in board membership without causing a change in the board legal status and authority. Individual members cannot exercise the power of the board unless authorized to do so by resolution of the board. The courts cannot interfere with the operations of the school board as long as the board does not exceed its powers as specified by law, as long as any irregularities in procedure which occur do not cause serious harm, or where the board, if it were mistaken, acted in good faith, and in general as long as the board did not act unjustly, prejudicially, or in bad faith. Traditionally, the main interest and function of school boards was considered to be financing education. In most jurisdictions this has changed. Other policy areas have become more important.

General Area of School Board Responsibility

duties
of boards

Contrary to the situation in earlier times, school boards normally administer school systems which have many schools and large staffs of professional and support employees. The eight general areas of school board operations listed below encompass most of the duties performed by the typical Canadian school board.

1. Legislation which covers policy development designed to meet the requirements of the provincial educational authority and the unique needs and problems of the local jurisdictions.

2. Compliance activities, wherein the school board ensures the laws and regulations of the province are implemented by the staff.

3. Inspection, observation and evaluation obligations require the board to evaluate the efficiency and effectiveness of the operation of the schools and the building and financial functions of the district.

4. Communication with the public, professional staff, and departmental officials are a central responsibility.

5. Interpretation of the wishes of the local community to the provincial authorities; the provincial directives to the local community, the parents concerns to the teachers and vice versa, and the expressions of the local educational community (parents, taxpayers, administrators and teachers) in policy and directives are an integral part of the trustee's and corporate school board function.

6. Adjudication of disputes which fall within their jurisdiction, usually student or teacher related, place school boards under a special common law, legal obligation to be governed by the principles of natural justice.

7. Budgets and contracts and other financial matters must be studied, debated, and approved by the board.

8. Operating its own business, for example, structuring of board committees, setting meeting times, electing officers of the board, deciding upon rules of procedure, expense and honorarium amounts, and the very important function of selecting the chief executive officer. The school superintendent responsibilities, not often recognized by teachers and the public, must be attended to diligently in order to limit confrontation and squabbling.

Policy Making Activities of the School Board

The provincial government would naturally view the compliances activities (seeing to it that provincial laws, programs and regulations are in place) as the most important part of the school board's activities. The staff and local citizens may hold a different view. For example, under its legislative authority (policy making function) the board usually establishes policies in the following areas.

policy making function

1. Professional and New Professional Staff

a. number to be employed, student-teacher ratios, hours of instruction time, preparation and marking, release time and when schools are to be granted, for example, a full-time teacher librarian, subject or grade-level coordinators, department heads, full-time release time for school principals, and a whole range of other staffing policy matters which impact directly upon the quality of the work life of the teacher;

b. pay scales, and other *collective agreement* (salary scale) benefit packages.

c. selection or rejection of teacher applicants for employment and other personnel contracting policies;

d. personnel policies including policies, for example, on recruitment, selection, orientation, staff development, and teacher performance appraisal procedures.

2. Curricular Offerings

a. decisions on the general scope and extent of local educational offerings to be provided in addition to those required by provincial statutes and regulations;

b. policies on general instructional procedures and students organization such as grading, multiple-grade organizations, double entry dates, etc.

3. Students

a. determining policies regarding age of school admission where the ages under consideration are outside the attendance requirements of the school act;

b. establishes school opening and closing dates, Christmas and the mid-year break within, of course, provincial guidelines;

c. establishing school attendance areas;

d. establishing special schools and classes within the parameters of provincial plans for special needs students;

e. provides for the protection and health of students;

f. providing for health and other special services including activities programs and off-campus trips;

g. making regulations regarding student discipline, truancy, dress and conduct.

4. Finance

a. approving budget;

b. establishing the level of local tax requisition;

c. approving accounts for payment;

d. entering into contracts for goods and services;

e. adapting regulations for accounting of funds;

f. receiving progress reports on expenditures (budget) and modifyng the budget where necessary.

5. Facilities

a. deciding, within provincial guidelines, what buildings should be built, when and where, and which buildings should be modified, and which schools and other facilities should be closed;

b. deciding upon the educational specifications, for example, library, gymnasium, shops, music rooms, and classroom sizes, required to be designed into new or modified buildings;

c. deciding upon furniture and equipment quantities and specifications;

d. selecting and purchasing school and other sites;

e. appointing architects, approves building plans, and accepts construction bids.

f. supervises construction and accepts completed building project.

6. Transportation

a. establishing policies regarding bussing distances, gate service (to the farm gate), bussing routes, and student conduct while on buses;

b. entering into contracts with the operators of non-district owned school busses;

c. establishing policies governing bus garage operations.

7. Community Relations

a. making policy decisions regarding community forms, annual meetings, printed advertising, open school board meetings, annual reports to the parents and other provisions to keep in touch with the community and especially the parents and ratepayers.

Policies

Downey, in *Policy Analysis in Education* notes that governing authorities such as school boards have two central obligations. First they must process the competing demands (needs) of the jurisdictions they represent and make choices, and second, they must allocate resources and set guidelines in order to bring their choices to fruition. Downey contends (p. 9) that a policy is an instrument of governance and can be defined in the following manner.

1. A policy is an authoritative determination, by a governing authority, of a society's intents and priorities and an authoritative allocation of resources to those intents and priorities.

2. A policy is also an authoritative guideline to institutions governed by the authority (and persons who work for them) as to what their intentions are to be and how they are to set out to achieve them.

Authorities agree that policies are guidelines which allow some discretion in their implementation. Downey notes later that policy making can be:

a. pure political action;

b. incremental precedent setting;

c. the exercise of a vested power; or

d. the legitimation of expertise.

School board policies are major guidelines for future discretionary action by the professional staff. Usually they are directed at the line officers of the school system such as superintendents, principals, teachers and heads of specific units of the organization. Policy statements are of four main types.

1. *Framework Policies.* These are policies which set forward, in broad terms, who the organization is and what it intends to do. Why do we exist? What is our preferred vision of the future? Who do we propose to serve?

2. *Governance Policies*. Policies which set forward the system through which the school jurisdiction will work including identifying the roles, responsibilities and functions of the Board and staff. By-laws and constitutions, and procedures for reaching decisions are referred to as governance policies.

3. *Operational Policies*. These are policies directed toward the functional effectiveness of the school system in terms of areas such as personnel administration, program implementation, and administration of finances.

4. *Issue Policies*. Policies which address major problems and frequently cause direction changes in policies under types 1, 2 and 3 above are referred to as issue policies. They are both specific and direct, and usually result from a direct interface with community, parents, staff, or sometimes with the Ministry, and sometimes with sister levels of government.

Policies are made or changed by positive action, usually in the form of a resolution or motion.

Those policies which are called administrative policies arise usually not from legislative action, but from professional decision making and have as their focus of attention the implementation of school board policy or government legislation and regulation.

Division of Powers Between Elected Trustees and Professional Staff

The reader will note that a major responsibility of the school board is to develop educational policies within the legal (statutory) confines of their mandate. But because the line between policy making and policy administration is so frequently blurred, a point of friction often develops at the board table. friction This is where the professional advice of the staff meets the sometimes politically motivated directions taken by elected trustees. The fight over the division of power between elected and professional people can become counter productive, even harmful, since the nature of the organizational climate has a tremendous effect upon the attitudes, beliefs, motivation (quality of the work life) of the people who work there.

Well functioning school boards have, through contract and procedural arrangements, moved to capture the advantages of open discussion by people who frequently see the educational world differently, without incurring the incapacities generated by aggressive conflict. The key players in the procedures are the school board chairman and the school superintendent.

Most school jurisdictions employ a system (cycle plan) to help reduce the potential conflict between the superintendent and the school board. The following (based upon the Davies-Brickell system of school management) illustrates the desirable division of rules.

For example, a number of children have been injured by slipping on icy sidewalks. The policy objectives would be to prevent student accidents. The policy statement (made by the Board) would require that every effort be made objective to eliminate accidents on school property. The policy regulations (issued by policy senior administration) would set out requirements governing student supervi-
regulation

sion for principals and teachers to follow, and perhaps requirements for caretakers regarding cleaning and sanding of sidewalks. The third phase would require reports on the number of teachers involved and hours of outdoor supervision, and probably when and the number of times that sidewalks are being shoveled.

Finally, the school boards would receive a report on the effectiveness of the student accident reduction policy in reducing student accidents. If trustees or the superintendency felt, after reviewing the report, that modifications were required, the policy would be redrafted and the cycle for this specific policy would proceed through a second revolution of the wheel.

In summary, the duties of the local school board can be categorized as: local duties

Compulsory Duties

In carrying out these duties, the board is acting as an agent of the provincial government. The duties specified by most provincial statutes are to:

a. ensure that all resident students have access to equitable educational opportunities;

b. engage suitable and qualified teachers as required for the school of the district;

c. provide adequate buildings and accommodation for the children of the district, and to keep these in good condition;

d. provide the instructional materials and equipment required for giving instruction to the various grades of the school;

e. make regulations for the management of the schools consistent with provincial laws and regulations;

f. hold regular meetings of the board in order to conduct the business of the district;

g. appoint or elect the officers of the board such as the chairperson;

h. keep financial and other records pertaining to the operations of the district;

i. ensure that school is conducted in accordance with the laws and regulations of the province, and that the prescribed program of studies is followed;

j. decide what school in the district a student shall attend, and to enforce compulsory attendance laws;

k. provide conveyance for students of the district under certain conditions;

l. allow students enrolled in programs of teacher education to practice in the schools;

m. pay teachers' and other employees' salaries regularly at the end of each month, or as required by contract; and

n. carry adequate insurance to protect the public and the staff.

Examples of Optional Powers

optional
powers

Optional powers allow the board to provide additional services to the schools and the district over and above the minimum services that are mandated by the province. Depending upon the wording of provincial laws, these usually permit the board to do at least the following:

a. employ doctors, dentists, or nurses to provide health services to the children in the district;

b. provide textbooks and other school supplies to students in the district; either through book rental plans or outright grants;

c. contribute financial support to such activities as school festivals and school fairs;

d. provide scholarships and bursaries to high school and university students from the district;

e. provide lunches to students at school during the noon hour;

f. expel students from school for gross misconduct, neglect of duty, or for other serious misdemeanors;

g. establish junior colleges in the district to offer studies above the usual high school level;

h. pay teachers for absences due to sickness over the minimum required by law, and make provision for sick pay to be cumulative;

i. dismiss teachers for various reasons, including misconduct, neglect of duty, or inefficiency; and

j. arrange to borrow money needed for educational purposes in the district.

Superintendent, Principal and Teacher

In some of the literature, the terms "superintendents" and "superintendency" are held to be two different things. The superintendent is an individual, the superintendency is that cluster of management, administrative and supervisory positions, usually working out of the central office of the school district or unit.

chief executive
officer

The superintendent is the individual professional educator who is designated as the chief executive officer of the school board; the person who is authorized to direct the school system in a manner consistent with the law and the educational and administrative policies of the board. As chief executive officer (in some jurisdictions chief educational officer or director), the superintendent of schools is ultimately responsible and solely accountable to the school board for the proper and efficient administration of the school system. Although, as chief educational leader, the superintendent may work with and through teams of professional educators (teachers, principals and supervisors) the ultimate responsibility to the school board cannot be delegated. The superintendent is accountable. As an agent of the school board, the superintendent is performance (results) oriented. The responsibility is to direct the school system toward achievement of its declared purposes. Results orient leadership is critical,

agent of
board

however, how the incumbent works with the teaching staff is usually more important to the day-to-day operations of the district than the power lodged in the position.

The superintendent, in conjunction with the school board, works at the strategic level in assisting the school system to relate to its environment through planning. At the operations level, the superintendent implements the plan, and at the coordination level, the superintendent's primary aim is to link the implementation strategies with the monetary activities and support services in order to move the organization in the desired direction. Part Three provides some extended definitions of the above terms, such as operations level, if the reader wishes to read further in this area.

strategic planning

The following list summarizes the duties of the school superintendent. Superintendents are usually held responsible for, and accountable to, the employing school board for the following areas.

duties of superintendent

1. General responsibility for advising the Board on matters arising in all areas of the Board's jurisdiction.

2. Recommending appropriate policies to the Board in these areas.

3. Implementing the policies adopted by the Board.

4. Determining present and future educational needs of the school district and developing short- and long-range plans for meeting identified needs and for communicating the *vision*.

5. Evaluating the operation of all aspects of the educational system including personnel, and providing reports to the Board which will keep it informed as to how the school system is functioning (performance monitoring system).

6. Coordinating educational programs with the physical facilities, financial, and human resources within the school system, and getting everyone going in the same direction toward the goal of effective education.

7. Providing educational leadership and fostering conditions which will ensure the improvement of educational programs, and the efficient use of resources. This would include the development and implementation of programs of instructional leadership, management development, teacher supervision, staff development and teacher evaluation.

8. Designing and staffing an organization which will ensure that educational and administrative functions are carried out effectively. This would include decisions regarding student-teacher ratios, the provision of teacher librarians, the hiring of generalist or specialist teachers and other decisions which directly affect the teacher's work and student learnings.

9. Interpreting the education program to the community and working to advance school community relations.

10. Carrying forward other specific duties which from time to time may be delegated by the board (i.e., all those other things not listed).

The superintendent, as the board's chief executive officer, inspires followers, mobilizes resources, generates ideas, performs services and assumes a *proactive stance*.

role conflict

When the above areas of superintendent duties are reviewed, it becomes obvious the superintendent may often be seen to be in a role conflict situation; on the one hand as agent of the school board, but on the other hand as spokesperson or leader for the teachers – a person in the middle. Part Three, "Administration of Canadian Schools," will direct the reader to the kinds of activities and skills involved in the process of educational leadership.

The Principal

instructional leadership

The principal, another person in the middle, is the link between the teaching staff and the central office (superintendency), and the community, especially the parents. The role of the principal is not identical to the role of the superintendent but is similar. The school principal is responsible for the management and instructional leadership of the school. The principal is the chief educational officer at the school level. The principal has the authority to make decisions and enunciate rules and regulations which are consistent with the school act, the regulations of the Department of Education, and of course, the specific authority granted by the employing school board. Again, part Three will be useful.

Interaction between those served by the school system, the students, and the professional educator occurs primarily in the classrooms, halls, and grounds of the school. It is the group of classroom teachers who will determine, to a large degree (consciously or unconsciously), whether the policies of the Department of Education and the school board are achieved. There are three basic units to our system of schooling: the Minister, the school trustees, and the teachers. The pedagogical and administrative skills of the teacher are central. Take a bow!

Role of the Teacher

School organizations are most often described as bureaucracies (also see Chapter 11). In these organizations there are many teachers at the base, fewer people in the middle (principals, directors, department heads) and usually only one superintendent at the top. A person at the bottom of the pyramid has much less power and a narrower range of responsibilities than an individual at the top. This would become especially obvious if one were to inspect the job descriptions of the teacher and superintendent, for example.

job descriptions

role and personality

Writers agree there are two factors within an organization which interact to determine the formal role of the individual within the organization, these being the structure of the organization expressed through a set of role expectations, and the nature of the specific person (needs, values, personality, lifestyle, etc.) who fills the role. People in different roles do different jobs but people in and of themselves are also different. The role of the teacher is not easy to define.

New teachers often find themselves struggling for definitions of the role of the teacher since the variations in definition held by others may be enormous. "Why should I straighten up the room? Why should I supervise the hallways and washrooms? Why should I collect money for school pictures? None of these jobs sounds like teaching to me. Should I expect anything and everything to be part of my role as a teacher?"

struggle

The list which follows is at best a generalized, and only partial, listing of the roles of the teacher. The roles of the teacher are to: instill in their students a desire to learn; to contribute to the educational development of the students; to set high expectations for student performance; to respect students as individuals; to show trust; to provide resource materials, information and experiences which will stimulate learning and development. The teacher is expected to provide a good role model. Teachers are responsible for promoting learning, upgrading themselves professionally, and participating in the activities and governance of the school.

roles of
the teacher

These statements, although satisfactory at the level of generalization, are not sufficient to describe the role of the teacher. What is included and what is excluded from the list will be determined in part by the reader's view of the nature of the teaching task. If one views teaching as *labor*, then the teacher is responsible for implementing the instructional program in the prescribed manner. The teacher will adhere to specific routines and procedures which are rationally planned, programmatically organized, and routinized. If, however, the reader views teaching as a *craft*, possession of a repertoire of specialized techniques will be central. The teacher will have a set of generalized rules to be applied, with modification of course, to produce desired outcomes. The key words are repertoire and habitual. On the other hand, if teaching is considered to be a *profession*, the teacher will not only have a repertoire of specialized techniques (usually based upon research findings) but will also be expected to exercise considerable judgment in their application. Sound professional judgment in the application of a body of theoretical knowledge is central (good pedagogy). We ask the professional to diagnose needs or problems, appraise solutions, and apply the appropriate one. The professional is responsible for strategy and techniques – professional problem solving. But when teaching is viewed as an *art*, then the techniques and their application may be unconventional, novel, and personalized rather than standardized. Theory is present, but it is one step back. If teaching is considered to be a *science* then the major role of the teacher is to apply verified and generalizable research results to the classroom situation.

views of
teaching

Which one is it? Obviously the role of the Canadian teacher contains aspects of all five views of the nature of teaching, however, the emphasis placed on a certain view will make all the difference (see Part Five, Teaching as a Profession).

academic role

Another way of looking at teacher roles is to consider them under a number of broad categories, in our example, five – academic, social, administrative, legal, and organizational.

The academic role of the teacher is generally the most commonly accepted one, wherein the teacher is responsible for transmitting knowledge and skills, sometimes culture and value, and teaching students how to explore, think, and creatively solve problems. Part of the teacher's role involves the socialization of the young, especially in those concepts considered fundamental to our society – democracy, free enterprise, equality, humanitarianism, human rights, and ethnic and cultural tolerance. The teacher is expected to teach the young (often by personal example) responsibility within society. The teacher is also expected to be an effective administrator of instruction, and the instructional setting. Teachers also have within their role a legal responsibility, not only for the safety of children, but also for the making and enforcing of rules of conduct. The last of the five responsibilities facing a teacher is his/her role as a member of the school organization – contributing, actively participating, doing one's share, being concerned. In actual practice there are many aspects of the role of teacher as member of the organization which are not so readily observable, and not nearly so easy to list and prioritize, however, these also make up part of the expectations of the individual as teacher.

Earlier a number of statements were provided to describe the general roles of departments of education, school trustees, superintendents, principals and other school officials, now we turn our attention to the classroom teacher.

What is the Role of the Teacher?

There are at least two broad questions to be answered. First, toward what social goal is the teacher's work directed, and second, what activities does the teacher undertake in working toward the accepted goal?

Each provincial department of education and each school jurisdiction has a set of goal statements designed to direct the organization's activities toward desired outcomes. Some provinces, Alberta for example, operate upon a two-tier system wherein a broad statement enumerates the educational goals which are the shared responsibility of the community and the school.

Goals of Education

shared
responsibility

Achievement of the broader goals of education must be viewed as a shared responsibility of the community. Maximum learning occurs when the efforts and expectations of various agencies affecting children complement each other. Recognizing the learning that has or has not occurred through various community influences, among which the home is most important, the school will strive to:

a. develop intellectual curiosity and a desire for lifelong learning;

b. develop the ability to get along with people of varying backgrounds, beliefs and lifestyles;

c. develop a sense of community responsibility which embraces respect for law and authority, public and private property, and the rights of others;

d. develop self-discipline, self-understanding, and a positive self-concept through realistic appraisal of one's capabilities and limitations;

e. develop the ability to understand and respond to change as it occurs in personal life and in society;

f. develop skills for reflective utilization of financial resources, community agencies, and leisure time;

g. develop an understanding of the role of the family in society and promote satisfying family relationships;

h. develop an interest in participating in the cultural pursuits of creative expression and appreciation;

i. develop a commitment to the careful use of natural resources and to the preservation and improvement of the physical environment; and

j. develop a sense of purpose in life consistent with one's ethical and/or spiritual beliefs.

The ultimate aim of education is to develop the abilities of the individual in order that he/she might fulfill his/her personal aspirations while making a positive contribution to society (Alberta 1978). ultimate aim

A second and narrower set of goals, goals of schooling, are stated as being the prime responsibility of the school.

Goals of Schooling

Schooling, as part of education, accepts primary and distinctive responsibility for specific goals basic to the broader goals of education. Programs and activities shall be planned, taught, and evaluated on the basis of these specific goals in order that students: primary
responsibillity

a. develop competencies in reading, writing, speaking, listening and viewing;

b. develop basic knowledge and skills in mathematics, the sciences, the social studies (including history and geography), and the practical and fine arts, with appropriate local, national and international emphases in each;

c. develop the learning skills of finding, organizing, analyzing and applying information in a critical and objective manner;

d. develop knowledge, skills, attitudes and habits which contribute to physical and mental health and safety;

e. develop an understanding of the meaning, responsibilities and benefits of active citizenship at the local, national and international levels; and

f. develop the knowledge, skills, attitudes and habits required to respond to the opportunities and expectations of the world of work.   (Alberta, 1978)

What activities does the teacher undertake in working toward the stated goals?

A useful way of viewing the role of the teacher is to cluster teacher activities into broad groupings such as pre-instructional activities, instructional activities, measurement evaluation and reporting activities, duties as a staff member, professional development, and collegial activities.

grouping of activities

Much of what the classroom teacher does is hidden in a sense from the view of the public and sometimes even the student body. For example, we know that effective teaching represents the culmination of a series of preparatory activities, but few see the long hours of careful preparation which often goes into a single class period. In setting the stage for effective instruction, the teacher must be a skillful predictor of events. Knowledge of students and a thorough knowledge of the subject being taught are necessary for instructional excellence. Teachers spend much time in developing yearly teaching units and lesson plans. These can be seen, but what of the thought, effort, time, training which go into *concept* development, for example. Is the concept (mental picture of an object, event or relationship) appropriate? What type of concept development (classificational, correlational, theoretical) do we have in mind? How will the problem be stated and clarified? How will the facts be sorted and analyzed? How will hypotheses, for example, be developed? What is the role of analytical thought? How will inferences be tested? How will conclusions be tested? What are the limitations and problems? As stated earlier, much of this part of the role of the teacher is unseen. Certainly the teacher can be seen in the library consulting references but most of the work is done *in the head*; sorting and re-sorting; stating and re-stating; priorizing and re-priorizing, in a sense rehearsing a lesson through *self-talk* and *mind's-eye* activities.

concept development

The second step in the pre-instructional activities part of the role of the teacher is the establishing of instructional objectives. Instructional objectives arise from the basic concepts or goals formulated by the teacher in conjunction with Department of Education and school jurisdiction goals, statements, and programs of studies. The teacher is once again planning and *thinking through* the lesson or unit. Are the objectives cognitive, affective, psychomotor, or a combination? What are the predicted behavioral outcomes? What are the expected entry, en route, and terminal student behaviors? What are the limitations and problems? How will student attainment be assessed? What kind of result is expected? What will non-goal related results tell the teacher?

instructional objectives

The most visible of the three preinstructional clusters of activities is planning for teaching. It is here that the teacher sets the planning on paper. Planning is part of the role of the teacher. The usual groupings are yearly plans, unit plans, and lesson plans. For good teaching, it is necessary that the teacher do well at this stage. But the actual series of instructional activities are most central to the role of the teacher. Teachers instruct. By definition, teachers teach. It is here that the teacher dips into his/her established and developing repertoire of motivational techniques, classroom management and discipline techniques, methods for providing for individual differences, procedures appropriate to the independent and semi-independent student, and the individualizing of instruction. The teacher's role requires the individual to consider student activities

planning

instruct

manage

methods

which are value focusing, and which encourage creativity. The teacher will question strategically, be able to use sociometric, sociodrama, and case studies methods, for example, when judged appropriate to meet the needs of students. The teacher will use class and small group discussion methods, debate procedures, inquiry experiences, large and small group procedures, panels, puzzles, laboratory exercises, demonstrations, dry runs, films and other audio visual devices, reading and library assignments, pantomime, skits, brain-storming, buzz groups, diagnostic sessions, role play, simulation games, and learning/teaching teams. Makes one out of breath, but the list is hardly a complete one of what teachers do in classrooms.

Part of the role of the teacher is to understand the organizational context of instruction (formal groups, informal groups, leadership, and organizational climate). As well, the role of the teacher includes an understanding of the goals and structure of the curriculum, the content of instruction, the learning goals desired, the social organization, typology, and climate of the classroom. And of course, the background characteristics of the students, including their knowledge, skills, attitudinal and motivational needs are included in the role of the teacher. *organizational context*

In summary, the instructional role of the teacher includes deciding upon instructional goals, diagnosing learners, specifying instructional objectives, and selecting evaluation procedures all within the organizational, legal, and interpersonal settings of the school and community.

The Canadian Teachers' Federation in 1976 stated among other things that it was the *responsibility* of the teacher:

a. constantly to review her/his own level of competence and effectiveness, and to seek necessary improvements as part of a continuing process of professional development;

b. to perform her/his professional duties according to an appropriate code of ethics, and appropriate standard of professional conduct;

c. to recognize that teaching is a collective activity, and to seek the most effective means of consultation and of collaboration with her/his professional colleagues; and

d. to support and to participate in, the efforts of her/his professional association to improve the quality of education and the status of the teaching profession.

Section 264 of the *Education Act* in the province of Ontario states in part:

It is the duty of a teacher and a temporary teacher:

a. to teach diligently and faithfully the classes or subjects assigned to him/her by the principal;

b. to encourage the pupils in pursuit of learning;

c. to inculcate by precept and example respect for religion and the principles of Judaeo-Christian morality and the highest regard for truth, justice, loyalty, love of country, humanity, benevolence, sobriety, industry, frugality, purity, temperament and and all other virtues;

d. to assist in developing cooperation and coordination of efforts among members of the staff of the school;

e. to maintain, under the direction of the principal, proper order and discipline in his/her classroom and while on duty in the school and in the school ground.

f. in instruction and in all communications with the pupils in regard to discipline and the management of the school,

i. to use the English language, except where it is impractical to do so by reason of the pupil not understanding English, and except in respect of instruction in a language other than English or as one of the subjects in the course of study, or

ii. to use the French language in schools or in classes in which French is the language of instruction except where it is impractical to do so by reason of the pupil not understanding French, and except in respect of instruction in a language other than French when such other language is being taught as one of the subjects in the course of study;

g. to conduct his/her class in accordance with a timetable which shall be accessible to pupils and to the principal and supervisory officers;

h. to participate in professional activity days as designated by the board under the regulations;

i. to notify such person as is designated by the board if he/she is to be absent from school and the reason thereof.

(Note: in the Ontario *Education Act,* this section and all others are also written in French.)

The Alberta *School Act* states in Section 13 that:

A teacher while providing instruction or supervision must:

a. provide instruction competently to students;

b. teach the courses of study and education programs that are prescribed, approved or authorized pursuant to this Act;

c. promote goals and standards applicable to the provision of education adopted or approved pursuant to this Act;

d. encourage and foster learning in students;

e. regularly evaluate students and periodically report the results of the evaluation to the students, the students' parents and the board;

f. maintain, under the direction of the principal, order and discipline among the students while they are in the school or on the school grounds and while they are attending or participating in activities sponsored or approved by the board;

g. subject to any applicable collective agreement and the teacher's contract of employment, carry out those duties that are assigned to the teacher by the principal or the board.

student and teacher performance   There are two measures of the outcome of the teacher's role – student performance and teacher performance.

Other Staff Members

1. *Supervisors.* The major responsibility of supervisors is to assist the teacher and school toward improvement of instruction. Sometimes the supervisor is responsible for a specific area of instruction, or a cluster of areas such as maths and sciences, or language arts, whereas in other jurisdictions the responsibility assigned may amount to the management of a unit of the organization. As used in this text, supervision will apply to the process of helping others improve instruction rather than a position on an organizational chart.

2. *Consultants.* These are professionals who consult with the teacher, usually in a specified area of instruction. They are in a helping role and rarely have any direct authority over the teacher. Supervisors sometimes are given the ultimate decision making power regarding teacher performance. Consultants rarely have this evaluative authority.

3. *Vice Principals or Assistant Principals.* These persons are the school principal's chief deputies. The scope and type of duties to be performed may be specified by school board policy, but more usually the duties assigned are at the discretion of the principal as part of the duties of the school administrative team. Rarely is this a full-time appointment. Some teaching duties are involved.

4. *Department Heads.* As the term implies, these educators are the coordinators of the work of the teachers involved in a specific subject area. They are usually expected to provide educational and management leadership at the department level. These persons normally have a shared responsibility for teaching and administration.

Organizational Chart of the Typical School System

The organization charts which follow illustrate what the structure of a large urban and a smaller rural school jurisdiction might look like. It is through these structures that the legal authority and formal communications of the school jurisdictions flow – down and up. Who is responsible for whom? Who answers to whom? Who reports to whom? Who does what? Part Three will define and explain the administrative, legal, power, and communication overlays involved in the process of putting life into the organization.

legal authority

The organization chart also provides the setting and the structure in which the teacher's role is placed. We see where *we* are. To whom do *we* report? Who report to *us*? The organization chart is the legal instrument. It is the formal organization. There is, of course, also an informal (not necessarily illegal) organization. Part Three will discuss this topic also. For the moment, we wanted to discuss the formal role of the teacher within the school organization.

organizational chart

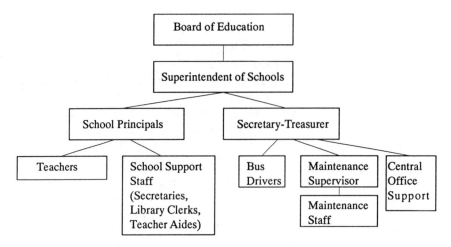

Exhibit 4-1
Organization Chart: Typical Small School Jurisdiction

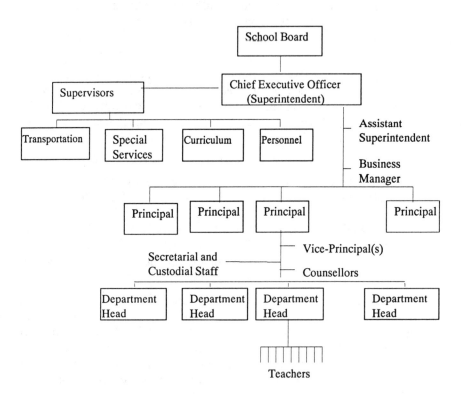

Exhibit 4-2
Organization Chart: Typical Medium-Sized School

5

Financing Canadian Education

A higher quality education is generally provided in school systems which spend larger amounts per pupil; lower quality education is generally provided in schools which spend smaller amounts per pupil.

National Education Association, U.S.A.

Educational Effort

Financing Education

Equalization Principle

Foundation Program

Incentive Grants

Flat Grants

Lighthouse Principle

Budgeting

Introduction

This chapter discusses the principles of educational effort, equalization, foundation programs, lighthouse districts, incentive grants, flat grants, and budgeting as they apply to financing Canadian education.

Two concepts which developed together in the Canadian design for education were compulsory school attendance and *free* public education. If schooling was to be provided for all children, then all must attend. This line of reasoning emerged early in Canada's educational development. If all must attend, then there is a public purpose to be attained. If a public purpose, then a public expense.

Education has become a major social service in society. It is also an expensive social service. Funds for education come from four sources: federal funds raised through the general revenue generating capabilities of the federal taxation authority (very limited amounts, mostly for language education), provincial funds raised through general provincial taxation sources (high yielding personal and corporate sources and retail sales taxes), perhaps federal-provincial transfer payments, and property tax levies on commercial and personal property. **sources**

supplementary requisition

Exhibit 5-1 illustrates two things. First, the rank ordering of the provinces with respect to the amount of money spent per student to provide free public **rank order of provinces** education is shown. Second, there exists a difference of approximately $1 800 per student in the amount of money spent by Quebec (first place) and Prince Edward Island (tenth place) – a difference which, even when allowances are made for local differences in costs of supplies and salaries, must have a considerable impact upon what is made available in the schools.

Province	1991-93 Per Student Expenditure	
	$	Rank
Canada	6 507	
Quebec	6 807	1
Manitoba	6 790	2
Ontario	6 739	3
British Columbia	6 725	4
Alberta	5 683	5
New Brunswick	5 668	6
Saskatchewan	5 664	7
Newfoundland	5 322	8
Nova Scotia	5 254	9
P.E.I.	5 054	10

Exhibit 5-1
Educational Expenditures by Province per Student
(Alberta, *Meeting the Challenge,* p. 18)

supplementary requistion

The local school tax levy on property is often called the supplementary requisition since it is considered to be supplementary to the other major sources of revenue. Miscellaneous other revenues come from tuition fees, user fees, sale of capital assets, rental of textbooks and school-owned properties. These latter sources are so small that they have become incidental to any discussion of public school financing. In the case of private school financing, the order of the above noted revenue sources changes. Government grants are smaller and tuition fees become a major source of funds.

restraints

burden shifts

The general historical flow over time has been toward an increased proportion of the educational costs being borne by provincial governments. However, the recent *restraint* atmosphere displayed by many provincial governments has shifted the burden once again more toward the local tax payer; toward increased student fees, and toward reduced program offerings. These are issues, however, that shift with changing political climates.

Expenditure figures on education as quoted through the public media and many government documents are never very helpful. They generally lump together federal and provincial spending on elementary, secondary, and post secondary education as well as grants to private schools, operating and capital expenditures, student aid programs, manpower and vocational training, federally funded language programs, and the costs of operating departments of education and the administrative and long-term interest costs incurred by local school boards. Recent deficit reduction efforts by both the federal and provincial governments are reducing the total amount of money available to fund education.

public media

Educational Effort

The relative amount of money that a society is willing to spend upon education is a strong indicator of the value placed upon education in that society. But any true measure of a community effort cannot be made in terms of absolute dollars (often done in public pronouncements) but should be done in relationship to its capacity to pay for education in comparison to other provinces or other communities.

There are two good indicators of educational effort (financial capacity). The first is the percentage of Gross Provincial Product (GPP) expended upon education where Gross Provincial Product refers to the total value of all goods and services produced in the province over a given period of time, usually one year. Gross National Product (GNP) is not a valuable statistic for most purposes because education at the basic levels is under the jurisdiction of the provincial government. The second is the average per capita cost of education. The average per capita cost of education is used frequently and certainly relates cost to the individual citizen of the province, but since the reference is to *all* citizens, those in the work force and those not, it bears little direct relation to wealth. Capacity (wealth) must be related directly to the level of educational expenditures in order to arrive at a useful measure of educational effort.

indicators
of effort

GPP

GNP

Financing Education: Two Illustrations

Illustration 1: Alberta

In the Province of Alberta, a large (province-wide approximately 55-60 percent) portion of the school revenues available to local school authorities comes from what is termed the School Foundation Program Fund (SFPF). The SFPF is composed of dollars raised by the Consolidated Revenue Fund (general revenues of the province generated from sources such as provincial income tax, resource royalties, liquor taxes, and from nonresidential taxation (property taxes on commercial properties, recreational homes, and privately owned utilities for example), which are paid into the School Foundation Program Fund. The money for other provincial grants for programs such as evening or adult education, small school assistance, support for declining enrollment assistance

School
Foundation
Program

grants, and assistance for districts who are experiencing conditions of student sparsity for example, also come from the general revenues of the province.

Of total budget expenditures for the Province of Alberta, approximately one quarter is directed to education. Public education (public, separate, private, and home schooling) receives 14 percent. Advanced education (universities, colleges, technical schools and adult training) receive nine percent.

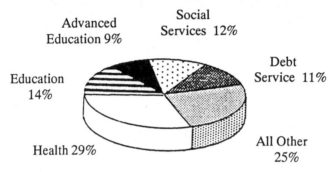

Exhibit 5-2
Alberta's Budget Expenditures
(Estimated $13 408 Billion in 1993-94)

In the 1991-92 school year, 535 000 students, 20 percent of the population, attended 1 950 schools.

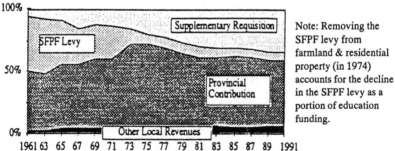

Exhibit 5-3
Relative Contributions to Education

Exhibit 5-3 displays the relative percentages of funding revenues drawn from the provincial general revenue contribution, the provincial School Foundation Program Fund, and the supplementary requisition on local property. This exhibit is interesting in that it demonstrates that local requisitions have increased steadily over the first 30 years of the Foundation Program.

local
requisition
sources

Exhibit 5-4 provides a visual display of the percentages of education funds coming from provincial grants (58 percent), supplementary requisition (38 percent), and other revenues (five percent). sources

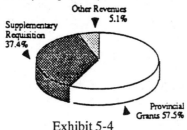

Exhibit 5-4
Provincial and Local Share of Basic Education Funding 1993-94

The reader should note that these percentages are moving gradually toward a greater amount of the cost being covered by local property taxes. At this time it is impossible to predict the consequences of the recent (January, 1994) Alberta government announcement that it will collect all property taxes, including corporate and machinery and equipment taxes, place them in the Provincial Treasury and then distribute the money according to the Provincial School Foundation Formula.

Property Taxation

Requisitions on local property are apportioned among the various Alberta municipalities on the basis of an equalized assessment program wherein all property assessment (placing a value upon land and buildings for taxation purposes) is determined on the basis of provincially determined criteria and is done under the supervision of the province. Assessments of the value placed upon buildings and land are normally done on the basis of a percentage of the true market value of the property. Recent assessment practices have been changed to evaluate property in such a way as to reflect more closely current sale prices. The schedule of factors to be considered to reach an *assessed value* is extensive. Provisions are made for different assessment levels for agricultural land as opposed to urban commercial property; for the variations in the size of the basic home (square metres) and for very many other factors such as distance from an urban centre, the presence or absence of what are labelled luxury items such as attached garages, fireplaces, and swimming pools. There are different sets of criteria for the various types and uses of property. By using assessment manuals and samples of the current selling prices of similar property on a community basis, to guide the process of evaluation of the numerous properties in Alberta, the provincial government is able to obtain a nearly uniform property assessment program. Other provinces use a similar process to equalize the relative burden placed upon the citizens (home owners) as a group, and upon industrial and commercial ventures as a group. Fairness within property grouping is the driving purpose.

equalized assessment

assessed value

ratio factors

oil and gas

As assessment manuals are revised, the inclusions and exemptions and ratio factors (for example, distance from a major commercial centre) may change but the determination remains that the assessment should remain equal for all parts of the province. This of course is essential in determining local tax effort in support of education since effort is usually expressed by educators either as mills of taxation, or dollar value of property assessment per child in school. What is assumed to be the case is not sufficient. Many sparsely settled rural areas have much higher assessment per child, usually due, not to the value of the farm land and buildings, but to the value of oil and gas well and petroleum processing and distribution systems.

Local Supplementary Requisition

uniform
school tax

The School Foundation Program Fund raises property tax revenues on Alberta property (with some exclusions) to add to the general revenues of the province in order to establish the provincial portion of school support. Until 1994, the local school authority (school boards) used to apply its own property tax on the property owners within the community. Beginning in 1994, the Province of Alberta will determine and collect a uniform school tax on all property. The equalization principle remains in force, however. Funding will continue to go to districts on the basis of student counts.

property
exclusions

A number of properties are excused from taxation. The first group is religious and charitable organizations. The second, and for most communities the larger groups, governmental (provincial, municipal, and federal) properties, are also excused upon the principle that one government should not tax another government. Senior governments normally make grants in lieu of taxes. Local governments and churches do not.

Control of School Board Expenditures

Provincial support, the largest part of which is provided on the basis of per student grants, is in all cases supplemented by the revenues generated by tax levies on local properties. The Provincial Government is responsible for determining the level of this tax and is held accountable for the amount of local (supplementary requisition) taxes imposed and the types of expenditures (expenditure priorities) authorized by the local budget. Accountability is through the provincial ballot box.

per student
grants

Per student grants (based upon student counts on September 30 and March 31 and averaged) are further modified by weighting factors which attempt to make provision for varying cost levels associated with the financial needs of the various grade levels. For example, in 1987, the block per student grant was $1 794. Early Childhood Services (kindergarten) were weighted at .58 of the block per student rate ($1 040); elementary students (grades 1-6) at 1.00 ($1 794); junior high students (grades 7-9) at 1.08 ($1 938); and senior high school students at 1.16 ($2 080) of the block amount. These number are modified each year.

In addition to per student grants, Alberta provides student transportation grants, capital funding support for the cost of a building or equipment projects, and special program grants for independent schools, native students, minority language education, language instruction in other than English and French, vocational education grants, and a broad category of grants for sparsity of population, isolation and other unique costs under the *Equity Program* of the School Foundation Program (these normally relate to isolated communities and sparsely populated schools). — *other grants*

Illustration 2: Ontario

The current provincial school support program in Ontario is called the Mill Rate Equalization Plan, a plan designed to incorporate the concepts of local responsibility (local effort and control) and equality of educational opportunity throughout the province. The taxation program is based upon the principle of equal yield (dollars) for equal effort. — *local responsibillity* / *equal opportunity*

All school boards have the same equalized mill rate for the same recognized dollar level of expenditure per student. The Province of Ontario's grant is based upon the difference between the school board's recognized expenditure levels and the amount of money which can be raised by applying a provincially determined mill rate on the value of the equalized assessment supporting the local school jurisdiction. Recognized expenditure levels are set each year by the province. Expenditures in excess of the recognized (approved) levels must be financed through local taxation. — *recognized expenditure level*

Funding

In 1991, Ontario spent \$13 125 200 000 on public education. In that year 55 percent went to basic per student grants (weighted) which recognize the different cost level, per student, of compensatory education, elementary education, secondary education, and vocational education, for example. Four percent went to what is termed board-specific grants, that is, recognition of the extra costs associated with teaching French as a first language; with operating small schools and small boards; with compensatory education programs and operating schools which are experiencing declining enrollments. Program-specific grants to cover new initiatives, language and special education, made up 21 percent of the total. Recognized capital grants for building and equipment renovating and replacement, new buildings and equipment and site purchases constituted six percent of the total expenditures. Teacher's pension fund payments and *other* programs made up 14 percent of the total Province of Ontario expenditures on public education. The *other* expenditures noted above covered approximately two dozen programs ranging from financial assistance for transfer of schools and programs between public and separate boards, programs in lieu of provincial services for blind and deaf students, support for the educational computing network, and to support for secondary school summer schools. (Thom, 1993) — *per student grants* / *board-specific grants* / *program-specific grants* / *capital grants* / *other grants*

Sources of Revenues

capital grants

    The amount of money available to the local school board is the sum of ordinary and extraordinary grants received from the Ontario treasury, and the revenues raised from the local property tax levy. School boards in Ontario also

other grants

enjoy authority to tax local residential and non-residential property. Each year the province sets assessed values, not directly representative of market value of the property, but which are determined by an analysis of a sample of local property sales in each municipality. Adjustments are then made which moderate the yearly fluctuation of property values in areas where property sales have either *heated* or *cooled* in excess of the average fluctuations.

Provincial	Percent
Consolidated Revenue	41.2
Provincially Imposed Property Tax	<u>34.6</u>
	80.8
Local	
Residential Taxation	<u>19.2</u>
	19.2

Exhibit 5-5
Sources of Revenue: Ontario Averages, 1991

Controls on Local School Boards

    Ontario does not impose direct controls on the level of local education expenditures. It too relies upon local voter pressures.

    Ontario (and Alberta, as well as many other provinces) has from time to time placed *ceilings* upon the level of permitted local increases in property taxes. The presence or absence of this type of control is probably the product of political forces.

Capital Funding

Capital Grants Plan

    In Ontario, local expenditures on capital projects must conform to the Ministry of Education published *Capital Grants Plan*, and are subject to prior approval based upon priority of need. Provincial capital grants, on average, support approximately 75 percent of approved building and equipment costs. The remaining 25 percent must be funded locally.

special programs

    Ontario, like Alberta, also makes grants available for special programs such as adult or evening education, technical education, independent schools, the education of native children, the funding of special education programs, and recognizes geographic cost difference, the additional costs associated with small schools and declining enrollments. Special grants are also available for minority language, second language education, multicultural education, and driver education.

Other Canadian provinces follow similar patterns wherein provincial resources (at least as large in percentage as the above illustrations) are blended
with local funds raised through local taxation. Thus, an equity in opportunity
principle (measured by dollars) is teamed with an ability to pay principle
(measured in the value of local property assessment) to provide for *fairness*.
The money goes to where the child is and comes from where the dollars are.

fairness

Equalization Principle

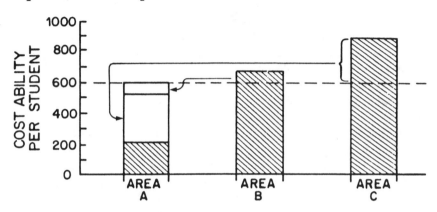

Exhibit 5-6
Illustration of Equalization Principle

The basic reasoning behind the equalization principle is that all children
deserve equality in educational opportunities, at least as far as this can be
measured in dollars and cents. Whether a child comes from a poor area or a rich
one should not be sufficient grounds for varying the quality of the child's
educational opportunities. Children frequently are victims of their environments. They have no choice usually, as to where they will receive their
education. Therefore, the financial resources for education must be distributed
on an equitable basis. Equalizing the financial basis does not of necessity mean
an adequate education for all, but rather an *equal educational opportunity* for
all – whether this is a poor or a good opportunity depends upon other factors.

equalization

equal educational
opportunity

To illustrate the equalization principle, consider three geographic areas with
the following abilities to pay for education:

Area A – ability to pay locally – $250 per student per annum

Area B – ability to pay locally – $650 per student per annum

Area C – ability to pay locally – $950 per student per annum

The average ability to pay would be $617 per student (assuming equal
numbers of students in the three areas). To equalize these three areas, Area A

would need $367 per student in assistance ($617 - $250). Area B would contribute $33 ($650 - $617) per Area A student and Area C would contribute $333 ($950 - $617) per Area A student. This is illustrated graphically in Exhibit 5-6.

This explanation is a vast oversimplification of the equalization principle. This becomes obvious when one attempts to work out details for such a system. For example, consider the possibility of Area C in the illustration as being an area in which the cost of living, of services, etc., is much higher than in Area A. After redistribution, both Areas A and C will have $617 available per student, but because the cost of living and general wage scale are higher in Area C, Area C may have to hire teachers with lower qualifications and less experience than those employed in Area A in order to compensate for this wage differential. Likewise for the availability of money to purchase supplies, building, and equipment. Therefore the quality of education in Area C could possibly be poorer than that which is available in Area A since each dollar expended in Area C would purchase less than each dollar expended in Area A.

adjustment

Therefore, a further adjustment to the funding program would be required to compensate for the decreased purchasing power of the dollar in some parts of the province.

Further, it may be that in Area A the people have decided that roads and hospitals are priority items before education. That is, after the other priorities are considered, they may have left only $250 worth per student as ability to pay for education. But Areas B and C may have placed education as a higher priority. If so, it would not be fair to penalize Areas B and C to compensate for the shortfalls of another community that has different local spending priorities. Therefore further adjustments must be included in the equalization program in order to recognize differing local spending priorities.

priority items

An analysis of nearly any school district financial statement will show that senior high education is more expensive to educate than elementary education. If one area has a different ratio of senior high to elementary as compared to another area, a compensating adjustment would need to be included in the equalization formula.

rural-urban

It may be that Area B is a rural area, requiring extensive bussing of students. A factor in the equalization formula would then be needed if Area A, in our example, was urban and therefore required little bussing. Further, what is meant by an area? Should Equalization take place province-by-province, with the *have* provinces equalizing the *have not* provinces; should the equalization be on a major regional basis; should it be on a school district basis; or perhaps compare school against school? Since education is a provincial responsibility, the federal government cannot equalize within a specific province for educational purposes per se, but through the federal government's transfer payment scheme the *have* provinces do assist the *have not* provinces, thereby directly affecting the equalization principle for education on a province-by-province basis. Also within each province the areas which have better fiscal abilities are required to assist the less fortunate areas. Even within a school jurisdiction (district, division, unit, county), the equalization principle can be made to work when appropriate policies have been made by the school board.

Another difficulty in establishing a fair equalization formula is to be found in establishing a specific community's ability to pay. In a very general way it is easy enough to say that Area C is richer than Area A, for example. But putting this belief into a formula expressed in exact dollar amounts is a more difficult task. Does one consider as evidence of wealth, the number of cars per house, the size of the house, to which clubs the people belong, or should the basis be the market value of the property? Should the evidence be the average income of the people as determined from the amount of income tax paid or perhaps the size of their bank accounts? Is property a good indicator of wealth? Is level of industrialization or the extent of commercialization a good indicator? Many would say no. One jurisdiction may be rural, another suburban, another inner city, thus further complicating any useful comparisons. One area may be older and thus have fewer children in school, and as a result have inflated ability to pay per student figures, when ability to pay is calculated on the basis of dollars of assessment per student in school. It is becoming more common to live in one area, say on an acreage or in an adjoining town (bedroom community), and work in the city. The problem then arises as to which area has the responsibility for the education of the children – the area from which the income is derived or the area in which the children live. Most contend that the money should go to where the child is, but there are political problems of *selling* this idea to those who have the money since they can just as easily plead the additional cost of some other service to the public, such as roads or mass transit, or parking structures, or parks.

The foregoing illustrates the difficulty of obtaining a workable equalization formula after accepting the desirability of the principle of equalization. The purpose of equalization is to force areas with a more substantial financial base to help areas with a less substantial financial base. However, this was the only base for determining educational financing if it could mean that instead of having *good* educational programs and *poor* educational programs, the net result could be an entire system of *mediocre* programs.

The Foundation Program

A modification of the equalization principle is the principle of the foundation program. There is a base program that is a minimum acceptable (foundation) educational program below which no schools would be permitted to fall. For the purposes of illustration, consider the same three areas as in the illustration for the equalization principle. Suppose the provincial department of education determined that an expense of $1 800 per student was necessary to maintain an acceptable minimum program. The provincial government would therefore be required to assist Area A by $1 550 per student. Area B would require $1 150 per student, and Area C would require grants of $850 in order to bring it to the foundation level.

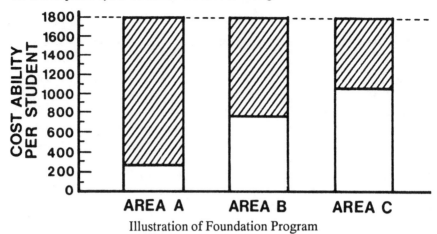

Illustration of Foundation Program

A foundation program, then, is basically not a redistribution of monies among areas, but rather the subsidizing of an area by the provincial government (either directly or indirectly) to bring the expenditures in that area up to an acceptable minimum level in order to provide the education program adequately. This is not true equalization but instead is equalization to a minimum financially expressed standard.

subsidizing

Incentive Grants

If the provincial government wishes the school jurisdictions to implement a particular program, the department of education could legally demand that the action be taken. As agents of the department of education, the boards of trustees would be forced to comply. That is, whether reading is taught in the schools is not an optional decision for school boards – they must ensure that reading is taught. However, there are many other programs which the departments of education may wish included in the school program, but for which they are not prepared to demand inclusion. Frequently this inaction grows out of a fear that the public will sense there is too much interference by the central authority. In such cases, *the carrot and the donkey* approach is used – if you want the donkey to move, dangle a carrot in front of its nose. For example, if the department of education wishes school systems to hire teacher-librarians, the department could offer a grant of a few thousand additional dollars per year/per teacher-librarian. In this way the school board would not be forced to hire teacher-librarians, but if they failed to act, there would ensue a *loss* of the grant, something that local parent/community pressure groups probably would not permit to happen.

encouragement

Often departments of education will use the incentive grant procedure to initiate a specific course of action or program which has not yet been well established. When the course of desired action is firmly implanted, the department can withdraw that incentive grant, realizing that local pressure (perhaps inertia) would ensure the retention of the idea.

withdrawal

An example of an incentive grant:

A grant of $15 800 is paid for each special education teaching position approved by the Deputy Minster in which a teacher is employed full-time exclusively for teaching students who require special instruction because of sub-normal mentality, defective hearing or eyesight or for other reasons determined by the Minister.

School boards themselves are prone to use the incentive principle when they make offers such as, "for equipment which is desirable in a school but which is not normally supplied by the school board, the school board will match the community-raised money on a dollar-for-dollar basis." Many computers and similar pieces of equipment have been purchased for schools on this basis.

local initiative

Incentive grants normally involve some spending on behalf of the school board and therefore the poorer the district the more likelihood of the district not taking advantage of the grants. In the case of the teacher-librarian illustration previously given, the incentive grant for librarians would not normally be the total cost of the librarian, but perhaps part of the base salary without provisions for additional training costs, benefit packages, and similar costs which would have to be borne locally. This illustration could be made to apply to the application of school-level incentive grants. Herein lies the problem with incentive grants. Shortages of funds locally limit the opportunities locally. This same problem can be observed when share-cost programs are initiated by the Federal Government. Those who have some can have some more!

Flat Grants

Flat grants are grants paid on a specific basis regardless of other factors such as ability to pay. For example, a grant may be paid on the basis of a specified number of dollars per elementary student, or per teacher. It is sometimes difficult to determine the difference between an incentive grant and a flat grant because of the overlap between the two. Let us say the department of education pays $20 000 per year for each special education teacher hired by the board. If the grant is the same as for other classroom teachers, then the $20 000 is probably a flat grant. But if the grant for other teachers is $12 000, then the $8 000 difference may be an incentive grant to promote special education. Or it may be that the $8 000 is recognition of reduced enrollment in special education classes, and therefore is only a flat grant which recognized additional costs of certain programs.

Flat grants and foundation program grants are not mutually exclusive categories of grants even though the principles involved are distinguishable from each other. For example, a department of education may pay $7 000 per teacher hired by the school board plus $1 200 per student enrolled; these two grants then become flat grants. However, if the department of education determined the payments would enable all school jurisdictions within the province to maintain a certain minimum acceptable level of education, the grants are also a foundation program grant. The true purpose is often difficult

not mutually exclusive

to determine without intimate knowledge of the working of the department and the priorities of the government-of-the-day.

Lighthouse Principle

Some communities may wish to provide for education above and beyond the foundation or average levels. Providing they do so with additional revenue raised in their own area, the area invariably is permitted to do so. That school, or that educational jurisdiction, then becomes a *lighthouse*, educationally speaking. While equality of educational opportunity is an important principle, lowering the standards of the above-average schools in order to achieve equality is not usually an acceptable procedure. Where communities wish to finance schooling beyond the capabilities of other areas, it should be their perogative to do so. In the example used previously in this chapter, each area could become a lighthouse area, but Area C would most likely do so since the amount of extra local effort would not be as great as in the other two, i.e., Areas A and B.

centralization

At the time of writing (early 1994), Alberta has chosen to tax all properties in the province at an equal rate and distribute the revenues raised (plus general provincial funds) to school jurisdictions on the basis of number of students, by the methods outlined by the foundation Program. The Province of Ontario is considering a similar plan. To the degree that centralization of decision making comes about, the lighthouse principle becomes an almost empty term. If all districts are funded equally through a Foundation Program and the provincial government taxes all jurisdictions equally, it is difficult to see how a district could become a lighthouse district since almost inevitably improvements cost money.

"in words"

From time to time, various terms become *in words* which are used in ways which make obtaining the true meaning quite difficult. A current example is, *block grants for generic services*, the meaning of which is not aided by use of a dictionary. Another difficulty in understanding grant structure is the mixing of types of grants. Quite often it is not possible to say with assurance whether a grant is equalization, foundation, incentive or flat because it may contain

overlapping

elements of several of these factors. Previous examples illustrate this difficulty. Sometimes a grant is labelled *foundation* when it really is a flat grant, that is, the basic terms are not always properly used. In spite of the difficulties of improper terminology and the use of terms which are not effectively descriptive, a basic understanding of the principles of equalization, incentive, flat, foundation, and lighthouse grants should improve one's understanding of financing education in Canada.

Budgeting

School jurisdictions, whether a school district, school division, or board of education of a county, receive financing for education from the following sources.

1. Foundation program grants which normally cover a major portion of costs of instruction, transportation, administration, debt retirement, and approved capital expenditures.

2. Other grants which provide specific dollar support for programs such as early childhood education, community schools, special education, declining enrollment schools, and other special projects such as film libraries and intern teachers.

3. Local supplementary requisitions. These are dollars raised from local tax levies which are used to make up the difference between the revenues derived from other sources (government grants, fees, investment income, etcetera) and the total amount of money required to operate the school jurisdiction. This principle is valid only to the extent that school boards are fiscally independent (able to collect their own taxes).

fiscally
independent

4. Miscellaneous sources. These include monies from the sale of capital assets, and from tuition fees, federal funds, textbook rentals, and the rental of school facilities, for example.

Ideally a school board, in developing a budget, would list the programs desired, then determine the cost of satisfactorily staffing, housing and maintaining these programs. The next step would be to determine the financing available from the foundation program and other grants from the province plus any miscellaneous sources. This amount would be subtracted from the total cost previously determined, leaving a balance which would have to be paid from additional local property taxation. In practice, this balance may result in excessive local supplementary taxation (requisition). Therefore, the school board reexamines the initial programs planned for; eliminating some, changing others, examining staffing and maintenance patterns and making adjustments until the extra amount to be levied against the local property taxpayer is reasonable and politically acceptable. The shirt is tailored to the cloth. Changing programs and shifting staffing patterns, in turn, affect departmental grants and other sources of financing and therefore there is further reshuffling at each stage of the budgeting process until the final budget is approved. The approved budget provides for the direction and control of the approved *educational plan* for that school jurisdiction for the current fiscal year, in some provinces the calendar year, in others the school year.

desired
programs

requisition

The reader is reminded that local taxes raised in supporting a foundation program, the funds are based upon equalized assessment, an assesssment which differs from the ordinary (actual) assessment. It is based on the principle that a standard mill rate applied to property across the province would not yield comparative revenues if the properties were assessed on different bases. For example, if a house (one community) is assessed (for taxation purposes) at $20 000, the maximum levy of 30 mill would yield $600. But if the exact same house in another community with other factors being equal, is assessed for $18 000, the yield would be $540. Therefore, equalized assessment is an attempt to ensure that when a standard mill rate is applied, the taxes paid would be equitable.

not taxed

All property is not necessarily assessed and/or taxed. There are three general categories of non-taxed property. First, there is property which is not taxed but for which an equivalent amount is paid; the best example is property (land and buildings) owned by the federal government. Usually the federal government pays the local municipality a grant which would be nearly the same as if the property had been assessed and taxed. Secondly, there is property which is not taxed but for which some compensation is afforded the municipality. An example of this is property under railways, and utility lines, and over pipelines.

churches

Usually the municipality receives some revenue from these sources but proportionately little in comparison to other taxed property. Thirdly, there is property

charity

which is not taxed and for which no compensation is afforded the municipality. Churches and charitable institutions generally fall within this category.

Another special category in some provinces involves residential property wherein the school foundation program levy is not applied to residential property. Perhaps more correct technically would be to say this property is assessed and taxed for the foundation program but this amount is then rebated

renters

or credited to the total property tax payable. Renters may also be given some assistance toward their rental costs. There is no necessary direct connection made between renter's assistance and the school foundation program levy, however, an inferred connection can certainly be made since renters, through their rent payments, are indeed paying indirect property taxes and assistance to them can be seen as a reduction on the local property taxes payable through rent.

The budget is a plan for the fiscal operations of the district which includes an estimate of the proposed expenditures for a given period of time (usually one year), and a plan for financing the proposed expenditures. Edgar Morphet (an American writer in the area of School Administration) ably and succinctly stated a very useful (for the school teacher) definition of a school budget:

> The budget is no longer viewed as a mere listing of probable expenditures and estimated receipts . . .A public budget is a well-conceived program of governmental action for a given period of time with reasonably accurate plans for making the financial outlays involved and raising the necessary revenues. (Oview & Castetter, 1960)

empowers

A school budget should be much more than a list of probable expenditures and revenues. To be effective, it is the educational plan for the district, stated in dollar terms. It should not be used as a financial strait jacket; but it does serve as a means of financial control. It is the way whereby the community is informed of what it costs to offer a particular type and level of educational program. It provides information on the educational activities for which public funds are being expanded. It indicates changes in program direction. It illustrates educational priorities. It serves as the basis upon which the amount of revenue that must be raised locally through taxes and fees can be determined.

It empowers the administration and professional staff with authority to expend funds on a pre-determined educational program.

There are essentially three phases to budgeting. First, the *planning phase* which consists of planning the educational program for the next fiscal year and estimating the dollar costs which will be involved in operationalizing the plan. The second phase, the *enactment phase*, occurs where the budget document is debated publicly, often modified, and subsequently approved by the school board. (The final act of phase two is the requisition of the funds required locally from the local tax raising authority, usually the local municipal government.) Phase three, the *operating phase*, is just as it states. It is the phase wherein the budget is put into operation. The budget is linked to the accounting system. The legal limits of approved expenditures are enforced. Administrators expend within the scope of their specific expenditure authority. The chief executive officer, usually through the secretary-treasurer or financial superintendent, makes periodic progress reports to the school board, in public, of course.

planning phase

enactment phase

operating phase

The budget is not all there is to planning education, but the budget is where virtually all the planning is resolved.

The budget does not itself achieve an educational program, but it is through the budget that achievement is realized. The budget is not only a plan for the distribution of money, it is a way to make money work for quality. A budget is financial stewardship.

financial stewardship

The reader will note that the cost of instruction is by far the largest single expenditure in a typical school district budget. As noted earlier, schooling is a very labor intensive business, but there is also a second factor at work. Over the years the number of students in any one classroom has decreased, thus adding to the per student cost. Further, largely because of urbanization, rural school populations have decreased noticeably. Since there are practical limits to the degree of centralization possible, many rural areas have had to operate with low student-teacher ratios in order to offer a reasonable educational opportunity to their children.

student-teacher ratio

	Percent
Instruction	67.50
Administration	5.00
Operation and Maintenance	12.50
Transportation of Students	3.75
Debt Services	8.75
Contributions to Capital (from revenue)	2.50
	100.00

Exhibit 5-8
The Distribution of Expenditures in a Typical School District Budget

Budget Development

experience

projections

In practical terms, the budget is formulated on the basis of both past experience and future projections of needs. Only rarely is a budget developed without heavy reliance upon past experience because past experience is a good teacher, provided that we do not become slaves to it.

The usual policy, in the past, has been to locate budget development in the central office of the jurisdiction and under the supervision of the superintendent of schools. In some instances, the processes fell under the control of the secretary-treasurer, with little input from the educational professionals. The swing toward a position wherein the superintendent of schools is named the chief executive officer of the district has resulted in placing budget plan-

superintendent

ning/budget operation phases under the direct control of the school superintendent. The school board, of course, maintains its authority to enact the budget on behalf of the community, but changes in attitude and policy have twinned with advancements in management skills to decrease the centralized tendencies of the past. Most people at more levels within the educational organization are becoming involved and contribute to the process.

objectives

As noted earlier, the budget is an educational plan. In order to accomplish this, decisions must be made with respect to the general purposes, objectives, goals of the school jurisdiction, including provisions for the re-assessment of the validity and attainability of previously accepted objectives. The impact of new provincial government initiatives and the emergence of changing educational, social, community and economic conditions must be assessed. Budgeting provides an opportunity for re-definition of purpose. The next question, since a budget is a financial document, is can the stated objectives, purposes, goals be attained through existing financial policies? Are shifts necessary?

Educational planning through the budget requires decisions respecting for whom the educational program should be planned? What provisions beyond the statutory requirements should be made, for example, for early childhood schools, adult education, cultural and recreational experience, home confined students, and out-of-school youth, children with learning or perceptual disorders?

program and
service reviews

Program and service reviews and decisions will be numerous. A considerable amount of professional and school trustee time will be involved in answering the following (and only a partial) list of questions.

1. What educational opportunities should be offered to elementary and secondary language arts (and all other instructional areas) students?

2. What adjustments must be made to the programs of a typical student? To what extent should the total school program be adapted to meet individual student differences?

3. What educational programs should be provided to improve physical, mental and emotional fitness?

4. What operational procedures, such as student grouping (homogeneous, heterogeneous) and mainstreaming of the handicapped child for example, should be implemented to facilitate learning and perennial development?

5. What should be the school district's policies on teaching living skills, controversial issues, and sex education? What additional teachers and educational materials will be necessary?

6. To what extent should specialized courses (vocational, technical, commercial, fine arts) be provided by the local school district? Could they be provided more efficiently by other means?

7. Should medical and nutritional help be provided through an educational budget? Is this an educational, municipal or provincial program?

8. What special provisions should be made for second language education, English for new Canadians, parent education for recent immigrants, and remedial instruction for parents or students outside regular school hours or in summer schools for example?

9. What portion of the planned expenditures should be devoted to parent and community involvement programs and continuing academic and general interest instruction?

10. What are to be the school district policies regarding joint use of school facilities and shared programs with police authorities and social service agencies?

The budgeting process will also require decisions regarding school employees:

1. How many classroom teachers, administrators, specialist, and non-certified personnel will be hired? Many school districts are restricted in these decisions by union contracts. (The battle between *management rights* and *working conditions* clauses.) school employees

2. What level of training and competency will be required for each class of employee?

3. What provisions will be made for selection, orientation and assignment of new employees?

4. What salary provisions will be made for non-unionized employees? non-union

5. What is the cost of the various collective (salary) agreements existing at budget time? Are changes in salary levels predicted?

6. What are the district's policies respecting staff development?

7. What are the costs of collateral (direct or indirect forms of compensation that do not require that additional services be performed – fringe benefits) and non-collateral employee benefits, beyond those specified in collect agreements, where part of the cost is generated by terms or policies outside the boundaries of the salary agreement? collatoral
non-collateral

These are major decisions since approximately 85 percent of a school district budget is allocated to personnel costs.

Approximately eight to nine percent of the total local educational costs are allocated to what is termed *fixed costs* such as utilities, insurance, and debt servicing. The remaining six to seven percent of the total budget is allocated to supplies, materials and equipment used in the system. This figure includes both instructional and non-instructional supplies.

1. What should be the quantity and quality of supplies?

2. Will classroom sets of texts be supplied?

3. Will students be charged *material* fees?

4. How large (or small) will school library (instructional materials) grants be?

5. Which existing piece of equipment and buildings will be included in the capital equipment purchase or maintenance program for the budget year?

6. Should existing buildings and grounds be upgraded?

7. What economics can be exercised in the existing structure in order to shift funds to essential or emerging needs?

8. What modifications are necessary in the existing administrative structure? Should the central office staff be downsized? Should proposed expenditures on additional supervisory or consultation staff be postponed? Are additional specialized staff necessary to implement the new provincially mandated or locally developed programs?

comprehensive plan

The budget is a comprehensive plan for facilitating the educational planning of a school jurisdiction. It includes a description of all the parts which make up the total program, an estimation of the expenditures required to operationalize each part, and an estimation of the sources and amounts of revenues required.

Categories of Expenditures

statistics

Departments of education, in order to gather statistics, provide a basis for foundation program grants, and to meet their own auditing requirements, require that school board budgets, and the accounting procedures attached thereto, be developed following a standard *program* format. Larger jurisdictions which usually have an increased number and variety of programs will have a more detailed format, but in general terms the categories are as follows.

1. School instruction, broken into sub-programs such as language arts instruction (sometimes language arts elementary, junior high, senior high), science instruction, vocational education, fine arts (art, music, drama), health education, education of autistic children, etc.

2. Administration, perhaps subdivided into central office, school based, educational, support services, consultative services, legal services, auditing costs, etc.

3. Operations and maintenance costs such as caretaking, electrical trades, bus/garage mechanics, painters, bookkeeping, etc.

4. Transportation of students, which would set forward the expected costs of implementing the transportation policy of the jurisdiction, set forward and detail the terms and costs of contracted school bus services, and perhaps the anticipated costs of bus fuel, tires, insurance, etc.

5. Debt services, including the yearly costs of debenture borrowing, long and short term loans and the bank and brokerage costs associated therewith, etc.

6. Contribution to capital fund. As noted earlier, the costs of many capital projects (buildings and equipment) are shared between provincial grants and local taxes. This program category of expenditures sets forward the anticipated local share of the costs of the new school, or new science laboratory upgrading project, for example.

Some jurisdictions provide for perhaps six types of budgets, each with its own expenditure categories which are then combined into one *superior* document called the budget. A common format is: the long-term budget which predicts the flow of expenditures and revenues over a period of perhaps three to five years, the capital expenditures budget (perhaps also a three to five year document), the current (performance expenditure) budget based upon functions and projects as outlined briefly above (work to be done – services to be rendered rather than things to be acquired), the building (site-based) budget which projects the expenditures necessary to carry forward the educational program in a given school, and perhaps a departmental budget (unit budget). Some jurisdictions also develop and pass special project budgets for expenditures which do not fall within the scope of conventional budgets.

ADMINISTRATION 100 SERIES
110. Salaries
120. Contracted Services
130. Other Expenses
INSTRUCTION 200 SERIES
210. Salaries
211. Principals
212. Consultants or
    Supervisors
213. Teachers
214. Other Instructional Staff
215. Sec. and Clerical Assistants
220. Textbooks
230. School Libraries
    Audio Visual
240. Teaching Supplies
250. Other Expenses
ATTENDANCE AND HEALTH
SERVICES 300-400 SERIES
300. Attendance Services

MAINTENANCE OF PLANT 700 SERIES
710. Salaries
720. Contracted Services
730. Replacements of Equipment
740. Other Expenses
FIXED CHARGES 800 SERIES
810. Employee Retirement
820. Insurance and Judgments
830. Rental of Land & Buildings
840. Interest on Current Loans
850. Other Fixed Charges
FOOD SERVICES AND STUDENT-BODY
ACTIVITIES 900-1000 SERIES
900. Food Services
910. Salaries
920. Other Expenses
930. Separate Fund or Account
1000. Student-Body Activities
1010. Salaries
1020. Other Expenses

310. Salaries
320. Other Expenses
400. Health Services
410. Salaries
420. Other Expenses
STUDENT TRANSPORTATION
SERVICES 500 SERIES
510. Salaries
520. Contracted Ser. & Pub. Carriers
530. Replacements of Vehicles
540. Transportation Insurance
550. Expenditures in Lieu of Trans.
560. Other Expenses
OPERATION OF PLANT
600 SERIES
610. Salaries
620. Contracted Services
630. Heat for Buildings
640. Utilities Except Heat
650. Supplies
660. Other Expenses

1030. Separate Fund
COMMUNITY SERVICES 1100 SERIES
1110. Recreation
1120. Civic Activities
1130. Public Libraries
1140. Custodial Care Children
1150. Welfare Activities
1160. Nonpublic School Students
1161. Instructional Services
1162. Attend. & Health Services
1163. Transportation Services
CAPITAL OUTLAY 1200 SERIES
1210. Sites
1220. Buildings
1230. Equipment
DEBT SERVICE, FROM CURRENT
FUNDS 1300 SERIES
1310. Principal of Debt
1320. Interest on Debt
1330. Paid into Sinking Funds
1340. Schoolhousing
1350. Other Debt Service

Exhibit 5-10
Example of Expenditure Categories Using Numbered Series of Accounts

School-Based Budgeting

site-based
budgets

decentralized

A recent modification to the budget and budget implementation process, has been the development of site-based budgets. Administrative dominated practices in budget development are giving way to shared practices. Professional staff, school principals and classroom teachers are taking a more active part in the process. Some school jurisdictions make provisions for school and also community involvement. Decentralized budgets are perceived as a mechanism to bring about accountability as well as permitting the flexibility necessary to ensure that the program developed will best fit the needs of the students. They help meet the demands from the emerging body of *professional* teachers. However, careful policy making and planning are essential to maximize the positive results.

A summary of the perceived advantages of the school-based program follows.

1. It provides teachers and principals with an effective role in educational planning and decision making.

2. It enables teachers and school-level administrators to decide upon the allocation of resources.

3. It encourages school staffs to examine the relationship between school-level program objectives, program outcomes, and the costs involved.

4. It encourages teachers to innovate.

5. It provides for flexibility and quicker response times to emerging school/community needs.

6. The budget process and the budget document experience an enhanced and educational focus.

7. It facilitates teacher and other staff participation in planning.

8. School principals are able to provide educational leadership more directly to the staff, student body and the community.

9. It can encourage community involvement.

10. Authorities believe that school-based budgeting is essential to decentralization and a forward-looking management style.

The degree of decentralization prevalent varies from provisions for staff determination of instructional supplies budgets through to decisions respecting student-to-teacher ratios, adult-to-teacher ratios, the presence or absence of school, instructional, marking, and library aides. However, these decisions must be made under the provisions of the broader district policy, and in recognition of statutes and collective agreements. These external forces often have a limiting effect, however, teachers are more often having an increased impact upon educational budgets and planning than they had through teacher/trustee advisory bodies, or though the working condition clauses and restrictions of local salary contracts.

ratios

personnel

external forces

Instruments of Budget Evaluation

Many school jurisdictions, and one expects provincial governments, evaluate the performance of the budget document only upon the basis of "did we come in under or over budget" Some rely upon the results of the annual audit to determine whether the budget had been executed (administered) properly. Many authorities contend that the budget is an instrument of accountability and therefore the evaluation of the budget's failure or success should be determined by output measures – student achievement, student growth – work done and its quality. What was the outcome? Sometimes the evidence is statistical, but frequently it is subjective. What do teachers think?

annual audit

The alternative to good budget evaluation procedures is to take last years figures and add a percentage for inflation, or "launch a new kite," in the hopes that it will fly. Surely this is not the intent of the definitions of budgeting and the processes enumerated earlier.

inflation

Teacher's Role

As new teachers, operating under the guidance of new administrative principles, assume their places in schools, it is anticipated that first there will be increased professional level involvement in educational budgeting, and second that the individual teacher will be required to gain a broad understanding of educational financing and a specific understanding of the program costs, and the relevant categories of expenditures necessary to financially activate a school or perhaps an instructional department at the very minimum.

Fund Raising

downward
pressure

The downward pressures regarding all public expenditures and especially spending on education will drive schools more and more toward school-based fund raising projects. We don't know the answer but one thing will become obvious to the teacher, and that is the professional dilemmas which are posed. First, should schools and teachers be involved in major fund raising projects? What does it do to our position of trust? What does it do to and for poor families? What does it do to public accountability? Will it introduce funding inequalities? Is this what we were hired for?

Summary

Although money is not everything in achieving quality education, and more money does not automatically produce better schools, expenditure levels per student remain an excellent indicator. If this were not so, provincial ministries of education would not be so concerned with the equalization of educational opportunities programs (the money goes where the child is) which are expressed through their *foundation programs* for funding education. Neither would they rely heavily on incentive grants (expressed in dollar amounts) to lead or encourage communities to implement certain programs (usually special education and instructional materials), nor would they concern themselves so directly with expenditure priorities within local budgets.

This chapter has hopefully provided the reader with a general understanding of the principles which are in play in making a budget. Little has been presented about the principles of taxation, however, taxes like death are everywhere and should not be ignored.

6

Federal Involvement in Education

However, rightly or wrongly, the federal government is involved in providing basic education.

> Areas of Federal Government Involvement
> Case for/against Federal Involvement
> Council of Ministers of Education

Delineation of Responsibility

The responsibility for education in Canada rests with the provincial government, a responsibility clearly stated in Section 93 of the Constitution. The single most important reason for making education a provincial matter was the presence of two nations, Lower and Upper Canada, unhappy in the bosom of a single state. Lower Canada (the Province of Quebec), overwhelmingly French and Roman Catholic, would never have consented to Confederation if their schools were to be removed from provincial control. Thus, the plan for Confederation would have been impossible unless each province was allowed to retain control of education within its borders.

resistance

In 1867 education was the least expensive of the government services. It was easy to administer and was financed by local parents and taxpayers with limited help from the Central Authority. The schools were frequently small, often one-room log houses, with heavy winter enrollments and a program which ended at the grade 4 or 5 level. Today the picture is quite different, in all parts of Canada, urban and rural, English and French, East and West.

Although Section 93, tradition, and practice are on the side of exclusive provincial control, the Federal Government is very much in the picture, educationally. The debate on the desirable degree of federal participation has continued since before Confederation, with no immediate solution apparent. The purpose of this chapter is to provide several examples of the current level of federal involvement, and to raise some of the questions which beg answers.

Other sections of the constitution are very explicit as to the powers and responsibilities of the Federal Government – national defense, postal services, census and statistics, excise tax, tariffs, to mention a few. The residual areas of responsibility, those not specified as being either provincial or federal, were considered to be under the federal umbrella. This may have appeared very neat and definite at the time of Confederation but subsequent events have shown a considerable area of jurisdictional greyness. At the time of Confederation universities were foreign to nearly all of the Canadian populace, vocational and technical schools were non-existent, and Native and Inuit (Indian and Eskimo in constitutional terms) education was in a relatively primitive stage of devel-

federal responsibility

opment. Education was simply not a high priority item in the minds of the pioneering populace – important, yes, but defense, food, shelter and clothing certainly were far more important and immediate.

There were many areas of responsibility which were not envisioned in 1867, or at least were not considered to be either in or out of the *education* package. When the label education was applied, then they were within provincial jurisdiction. But there are some areas which may, or may not, be *education*; if they are not, then they become a federal responsibility (assuming these areas were not specifically mentioned in other parts of the Constitution). An example of this is the use of the word *training* instead of *education* in the Federal Government Vocational Training Acts described later. Teaching arithmetic to grade three students is definitely *education*, whereas drilling soldiers on the parade square is generally accepted as *training*, but which word best describes the program of academic subjects plus apprenticeship training or on-the-job training and vocational education which is now a relatively common route for many Canadian high school students?

It is clear that the Fathers of Confederation intended to exercise careful control over the enactments of provincial legislatures. Presumably this intention included education and consisted of more than ensuring those minority guarantees contained in the sub-sections of Section 93. The *Constitution* which they drafted granted the Governor-General-in-Council the power (without limit) to disallow any provincial statute within one year of its passage. Because the struggle for provincial rights is an ongoing struggle, an important part of our political history, and because the provinces have vigorously pressed their interests (for example, the Meech Lake negotiations), federal disallowance is a rare occurrence. But, the power still resides at the federal level. Present day practice tends to call upon the courts to decide whether a specific provincial state is *ultra vires* (beyond their powers) or not.

Our neighbors to the south have attempted to delineate more specifically the responsibilities of the state versus the federal government by way of a series of successive amendments to their Constitution. Canadians have chosen instead to depend upon negotiation, discussion, and sometimes referral to the courts. Perhaps Canadians are still not sure in their own minds of the distinction between federal and provincial responsibilities and thus would prefer to retain a number of grey areas, including certain aspects of *education*.

However, rightly or wrongly, the federal government is quite involved in education in Canada. Federal monies constitute approximately 20 percent of the monies spent on education today (direct expenditures and estimated expenditures out of federal equalization transfers and tax credits). Federal Government actions create the social framework within which we operate our schools, and their fiscal policies create the economic realities within which provincial legislative assemblies choose their own fiscal and political priorities for action or inaction.

education vs. training

control

uncertainty

Areas of Federal Involvement

1. *Non-provincial Parts of Canada*. The northern parts of Canada (the Yukon and Northwest Territories) are not included in the provinces and therefore the education for people in these areas becomes a direct responsibility of the Federal Government. Until recently educational affairs were handled directly from Ottawa. In recent years, departments of education for the Yukon and Northwest Territories have been formed, located at Whitehorse and Yellowknife. The relationship of the Federal Government to these departments tends to parallel the relationships with the provincial departments of education, even though jurisdictionally the northern departments are ultimately responsible to Ottawa. Financially, the education in these territories is supported by the Federal Government, offset to a small degree by local property taxes and other miscellaneous revenue sources. Perhaps the best piece of advice for the teacher is to remember that in matters of school governance little remains as it was. The formation of the two new northern districts, in the east, Nunavut and in the west, Denedeh, will induce new alignments of power respecting school matters. (Indian and Northern Affairs)

> non-provincial

2. *Education of Native Peoples*. In accordance with formal treaties and other agreements, the Federal Government has retained the responsibility for the educating of the Native and Inuit Peoples in Canada. While there never has been a federal office or department of education, various departments in the government over the years have supplied that function for the education of Canadian native peoples. During the last two decades, there has been an accelerating movement to have the respective provinces provide educational services for the Native Peoples, with complete reimbursement of costs by the Federal Government. In effect, the Federal Government retains its responsibilities (demonstrated by its complete cost coverage) through contracts for educational services with school boards in the various provinces. Such contracts, however, are now always subject to the approval of the native peoples involved. The Assembly of First Nations has been pressing for native self-government. Control over the education of native children will obviously be part of the definition. Indeed the role of Ottawa has changed measurably in the last two decades.

> Native Peoples

3. *Education of the Armed Forces Children*. The Department of National Defense provides schooling for the children of servicemen. Since the families of servicemen are normally provided housing adjacent to the military bases, the Department provides for a school within the confines of the *base* community. Buildings, teachers and supervision are supplied by the Department. The program of studies follows the program for the province in which the base is located, and generally follows the Ontario curriculum for overseas bases. In a number of instances, especially at the high school level, servicemen's children are educated in nearby public or separate schools through a tuition fee arrangement. In some instances the public school

> armed forces

jurisdiction has accepted complete responsibility for the operation of the school and has charged the Department of Defense for the actual costs involved.

vocational
technical

4. *Vocational and Technical Education (Training).* The history of the interest and involvement of the Federal Government in vocational and technical education dates from 1901 when representatives of Boards of Trade and the Dominion Trades and Labour Council met with Prime Minister Laurier. From then until the present there have been a number of incursions into this area by Ottawa. For example, there was: the *Royal Commission on Industrial and Technical Education* of 1910; the *Agricultural Aid Act* of 1912; the *Agricultural Instruction Act* of 1913; the *Technical Education Act* of 1919; the *Youth Training Act* of 1940; and the *Vocational Training Coordination Act* of 1942. One of the more recent examples was the *Technical and Vocational Assistance Act* of 1960, under whose auspices dozens of vocational schools and additions to existing schools were built. These institutions provided vocational and technical education to high school students and job re-training for older and unemployed people, all on a cost-sharing basis with provincial governments. Partly because of the pressure for provincial autonomy in education, this act was phased out and replaced by an agreement whereby the Federal Government would pay one half of the operating costs of all post-secondary institutions in Canada (including grade twelve students) and provide for a reshuffling of grants so that monies formerly paid directly to provinces for technical education would be paid into provincial coffers with no specified education *strings* attached.

External
Affairs

5. *Department of External Affairs.* The Federal Government, through the Department of External Affairs, is involved in several programs which have educational components. This department maintains links with the United Nations Educational Scientific and Cultural Organization (UNESCO), the Organization for Economic Cooperation and Development (OECD), the International Bureau of Education, and the Commonwealth Education Liaison committee. Education, one facet of the Canadian International Development agency (CIDA), provides for the administration of educational and technical assistance to other countries. Through this plan students and trainees from developing countries study in Canada, and Canadian teachers teach and assist in program development for developing countries.

research

6. *Research Support Programs.* Research in physical and natural sciences, in the social sciences, and in the humanities is assisted by grants from the National Research Council, Canada Council and Medical Research Council as well as other agencies and departments such as Atomic Energy of Canada, Central Mortgage and Housing Corporation, and the National Research Board.

other areas

7. *Other Areas of Federal Involvement.*

a. Canadian Broadcasting Corporation. Production of radio and television programs at public school, university, and adult education levels.

b. Department of Veterans' Affairs. Academic and vocational correspondence courses for public servants, armed forces members, and others.

c. Statistics Canada. Collects, coordinates and publishes statistics and information on all levels of education.

d. Department of Justice. Educational and training programs for the inmates of penitentiaries.

e. Public Service Commission of Canada. Bilingualism, including training and education of public service staff members, including intensive courses in French and English.

f. National Film Board. Production of educational slides, films and filmstrips, many of which are used in school; also of educational value are the National Museum and National Gallery.

g. Department of Agriculture. Prepares publications, motion pictures, videos, and displays for educational purposes.

h. Historic Sites and Monuments Board of Canada. Advises on the marking and commemoration of national historic sites of interest and significance in Canada, and provides educational materials.

i. Department of National Health and Welfare. Promotion and preservation of the health, social security and social welfare of the people of Canada.

j. Public Archives. Assembles and makes available to the public and educational institutions a comprehensive collection of source material relating to the history of Canada.

k. Department of National Defense. Maintains military colleges at Kingston, Royal Roads and Saint-Jean (the latter two are in the process of being closed). Provides regular officer and enlisted personnel training programs, and other service training programs which often have a substantial *education* component. As well, the Department provides cadet corps for youth.

8. *Teacher as Worker*. Federal laws directly affect the teacher as a worker, and also the economic and social well-being of the parents, and thus the children who enter the classroom as students.

worker

9. *Copyright Law*. Copyright violations and alleged copyright violations come under criminal law and are, as a consequence, under federal jurisdiction.

copyright

10. *Post Secondary Education*. Ottawa's involvement includes not only financial transfers but also includes the *Canadian Students Loan Act*.

post-secondary

The Case for Federal Involvement in Education

Previous parts of this chapter illustrated that the federal government is involved in education. The question now is whether it should become more involved, less involved, or retain the present level of involvement. The following illustrates some of the difficulties encountered in expecting an entirely satisfactory solution.

difficulties encountered

1867
education

1. On a constitutional basis, the provinces were provided with the responsibility for education and on that basis alone, incursions into the area by Ottawa are unconstitutional. However, the Constitution also made some direct references to federal involvement in education (Indian education and separate school protection, and language of instruction, are examples) and therefore, even on a constitutional basis some federal involvement may be justified. Some writers claim that Section 93 related only to the kind of education in vogue in Canada in 1867, and therefore extensions to the educational program (university, vocational, second language, and adult education, for example) properly fall within the federal jurisdiction.

not definitive

It becomes clear that the *Constitution* does not provide a definite statement on jurisdictional rights. But the *Constitution* and the laws of the country should reflect the wishes of the people (assuming that the wishes of the people can be determined). As was mentioned earlier, there also appears to be a certain willingness on the part of the general public to retain some undefined (grey) areas between federal and provincial educational jurisdiction. To legislate definitively can mean future rigidity and Canadians are perhaps not ready at this time to solidify educational control.

mobility

2. Canadians are very mobile; they move from place to place within their provinces, and from province to province. This mobility creates hardships for children attending school – stories are told of children being in one grade in one province and then being placed either a grade ahead or a grade behind upon moving to another province. Frequently, material studied in one grade may appear in another grade in another province, thus forcing either a repetition or creating an omission of certain topics. Often parents are faced with the necessity to purchase or rent different texts and workbooks as a result of a family relocation. This can become a considerable additional burden upon an already over-extended family budget. The proponents of greater federal involvement in education state that greater uniformity could be achieved (through such devices as developing a national curriculum) and would relieve the mobile population of many of the hardships associated with different textbook and instructional material requirements.

While some of the hardships suggested must be accepted as being true hardships, perhaps a more accurate description of many of the difficulties faced would be to call them inconveniences. Population mobility also occurs within a province, often with very similar disruptions. That is, the school systems within a province, practising local autonomy, often differ greatly as to when various topics are taught, and frequently differ in textbook and reference material requirements. This can happen even within a school system; it may happen within a school itself, from classroom to classroom. Thus perhaps the uniformity that could be achieved on a national level is more mythical than real.

national
uniformity

On the other hand, it may be incorrect to assume that materials and curricula are so very different from province to province. There exists a great deal of borrowing and consulting among the provinces, expedited by the Council of Ministers of Education. Further, publishing houses, through their interests in gaining national rather than provincial markets, influence the purchasing practices of educators, thus perhaps assisting in creating greater national uniformity.

3. The development of curricula is usually very expensive. The resources of school boards (and even provincial departments of education) are often insufficient to finance the constantly changing curriculum needs. Therefore, the federal government, if it was permitted by agreement, could provide financing on a national basis, thus eliminating much of the need for area curriculum development. Further, much of the present planning could be termed wasteful in that many groups are going through the same planning processes. However, this reasoning may tend to ignore those regional differences which are difficult to incorporate within national curricula. Moreover, perhaps cooperation among provinces could achieve sufficient national perspectives without having national control. Financing could also be on a pooled basis. However, national curricula, to overcome the problems of mobility, would of necessity be more rigid. This violates the presently accepted premise that what is needed is more, not less, flexibility in curricula. Another point which should not be overlooked is the value in the planning process itself; that is, the reinventing of the wheel does not add to the overall scientific knowledge, but the experiences obtained by the teachers who are reinventing the curriculum wheel can be in themselves a valuable education for them.

curricula

4. The equalization of educational opportunity, and costs, across Canada can best be achieved on a federal basis. Federal aid to education could assist the poorer provinces. The matter of equalization of educational costs and its consequences was discussed in the previous chapter on financing education.

equalization

5. Uniformity of curriculum could lead to standardization of university entrance requirements, making it easier for students to enter a university of their choice. Although this possibility exists, the trend appears to be in the opposite direction, with entrance requirements being different even for the universities within a province. Teacher training and teacher certification could perhaps be made more uniform as well, facilitating the movement of teachers from province to province. However, school districts and provincial teacher licensing authorities often have unique requirements and special preferences which could not be met by teachers studying in a common pedagogical and content route.

uniformity

6. Through the previous five points runs the theme of the importance and desirability of national unity. Canada is one country, not ten, eleven or twelve countries. Regional differences, as reflected through provincial structures, are important, but a unified Canada is even more important. Recognition of the importance of education for the strengthening of Canada as a country necessarily involves a degree of federal involvement in education, or for those who do not like the word *involvement*, at least a deep, real concern of the federal government for education in Canada. Obviously the educational requirements of 1867 are not the requirements of a modern Canada. The needs are new; perhaps the solution should also be new.

national unity

Council of Ministers of Education

coordination
information
liaison

Canada has no federal office of education. Each province has its own department of education. The Council of the Ministers of Education has, since 1967, served as an avenue for coordination, information exchange, and liaison.

The secretariat of CMEC, located in Toronto, is under the direction of a permanent secretary-general who carries out the work through committees which have inter-provincial representation. The Council prepares reports on such matters as manpower training, financing of post-secondary education, and coordinating the programing of school broadcasts, bilingualism, biculturalism, Canadian studies, environmental education, and other topics of mutual interest.

Summary

extent
not static

The extent of federal involvement in education is not something static. There exists no clear-cut political party lines, respecting whether the federal government should be more or less involved. The debate has raged since 1867 with no apparent resolution. As Wilson, Stamp and Audet point out, the period between 1945 to 1966 marked the apex years of federal government involvement, and can be attributed to the World War II war effort, the dislocation, and then the rebuilding of Canadian society. They label the late 1960s and onward as the time of retreat.

> The Federal-Provincial Conference of October, 1966 was significant in the development of Canadian federalism in that Ottawa began to withdraw from two important areas of educational assistance – vocational training and university education. . . . These attacks were in part political, in part a manifestation of Quebec's Quiet Revolution of the 1960s, in part a question of administrative efficiency, and in part a criticism of Ottawa's effectiveness in the education of native peoples. This trend is holding steady, perhaps with the exception of the pressures due to official bilingualism. (Wilson, Stamp, Audet, 1970, p. 461)

conformity
and flexibility

The strength of the Canadian educational system may be achieved by determining the optimal balance between the needs of conformity and flexibility, as they are reflected in national, provincial and local interests. It appears at this time that federal involvement in education is necessary and desirable but the optimal extent of this involvement remains unknown. Any changes in the present federal-provincial balance will, of necessity, involve political action and politicians have learned that one way to deal with a hot potato is not to touch it. The Council of the Ministers of Education, insofar as they reach consensus on major educational issues are, in part, operating as a national office of education and could operate in the common interest. The level of involvement of the council is informal. Its decisions are not binding and thus, on the other side, it lacks the necessary force to serve a national interest which could from time to time be contrary to provincial interests.

Part Two

Legal Concerns

The Teacher and the Law

What is your legal literacy quotient?

> School Law
>
> Classes, Systems and Sources of Law
>
> Natural Justice
>
> Categories of Wrong Doing
>
> Children and the Law
>
> Juvenile Justice
>
> Freedoms
>
> Malpractice
>
> Defamation
>
> Privacy
>
> Discrimination

Introduction

Just as preventative medicine is the best cure, so attention to safety and sensible teacher conduct are the best defences against litigation directed at teachers and their employers. Teachers should think about their legal literacy quotient. For most educators, it is not as high as they would like it to be. After all, they have been concerned about the education of boys and girls, but possibly they have been skating upon thin ice, legally. *(attention to safety)*

Parents are haunted by the fear that harm will come to their children. Litigation involving schools and school teachers seems to grow and grow. Many individuals and groups alike are seeking legal changes. In moving to assert their rights, they often come into conflict with the school teacher. Changes in schooling and society have placed legal pressures upon teachers and their employers. For example, increased numbers of field trips (off campus activities and outdoor education) have increased the student's exposure to potential accidents. In-school activities in physical education, the sciences, music, vocational education, home economics, indeed almost all parts of the curriculum have shifted over the years toward more activity, experimentation, and creative problem solving. Even the nature of children's play and recreational activities have changed. And of course, violence in schools is the centre of much public and parent concern. Students are bringing weapons to school. Some commentators refer to our junior and senior high schools as *combative enterprises*. The transmission of *AIDS* and other sexually transmitted diseases *(litigation)* *(violence in schools)* raise a great concern. The question of permitting condom dispensing machines in schools would not even be uttered in public only a few years ago. This section of the text will stress that in many ways the teacher must act in the place of the parent, and so in this new setting the teacher is not only concerned for his or her safety and legal rights but also for those of the students.

School Law

overcome fear

Educators cannot stem the tide of litigation, but they can improve their chances by overcoming their fear of the law, and by developing a better understanding of how it affects all of us. Many of our problems result from the fact that education law is less than a cohesive field of study. It is a bits-and-pieces business. Indeed there is no such field of study as educational law, in the technical legal sense. What we will be discussing is the application of legal principles and case law to the field of education with some mention of specific statutes as they apply, and of course under the broad recognition that children are citizens with all the rights that flow therefrom, but citizens with some additional legal shields provided to them due to their immature nature. The

juvenile justice

broader term *juvenile justice* is even more nebulous in that it is more a frame of mind, a philosophical approach to children and their rights, than it is something to be studied.

There is a saying among lawyers that their business is much less a matter of winning court cases than it is a matter of keeping their clients out of court. A sensitivity to potential legal danger points is the best way to stay out of court. A few simple rules and a clearer understanding of the legal system will take the teacher a long way in the desired directions.

guarding against hazards

Have classroom, school, and school yard hazards been guarded against, and prompt, corrective actions taken? Are student activities in the classroom, hallways and on the playground observed with care so that accidents which could arise from student misconduct can be prevented? Are students regularly informed of potential school-associated dangers? Have provisions been made for controlling student conduct when the teacher is called from the classroom to attend to an emergency or to respond to an urgent call? Have prepared talks about student-oriented behavior rules for their own safety been presented to the students? Have the physical facilities and instructional equipment been inspected for defects which may cause harm to the students? How about the special machines that are used? Has careful planning been conducted for supervision against injury resulting from potentially hazardous activities on field trips and other outings as well as for classroom experiments? Are the classroom activities appropriate to the physical and mental level of the student? Has this activity been used successfully in the past? Are the activities within the scope of the teacher's duties? Are they within the level of competency of the particular teacher? Have provisions been made for supervising the work of teacher aides, student helpers, student teachers, adult volunteers, and others who are answerable to the teacher? This list could go on, but it should be sufficient to highlight the areas in which teachers must exercise care in order to guard their students against unreasonable harm. Is the educational value of the activity worth the risk?

The Concept of Law

Each society finds it necessary to have an agreed upon set of basic rules which will govern the conduct of its members. Lacking this, disagreements, conflict, and anarchy set in and the society becomes unstable. It may destroy itself.

basic rules

Three areas in which societies find it imperative to formulate such rules are the values placed upon human life, the ownership of property, and the ways in which one member may or may not behave toward another. There are of course others, but the point being that the system of agreed upon values held by that society becomes formalized into a body of law – a set of rules.

In earlier societies, conflicts between individuals were taken before an elder or chief who was respected by both persons. The elder would listen to the arguments and pronounce a decision. If a current dispute was identical to a previous dispute in matters of fact, or nearly so, the previous decision of the elder would be re-stated as being the decision upheld for this dispute. Thus, the decision became a customary rule for settling similar future disputes, that is, precedent was set.

customary rule

In every society there are those who are unwilling to abide by the agreed-upon rules. A system of penalties was developed which were imposed upon those deviants who failed to conform, in order that the harmony of the group would not be destroyed.

Modern laws reflect the agreed-upon values of a modern society. As these values change, so do the law and the penalties.

Not all behavior contrary to the value system of the society is a threat to the interest of the society as a whole. Many laws are formulated for the protection of individual freedoms and liberties. The breaking of these laws did not threaten society as a whole, at least not initially. Of course, numerous and flagrant violations of any law, which has a reasoned base, will threaten the fabric of the society as a whole. The point being that different classes of laws were being developed in each society as it grew and matured.

freedoms and liberties

Class of Law

There are two main classes of laws in our society, these being public laws and private laws. Public laws speak to the relationships between the branches of government, often the relationship between levels of government, municipal, provincial, federal, and frequently to the relationships between government and the individual. Private laws govern the relationship between private persons or groups of persons and are described as being civil laws. Criminal law, constitutional law, and administrative law are examples of public law. Later in this

public laws

private laws

section the reader's attention will be drawn to the importance of the principles of tort law in the daily life of the classroom teacher.

Systems of Law

common law

codified law

There are two main systems of law operating in Canada today. A major part of the Canadian legal system has its roots in the British civil system, which is a common law system. The other is reflected in the provincial laws of the Province of Quebec (see chapter one). In the codified legal system, all laws issued were from the monarch or emperor through a system of declared "codes" of law. Frequently gods were given credit for the edicts and the ruler simply claimed to be the messenger through which the wishes of the gods were made known. Perhaps the three best known codes of law are those of Hammurabi, King of Babylonia, Justin of Rome, and the Napoleonic Code which became the foundation of Quebec provincial law.

rule of
precedent

The legal system common to the most of Canada is the common law system originated in Anglo-Saxon England. It consisted of common sense rules by which community members resolved their differences. The common law system is quite different than the codified law system in the sense that the former derives its power from usage, the latter from the wishes of a ruler. The common law system of England moved toward standardization following the Norman conquest. The conquerors introduced travelling judges who decided cases based upon local custom, but who, however, began to compare cases and began to follow the patterns of deciding like cases in a like manner. Thus the rule of precedent was established, a rule which assists us as teachers in understanding the probable direction which a case of teacher negligence, for example, is likely to take. The rule of precedent brought with it uniformity and impartial judgments. Personal preference or favoritism are less likely to enter a legal system based heavily upon precedent.

In Canadian civil law, judges follow precedent decisions in those cases where there is sufficient similarity between a present case under consideration and some previous cases. Fresh interpretations produce new precedents. As noted earlier, law is based upon a system of values held by a society. As the value system changes, precedent may no longer reflect the values held. Judges may overturn the precedent with a fresh interpretation. Precedent law does not promote stagnation, but tends to promote consistency and impartiality and introduces a considerable degree of predictability into the bits-and-pieces field of study which is the subject of this section of the text.

Sources of Law

writtten law

enacteed law

There are two main sources of law, i.e., the rules which govern our behavior or relationships. The first is written or enacted law, which in our society is called statute law. Enacted law is sometimes referred to in the law literature as positive law in that it results from an act of proclamation by a monarch or more usually from a legislated enactment by elected representatives of the people. Statute law of special interest to the teacher exists in two forms. The first of these are those laws which result from an act of parliament or a legislative assembly. The *Criminal Code* as passed by the Federal Parliament or a school act as approved or amended by a provincial government are good examples. The second form of statute law, those enactments which are the result of delegated legislative authority, are frequently overlooked by the teacher, or are not given the attention they warrant. Examples of these are local orders-in-council or by-laws. Of greatest importance to the teacher are the regulations and policies of the employer, the school board. When the school board is acting within the authority granted to it by the provincial legislature, usually through the school act, its regulations and policies have all the weight of law and are as binding upon teachers as they would be if they were a section of the act. Chapter 4 illustrates some of the policy making areas and practices of a typical school board.

Criminal Law

Statute law is said to be a law enforced by a sovereign political authority – in our system, the Governor-General-in-Council or the Lieutenant-Governor-in-Council.

Statute law

The second source of laws arises from the principles and rules of action developed over time to govern the affairs of people. They derive their authority from custom and usage, or the judgments and decrees of the courts. This source is known as common law, case law, unwritten, not enacted, or discovered law. British common law principles have much to say to the Canadian school teacher. More about this later.

custom and usage

Natural Justice

There exists a set of rules which usage dictates must be applied in every situation where a person or body is charged with the duty of adjudicating disputes between people or adjudicating upon the rights of others. This set of rules is referred to as the rules of natural justice. They are written in many forms, pervade most of our rules of action, and are usually stated as follows. Those who adjudicate must act fairly and in good faith, without bias, and with a judicial temper. They must provide each party with an opportunity to understand what case has to be made and further, must provide them ample opportunity to state that case.

The legal principle of *natural justice* and the *duty to be fair* (due process in the U.S.A.) is a common thread which runs through the courts and administrative tribunals such as the various boards, for example, which adjudicate on teacher dismissal or student attendance and placement matters. When these boards fail to follow the rules of natural justice, the decisions rendered will be voided by the courts.

In addition to the set of rules referred to above, two fundamental principles must be applied in order to achieve natural justice:

rules

1. the right to be heard;

2. the right to an unbiased decision.

The more impact a board has upon a person's rights, the more closely these two principles must be followed.

The right to be heard includes a number of issues. However, the fundamental question is, "have the affected individuals or parties been given an adequate opportunity to present their case and to meet the case against them?"

hearing   Usually this is accomplished through entitlement to a *hearing*, and the opportunity to present written materials.

The right to be heard principle usually covers:

1. the right to adequate notice. This requires that the affected persons must be given sufficient time and adequate information so they are able to know the case against them, and thus have an opportunity to adequately prepare their case;

2. the right to cross examination in order to more fully present their case and meet the charges against them;

3. the right to counsel ensures the persons have access to support and advice, usually legal in the solicitor/client sense, but for children this may include advice in the parental sense. The references in the *Young Offenders Act*, for example, (see later sections) suggest there can be more than lawyers involved in providing the necessary counsel.;

4. the right to present evidence in support of the positions held by the parties;

5. the right to request an adjournment of the proceedings usually in order to seek additional supportive evidence;

6. the right to know the reasons for the decision. Usually this evolves into a written statement of the decision, a setting forward of the findings of fact upon which the decision was made, and a clear statement of the reasons for the decision. These provisions ensure the persons or parties know why the tribunal reached the decision that it did, they know the decision was not arbitrary, and further, the written statement enables the persons or parties to decide whether there is a basis for an appeal or not.

unbiased   The second fundamental principle, the right to an unbiased decision, is tested by asking the question, *would a reasonable person have considered the decision is likely to be biased?* This decision usually centres upon questions as to whether a tribunal member has a direct or indirect pecuniary interest in the outcome; whether the tribunal member has a personal friendship or business relationship with the persons or parties appearing before the tribunal, or whether there is a history of animosity or bias between the tribunal member and the appellant.

practical steps   There are a number of practical steps which adjudicators take in order to ensure an unbiased decision.

1. Hearing procedures (rules) are developed which respect the rules of natural justice and procedural fairness.

opening statements   2. Procedures centring around the format of the *opening statements* will ensure the parties have an opportunity to set forward what they consider the issues to be, what has to be proven, and what kinds of evidence both parties will be presenting.

3. Procedures regarding what the terms of *preliminary application* are must be decided upon. These procedures consider the matters of jurisdiction, that is, whether the tribunal is legally empowered to hear the issue, determination of whether adequate and sufficient notice has been given, requests for any procedures for adjournments, and the *rights of other parties*, that is, who has the right to *standing* (entitled to attend) the hearing. preliminary application

4. Evidence is usually presented by witnesses and perhaps written statements. Tribunals will, in an effort to ensure an unbiased decision, make provisions for evidence under oath, the right to cross examination, the establishment of time limits which are fair, provisions for recording the proceedings, decisions regarding public or private (*in camera*) hearings. Note that tribunals are normally provided with sufficient powers to compel the attendance of witnesses and the producing of documents. evidence

5. Finally, administrative tribunals will formalize the procedures through which their judgment will be rendered, and communicated to the parties. The timing, route, and format of the communication of the decision will be indicated. formalize

Categories of Wrong Doing

The legal repertoire of the teacher should include an understanding of the two main categories of wrong doing. The first, criminal wrongs which are wrongs against the values or rules of a society, where the aim of the court is to punish the defendant, in part for punishment's sake, but in part in order that the punishment will serve as a deterrent or lesson to others who are considering a similar illegal act. The second category of wrong doing is a civil wrong. It is a wrong against a person or group of people. The aim of civil actions is to enforce some right claimed by the plaintiff. There are essentially four types of civil wrongs, those which are breaches of trust, those which are breaches of contract, those which give rise to an award of money for damages, and those which give rise to a court order requiring that something be done. The latter is called a *mandamus* and enters into such matters as a child's right to attend school or to attend a specific program. criminal wrong civil wrong mandamus

Children and the Law

The law recognizes children as legal persons who are entitled to the same basic human rights and legal protections as those awarded adult members of our society. The *Constitution Act* of 1982 awards the same fundamental freedoms to everyone. Children are entitled to the same legal protection from criminal acts as are adults. The principles of civil law apply to children in that no person may usurp the property of the child, for example. But as history teaches us, children were often regarded as being the property (chattels) of their parents and as being dependants. Current expressions of children's rights are children as chattels

providing a wrenching experience for some. Changes in basic beliefs are slow to take place.

The problem is that children suffer one serious handicap – they are so young and immature. Consequently, the law relating to children does not stop with such statements as "children are people and must be recognized by and given the full protection of the law." English common law recognized this problem. There developed an important set of legal principles which have been continued and expanded upon to form the body of law known as *children's law*. The term refers to some unique principles and statutes directed specifically toward a societal concern for the legal welfare of children. For example, legal historians believe that sometime in the eighth century two legal principles with respect to children began to develop. They were:

1. because the child is immature, someone must provide care for that child, and that person was ordinarily the child's father;

2. the father's authority over his child was subordinate to the authority of the monarch who, as *parens patriae* (father of his country), was thus responsible for the protection of all the children within the realm.

These two principles were enshrined into the law by the *Magna Carta* in 1215.

By the 18th century, the duties of the father with respect to his children had been defined to include the duty to maintain, the duty to protect, and the duty to educate. And of course, the responsibility of the *monarch* as *parens patriae* was expanded to include the same three areas. These responsibilities accurately describe the duty of the present-day parent. Two important modifications have taken place, however. First, the mother now shares joint legal authority and responsibility with the father for the care of the children, and second, the monarch's authority as *parens patriae* has been delegated to the courts of our nation. In addition, we have established agencies of government to monitor the degree of parental care, and provide many of those services required by children which were provided by parent or church in the past.

In antiquity, these duties were wholly moral, but as time passed they became legal duties enforceable by the power of the legal system. Further, it is important to note these duties gave rise to a corresponding authority. Thus, the duty of parents gave rise to the authority of parents to have custody of their children or to direct their education as well as to discipline them, if done in a reasonable manner. Parents are usually required to maintain children up to the age of 16 years. This duty may be extended beyond age 16 if the child is handicapped, or impotent, or destitute. Correspondingly, the authority of the parent to have custody, to direct the education of, and to discipline the child extends to age 16 and beyond depending upon the extension of the duty as noted above. In some situations, the parents' rights have been extended to 18 and 21 years of age, but in common practice, it is a declining parental right, i.e., from direct control to something which is little more than advice giving.

[margin notes]
young and immature

Magna Carta

parens patriae

parental duty

Also, it should be noted that divorce laws have modified the general situation described above to the extent that, in at least one legal case, a university student was ruled to be impotent and thus a responsibility of his divorced father.

Where an injustice has been done against a child, there are only two ways of enforcing the parents' duty, either by bringing criminal charges against the parent, or by having the courts invoke the *parens patriae* principle. The courts are very cautious about exercising their authority to claim custody over a child, however. They treat the parent's right to custody as almost sacred and terminate it only when the parent is judged unfit or is not properly carrying forward the duty to protect the child, or where there is sufficient evidence of serious immorality of conduct. The court's position seems to be that the state cannot replace the natural love and affection of parents. To make a child a *ward* of the state is a harsh measure. Opportunities for rehabilitation must be provided.

parents' right

The Child's Best Interest

It is not only the parents' duty to protect the child, but also this duty must be performed in the child's best interest. British common law has established the principle that not only must the parent carry out parental duties but they must do so in the *best interest* of the child. The *best interest test* is frequently applied with respect to medical treatment. For example, where a mother proposed to have an 11-year-old mentally disabled girl sterilized, the court intervened to prevent the operation on the grounds that the proposed action was not in the *best interest* of the girl.

best interest test

Most often where a mother is charged with parental neglect of duty toward the child, the situation is handled by the child welfare department or the provincial government on the basis of a third party complaint. Sometimes schools become involved, especially in the area of suspected child abuse. Some provinces use the phrase *child in need of protection* which is much broader than child abuse and its consequences more far-reaching for the school. Usually a more central issue for the school is the matter of the duty to educate and the type of education to be offered.

need for protection

The principle of the child's best interest and the emergence of specific statutes which have enshrined certain basic freedoms within enacted law have given rise to many issues which are of special interest to classroom teachers. For example, the *Canadian Charter of Rights and Freedoms* supersedes and takes precedent over any other piece of legislation. These rights and freedoms apply to all Canadians, including children. The presence of these principles has opened the way for the courts of Canada to do much more social engineering – some would say interfering!

As a result of passage of the *Charter*, the emphasis has shifted from the rights of the majority to the rights of the individual.

To this point, the rights of the community have been narrowly and poorly expressed and often could be summarized in this way – *Children, conform to the norms of society. Do not deviate too much. Graduate and get a job.* The rights of the school system are expressed in school acts, school trustee acts, teaching profession acts and other pieces of legislation, many of which are essentially peace, order, and good government statements. Changes are taking place in Canadian society. Today, legislation has placed little priority on student rights. However, more often now than ever before, our children are saying, "It's our future, isn't it?"

Students are apprehensive about compulsory attendance laws, about restrictions which schools have placed upon publications, and about the kind of literature they are permitted to see. They are concerned about teacher evaluation and the course selections available. They are, of course, apprehensive about drugs, alcohol, and tobacco. Freedom to govern themselves is a major concern. The nature of society and its survival are uppermost in the minds of many of them.

nature of
society

Juvenile Justice

Too often the concept of juvenile justice becomes confused with the system of courts, probation officers, social workers, detention centres, police officers, and those who devote special attention to the legal problems of the youth of our society. Juvenile justice, however, is better defined as *fair and reasonable treatment for all children.* The point to be made is not that these persons and institutions have failed, but every teacher must remember teachers are very much a part of the juvenile justice system. Indeed, teachers play a central role because they stand in *loco parentis.* This legal term means the teacher stands in the place of the parent, and thus is placed in the position of the *caring* parent and is not solely an agent of the government. Further, this legal concept allows the teacher many of the privileges of the parent, especially respecting control and discipline. To be a *caring* parent is a tremendous responsibility. Teachers are the parents for a part of every child's life. Mothers and fathers send their children to teachers, in trust. Teachers must do as well in protecting children legally as they would do in protecting them physically.

loco parentis

Search of Locker; Search of Person

Under the provision of Section 8 of the *Charter of Rights and Freedoms,* everyone is protected from unreasonable search and seizure. This includes children. As a general rule, if the person does agree to a locker search, a search warrant is required. As a rule, if evidence is obtained by infringing upon freedoms which are secured by the *Charter,* it will not be admissible in court. As a rule, when it comes to personal search, school people have no authority whatsoever. If the student is searched, the searchers are probably guilty of a civil wrong. Teachers would leave *search of a person* to a proper civilian authority.

personal
search

The following general guidelines are presented in a hope they will be useful in ensuring justice:

1. respect the student's right to property;

2. make them aware of any school policies authorizing periodic locker searches;

3. have reasonable and probable grounds before undertaking a search;

4. seek their consent;

5. have a student and a witness present, if possible;

6. if illegal acts are suspected, contact the proper civilian authorities;

7. if police officers are conducting the search, the teacher (in *loco parentis*) should seek a search warrant on behalf of the child.

Interviewing Students

The manner in which the student is interviewed will have much to do with what can be done with the evidence obtained. In general, courts must be satisfied that the answers were given freely and were voluntary, without the presence of threat, or promise, or other inducement. This is especially true for young persons. Even high school students are persons of tender years in the view of many courts of law.

methods used

The absence of these safeguards does not, of necessity, mean the evidence so obtained will be thrown out but it certainly would work towards that direction.

The *Young Offenders Act*, a federal statute, came into effect in 1984. It applies to youthful offenders who are twelve years of age, not yet eighteen, and deals with possible criminal conduct.

young offenders

Since many young offenders are also school students, and since teachers may, in some instances, be regarded as parents for purposes of the act, it is useful to review the requirements of the act with respect to the taking of statements by peace officers and other persons who are in law, a person in authority. Section 56 of the *Young Offenders Act* states:

1. Subject to this section, the law relating to the admissibility of statements made by persons accused of committing offences applies in respect of young persons.

2. No oral or written statement given by a young person to a peace officer or other person who is, in law, a person in authority is admissible against the young person unless
a. the statement was voluntary;
b. the person to whom the statement was given has, before the statement was made, clearly explained to the young person, in language appropriate to his age and understanding, that
i. the young person is under no obligation to give a statement,
ii. any statement given by him may be used as evidence in proceedings against him,
iii. the young person has the right to consult another person in accordance with paragraph (c), and
iv. any statement made by the young person is required to be made in the presence of the person consulted, unless the young person desires otherwise;
c. the young person has, before the statement was made, been given a

reasonable opportunity to consult with counsel or a parent, or in the absence of a parent, an adult relative, or in the absence of a parent or an adult relative, any other appropriate adult chosen by the young person; and

d. where the young person consults any person pursuant to paragraph (c), the young person has been given a reasonable opportunity to make the statement in the presence of that person.

3. The requirements set out in paragraphs (2) (b),(c), and (d) do not apply in respect of oral statements where they were made spontaneously by the young person to a peace officer or other person in authority before that person has had a reasonable opportunity to comply with those requirements.

4. A young person may waive his rights under paragraph (2)(c) or (d) but any such waiver shall be made in writing and shall contain a statement signed by the young person that he has been apprised of the right that he is waiving.

5. A youth court judge may rule inadmissible in any proceedings under this Act a statement given by the young person in respect of whom proceedings are taken if the young person satisfied the judge that the statement was given under duress imposed by any person who is not, in law, a person in authority.

6. For the purpose of this section, an adult consulted pursuant to paragraph 56(2)(c) shall, in the absence of evidence to the contrary, be deemed not to be a person in *authority*. (added by S.C. 1986, c.32, 2.38)

person in
authority

Since school principals, and on occasion school teachers, may be taken to be in law, a person in authority it is essential for the school person to understand his or her legal rights under Section 56. Failure to do so may destroy the case by having the youth's statements excluded from the hearing. Also it is essential that as 56(2)(b) specifies the young person be cautioned in language appropriate to his or her age, and that he or she therefore understands his or her rights.

Following is a suggested form of cautionary wording which modified the language of Section 56 but maintains the intent. Section references are provided in order that the reader may check the new wording for its *appropriateness* in communicating the student's rights to him/her.

Suggested Sample Caution

1. You may be charged with _____ in relation to _____.

2. You don't have to say anything about this unless you want to.

(Sec. 56(2)(a)(i))

3. If you say anything to me I could tell it to the judge at your trial. The judge could use what you say to me to help him/her decide whether or not you are guilty.

(Sec. 56(2)(a)(ii))

4. Before you say anything to me you can talk to your mom or dad. Do you want that?

(Sec. 56(2)(a)(iii))

5. Before you say anything to me you can talk to a lawyer. A lawyer is somebody who knows about the law and can tell you about it. Do you want to talk to a lawyer?

(Sec. 56(2)(a)(iii))

6. If your mom or dad cannot be here you could talk to a grown-up relative. If a relative cannot be here you can pick another grown-up to talk to. Do you want to talk to a grown-up?

(Sec. 56(2)(a)(iii))

7. If you talk to a lawyer or your mom or dad or another grown-up you can have that person there while you talk to me if you want.

(Sec. 56(2)(a)(iv))

(If the young offender does not wish to consult with anyone, obtain a properly executed waiver.)

On the surface, it may appear that teachers (in *loco parentis* or as consultants under 56(2)(a)(iv) to a young person) stand in opposition to the police and legal system. This is not so, but they have a prior obligation and that is to the child and his/her parents who are required by law to send the child to the teachers. The parents have sent the child to the teacher, in trust. prior obligation

If the officer questioning the child states the matter is urgent, then what should the teacher do?

1. Question the officer regarding the urgency and seek to have the child questioned at his or her residence in the presence of the parents or guardians.

2. If the officer persists, then permit the questioning after having obtained the officer's reasons for the questioning. (Get these in writing if possible.)

3. Advise the student of his/her rights.

4. Advise parents or relatives of what is happening and request their attendance.

5. Advise school officials, especially the principal.

6. Make a written record of all that was said, or at least make a rough outline of what was said.

7. If the student is arrested before the parents arrive, then advise the student of his/her rights and inform the administration and/or district legal counsel immediately.

As an absolute minimum, a clear record of events should be kept and, if possible, the teacher should be there when the student is interviewed. record of events

A word of caution. Children's rights are not the only rights to be considered but the school's job is to take positive action with respect to the child's rights, again because of the teacher's position of trust. position of trust

Testimony

conversation inviolate

Teachers are reminded that the only conversation which is legally inviolate in Canada is the conversation between solicitor and client. All other conversations must be admitted by the courts.

Civil Rights for Students

Students, especially those at the secondary school level, are well aware of the *Constitution Act* of 1982, especially the *Charter of Rights and Freedoms* (the *Charter*) as contained therein as Part I, Schedule B. On occasion, a student or group of students will become the proverbial Philadelphia lawyer. They will argue their *Charter* civil rights with immense vigor.

rights enjoyed

Teachers should acquaint themselves with the rights enjoyed by the student body and also in response the rights enjoyed by teachers and school administrators as part of the educational establishment. In summation, *Charter* rights are somewhat restricted in the school context.

The *Canadian Charter of Rights and Freedoms* states, under Section 2, fundamental freedoms:

> 2. Everyone has the following fundamental freedoms:
> a. freedom of conscience and religion;
> b. freedom of thought, belief, opinion and expression including freedom of the press and other media of communication;
> c. freedom of peaceful assembly; and
> d. freedom of association.

Before the reader concludes that the *Charter* rights are wide open, note should be made of Section One which states:

> The *Canadian Charter of Rights and Freedoms* guarantees the rights and freedoms set out in it subject only to such reasonable limits prescribed by law as can be demonstrably justified in a free and democratic society (the judicial limitations), and the political limitations imposed by Section 33 which permits the federal or provincial governments to opt out of certain *Charter* protections (the notwithstanding clause).

The arguments surrounding these sections suggest they were intended to restore an important measure of legislative supremacy to government.

Freedom of Conscience and Religion

religious and patriotic exercises

Disputes in this area usually centre upon the presence of patriotic exercises and instruction, and religious exercises and instruction. Since the school acts of the various provinces, in one form or another, make provision for some local autonomy in these areas, the teacher may wittingly or more probably unwittingly become embroiled in one of the more *conflict prone* areas of the Charter.

The *Alberta School Act*, for example, states:

> 33(1). A board may:
> a. prescribe religious instruction to be offered to its students;
> b. prescribe religious exercises for its students;
> c. prescribe patriotic instruction to be offered to its students;

d. prescribe patriotic exercises for its students;

e. permit persons other than teachers to provide religious instruction to its students.

Section 32(2) makes provision for student exclusion upon written request by the parent or guardian. Section 50 of the *Education Act* of Ontario states:

> 50(1). Subject to the regulations, a pupil shall be allowed to receive such religious instruction as the parent or guardian desires or where the pupil is an adult, as he desires.

> (2) No pupil in a public school shall be required to read or study in or from a religious book, or to join in an exercise of devotion or religion, objected to by his parent or guardian, or by the pupil, where he is an adult.

There have been several legal confirmations. For example, in an Ontario case *Donald v. Hamilton Board of Education* (1944), 4 D.L.R. 227; [1945] 3 D.L.R. 424 a parent sought to justify a child's refusal to participate in the flag salute on the basis that it was a religious exercise, the trial judge ruled that the requested exemption did not apply to Section 50(1) of the *Education Act* of Ontario as quoted above. flag salute

The Ontario Court of Appeal held, however:

> That certain acts, exercises and symbols at certain times, or to certain people, connote a significance or meaning which, at other times to other people, is completely absent is a fact so obvious from history, and from observation, that it needs no elaboration.

> The fact that the appellants conscientiously believe the views which they assert is not here in question. A considerable number of cases in other jurisdictions, in which a similar attitude to the flag has been taken, indicates that at least the same view has been conscientiously held by others. The statute, while it absolves pupils from joining in exercises of devotion or religion to which they or their parents object, does not further define or specify what such exercises are or include or exclude. Had it done so, other considerations would apply. For the Court to take to itself the right to say that the exercises here in question had no religious or devotional significance might well be for the Court to deny that very religious freedom which the statute is intended to provide.

Earlier sections of this text, especially chapters 1 and 2, illustrate the central place of religion in the development of our educational system. Canada does not have the traditional separation of church and state as required by the Constitution of the United States. So in Canada, is freedom of religion an absolute freedom for the Canadian school student? church and state

An Ontario case, *re Zylberberg et al., and Director of Education of Sudbury Board of Education* (1986) 25 CRR 193, dealt with an application by parents to have the Ontario regulation requiring prayers declared as being contrary to Section 2(a) of the *Charter*. The reasoned opinions of the justices who heard the case provide the teacher with a good sample of future possible directions respecting the student and Section 2(a) of the *Charter*. Justice O'Leary stated: prayers

The recognition in the Constitution of the existence of God and that our society is multicultural in nature cannot, of course, excuse a violation of s.2(a) or s.15(1) of the *Charter* but must be kept in mind when such violations are alleged . . . .

I accept that there is or may be pressure on all who are culturally or religiously different to conform to the ways of the majority. In particular, I accept that the holding of religious exercises in the school may constitute some pressure on students to participate rather than disclose to teachers and fellow-students that their conscience or religious beliefs dictate they should not participate . . . .

The type of coercion complained of is pressure to conform rather than face the embarrassment of disclosing that a different belief is held. If such coercion infringes the guarantee of freedom of conscience and religion then such freedom is likewise infringed whenever prayer is said at functions provided for by statute. For example, a religious exercise or prayer in Parliament or the Legislature would infringe upon the right to freedom of conscience and religion.

In my view the pressure to conform complained about here does not constitute coercion to such an extent as to infringe the right of freedom of conscience and religion.

If contrary to the view I have just expressed it can be said that the pressure to participate in religious exercises . . . is an infringement of freedom of conscience and religion, then, in my view, it is such an infringement as can be demonstrably justified in a free and democratic society and so . . .

religious exercises

The directions with respect to religious exercises in schools which are taking place across Canada point toward the continuing use of opening prayers and religious courses of study in separate schools, where these schools are provided for under the *Charter*, and also in private religious schools, and for the local public boards *not* to exercise their authority to prescribe religious exercises and instruction. Many public (common) schools have had neither for many years now, however, the teacher should carefully check local policies before initiating anything in this area.

Freedom of Expression

student grooming

Two issues frequently arise in the school setting. One, what authority does the teacher and school system have over the student dress and grooming as a form of personal expression of the student (hair length, shorts, mini skirts)? Two, what are reasonable limits on verbal and pictorial messages on T-shirts, and the content of and the distribution of leaflets, newspapers, and other similar literature within the context of the school?

The Ward (Saskatchewan) and Tuli (Alberta) cases provide a suggested direction. Let us review, in part at least, the court's thinking on the issue of dress regulations.

hair length

In the Ward case, *Ward v. Board of Blaine Lake School Unit No. 57* [1971] 4 W.W.R. 161, an 11-year-old student was suspended from school for failing to comply with the school board's policy on hair length for male students. The judge concluded in part:

In my opinion, the Education Acts are intended to provide for education in its truest and widest sense. Such education includes the inculcation of habits of order and obedience and courtesy: such habits are taught by giving orders, and if such orders are reasonable and proper under the circumstances of the case, they are within the scope of the teacher's authority, even although they are not confined to bidding the child to read or write, to sit down or to stand up in school, or the like.

In *Hutt et al. v. Governors of Haileybury College et al. (1888)*, 4 T.L.R. 623 at 624, Field, J. said: 'the master must take into consideration the interests, not only of one boy, but those of the whole school.' ... I am of the opinion that the power of prescribing within reasonable limits the extent of cleanliness required of pupils attending school, the extent of clothing they should wear, their general appearance, including hair grooming, was within the power of the Board under the heading 'administering and managing the educational affairs of the school district' and 'exercising a general supervision and control over the schools of the unit.' In these days of the so-called 'permissive society' one does not need to indulge in much in the way of flights of the imagination to envisage how difficult it would be to conduct a class of boys and girls where they could wear as little or as unusual clothing as some children or some parents might see fit. This would include not only care, cleanliness and covering of various parts of the body but also prevention of unusual types of dress and hair styling which might be calculated to distract the pupils from their work in the classroom or adversely affect a proper and reasonable air of discipline in the school.

If the resolution was necessary or wise and required more conformity than reasonably necessary, is the remedy to go to the courts or to the electors who elect the legislators and members of the School Board?

One of the authorities cited, in my opinion, on all the evidence, the Board was acting bona fide in the exercise of its powers under the sections cited of the School Acts and it was within its jurisdiction in passing this regulation and in so acting it was not performing a judicial act and so its action in passing the regulation is not reviewable on *certiorari* ....

It is not for this court to substitute its opinion, as to whether the resolution should have been enforced by reasonable disciplinary action, for the opinion of the duly elected Unit Board. As stated by the Chief Justice of the Supreme Court of Canada 'it is necessary for good administration, municipal or school, that those who are charged with it ... are not hampered in the exercise of their duty by intervention of the courts of justice except for grave reasons.'

Officials of the St. Albert Protestant Separate School District had refused to grant permission to Suneet Singh Tuli to wear his kirpan (ceremonial sword) in school. *Tuli v. The Board of Trustees of the St. Albert Protestant Separate School District No. 6* (1987) 8 C.H.R.R.D. 3906. Tuli applied to the Alberta's superior court for an interim injunction against the Board's action until the case had been heard by the Alberta Human Rights Commission. In granting the injunction, the court stated:

kirpan

Surely the fact that this person would be seen to have fallen from his faith in my view is sufficient to warrant the relief that he seeks, to say nothing of his possible loss of a scholarship and potential loss of a school year. It is my view that within this application to wear the requirements of his religion upon baptism, including the kirpan, would provide those who are unfamiliar with the tenet of his faith an opportunity to be introduced to and to develop an understanding of another's culture and heritage. In this case, that being the traditions of a very well established, respected and old religion.

That does not mean that everyone who wishes to wear such an instrument is entitled to do so. The case must be made out, as was made out in this particular application. It is in my view a positive educational tool which can far outweigh the potential danger as analyzed by the respondent, so long as it is recognized, at least at this time, that it is a privilege and still not a right.

Tuli continued to attend school wearing his kirpan. The Human Rights Commission found there had been no discrimination under Alberta's *Individual Rights Protection Act.* In part, the Board of Inquiry decision stated:

Here the complainant was not denied permission to use the school services or school facilities. He was denied permission to wear a kirpan to school. He was not, in fact, treated differently . . . .

It may well be reasonable and justifiable for a school board to make a general rule prohibiting all non-Khalsa (unbaptized) Sikhs from using school services or facilities while wearing a kirpan. In light of the degree of commitment, involving both spiritual and personal maturity, which must be exhibited by a person accepted for baptism into the Sikh faith, that general rule would likely not be reasonable and justifiable if it also applied to a Khalsa Sikh. That is not to say that a school board would not be entitled lawfully to pass a rule requiring advance notice to be given to it and a hearing to be held before the date when a student intends to become a Khalsa Sikh. An individual Khalsa Sikh might lawfully be prohibited after a hearing from using publicly funded school services and facilities generally or in limited circumstances or on certain conditions while wearing a kirpan. The circumstances for such determination would have to withstand the test of reasonableness and justifiability in each case. (Board of Inquiry, (1987) 8 C.H.R.R.D. 3736)

On the matter of freedom of expression respecting communications, only the *Regina v. Burko* (1968) 3 D.L.R. (3d) 303 case which predates the *Charter* enactment could be considered to impinge upon the subject. But, since the central issue was the denial of the rights of university students to enter a high school and distribute literature to students during class change, little direct guidance is provided by the courts except for the inferences which may be drawn from the last part of the magistrate's statement.

literature
distribution

. . . it is contrary to the public good to permit individuals on public or secondary school property without the permission of the proper authorities for the purpose of disseminating information or ideas, particularly when such information or ideas may not be in accordance with the curriculum established by the state for the public good.

American precedent suggests that considerable authority in these matters rests with the school administration if the actions are taken for the purpose of the orderly administration of the school.

Freedom of Assembly

The *Charter* right of freedom of assembly usually becomes an issue for school authorities when they attempt to limit student rallies and protest assemblies. There are no post-Charter cases in Canada but United States precedents suggest the courts will find in favor of the authorities if their motives for action are good school order and they are not biased for or against the subject matter of the protest.

rallies and assemblies

Freedom of Association

This right becomes an issue for teachers when attempts are made to restrict student movement within the school building or to forbid a student from associating with others. We are of course addressing restrictions which are placed upon one student or a small group of students, and which do not apply to the student body generally.

A 1987 Saskatchewan case speaks directly to this issue. In *G.H. et al. v. Board of Education of Shamrock School Division 38 of Saskatchewan*, [1987] 3 W.W.R. 270, some students were restricted in their in-school movements following charges having been laid against them relating to the sexual assault of another student from the same school. The applicants charged that the action of the school authorities was beyond the powers granted by the *Education Act*. Since the application did not argue that *Charter* freedoms were violated, it remains open to speculation as to what the Supreme Court of Canada, for example, may have decided. However, the judge's ruling provides valuable insights as to the probable outcome.

in-school movements

> In my opinion, the action of the board in restricting the movement of students within the school fell within the power of the board to "administer and manage the educational affairs of the school division" and also came within the duty to "exercise general supervision and control over the schools of the division."
>
> If the board perceived the potential conflict between certain students, for whatever reason, the board most certainly had the power to restrict, in a reasonable manner, the movement of students so as to prevent any possible confrontation. It is not uncommon for the courts, for example, when granting bail to impose a condition upon an accused that he or she refrain from contact with the alleged victim. The action by the board amounts to no more than that.
>
> Students are not free to move throughout a school as they wish. The board must have the power to control their movements. If the board did not possess that power, it would be impossible, for example, to maintain separate washrooms or locker rooms.
>
> On this application, the board does not have to justify the necessity of the "short bounds" placed on the applicants. It is not for me to decide the rightness or wrongness of the decision of the board. I do not sit on appeal from the board. I am only asked to determine whether the board possessed the authority under the Act to impose the restrictions.
>
> There was no suggestion by the applicants, for example, that there had been a denial of natural justice. Nor was there any argument that there had been in

infringement of any of the rights and freedoms guaranteed to the applicants under the Canadian *Charter of Rights and Freedoms.*

The reasons that the board gave for its action, as contained in two affidavits filed on its behalf, may or may not be convincing. I note your decision on that point. I am satisfied that the board acted bona fide in a matter within the scope of its powers. As for the wisdom or unwisdom of the board policy, it is for the electors and not the court to decide that issue.

political clubs
Another area of teacher concern regarding freedom of association is with respect to the formation of partisan political clubs at the secondary school level. No Canadian legal precedent is available at the time of writing, so prohibitions regarding political clubs are open to first challenge.

In summary, litigation against school teachers and their employers are on the increase. A number, but by no means all, of the available judgments on human rights issues have been presented for the teacher's guidance in several legal areas. Also of special importance are the principles of natural justice and the sections on children and the law, the child's best interest, and juvenile justice which initiated the chapter.

Privacy

The right to privacy is not one of the rights set forward in the *Charter.* It was in the 1980 draft but did not survive. However, the right to privacy is a substantive right. The petitioner (student or parent) will proceed through
student
records
provincial legislated clauses, probably with equal success. Most frequently privacy matters relate to student records.

Discrimination Based on Sex

Like the right to privacy, the right not to be discriminated against based on the sex of the individual, the matter, since it is not addressed in the *Charter,* will be decided on the basis of provincial human rights legislation. The kinds of questions which will be brought forward from the teacher's point of view will include equal employment, equal pay and equal opportunities for promotion. From the student/parent perspective, they will probably be matters of curricular offerings (rights to attend specific courses such as home economics or industrial arts, or participation in athletic programs.)

The Province of Ontario attempted to solve the problems surrounding discrimination based on sex in athletic programs by inserting Section 19 into their *Human Rights Code.*

19(1) The right under section 1 to equal treatment with respect to services and facilities without discrimination because of sex is not infringed where the use of the services or facilities is restricted to persons of the same sex on the ground of public decency.

(2) The right under section 1 is equal treatment with respect to services and facilities is not infringed where membership in an athletic organization or participation in an athletic activity is restricted to persons of the same sex.

(3) The right under section 1 is to equal treatment with respect to the services and facilities is not infringed where a recreational club restricts or qualifies access to services or facilities or gives preference with respect to membership dues and other fees because of age, sex, marital status, or family status.

The Ontario Court of Appeal in *Re Blainey and the Ontario Hockey Association et al.* (1986) concluded that 19(2) was inconsistent with Section 15 of the *Charter* and thus of no force or effect. The case concerned a girl who had been prohibited from playing in a boy's hockey league because of Section 19(2). The matter was then sent back to the Ontario Human Rights Commission. The board concluded that the Ontario Hockey Association could not exclude females who were otherwise qualified to play. The same tribunal ruled that the Ontario Women's Hockey Association could exclude males by virtue of the association's status as a special program designed to assist disadvantaged persons. There are definitive rulings by the members of a Human Rights Commission in one province. The issue, however, is far from solved. *Hoover v. Meiklejohn*, a U.S. case, suggests the courts will not get directly involved in sex discrimination cases. They will probably leave the solution to human rights commissions.

female hockey players

Whatever may be the validity of the two-tiered analysis to other questions of equal protection, it should be avoided in athletics as education to keep the courts out of the thicket of an acute analysis of rules and games. The question should not be whether there is a basis for each classification; but what is the relative importance of the individual interest affected compared with the governmental objective.

Mental and Physical Disabilities

David Cruickshank in *Courts in the Classroom* warns there are three things worth noting by those who would initiate litigation under Section 15 (equality rights, equal rights, equal benefits). They must first prove there is some inequality in a law or some unequal benefit of the law. Second, most provinces do not have in their school legislation statements of a child's right to an education, let alone a right to an appropriate education. Manitoba has a declared right. Ontario and Saskatchewan provide for regular and disabled students but under the control of the Minister. The rest require students to attend school between the ages of six and sixteen. Third, there exists a great danger that any special treatment can be said to be affirmative action and thus beyond 15(1).

mental physical disabilities

Educational Malpractice

Teachers play a central role in the lives of the children of our country. Teachers must protect the children educationally as carefully as they protect them physically and legally.

Children are sent to school in order to learn. Sometimes they do not. Suits for educational malpractice are uncommon. To date there are no Canadian cases and only a scattering in the United States. To this point the parents who have sued in the United States have not been successful. It is only a matter of time,

competence and care

however, when this happens, and a new era in school law will be introduced. The best defense then will be the same as it is now – competence and care.

Defamation

slander

libel

Defamation is defined as inflicting injury to a person's character or reputation by false or malicious statements. Slander is the non-permanent (oral) form of defamation. Libel refers to the permanent form through writing, pictures, or other visual arts. The essential feature of the action for the teacher is that they are deigned to have damaged a person's reputation (often students, sometimes parents) by either written or spoken statements, or that the teacher's reputation has been damaged by the defamatory remarks of parents, administrators or other teachers. Since teachers are frequently involved in often heated discussions concerning education where differences of opinion run deep, and are often called upon to make written or oral comments upon the work or character of others, the teacher should familiarize himself/herself with the law on defamation and understand the defences to a charge – the complainant consented, the statement was completely truthful, or that the comment was a *fair* comment on

fair comment

a matter of public interest. Further, the teacher is required also to maintain the custody of records, to receive and record student-related information (and other), and to transmit this information. Its transmission should not be damaging to the reputation of those persons. The rule of law applies. The legal concept of *tortious acts* provides the framework. Also, specific provincial statutes and professional codes of ethics may apply. (See also the sections on student reports and student records.)

Summary

Many aspects of the teacher's professional life touches upon the legal rights and responsibilities of the children, their parents, and the community in its larger and pervasive context. The purpose of this chapter has been to set a framework for the teacher's expanded interest and study in this area. Law is public policy. Ignorance is a poor defense. Litigation against teachers and their employers continues to grow. Teachers may not stem the tide but should prepare through sensible conduct to withdraw the forces. Chapter 8 elaborates upon one such force, the legal suits claiming the teacher was negligent in failing to act properly to protect the safety of students.

Legal Liability of Teachers

Almost all litigation against teachers stems from the negligent conduct of the teacher . . . what is needed is a sense of safety.

Law of Torts

Negligence Tests

Master/Servant

Duty to Supervise

Factors Influencing Standard of Care

Student Illness

Insurance

Transportation

Introduction

The school year has barely begun before the teacher is expected to act or react to pressing statements and queries such as "I feel sick – I wanna go home," "I need an aspirin for my headache," "Jimmy poked his pencil in my ear." It may be that the teacher receives a telephone call from an irate parent, "My daughter was hurt while on that science field trip and I'm going to sue you," or perhaps it is the parent saying, "My son was sold marijuana during your physics class today. You will be hearing from my lawyer," or maybe it is a word of caution, "My daughter is an epileptic – you do know what to do when she has a seizure, don't you?" It is unlikely that any individual teacher will be confronted with all of these situations, but such confrontations force the teacher to an increased level of awareness of a very real problem: what is expected of a teacher and where does the teacher stand from a legal viewpoint? The educator begins to realize there is more involved in teaching than the dispensing of knowledge.

expectations

This chapter will provide the teacher with some basic legal knowledge which should be helpful in determining where teacher actions (or lack of action), regarding student safety would have the potential for causing legal problems for the individual and his/her employer, the school board.

Almost all litigation against teachers stems from the negligent conduct of the teacher or from uncontrolled emotions. Seldom does the problem arise from a lack of *knowledge* of what should be proper conduct. If teachers were given sufficient time to consider each situation they would most often choose the proper course of action. The problem for us, as teachers, is that we must make quick decisions. When little John is found perched on the ledge of the fire

litigation

escape, there is little time for pondering either the legal technicalities or the pedagogical intricacies inherent in the event. What we must develop is a *sense of student safety.*

sense of
safety

The average teacher spends approximately 1 400 hours per year with students, and can expect to have approximately twenty-five students enrolled in any given class; this means the teacher has something in the order of two million student contact minutes per year. With only a split second required for a playful boy, for example, to injure a classmate, the potential for teacher liability is staggering. The small number of actual accidents is a credit to the teaching profession.

The teacher must act, not as fellow teachers would act, but as a professionally skilled teacher *ought* to act. This rule does not require the teacher to act as the *most* skilled teacher would act, or as the *least* skilled would act, or necessarily as the *average* teacher would act. The court will use legal precedent (and perhaps expert witnesses) to determine how the professionally competent teacher should have acted in the specific case under review. The best guard against this seemingly impossible situation is to become sensitive to the major danger points. Accidents can happen in classrooms, laboratories, gymnasia, hallways and playing fields. The prudent teacher understands this and plans accordingly. This same prudent teacher has general supervisory duties where the number of students is greater than the number normally found in the classroom, or where handicapped children are present, or where the students are not in familiar surroundings, or where the events take place either before or after regular school hours, or where the presence of uncertified other personnel introduces additional responsibility. Each situation introduces an additional burden. Again, the teacher plans carefully.

level of care

accidents
happen

Just as homeowners may find, much to their chagrin, that the icy patch on the sidewalk could lead to a liability suit when the next door neighbor slips and breaks a leg, so also the teacher is aware of the wide range of opportunities for parents, and others, to initiate legal action to recover for damages suffered. Whether the actions are justified or not is only part of the problem. When legal action is taken and a teacher is involved, there are legal fees, loss of salary, mental stress, breakdown of parent-teacher relations, strain on student-teacher rapport, and perhaps deteriorating employer-employee relationships to consider, regardless of whether or not the teacher was responsible for a negligent act. If the courts find the teacher responsible, there is the possibility of required payment of damages, which often are considerable. The following recent case illustrates the extent of damages which may be awarded. (*Thornton, Tanner et al v. Board of School Trustees of School District No. 57 (Prince George) et al.* (1976) 3 W.W.R. 662, 57 D.L.R. (3d) (1976) 5 W.W.R. 240, (1978) 1 W.W.R. 606.)

consequences

> Plaintiff, a 15 year old boy, was a student in a school administered by defendant trustees; he was a member of a gymnastic class in the charge of defendant E. The boys were performing somersaults by jumping off a spring-board and landing on a pile of foam rubber chunks contained in a large net. In order to

obtain a better take-off from the spring-board the boys had placed a box horse in a position from which they could jump from it onto the end of the spring-board; they did this with E.'s permission. The boys were inexperienced gymnasts and they were given no warnings or instructions by E., who, while they were performing their somersaults, was sitting at a desk writing report cards. One boy made a bad landing and injured his wrist, which was later found to be broken. Despite this mishap, no warning was given to the class; some additional two-inch thick foam rubber mats were placed around the perimeter of the landing area, E. returned to his desk and the somersaults continued. Shortly after, this plaintiff, attempting a somersault, landed on his head on one of the two-inch thick pads and suffered severe spinal injury which rendered him a quadriplegic. He would require total care for the rest of his life expectancy, which was found to be 49 years.

In the judgment, the judge reviewed the degree of teacher negligence and the needs of a quadriplegic requiring total care, and the cost thereof.

The judge concluded that the use to which the gymnastic apparatus was put was inherently dangerous, a fact E. knew or ought to have known; the first mishap ought to have put him on notice. This, and his failure to supervise closely his inexperienced students, or to warn or instruct them, amounted to negligence for which he was liable. Since he was acting within the scope of his employment, defendant trustees were also liable. The plaintiff, Thornton, was not contributively negligent. He would require total care on a 24-hour-a-day basis for the rest of his life and had lost his whole enjoyment of life and his ability to work. He was entitled to the following damages: special damages - $42 128.87; cost of future care, including home, furnishings and special equipment - $1 133 071.80; loss of ability to earn income $103 858.26; loss of amenities and enjoyment of life – $200 000.00; in total $1 534 058.93.

inherently dangerous

In the subsequent appeal to the British Columbia Court of Appeal, the damages were reduced to $650 000; then raised to $810 000 by the Supreme Court of Canada. Total judgment therefore became $859 628.

Caution

Therefore, because of the very nature of the teacher's role – that of working with impulsive, capricious and adventuresome students who are the sons and daughters of worrisome, sagacious and protective parents – the teacher must be at least as cautious and responsible as the real parents. In this chapter some suggestions will be made, and inferences drawn, from the experience gained from other teachers in Canada who are now wiser, but often poorer, for their experiences. The cases used in the discussions, even though they are actual cases, must be considered as illustrative only. The reader is cautioned that, while some generalizations are made which may be of assistance in guiding the teachers' actions, each case is dependent upon the particular facts and the value judgments involved therein. There are no *cut-and-dried* cases. The main purpose here is to provide some insight for teachers as to which situations are

inferences

potentially dangerous and to give them some advice which may temper their actions or strengthen the ability of the teacher to deal with the situation.

While the purpose of this chapter is to emphasize the position of the teacher, it should be remembered that very seldom is action taken against the teacher alone. Usually, the defendants named are the teacher, the principal and the school board. There are two main reasons for this. First, the actual responsibility is usually very difficult to define and therefore the plaintiffs have a better change of winning the case if they include all those who could in any way be implicated, namely: the teacher, the principal, the bus driver, and the board of trustees. Secondly, the testimony of one party may strengthen the case against another party. In other words, teachers could be included in a damage claim whether or not they remain actual defendants.

When actions against teachers are initiated, the teachers are well advised to contact the professional association to which they belong. To attempt a defense against an action without the assistance of dependable legal counsel is foolhardy.

The Law of Torts

The law of torts deals with those situations in which one person, the plaintiff, sues another person, the defendant, because the defendant has allegedly caused some harm to, or interfered with, the interest of the plaintiff. This holds only when it can be proven that the defendant's actions were wrong actions. The key words are *I'll sue*. It should be noted that when the word *person* is used it refers not only to person in the usual sense but also to persons as recognized in law, and thus to trade unions, school boards, and corporations, for example.

Definitions of a tortious action tend to be somewhat vague. However, one of the more commonly accepted definitions is that from Prosser.

> Tort is a term applied to a miscellaneous and more or less unconnected group of civil wrongs, other than breach of contract, for which a court of law will afford a remedy in the form of an action for damages. The law of torts is concerned with the compensation of losses suffered by private individuals in their legally protected interests, through conduct of others which is regarded as socially unreasonable (Prosser, 1971, p. 1).

There are three parts of tort law, which are of special interest to the teacher: intentional interference with the interests of the plaintiff; unintentional interference with the interests of the plaintiff (fault-based); and strict (vicarious) liability wherein the master is responsible for the actions of the servants.

Intentional torts are, as suggested by the term, wrongs which one person does to another intentionally. If someone hurts someone else by hitting that person on purpose, an intentional tort has been committed. In a general sense an intentional tort is a trespass to a person or their chattels and so not only does it include alleged physical assault but it could also include alleged product deficiency, for example, where the producer did, or should have known about the defect. In this example, a criminal wrong, in the form of assault, may have

[margin note: multiple defendants]

[margin note: intentional torts]

also been committed. Other illustrations include situations wherein the property of the plaintiff was damaged, or where the liberty of the plaintiff was restricted by, for example, false imprisonment.

An unintentional tort refers to those actions found in situations where there is non-intentional interference with the interest of the plaintiff. Citizens are required to live their lives being mindful that they owe a duty of care to others. If they fail in this care and their failure results in damage or injury to others, the purpose of the law is to determine fault and award damages. The most common example of an unintentional tort is the legal situation described as the tort of negligence.

unintentional torts

Prosser, in a text entitled *Handbook of the Law of Torts*, defined negligence as follows: "A person is negligent when they omit to do something which a reasonable person would do, or when they do something which a reasonable person would not do." Prosser continues by describing this hypothetical person, the reasonable person/the *reasonable man* as follows:

negligence defined

> He is an ideal, a standard, the embodiment of all those qualities which we demand of the good citizen . . . He is one who invariably looks where he is going, and is careful to examine the immediate foreground before he executes a leap or a bound; who neither star-gazes nor is lost in meditation when approaching trap doors or the margin of a dock; . . . who never mounts a moving omnibus and does not alight from any car while the train is in motion . . . and will inform himself of the history and habits of a dog before administering a caress; . . . who never drives his ball until those in front of him have definitely vacated the putting-green which is his own objective; who never from one year's end to another makes an excessive demand upon his wife, his neighbors, his servants, his ox, or his ass; . . . who never swears, gambles or loses his temper; who uses nothing except in moderation and even while he flogs his child is meditating only on the golden mean . . . (Prosser, 1971).

The essential feature of the tort of negligence is that persons must not do those things which can be foreseen to do damage to people who come into contact with them. Has the person foreseen the risk as a reasonable person would have? How can it be determined what a reasonable person would have foreseen? Simple, by experience over time. Often the level of reasonable care is determined in complex situations, such as medical operations, by the use of expert witnesses. Frequently a statute will define a standard, however these definitions may not be *prima facia* help in determining negligence. Travelling 80 in a 50 kmh zone would suggest negligence, but would not determine it. It is always up to the plaintiff to prove the case. The principle applied in civil cases is that proof is determined on the *balance of probabilities* rather than on the standard of beyond a *reasonable doubt* as is the situation in criminal law. This distinction suggests that there is an order of importance, in the public's mind.

reasonable person

There are four broad classes of unintentional negligence: ordinary negligence where the person fails to use ordinary care; slight negligence where the

broad classes

person failed to use great care (this applies only where great care is required); gross negligence which describes the situation where the defendant failed to demonstrate a standard of care toward the plaintiff which is judged to be not even the standard for a careless person; and a class of negligence described as being willful or wanton. This terminology is used to describe actions which border on intentional negligence, that is, a disregard for risk.

The Successful Action for Negligence

It is not easy to prove negligence and thus be awarded the large sums of money for damages that have been conjured up in the public's mind as being available.

probabilities
tests

The facts in the case and the balance of probabilities (as noted earlier) must point to the results of four tests. First, there must be a legal duty. That is, the law must recognize that the defendant was required to display a standard of care toward the plaintiff or his or her chattels for the purpose of protecting the plaintiff from unreasonable risk. The plaintiff must next demonstrate the defendant failed to conform to the standard. Third, the plaintiff must show there was a reasonable, close relationship between the defendant's actions or failure to act and the injury or loss which occurred. Finally it must be demonstrated that the plaintiff suffered some actual loss or damages to *person* or *interests*. This is not an easy task, and the requirements of these tests (in part at least) explains the limited number of successful cases for damages due to negligence. Examine each of the four elements in more detail.

1. The Legal Duty

The Legal Duty of teachers and their employers arises from two sources. The first source is from the statutes; the acts, by-laws, and policies of elected legislative authorities. Legal responsibility results in either a claim for *non-fea-sance* which refers to the failure to provide, for example, guard rails, or *mis-feasance* which refers to the situation where the guard rails were provided but they were faulty. Or, the school board provided gym mats, but they were faulty mats.

non-feasance

mis-feasance

The second source of the legal duty arises out of the common law standard of care. The standard of care which is normally required is that the performance of the duty be to the level of the care provided by the *reasonable man*. This person, the reasonable person, performs to the level of the community's expectations of reasonable behavior.

What is assumed under the reasonable person principle, is that the person has normal physical attributes, normal intelligence and memory, the minimum of experience and information common to the members of the community and added to the above, whatever superior skill the person holds.

2. The Standard of Care for Teachers

Due to the fact that teachers are licensed to teach and thus occupy a distinctive role in our communities, the *standard of care* level of expectation for teachers is raised considerably above the standard for the *reasonable person*. Teachers are said to act in *loco parentis*: they stand in the position of parent and perform the role of a careful parent. Teachers are required to guard their many children from harm in the same manner that *careful parents* would protect their many children. The reader's attention is drawn to the term *many*, for although the teacher acts as a careful parent, the teacher is not expected, by the numerous justices who have pronounced on this matter, to act in the one-to-one or one-to-two (or three) manner of supervision found in the traditional family unit. The concepts of *loco parentis* and careful parent will be expanded upon later by way of illustrative precedent-setting legal cases.

careful parent

Teachers, because of their position as *occupiers* and because their employers (the schools boards) are *owners* of buildings, equipment and grounds, are subject to the application of another common law standard. Children, when they are in school, are a legal class of person called an *invitee*. Teachers as occupiers and their employers as owner owe the highest standard of care to the invitee. In a person's own home the highest standard of care is owed to the invitee. The next group of persons, known legally as the *licensee*, are owed a somewhat reduced standard of care. These are people who are on the property (without charge) by the expressed or implied permission of the occupier/owner. They must be warned of hidden dangers but do not require the degree of care owed to the invitee. Children on the school grounds before or after school hours or on weekends are of this class of person unless the school has taken on special responsibilities. The third class of person, the *trespasser*, is owed no duty of care but does enjoy some rights. For example, owners or occupiers must not create deliberate danger, if they know or should know that the trespasser is present. Also they must not create hidden dangers (traps) to forestall trespassers.

occupier's
liability

invitee

licensee

trespasser

The standard of care owed by the teachers to the students may become modified by the voluntary assumption of risk by the student. It is not necessary for the student to assume all the risk, but if the student and teacher are engaged in some inherently dangerous activity, a court may find that the injured student assumed some of the risk and therefore a share of the responsibility for what ensued (*the person consents*). What happens in these situations is that the court will award a sum of money as total damages and then proportion the responsibility out to the plaintiff and the defendant. Each case is judged on its own merits. For example, in a 1934 Canadian case, the plaintiff fell into an open elevator shaft. The door had been left open by the defendant. The court found the defendant negligent for leaving the door open, but also found the plaintiff negligent for not looking where he was going. The upshot of the matter was that the defendant was held to be 90 percent responsible, and the plaintiff 10 percent. The standard of care demanded of teachers appears also to vary according to the age of the child. This seems reasonable. The younger the child, the greater the amount of responsibility which the teacher must shoulder for the child's safety. The level of responsibility can also become greater or lesser depending upon the nature of the activities being undertaken. The level of the

consent

standard of care thus becomes particularly onerous for the teachers of pre-school and primary level children, especially when they are involved in trips to the farm or zoo.

3. Causal Relationship

The third matter to be considered in cases of negligence is whether there was a causal relationship between the level of intelligence present and the harm caused. Frequently this connection is difficult to demonstrate. Would the presence of the teacher as supervisor have made any difference? Indeed, in *Gard v. Board of School Trustees of Duncan* (1946) 2 D.L.R. 441, the court concluded the presence of the teacher would not have changed the situation. This case involved a student injury during a grass hockey game when the teacher was absent attending a staff meeting. In the Butterworth case,

(*Butterworth et al. v. Collegiate Institute Board of Ottawa* [1940] 3 D.L.R. 466) the teacher had assigned supervisory duties to two senior boys. The teacher was absent from the gymnasium at the time of the injury. In its judgment the court stated that it could find no causal relationship between the absence of the teacher and the injury to the fourteen-year-old Butterworth boy. In most instances, however, it appears that teachers are expected to be present, and if they are absent the court will seek to determine what steps the teacher had taken and what arrangements the teacher had made to shield the student from harm.

A delicate legal situation arises frequently when younger students are involved. In situations where the teacher is the defendant and the plaintiff is a young child, the court is faced with the problem of obtaining credible evidence. Since the defendant may be the only person who knows the true cause of the accident, the courts have employed the procedure of *inferring negligence* from the facts which it is able to establish.

4. Actual Loss

Actual loss or damage is the fourth element necessary for a successful action for damages due to negligence. The damages sought usually cover such things as out-of-pocket medical expenses, loss of present and future earning power, the cost of custodial care, and an award for pain and suffering. Because there are, in most school accidents, few medical expenses which are not covered by

medical insurance or school insurance, and since pain and suffering are ex-tremely difficult to document and quantify, in most successful liability cases the awards are for loss of future earning power, or the costs of custodial care and the cost of special medical apparatus not covered by insurance (private or state). The number of cases are few, but the awards are usually very substantial.

In summary there are two main sources of liability action:

1. the school board was negligent in not providing a safe place or in permit-ting the use of unsafe equipment;

2. the school board was negligent in not providing supervision through its servants and agents, equivalent to the supervision which would be pro-vided by a careful parent.

Courts will search out answers to the question as to whether the practices had been adopted generally. This is the question of general use in the education community. New or unusual types of activities are open to considerable scrutiny.

Finally, courts will also seek to determine from the records, and from witnesses, whether the practices in question had been followed successfully in the past. This is the test of the adequacy of safety instruction which helps to determine the level of risk the teacher should have anticipated.

safety
instruction

Teacher-Employer Relationships

The relationship between a teacher and the employer, the school board, is that of a master and servant, or for those who prefer to avoid legal terminology, an employer-employee relationship. Under this relationship the employer can be held responsible for the tortious actions of a teacher it employs, providing these actions were taken within the parameters of the responsibilities for which the teacher was hired.

master/servant

The legal concept is often described as *vicarious liability* in that one party is held responsible for the negligent acts of another person even when the first party (in our example, the school board) has committed no *actual* act of negligence. The school board is responsible for the actions of its teachers and agents.

vicarious
liability

This relationship between the school board and the teacher passes responsibility on to the board for certain of the teacher's actions which have resulted in legal recourse through the courts. However, the teacher must not assume the passing on of the responsibility necessarily relieves the teacher of responsibility. It can be stated that there is added protection and support for the teacher because of the employer-employee relationship, but that this is not a blanket protection which will protect the teacher in all ways. Lack of job security, legal costs associated with the teacher's defense (if not paid for by the professional association to which the teacher belongs or by the employer), loss of salary while attending court are but a few possibilities, not to mention the possibility of the employer subsequently taking action against the teacher. An example of this possibility is illustrated in the following case. (*Sleeman v. Foothills School Division* (1946) 1 W.W.R. 145).

other factors

> The action was one for damages for injuries to a child, sustained in a collision between a school bus and a farm truck loaded with wheat. The court held both drivers to have been negligent, in that they both approached a "blind" intersection, familiar to both of them, at an excessive speed, and collided in the intersection. The school bus was overturned and the child, partly thrown out of the bus, was pinned underneath the bus and severely injured. Damages totalling $5 539 were assessed equally against the two drivers, the school board, and the farmer who owned the truck.

> The bias of the board's liability was twofold. First it had a statutory duty to provide transportation. Secondly, the driver of the bus was not, in fact, liable

for his act. However, because it was the negligence of the driver that caused the school board to be liable, the court directed that the board was entitled, on the cross claim against the driver, to have contribution from him for any sums that the board was required to pay.

This case involved a bus driver, but the possibility of gross negligence claims exists in teacher-related suits.

Even though boards, as employers, can be held liable for negligent actions of their employees, including teachers, the assumption should not be made that the board will, through its insurance company, be picking up the costs automatically for any successful action arising from teacher negligence. Sometimes an

personal
liability

assessment is made against both the school board and its teachers, in which case the teachers are liable for their own share of the damages. It should be remembered, therefore, that the master-servant relationship exists and may provide considerable protection for the teacher but only when the teacher was acting as a teacher – within the scope of his/her professional competencies. This means that if the board is able to show the actions of the teacher which led to the court action were, in fact, not within the normal circumambient authority as a teacher, or if the teacher did not act in ways approved or condoned by the board, the master-servant relationship does not exist and therefore the teacher could be left totally responsible for the damages.

The following case, *McKay et al. v. Board of Govan School Unit No. 29 et al. Saskatchewan,* (1976) 60 W.W.R. 513; (1968) 64 W.W.R. 301; (1967) 62 D.L.R. (2d) 503, illustrates the importance to the teacher of this master and servant relationship while still holding the teacher in an almost untenable position. Also the case is of particular interest to the teacher since it is one of the few such cases heard by jury instead of judge alone.

> In this case McKay was taking part voluntarily in a gymnastic display. While practicing, he fell between the bars of the parallel bars. As a result of the accident, the boy was paralyzed from the neck down. The jury found that the physical education teacher had been negligent in not providing competent instruction on the parallel bars, in that he had not given sufficient demonstration on their proper use, in rushing the student through the progression of activities on the bars, and in not giving sufficient attention to spotting during the exercise. In general, the jury found the safety precautions taken to be insufficient. They concluded that although the teacher was qualified to teach gymnastics, he did not have experience with the parallel bars.

The judgment was appealed to the Supreme Court of Canada. The superior court upheld the lower court. The award was $183 900.

prohibitive
expenses

Even though, in this case, the action against the teacher was dropped, this did not prevent prohibitive expenses from being incurred. This is forcibly stated in a communication from the solicitors to the Saskatchewan Teachers' Federation. A letter from Francis, Gauley, Dierker and Dahlem, Barristers and Solicitors to the Saskatchewan Teachers' Federation, February 22, 1965 stated in part:

Since damages as well as costs in the McKay and Molesky case were over $200 000 the legal costs are accordingly tremendously high. In effect we suggest that if the Teachers' Federation was not looking after the interests of the teacher, the costs in itself may well be prohibitive to any teacher to fight such a law suit because even if the teacher is released pursuant to the above mentioned authorities from legal liability, the efforts that his solicitors will have to put into this case are well beyond what the teacher will ever recover in legal costs from his opposing sides, even if he wins.

The McKay case also illustrates the importance of a section of the *School Act* of Saskatchewan which was at that time unique in Canada and which provided more protection to teachers than was provided in other provinces. The section stated, in part, "Where the board, the principal or the teacher approves or sponsors activities during the school hours or at other times the teacher responsible for the conduct of the pupils shall not be liable . . . for personal injury suffered by pupils during such activities."

district liability insurance

While the discussion in this section focuses on negligence within the framework of a master-servant (employer-employee) relationship, the teacher should be aware this relationship affects a number of other areas of concern besides negligence, for example, ownership of copyrights and patents, matters which are discussed in Chapter 10.

A Duty to Supervise

1. **The Teacher Acts in** *Loco Parentis (Careful Parent Test)*. The teacher is required legally and morally to ensure that a system of supervision for student safety is established in the classroom and in any other locations where instruction takes place. The teacher is required to ensure that warnings of danger and *safety* instructions are *given* and *understood* by the students. Experienced teachers can rely upon their own experience in large measure, but the reader is cautioned that when instructional assignments are changed, new supervisory problems arise and new safety instructions may be required.

warnings

Since new teachers do not enjoy the luxury of much previous student supervisory experience, the following pages attempt through case descriptions and commentary to make some suggestions in this important area.

The teacher acts as a parent or guardian would act. The British common law (Canadian case law) principle that the teacher should act in *loco parentis* (as the careful parent would act) brings with it some privileges such as the right to discipline the child, but it also delivers a substantial degree of responsibility for the safety and well-being of the student. Courts have not anticipated that the teacher will stand in the same relationship to the child as parents would with respect to their one or two children. The courts have long since recognized the teacher has many, many children. The safety relationship is not a one-on-one relationship, however, the teacher must take the necessary and prudent steps to guard against injury to the students. The teachers are expected to have the foresight of a prudent parent and whatever additional special skills that their

responsibility

training has provided them and expected to be governed by the nature of the activity being undertaken demands. It is these latter two requirements which raise the expectations for the teacher well above those of the careful parent. (See *Law of Torts* earlier in this chapter.) The concepts of in *loco parentis* and careful parent test are useful legal concepts if one remembers that the level of expectation is that of a competent, prudent, insightful, professional teacher whose level of care for *student safety* would match that of other competent, prudent, insightful, professional teachers. The careful parent test could well be called the *careful teacher test*.

2. **The Duty to Supervise.** Defendant J.M. was employed by defendant board as coordinator of the outdoor educational program of one of the board's high schools and at the relevant time was one of the supervisors of a "field trip" organized by the school and sponsored by the board. . . . Two girls, M and G, both 14 years old, were drowned in a swimming accident during the trip. On the evening in question a small group of the children persuaded defendant to take them swimming, for which purpose they went to a swimming area created by a conservation authority. A natural creek had been dammed and the surrounding areas flooded, and an artificial sand beach had been made. There was an area of shallow water but along the line of the old creek bed there was a sharp drop-off and the water became suddenly deep. The safe area had not been marked with buoys but there was one marker in the water and defendant, who knew the area well, had explained the limits of the shallow water carefully to the children and instructed them to say within it, which they did. Defendant himself was unable to swim as was the infant G. The infant M was an average swimmer. A fresh breeze suddenly developed which created a surface current on the water. As a result G and another child were carried over the drop-off area into the deep water. The infant M immediately swam to their assistance and though successful in rescuing the other child she drowned in her attempt to rescue G, who also drowned despite the efforts of others, including J.M. who ran into the water as far as he could, to save them.

It was held that J.M. was liable in negligence for the death of G. The duty owed by a teacher or supervisor towards children in his charge is to take such care of them as a prudent father would of his children. It was therefore the duty of J.M., within the scope of that duty, to guard against the foreseeable risks to which G was exposed. . . . Since he was acting within the scope of his employment the defendant board was also liable.

exposes others to danger

It was held, further, he was also liable for the death of M. When a person by his negligence exposes another to danger it is a foreseeable consequence that a third person will attempt to rescue the one in danger. . . . (*Middejonge et al. v. Huron County Board of Education et al.* (1972) 25 D.L.R. (3d) 661)

approval slips

Note should be taken of the fact that even though the parents had given written permission for their children to go on a field trip, the presence of *approval slips* did not shield the teacher from liability where it was found the children were placed in a situation which carried with it an unreasonable risk of injury.

In another case, the scene of the accident was a grade twelve chemistry classroom. This was the case of *James et al. v. River East School Division No. 9 and Peniuk,* heard in 1975 at the Manitoba Court of Queen's Bench. The circumstances were as follows.

> On the morning of September 22, 1972 Joni Lou James, a grade twelve student, was carrying out an experiment for the purpose of determining the precise atomic weight of tin. The experiment was found in the Manitoba Department of Educational laboratory manual for this subject. The teacher had provided verbal instructions in the previous day's lesson and had placed written instructions on the blackboard.
>
> The experiment involved placing predetermined amounts of tin and concentrated nitric acid in a pre-weighed, covered evaporating dish. The nitric acid oxidized the tin, producing a reddish gas. The reaction was considered complete when the gas was no longer visible. The plaintiff and her laboratory partner, after deciding that the oxidation process was completed, began heating the evaporating dish to dry the residue prior to weighing it. The experiment stated that the amount of heat applied could be increased when the material had turned powdery and white. The teacher was not available when the plaintiff and her partner attempted to verify that the residue was ready to receive increased heat. The students considered the situation for a few moments, then proceeded to increase the amount of heat. The material suddenly bubbled in the middle and exploded into the face of Joni James. She received permanent damage to the tear ducts of the left eye and facial scarring.

The teacher was found guilty for not foreseeing that the accident might happen in an experiment as dangerous as this one. The court found the written instructions badly worded. Further, it found a general failure on the part of the teacher to give proper instructions on correct methods and on the dangers to be guarded against. The court was particularly critical of the teacher's failure to provide safety goggles as was recommended in the laboratory manual. Joni James was awarded almost $6 000 in special damage and $25 000 in general damages.

foreseeability

When a student is at home, the child is under the effective control and responsibility of the parent. When the student is in the classroom at school, the student is under the effective control and responsibility of the teacher (as well as the administrators and school board). That is, at school the teacher stands in *loco parentis*; the teacher is the substitute for the real parents.

loco parentis

Where the responsibility of one set of parents ends and the responsibility of the other set of parents begins is not very clear. It seems there is much over-lap; the real parents (or for the more mature students, the student) must assume some responsibility for the actions of their children (or themselves) while outside the classroom but, on the other hand, the teachers must assume responsibility for providing adequate care of the children somewhat beyond the bounds of the classroom door. In general, the courts indicate the teacher stands in *loco parentis* with respect to the student during the time the student is under the jurisdiction of the school.

A 1955 case involving a British nursery school teacher, an unlatched gate, and a dead motorist is illustrative of the degree to which responsibility can be extended even in the face of an emergency. (*Carmarthenshire County Council v. Lewis* [1955] A.C. 549)

> In this case a four-year-old nursery school student left the teacher's classroom and wandered across the school playground, through an unlocked gate and out onto a busy street. A driver, in an attempt to avoid hitting the child, swerved and struck a telegraph pole, killing himself. His widow sued both the teacher and the employer. She claimed that the negligence of the teacher had been the cause of her husband's death.
>
> The teacher had expected to leave the children for only a few minutes while she checked the washroom. The child had been told to wait. While the teacher was in the washroom she discovered another child who had cut himself. She spent approximately ten minutes washing and bandaging the second child's cut and in making arrangements to leave the injured child with the Headmistress. During this time, the first child left the school and entered the street.

mis-feasance

Two lower courts found in favor of the widow. However, the House of Lords reversed the decision, contending that the teacher had acted as any other parent would have acted considering the emergency situation, but they held that the school authority was negligent for not locking the gate or having a latch above the child's reach. The Lords held this was a reasonable expectation considering the age of the children and the business of the adjacent street.

Being under the jurisdiction of the school is not the same as being at school. Resources beyond the school grounds are often used to supplement the educational program, for example: field trips to the legislative buildings and to the local airport, or, as in the case cited in this section, swimming during an outdoor educational field trip. During these times the students are under the jurisdiction of the school. Conversely, the student may be in the school or on the playground during times beyond which the school could normally be considered to be in session. In the first instance, the teacher normally continues to assume certain responsibilities but in the second instance the teacher normally is exempt from responsibilities.

trespasser

The claim resulting from accidents beyond the school grounds (excluding those happening on school sponsored excursions of various types) as well as those on the school grounds or within the school building which happen after normal school hours invariably are launched against the school board but they sometimes can include the principal and teacher. An important distinction is made by the courts in these cases as to the status of the individual concerned – whether that person be judged to be a *compulsee, invitee, licensee,* or *trespasser*. As a trespasser he would have no right to be on the premises, or certain parts of the premises, and therefore courts are very reluctant to provide any compensation for injuries sustained. This is illustrated in the case where a school boy was using the grounds of his school during a holiday with tacit permission of the school authority and playing on a descending fire escape on which he knew he was not supposed to play. (*Storms v. Winnipeg School District No. 1 (Man.)* (1963), 44 W.W.R. (1963-64) 41 D.L.R. (2d) 216)

The judge ruled that, since he was a trespasser he was unable to receive compensation for injuries sustained on the fire escape. The judge ruled also that the boy was a bare licensee with respect to the school grounds. The following case illustrates the attitude of the courts to those seeking compensation for accidents sustained when they were considered as a licensee. (*Edmondson v. Moose Jaw School Trustees (Saskatchewan),* (1920) 3 W.W.R. 979; 13 Saskatchewan L.R. 516; 55 D.L.R. 563 (C.A.):

> A previous award of $7 200 was quashed on appeal. An eight-year-old boy, who was blind in one eye, was watching his nine-year-old brother high jumping after school hours. The broken end of the crossbar struck the boy, causing him to lose his good eye. The jury in the original trial held that the equipment was dangerous. However, the appeal court held that the boy could claim against the school board only as a licensee, not as an invitee, because he was on the school property after school hours.

One might speculate on the outcome of the case if the court had considered the injured boy an invitee instead of a licensee. Within reasonable limits, therefore, a trespasser and, to a slightly lesser degree, a licensee must accept the conditions of the property as he finds them – if licensees are hurt in some manner, they must assume the responsibility themselves. But where the student becomes an invitee or, more especially, a compulsee, the onus on the school board and its employees becomes much greater. For example, in *Pook, et al. v. Ernesttown School Trustees* (Ontario) (1944) 4 D.L.R. 268; O.R. 465; O.W.N. 543:

> Damages of $519.36 and $350 were awarded for fracture of the fibula and tibia of the right leg. A fourteen-year-old boy fell on the school ground during a recreation period and when he was lawfully and properly playing in the school ground. It was shown that the ground had been littered with stones and brickbats for some time.

It appears obvious that the school board has a responsibility to provide reasonable and safe facilities for the students – in the school as well as on the school grounds. But it must be remembered that the board must have some way of obtaining information about potentially hazardous conditions: that broken step, that hole in the school grounds surface, that light fixture in a state of collapse. This information is usually obtained through the employees of the board, including the teachers. Who is in a better position to be acquainted with potentially hazardous conditions than the teacher who uses them? The responsibility of the teacher is not necessarily to correct these conditions but to ensure the message is given to the appropriate authorities so they can act appropriately on the matter. A teacher who knows there is a hazardous condition but who does nothing about it should expect to be involved in any legal actions resulting from injuries obtained therefrom. The normal channel of communication respecting these matters would be to the principal of the school. If the situation

informing board

persists, then the teacher has an obligation to report the matter in writing to the employer, the school board.

The successful actions against teachers resulting from accidents within the school or on the school grounds during school hours or within the school during *out of school* hours invariably emphasize the lack of sufficient supervision and that this lack had a causal effect. This lack of supervision is used to illustrate *negligence*. From this standpoint the word negligence is used in situations where care must be taken, but the reader is cautioned not to equate this with *incompetency*. Although incompetency would point towards negligence, it would not be right to use these terms in the reverse order. That is, a competent, conscientious person can be shown to be legally negligent in many cases. Prosser cites four elements (stated earlier in the chapter) which must be present in order for a cause of action to show negligence, but the four points, in and of themselves, do not define negligence. The four points are (Prosser, 1971 p. 426):

incompetence

a. there must exist a legal duty for a person to maintain a standard of conduct for the protection of others against hazardous risks;

b. there must exist a failure on the part of the same person to conform to the standard required;

c. there must exist an injury to another person or persons as a result of the failure of the first person to maintain the proper standard of conduct; and

d. there must exist a causal connection between the failure of the first person to maintain an acceptable standard of conduct and the resulting injury sustained by the other party.

It has been stated earlier that teachers are expected to act in lieu of the real parents, that is, to stand in *loco parentis*. Added to this is the question as to whether the teacher acted in those circumstances as would a reasonable person under similar circumstances. Bargen quotes the characteristics of this artificial and unreal character as follows (note the potential conflict between points 3 and 5).

artificial
character

1. The reasonable man will vary his conduct in keeping with the circumstances.

2. The reasonable man will be made to be identical with the actor in the matter of physical characteristics. The man who is blind, lame or deaf is not required to do the impossible by conforming to physical standards.

3. The reasonable man is accorded no allowance for lack of intelligence short of insanity. For a defendant to do the best he knows is not enough.

4. The reasonable man is considered to be an adult. Children, therefore, are not required to meet the same standard of conduct as that of the reasonable man.

5. The reasonable man will be accorded special abilities and skills and will be held responsible for them when the circumstances so warrant. In other words, the law will take knowledge of the fact that some people are of superior knowledge, skill, and intelligence.

6. The reasonable man is required to maintain a higher degree of standard of conduct when he has had time to reflect on his course of action than when he must act in an emergency.

7. The reasonable man, under many circumstances, will be charged with the duty of anticipating and guarding against the conduct of others. For instance, where children are in the vicinity, greater caution and anticipation are required than if they were adults. (Bargen, 1961, p. 137)

If the novice teacher now knows the basic elements which go toward proving negligence and has a sense of how a reasonable person would act, then the teacher is in a better position to adjust his/her actions so as to act as a reasonable, careful parent would act. The degree of supervision, or lack of supervision, seems to be basic to much of the difficulties in which teachers find themselves. Consider what constitutes good supervision. In the case of the student, Ramsden, (*Ramsden v. Hamilton board of Education*, (1942) 1 D.L.R. 770) it was noted that:

> Ramsden had left his bench to get a chisel. Instead of returning directly to his bench, as he had been warned to do on previous occasions, he flicked the chisel at the sanding wheel. The chisel caught in the wheel, driving it into Ramsden's thigh, resulting in a leg amputation below the knee. It was held that the sanding machine was not inherently dangerous and did not require a guard even if it were possible to devise one. Supervision was held to have been sufficient and the action was defeated on the grounds that the negligence was completely that of the sixteen-year-old plaintiff.

degree of supervision

Courts recognize that in spite of the best efforts at competent supervision, accidents will happen. Perhaps the above case would have been different, however, if the teacher had been absent from the room at the time. In the following case the teacher was absent (*Gray et al. v. McGonegal and Trustees of Leeds and Lansdowne Front Township School Area*, (1949) 4 D.L.R. 344; O.R. 749; O.W.N. 127; app. (1950) 4 D.L.R. 395; O.R. 512; O.W.N. 475; app. (1952) 2 D.L.R. 161; 2 S.C.R. 274).

accidents

> Damages of $8 000 and $1 208.75 were awarded. The case was appealed to the Supreme Court of Canada but with no change, the liability of both board and teacher being upheld. In this incident, a boy attempting to light a gasoline stove to serve a hot lunch, was burned after the teacher left him. Hot lunches were not part of the statutory or public duties of the board. However, the board knew of and encouraged the serving of hot lunches in the school and was therefore liable for negligence through the teacher.

It is sometimes possible for the teacher to be absent but still provide adequate supervision, as was shown in the following case. (*Butterworth et al. v. Collegiate Institute Board of Ottawa* (1940) 3 D.L.R. 446; 1940 O.W.N. 332)

teacher absent

> A fourteen-year-old boy was injured in the gymnasium of Lisgar Collegiate. The instructor was absent, but two senior boys were present. The boy's elbow was damaged to the extent that it caused fixation of the joint at a right angle. The action was dismissed because:

1. The senior boys were capable.
2. The cause of the accident was not known.
3. The plaintiff was *sciens et volens* (knowing and willing).
4. Fourteen-year-olds must exercise reasonable and intelligent care of their own safety.

presence
not enough

Sometimes negligence, through lack of supervision, can be shown even when the teacher is present. The first case (Thornton) in this chapter illustrates this situation.

Supervision of the playground during recesses and noon hour should be on a planned, organized basis, as is illustrated in the following case. (*Brost v. Tilley School District Alberta* (1955) WWR. 241 (C.A.)

> On appeal from a previous judgment which had dismissed the action, the board and principal were found negligent. Damages of $1 000 and $160.25 were awarded. A six-year-old girl fell from a swing in the school grounds at morning recess. In this case no evidence was given of the provision of supervision. The local handbook seemed concerned with discipline supervision rather than supervision for safety.

While there is a lack of organization for supervision, much of the burden of responsibility must then rest upon the shoulders of the principal. However, when supervision is organized, it is up to the individual teachers to fulfill the responsibilities set out for them.

A recent illustration of this is the *Johnson v. Ryall* case.

car wash

> During a school supervised car wash, a student was struck and pinned against a school wall by a vehicle driven by another student but owned by a patron of the car wash. The student was deemed to have operated the motor vehicle with the owner's consent. The parents of the injured student sued the owner of the vehicle and the supervising teacher. The court held that the owner was liable and that the teacher was not. The negligent operation of the motor vehicle, not the level of supervision was judged to be the cause of the accident (*Johnson v. Ryall* (1989) 76 Newfoundland and P.E.I.R. 121).

The extent of supervision necessary is illustrated in the case which follows. (*Dziwenka et al. v. The Queen and Mapplebeck* (1972) W.W.R. (Vol. 1) 350.) Note that the accident described in the action took place in 1961. The Supreme Court did not hear the matter until the early 1970s.

> An eighteen-year-old deaf-mute, a student in the Alberta School for the Deaf, was seriously injured when his hand came into contact with the blade of a power saw in an Industrial Arts class. It was shown that the teacher was competent with power tools and that the student had been shown how to use the saw. The teacher stood 15 to 25 feet away, helping other boys and occasionally glancing over to the student (Dziwenka) using the power saw.

> Damages were assessed at $10 716.60, with 40 percent the responsibility of the student (contributory negligence) and 60 percent responsibility directed to the teacher and the Crown (the school was operated by the Government of Alberta) by the trial judge. The Appellate Division of Alberta reversed the decision. The Supreme Court of Canada subsequently re-instated the original judgment.

The Supreme Court noted that Dziwenka was the only student working with power tools at the time and the high risk of injury should have been obvious. They contended that in this instance the teacher should have either supervised the entire project, or made the task safer.

Finally, the Court considered the child's handicap. They reasoned that since teachers are acting as *careful parents* and since the parents of handicapped children must use more care, the teachers of handicapped children owe their students a higher level of care.

handicap

In a 1989 British Columbia case involving a table saw, (*Dunbar v. British Columbia School District No. 71* (1989) Doc. No. CA008589 (B.C.C.A.)), an 18-year-old student was injured while using a saw in a woodworking class. The court held that the defendant teacher, as a servant of the board, had used the care of a *careful or prudent parent.* The teacher had taken reasonable care to ensure the table saw was as safe as possible. Supervision was deemed to be adequate.

table saw

In the case of *Myers v. Peel County Board of Education* (Ferguson, 1982) the Supreme Court of Canada was again involved.

gymnastics

> The litigation concerned a gymnastics accident in which a fifteen-year-old boy, while attempting to dismount from rings without the aid of a spotter, fell onto the mats and broke his neck. The Myers boy was practicing in an exercise room out of the view of the teacher who was located in the gymnasium. Further, extra matting was not used, although it was available in the school.

The teacher was found liable, but the Myers boy was held partially responsible because he had attempted the exercise without the aid of a spotter. Responsibility was determined to be 80 percent on the part of the teacher and 20 percent on the part of the student.

Field Trips

The supervision of students during an excursion or field trip is often much more difficult than within the school premises. There are different dangers in unfamiliar surroundings, making it necessary to provide greater supervision than in the school. Even though it is commonly recognized that field trips are an important adjunct to the school program, they must be organized and conducted in such a manner that the chance of accidents is minimal. This entails more detailed planning, including planned procedures for handling emergencies.

A common practice adopted by most schools is the consent slip, sometimes erroneously called a waiver slip. This is a form which is signed by the parents indicating their approval of the proposed field trip. To call this slip a waiver is erroneous in that a parent is not able to sign away the rights of the child in this manner. Even when the parents have indicated in some manner that they waive the right to take legal action in the event of some accident to their child, the parent is not bound by this. The consent slip does provide other useful purposes,

waiver slip

however. The communications between the school and the parents usually are quite inadequate; the parents frequently do not know what is going on in school. The consent slip is an opportunity to describe a particular activity so that the parent not only understands what the activity is all about but also has an opportunity to indicate approval. By indicating knowledge of the excursion to be undertaken, the parent thus gives written acceptance of the corresponding inherent dangers involved, thus strengthening the stand of the teacher should litigation occur. A teacher is well advised to check the written policies of the school board regarding field trips and to plan field trips only with the knowledge and consent of the principal and senior administration, as well as the parents of the children.

board policies

An unfortunate part of the act of gaining parental approval is the gentle, and sometimes not so gentle, inclusion of the prospect of coercion. What parent dares to indicate disapproval when the message, through the child, is that every other parent involved has said yes? Teachers should do as much as possible to avoid this type of situation since, from a public relations standpoint, more harm may be done than benefits achieved from the field trip. Recall that consent obtained under coercion is not consent.

coercion

Since there is often a greater freedom of action in surroundings which are not very familiar, there is often a greater chance of injuries being sustained on a field trip than in the classroom. To compensate for this, it is suggested that additional adult personnel be included so that the ratio of students to responsible adults is considerably lower than in the classroom setting. Also the students must be fully apprised of behavioral expectations, the purpose of the trip, and some of the *potential dangers* involved. There is a fine but wavering line between over-supervision and inadequate supervision. There is no real way of knowing just where this line is, but the teacher apparently is expected to know. The courts are aware of this, as is illustrated in the following court decision (*Schade v. Winnipeg School District No. 1 and Ducharme* (1959) 28 W.R.R. 577, (1959) 27 W.W.R. 546, 66 Man. R. 335, at 360, (1959) 19 D.L.R. (2d) 299).

potential dangers

The courts' realization of the necessity of developing a sense of responsibility has led to a changing attitude and a more practical approach to the question of supervision by school authorities. While there is a duty to supervise certain activities, such duty bears some relation to the age of the pupils, the special circumstances of each case and particularly the type of activity.

A 1924 court decision continues to remind us of the importance of a board being informed as to anything different or special the school is doing. This is particularly true of any field trips; if the board is not aware of a field trip, and there is an accident, there is the opportunity for the board (or the insurance company which carries the insurance for the board) to claim the teacher was acting beyond the scope of the teacher's duty. This would leave the teacher (and possibly the principal) to face the action without school board help. This 1924 case is summarized as follows (*Walton v. Vancouver Board of School Trustees and Thomas*, (1924) 2 D.L.R. 387; 34 B.C.R. 38).

inform board

Damages of $2 000 against the board were awarded, but the action against Thomas, the principal of the school, was dismissed. The appeal was dismissed. The board had decided that all schools should have a sports program for the 23rd of May holiday. Specific arrangements were, however, left in the hands of the individual principals. Thomas decided to have a shooting contest and asked the boys to bring rifles. One of the rifles was defective. There was some trouble and after a second try with the same cartridge, the gun backfired and a particle went into Walton's eye, which became inflamed and later had to be removed. The board claimed that the shooting contest was outside the powers of the school board and that Thomas was acting beyond the scope of his authority. It was held that the board knew that such a contest had been held for several years, and that it was, therefore, their duty either to prevent the contests, or to ensure they were properly supervised.

shooting
contest

Had the board been able to show they were, in fact, not aware of the shooting contests, Principal Thomas probably would have found himself on his own in the action. It is imperative that teachers receive board permission for field trips. For example, in the Beauparlant (truck) case, *(Beauparlant et al. v. The Appleby Separate School Trustees et al.* [1955] O.W.N. 286):

> The children from two separate school classes were awarded a half-day holiday by their teachers in order that children could attend a concert in an adjacent town. Sixty-six children were loaded into the back of a truck. As the vehicle proceeded down the road, the sides gave way and many children fell out onto the roadway. The school board had not approved the trip nor had they given approval for similar trips in the past. The parents did not regard the outing as an educational field trip.

The solicitor, on behalf of the family of one of the injured students, initiated an action against the school board. The trial judge stated:

> I have no hesitation whatever in holding that there was negligence on the part of the teachers responsible for seeing that the children were on the truck. It was heavily overloaded, no examination was made of the sides of the truck to see if they were reasonably strong for the purpose, and during the course of the journey there was some singing and swaying by the pupils, and Gilles Lefebre, the teacher who went along on the truck, presumably to supervise it, was apprehensive.

But the Appleby school board was able to avoid responsibility. The trial judge continued:

> There is no doubt that a school board is liable in law for an accident due to a teacher's negligence if it is in a matter which may reasonably be regarded as falling within the scope of his employment.

> The chairman of the school board and the secretary-treasurer, both of whom gave evidence, say that no request of any kind was made to the school board by any of the teachers, nor was any permission given.

> After much careful thought and anxious consideration of this matter, I have come to the conclusion that the teachers, in organizing this trip and in allowing the children their freedom from their regular studies, were exceeding their

authority and were not acting within the scope of their authority, express or implied.

It does not seem to me that this expedition can even be brought within the broad and comprehensive general subject of *social studies*.

snowball
fight

The 12-year-old plaintiff (Mainville v. Ottawa (City) Board of Education (1990) 75 O.R. (2d)), was injured when struck on the head by an iceball thrown by another student. The incident occurred on school property shortly after school had been dismissed for the day. The student required two stitches to mend the wound. The defendant board had not assigned anyone to supervise the school grounds following dismissal of the students. The plaintiff claimed that the school had neglected to provide adequate supervision. The court dismissed the action, noting there was nothing inherently dangerous about leaving school. Children who walked home were of sufficient age to realize the dangers of participating in a snowball fight. The court concluded that *no amount of supervision or surveillance could have prevented the accident.*

metal
lathe

In 1990, a student lost an eye while working on a metal lathe. The student was under the supervision of a substitute teacher. The student had been given safety instructions, which he failed to follow. It was demonstrated that the student had missed the initial class on the unit at which time many of the safety instructions were given. The court held that the student had been given safety instructions, but also held that the employing district had been negligent in employing an unqualified (for metal work) substitute teacher, but this did not contribute to the injuries. No damages were awarded (Anderson in *Canadian School Executive* (1991).

recess
supervision

In 1991 a group of Ontario students were playing on a high jump mat outside the school building, at recess. Students had been given several warnings not to play on the mat, but they continued to do so. One student fell and broke his arm. No teacher supervisor was on duty in the immediate area. Two teachers were on duty elsewhere in the school yard. The court found shared liability, 80 percent school board, 20 percent student. The court stated that simply *telling* students did not constitute adequate supervision. Positive action to prevent students from playing on the mat should have been taken (Anderson in *Canadian School Executive,* 1992).

Factors Influencing the Standard of Care

In summary, the standard of care required may vary according to:

a. the age of the child;

b. the physical attributes of the child;

c. the mental capacity of the child;

d. the experience level of the child;

e. the class of person (invitee/licensee/trespasser);

f. the nature of the activity;

g. the kind and amount of instruction received;

h. the level of the student's awareness of the risks involved (the man consents);

i. the nature and purpose of the rules formulated to govern student behavior;

j. whether the activity was approved as a general practice for schools and children of that age;

k. the foreseeability of the danger;

l. past experiences with the activity/equipment; and

m. whether the object is considered to be potentially dangerous or inherently dangerous.

Indicators of Sufficient Supervision

There are a number of indicators that sufficient supervision was being provided by the school staff but in general terms, the following four provide an adequate summary of what the courts are seeking.

indicators

1. Discipline was good and the students were conducting themselves in an orderly fashion.

2. The teacher had formulated student-oriented rules for the guidance of students in order that they will understand the inherent dangers and in order to provide for instruction regarding safety. (Courts tend to draw a distinction between discipline rules and safety rules.)

3. The teacher (supervisor) was competent. The level of expected competency has been extended well beyond the general competency of supervision of play groups to include specific competencies concerning specific activities in a gymnastics program, for example.

4. The teacher (supervisor) was present. Although as noted elsewhere, the absence of the supervisor is not an automatic determinant of liability, the circumstances will be probed extensively to determine what actions the teacher took to cover the absence and whether the presence of the teacher would have made the difference.

Student Injury or Illness

Whether teachers should, or should not, give first aid to injured students is a question often discussed with some concern. The answer invariably is: teachers will always do whatever is within their power to assist a student who is injured or ill. Sometimes this means providing first aid and sometimes it means obtaining help for the student through more competent personnel (medically competent).

first aid

When a student is injured and the teacher does not give first aid, with resulting aggravation of the injury, the teacher may have acted negligently. However, when the teacher gives first aid, and as a result of the first aid treatment the injury is aggravated, then the teacher may also have acted in a negligent manner. This may appear as double jeopardy. Knowledge of first aid is not usually a legal requirement for teachers but, seen from the parent's viewpoint, there exists the expectation that the teacher possesses at least minimal first aid expertise.

medical
competence

The professional competence of a teacher is an educational competence, not a medical competence. The teacher should never attempt to play the role of a medical professional. When a student is ill or injured, the competence required is that of a doctor or nurse, rather than that of an educator. However, the educator (the teacher), must remain in control of the situation until relieved by another person, whether this be the parent, the school nurse, a paramedic, an emergency ward of a hospital or a physician. Further, teachers must never prescribe drugs for students (aspirin, 222s, etc.) since this is also viewed as being beyond the competency of the educator.

emergencies

Teachers must familiarize themselves with the emergency procedures established by the school. Where is the emergency list of telephone numbers for parents at home and at work? Who is the family doctor? Are there special medical situations the teacher should be aware of and be prepared for (possibility of epileptic seizures, for example)? Where are the first aid kits and what are their contents? How is transportation provided in emergency medical situations? How is the reporting of accidents to be conducted? What is the procedure to be followed when students become ill during school hours? These and other questions should be considered before an emergency arises, not during or after.

reasonable
procedures

The following Saskatchewan case emphasizes the need for alertness and the establishment of reasonable procedures to be followed (*Poulton et al. v. Notre Dame College et al.* (1975) 60 D.L.R. (3d) 501). In Poulton, it was noted that:

> The plaintiff, aged 17, came to live in residence and attend grade 11 at the defendant school. The defendant S was a teacher in the school. S was in charge of the residence in which plaintiff lived, and was coach of the hockey team on which plaintiff played. At the beginning of the hockey season the plaintiff got a cut on his big toe from ill-fitting hockey skates, which he had bought. The plaintiff did not regard this as a serious injury. He received an antiseptic for it from S. A few days later the plaintiff was hit on the hip by a hockey puck. Over the next several days the hip injury became progressively worse as a result of an infection in the region of the hip, apparently caused by the cut on the toe. On a number of occasions the plaintiff asked S to let him go to see a physician but S refused him permission. S forced the plaintiff to dress for hockey games when he was in no condition to play. Eventually the plaintiff became so seriously ill that he was taken to hospital by some of his fellow students. At one stage the plaintiff was near death but he eventually made a good recovery.

> In a negligence action by the plaintiff against the defendants to recover damages for personal injuries and for loss of clothing, held, the plaintiff was entitled to succeed. The standard to be applied in judging S's conduct was that of a careful father. Applying this standard, S was negligent. A careful father, when faced with requests from his son for medical attention, would have arranged for such medical attention or, at the very least in the case of a 17-year-old, would have urged him to seek or consented to his seeking medical attention. The defendants

were not at fault with respect to the cut on the plaintiff's toe or the injury to his hip. Nor did the plaintiff establish that the infection was caused by any fault on the part of the defendants. However, it is probable that earlier treatment with antibiotics and an earlier presentation of this infection for medical attention would have had a beneficial effect. Under the circumstances, damages should be more, but only slightly more, than nominal.

punitive damages

Further, many school-aged children suffer from conditions which require them to take medication during school hours. For example, children suffer from infections, attention deficit disorder, epilepsy and toxic reactions. So the teacher assumes the position of parent in administering prescribed medication. The situation cannot be avoided, so work out the procedures carefully with parents and administrators.

medication

Accident and Liability Insurance

Although negligence suits have not been as numerous in Canada as in the United States, the number that have been referred to the courts, and the magnitude of some of the judgments make the educator quite concerned about protecting him/herself. The employer-employee relationship helps, but further protection is needed. One of the ways to provide protection is through the purchase of insurance. Keep in mind that insurance does not provide complete coverage. The presence of an insurance policy may in fact result in a false sense of security.

The first clear distinction the teacher must make is between accident insurance and liability insurance. Most school boards in Canada either provide *accident insurance* for their students, or permit this to be done on a group basis through an insurance company, with the premiums being paid by the parents. When there is accident coverage, and a student is injured, payment to cover most or all of the incurred expenses can be expected from the insurance company. This normally would be regardless of whether or not the accident arose as a result of a negligent act of the board, principal or teachers. Because the immediate expenses are paid for by the insurance company, usually promptly, the parents are less likely to bring court action against the teacher. After all, if the accident did not actually cost the parents anything there would be little point in trying to convince a judge they should receive extra remuneration. However, the limitations of the accident insurance policy may be such that all the costs are not recovered from the insurance company, or there may be exclusions which are not covered by the policy. For example, even though the policy may pay a certain sum for the loss of an arm, the parents may feel this sum would not compensate for the loss of earning power throughout the lifetime of their child. Consider also the price of disfigurement of the face of a pretty girl, the loss of mental capacity of a child, or facing the future having to wear artificial limbs and braces. There are many such possibilities. There are many accidents where insurance does not cover the total costs, and where the parents may feel inclined to seek additional compensation on behalf of their children. There exists also the *punitive damages* aspects in a civil action. These

limitations

damages can be substantial and cost the teacher mental, as well as financial, hardship.

Some school boards insist that students engaging in school activities which are potentially more hazardous than other activities, be covered by accident insurance. These activities are usually competitive sports, such as football and hockey, but sometimes may include vocational subjects, such as automotives and welding. Such insistence may result in duplication of insurance for some students but the cost of accident insurance for the individual student, on the basis of a group plan, is usually minimal so parents go along with the requirements.

hazardous
activities

Even when the parents are satisfied they have been suitably compensated through the insurance coverage, this does not mean the insurance company is necessarily satisfied. They have paid out a sum of money (often large) which may have been for the result of negligent act of a teacher. If so, there is always the possibility of the insurance company instigating action against the negligent teacher to recover the costs incurred. Therefore, as desirable and as useful as accident insurance for students may be, it still cannot in any way be considered as liability insurance.

counter suit

For all school boards in Canada it is compulsory to carry *liability insurance* to protect the interests of both the board and its employees.

Teachers would be well advised to check the policy the board carries to determine the actual coverage the teachers have (provided they are prepared to unscramble the complexity of terms in the policy). This would enable teachers to decide whether they are adequately covered or not. The limitations of the policy should be carefully considered. The coverage no doubt will be limited to actions of teachers acting within their responsibility and authority as teachers.

Transport Students

Teachers who use their own automobiles to transport students (this is usually for off-campus and athletic events) should be sure they consider the sources and adequacy of the insurance coverage which is available to them. First, they should consult with their agent or broker concerning the adequacy of their own public liability insurance coverage. Special endorsements may be required if the business use or student transportation use of the automobile is anything more than *occasional and infrequent.*

car
insurance

Second, teachers are advised to check the nature and extent of liability insurance coverage provided by their employer. This involves checking with an official of the school board or the teachers' associations (provincial or local). Teachers are urged to press the question and not simply rely upon the often off-handed, often uninformed opinion of a colleague.

Some school board insurance programs make provision to provide additional insurance coverage for employee vehicles when used for school board purposes. Some insurance policies provide coverage for teacher-owned vehicles used to transport students, and some provide coverage for non-owned vehicles supplied by parents to transport students to school-sponsored events.

Summary

Much of the litigation against school boards stems from the negligent acts of school teachers. Every effort must be expended to develop a sense of student safety. When preparing for student activities, especially those which are inherently dangerous, the teacher is reminded to plan and act as a professionally skilled teacher ought to act. Be mindful of the age, physical attributes, mental capacity and experience level of the students. Make sure safety oriented instruction is received. Make the students aware of the risks involved. Give competent instruction not only in the procedures or activities involved in the lesson, but also on personal safety and first-aid procedures.

Be safety conscious. Review your own competency level to instruct the lesson. Follow good practices.

Law Reports

A.C.	Appeal Cases, Canadian Reports
Alta.L.R.	Alberta Law Reports
B.C.R.	British Columbia Reports
D.L.R.	Dominion Law Reports
Man.R.	Manitoba Reports
M.P.R.	Maritime Provinces Reports
N.B.R.	New Brunswick Reports
N.L.R.	Newfoundland Law Reports
N.S.R.	Nova Scotia Reports
O.L.R.	Ontario Law Reports
O.R.	Ontario Reports
O.W.N.	Ontario Weekly Notes
O.W.R.	Ontario Weekly Reports
Q.K.B.	Quebec Queen's Bench Reports
Que.Q.B.	Quebec Queen's Bench Reports
Sask.L.R.	Saskatchewan Law Reports
S.C.R.	Canada Supreme Court Reports
T.L.R.	Territories Law Reports
W.L.R.	Western Law Reports
W.W.R.	Western Weekly Reports

9

Family Law

Juvenile justice refers to the conditions and circumstances which will bring about fair and decent treatment of children, including satisfying their basic human needs for love, care and safety, food and shelter, and a positive role model. . . .

> Child Welfare Legislation
> Child Abuse/Child Neglect
> Failure to Report
> Youth Justice System
> Types of Offences
> Probation

Introduction

Chapter 7 provided the reader with some legal concepts which were considered important to the work of the educator. Among these was the concern for the *child's best interest*. Also, throughout the text there are many illustrations of the hand-in-glove relationship between social and educational development. Some see society leading; others see education leading. However, in every case social institutions, family, church, monarch, government, and schools have expanded in their responsibility to the young of the society. As educators we may wish that new and expanded responsibilities would not be laid on our shoulders. We may wish that all we had to do was teach reading. For example, you may wish that your class could study geography and not social adjustment, living skills, health and other *soft* topics, first period after lunch. You may wish that all the children had adequate clothing, shelter, and nutritional meals. You may wish that no child suffered physical, emotional or sexual abuse in his/her home life. You may wish that no children were *abandoned*. You may wish! But our rational selves tell us this utopian condition does not exist, and our pedagogical selves tell us poor nutrition, for example, influences learning negatively; that frightened children do not learn well; that abused children have special needs. So you may wish all you want, and although the reading or geography lesson is very important, that is not all there is to the role of being a teacher.

child's best interest

abandoned

sentenced
to school

The topic, family law, in many respects is well beyond the limited scope of this text; however, teachers face many additional legal situations which do not relate to potential student injuries on the field trip, for example, and the teacher's responsibilities under civil (court) law attached thereto. Abused children are in classrooms. Many young people in trouble with the law are in classrooms. Many are *sentenced to school*, or are educated by teachers working within the confines of the penal system. Children commit crimes, sometimes within the physical surroundings of the school, and sometimes within the larger confines of the community. They are nevertheless more often considered as being part of the student body of the school rather than members of the community at large. As teachers, we may wish this was not so. We may insist that these are family matters, but in reality the professional teacher may not be able to avoid these issues, and indeed may consider direct involvement as part of the role of a helping professional. The pages which follow provide but a few examples of the moral and legal issues which must be faced in the teacher's pedagogical and administrative roles.

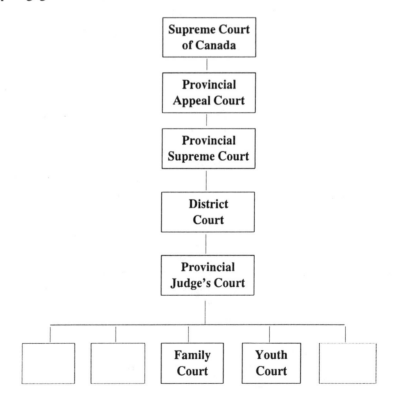

Exhibit 9-1
Court System

Child Welfare Legislation

Each Canadian province has passed legislation directed toward protecting children from physical, emotional, or sexual abuse. Alberta, Manitoba, and Newfoundland call their legislation the *Child Welfare Act*. The Territories labels its specific legislation the *Child Welfare Ordinance,* while Quebec labels its legislation the *Youth Protection Act*, British Columbia and Prince Edward Island use the label *Family and Child Services Act*, Saskatchewan, the *Family Services Act*, and the Yukon Territories, very simply, the *Children's Act.*

Teachers should become thoroughly knowledgeable about the criminal and civil requirements imposed upon them in the province of employment; however, central to each piece of legislation is the requirement that the teacher must report instances of suspected child abuse. The reason for the reporting requirement is obvious. Also, the teacher usually performs a therapeutic role in the treatment of abused children, a role which may add considerably to the teacher's responsibility. Further, many local school jurisdictions have developed policies and procedures on child abuse. These should also be sought out and studied.

criminal and civil requirements

Child Abuse/Child Neglect

This section discusses how the teaching profession, a profession closely associated with children, becomes involved in issues associated with children *in need of protection.*

protection

Alberta's *Child Welfare Act,* passed into law on July 1, 1985 requires that:

> Anyone who has reasonable and probable grounds to believe and believes that a child is in need of protective services shall forthwith report the matter to a director [of Alberta Social Services].

Anyone who fails to report:

> is guilty of an offense and liable to a fine of not more than $2 000 and in default of payment, to imprisonment for a term of not more than six months.

And if the teacher (a professional) fails to report, Alberta Social Services is obliged to advise the proper governing body of the occupation or profession (i.e., the Alberta Teachers' Association).

Alberta law also makes provision for the protection of people who report the names of children in need of protective services provided that the reporting:

> is not done maliciously or without reasonable and probable grounds for the belief.

The confidentiality provisions of the Act protect the reporting person further by preventing anyone from disclosing his/her name.

shields

British Columbia legislation provides that:

> Every person who has reasonable grounds for suspecting that a child:
> a. has been or is being abandoned, deserted, or maltreated; or

b. is otherwise in need of protection, shall, notwithstanding any claim of confidentiality, or privilege that may exist or be made;

c. forthwith make a complete report of the circumstances to the superintendent
...

And furthermore:

No person is liable for any loss or damage suffered by any person by reason only of making or providing, in good faith, a report. . . .

Each provincial legislature and department of social services has devised its own wording and definitions of what constitutes *a child in need of protective services*, however, the following explanations taken from an Alberta publication (Child Welfare Act: Information Package, 1987) should prove useful to the reader. Also, many local school jurisdictions have developed their own unique policies, procedures, and published materials. The teacher is urged to consult the school principal regarding local policies and procedures.

When does a child need protective services?

protective services

The *Act* (Alberta) states that a child is in need of protective services when there are reasons to believe that the survival, security or development of the child is endangered. This may occur when the condition or behaviour of the child prevents the parent or guardian from giving the care necessary to meet the child's needs.

But it may also occur under a number of other conditions, such as if the child has been abandoned or lost, or the parent or guardian is dead and the child has no other guardian. A child also needs to be protected when the parent or guardian can't or won't give the child the necessities of life, including medical, surgical or other necessary treatment suggested by a doctor.

Parents are also obliged to protect their children from cruel or unusual punishment, and from serious risk of physical injury, emotional injury and sexual abuse. If the parent can't or won't protect the child from these things, the child may need protective services from the community.

physical abuse

Physical abuse includes cases where there is substantial and observable injury to any part of the child's body as a result of the non-accidental use of force or an agent to the child's body. This is shown by:
a. cuts, bruises or welts;
b. a fracture or other bone injury;
c. a dislocation or sprain;
d. hemorrhaging, internal injury, a burn, a scald, or frostbite;
e. the loss of consciousness, physiological functioning, or
f. the loss of hair or teeth.

sexual abuse

Sexual abuse includes cases where a child is inappropriately exposed or subjected to sexual contact, activity or behaviors. Emotional injury includes cases where the child's mental or emotional actions are substantially harmed and this harm can be shown by a mental or behavioral disorder such as anxiety, depression, withdrawal, aggression or delayed development.

There must be reason to believe the emotional injury is the result of one or a number of factors – rejection, loss of affection or cognitive stimulation, exposure to violence, or severe disharmony at home. A child may also be emotionally injured if he or she is exposed to improper criticism, threats, humiliation, accusations or expectations. It is also necessary to consider the mental or emotional condition of the guardian, and whether anyone living in the same place as the child has a chronic alcohol or drug abuse problem.

emotional injury

The *Criminal Code* of Canada provides some helpful definitions.

197.(1) Every one is under a legal duty (a) as a parent, foster parent, guardian or head of a family, to provide necessaries of life for a child under the age of sixteen years. . . .

197.(2) Every one commits an offence who, being under a legal duty within the meaning of subsection (1), fails without lawful excuse, the proof of which lies upon him, to perform that duty, if (a) with respect to a duty imposed by paragraph (1)(a) . . .
(ii) the failure to perform the duty endangers the life of a person to whom the duty is owed, or causes or is likely to cause the health of that person to be endangered permanently;

200. Every one who unlawfully abandons or exposes a child who is under the age of ten years, so that its life is or is likely to be endangered or its health is or is likely to be permanently injured, is guilty of an indictable offence and is liable to imprisonment for two years.

202.(1) Every one is criminally negligent who (a) in doing anything, or (b) in omitting to do anything that it is his duty to do, shows wanton disregard for the lives or safety of other persons.

As the teacher considers his/her responsibilities under the appropriate policies and legislation, the above-noted distinction is usual in determining potential courses for action. The guiding principle is that teachers have a moral and professional obligation to protect children. Also, abused and neglected children may have special learning and behavior problems. Excellent self-instruction and classroom-use materials are readily available to assist the teacher, almost always without charge, from departments of education, local library materials centres, service agencies, and the services of professional teachers' associations.

guiding principle

Sexual Abuse

Provisions for protecting children against sexual abuse are universally a part of all child welfare legislation, but the classroom teacher is also encouraged to consider the appropriate sections of the federal *Criminal Code*. These sections are especially useful in providing definitions of what is sexual abuse and who may be charged.

140. Every person who, for a sexual purpose, touches, directly or indirectly, with a part of the body or with an object, any part of the body of a person under the age of fourteen years is guilty of an indictable offence and is liable

to imprisonment for a term not exceeding ten years or is guilty of an offence punishable on summary conviction.

141. Every person who for a sexual purpose, invites, counsels or incites a person under the age of fourteen years to touch, directly or indirectly, with a part of the body or with an object, the body of any person, including the body of the person who so invites, counsels or incites and the body of the person under the age of fourteen years, is guilty of an indictable offence and is liable to imprisonment for a term not exceeding ten years or is guilty of an offence punishable on summary conviction.

146.(1) Every person who is in a position of trust or authority towards a young person or is a person with whom the young person is in a relationship of dependency and who

(a) for a sexual purpose, touches directly or indirectly, with a part of the body or with an object, any part of the body of the young person, or

(b) for a sexual purpose, invites, counsels or incites a young person to touch, directly or indirectly, with a part of the body or with an object, the body of any person, including the body of the person who so invites, counsels or incites and the body of the young person, is guilty of an indictable offence and is liable to imprisonment for a term not exceeding five years or is guilty of an offence punishable on summary conviction.

(2) In this section, "young person" means a person fourteen years of age or more but under the age of eighteen years.

150.(1) Every one commits incest who, knowing that another person is by blood relationship his or her parent, child, brother, sister, grandparent or grandchild, as the case may be, has sexual intercourse with that person.

(2) Every one who commits incest is guilty of an indictable offence and is liable to imprisonment for fourteen years.

153.(1) Every male person who (a) has illicit sexual intercourse with his step-daughter, foster daughter or female ward . . . is guilty of an indictable offence and is liable to imprisonment for two years.

166. Every one who, being the parent or guardian of a female person, (a) procures her to have illicit sexual intercourse with a person other than the procurer, or (b) orders, is party to, permits or knowingly receives the avails of, the defilement, seduction or prostitution of the female person, is guilty of an indictable offence and is liable to (c) imprisonment for fourteen years, if the female person is under the age of fourteen years, or (d) imprisonment for five years, if the female person is fourteen years of age or more.

168.(1) Every one who, in the home of a child, participates in adultery or sexual immorality, or indulges in habitual drunkenness or any other form of vice, and thereby endangers the morals of the child or renders the home an unfit place for the child to be in, is guilty of an indictable offence and is liable to imprisonment for two years.

246.(1) Every one who commits a sexual assault is guilty of (a) an indictable offence and is liable to imprisonment for ten years; or (b) an offence punishable on summary conviction.

(2) Where an accused is charged with an offence under subsection (1) . . . in respect of a person under the age of fourteen years, it is not a defence that the complainant consented to the activity that forms the subject-matter of the charge unless the accused is less than three years older than the complainant.

The textbook *Teacher Beware* summarizes some appropriate case law which helps to define how society, through its courts, defines such terms as *sexual purposes and labels the parts of the body* which must not be touched.

Further, after reviewing the requirements to report the names of children in need of protection, and the literature on what constitutes child neglect and abuse, the teacher may conclude that many cases go unreported, and may wonder why. The numbers of abused and neglected children appear to be shockingly high. Obviously there exists limited firm research evidence, and although government and agency fact-finding and investigative tribunals are adding new evidence, the data is *soft* and even the reasons for this state remain largely speculative. `unreported`

Some barriers to reporting are cultural. Community (often cultural) standards and beliefs regarding child-rearing influence the person's decision as to what constitutes abuse. Is not the family situation, by-and-large, a private matter? Is not a reasonable level of corporal punishment an appropriate method to discipline children? Should the *state* interfere in family matters? What makes an individual capable of making judgments like that? `barriers to reporting`

Other barriers to reporting are administrative and relate to the lack of clearly defined policies and procedures. What are the legal requirements? What happens if I fail to report? What *must* I do? What happens if I am wrong? Will the administration find fault? What legal protection do I have? If I report, will the school and the surrounding community lose respect in the eyes of outsiders – the media, perhaps?

The third general cluster of barriers to reporting child abuse and neglect relate to the individual's fear of personal involvement, fear of error and what reporting will do to others: Will reporting destroy the family? Nothing will happen. I'll be sued. I don't want to go to court. If it is true, how can I face them again?

Failure to Report

Under provincial legislation, failure to report a suspected case of child abuse can result in legal prosecution. Since teachers are required to report, the question becomes, what is the legal penalty for failure to report? In Alberta it is a fine of up to $2 000 or imprisonment not to exceed six months' duration. The moral penalty is obvious! `penalty for not reporting`

At the time of preparing this manuscript there were no known cases where teachers had been tried for failing to report. An Ontario case involving a practising doctor offers some guidance. In *R. v. Cook* (1983) 37 R.F.L. (2d) 3, a family doctor failed to report to the proper authorities when informed by a mother that her 15-year-old daughter had been touched in a sexual way at various times by the step-father. The doctor was required by Section 49 of the *Child and Family Services Act* to report suspected abuse.

> 49(1) Every person who has information of the abandonment, desertion or need for protection of a child, or the infliction of abuse upon a child, shall forthwith report the information to a society.

The mother had, however, later informed the doctor that her husband had admitted to the offence, but that he was seeking counselling. Dr. Cook took no action. Later the step-father was charged on the basis of another report of sexually molesting the girl. This brought Dr. Cook's failure to report to the attention of the Ontario authorities.

second-hand information

The trial judge considered two issues, first did the doctor have sufficient information to have *reasonable grounds to suspect* and concluded that she had only sketchy and second-hand information. Second, the judge wondered whether, even if the doctor had grounds to suspect, could she have a *bona fide professional belief* that the problem would be solved without reporting it to the authorities. Does professional discretion override mandatory reporting? Again the judge concluded in the doctor's favor.

The Crown appealed the acquittal. A new trial was ordered.

Dr. Cook then appealed the district court finding to the Ontario Court of Appeal. The court stated in part:

> The principal issue in this case is whether or not the Crown has proved that the appellant 'who has reasonable grounds to suspect ... that a child is suffering' from abuse failed to report as required by the Child Welfare Act. It is significant to note that the charge did not allege, as it might have done, that the appellant had reasonable grounds to suspect that a child has suffered or is suffering from abuse.

> It is therefore not sufficient to support the charge that the material before Dr. Cook constituted reasonable grounds to suspect that child abuse had taken place at some time in the past. It was necessary to prove the charge as laid and prove that there were reasonable grounds to suspect that 'a child ... is suffering from abuse.' The trial judge recognized this issue in his reference to the need to prove reasonable grounds to suspect 'ongoing abuse in February, March and April.' The trial judge was not satisfied that the crown had proved its case. I find no error in the conclusion reached by the trial judge. . . .

> I agree with Haley, D.C.J. in her characterization of the issue in this case as a question of law. It is apparent from her reasons that the learned District Court Judge disagreed with the trial judge because she was of the view that the information available to Dr. Cook constituted reasonable grounds to suspect that child abuse had taken place. However, as pointed out above, this was not the allegation in the charge against the appellant.

The teacher owes to the child the right to legal safety, and although the results of the cases against professionals who fail to report are inconclusive, perhaps the more serious consequence of failure is not a legal one, but a moral one.

Recognizing a Child in Need of Protective Services

There are a number of physical symptoms of behaviors which, when demonstrated by a child, may indicate abuse or neglect. When considering these symptoms and behaviors, it may be helpful for a teacher to consult with a school guidance counsellor, a community health nurse or a school district psychologist.

Concern is needed about a student who is:

1a. often tardy;

b. very reluctant to attend school;

c. often absent from school (especially if justified by guardian or parent);

d. apparently reluctant to go home after school; and/or

e. often inadequately dressed for the season or the weather.

But with these symptoms in mind, it should be remembered that truancy alone does not demonstrate that a child needs protective services. Truancy is not considered grounds for neglect under the Act unless it is one of a number of factors showing that the child is in need of protective services. Truancy is covered under the *School Act* and teachers should be aware of school board policies and the *School Act* provisions regarding truancy.

In addition to truancy-related problems, there are a number of behaviors that may indicate abuse or neglect. Teachers should be aware of students who:

a. appear to be undernourished;

b. have obvious medical needs that are not receiving attention;

c. have physical injuries such as bruises, welts, cuts or burns and whose explanations appear to be incompatible with the nature or extent of the injury;

d. appear to be unusually afraid to undress at appropriate times, such as for a gym class;

e. complain of pain around the genital area or mouth; and/or

f. mention that "it hurts when I go to the bathroom."

Teachers should be aware that quite often students who show these symptoms are afraid when asked about their injury or injuries.

Also, when students show patterns of extreme behavior – whether overly compliant and passive (possibly even appearing to be afraid of physical contact) or aggressive and destructive – consideration should be given to the possibility of abuse or neglect.

There are other situations that should be watched, such as students whose drawings of people frequently include disproportionately shaped sexual organs. Also of concern are students who show interest in or preoccupation with sexual acts or sexual language, beyond the scope of interest normally expected for their age. (Sometimes the child will tell of sexual involvement with an adult, or other children will tell what the child has said about his/her sexual involvement.)

afraid to be left alone

Teachers should be aware of students who appear to be extremely afraid of being left alone with certain adults or with adult men or women in general. These students may also try to draw attention to themselves through acting out behaviors such as drug and alcohol abuse or sexual promiscuity.

parental behavior

Parental behavior may also indicate possible abuse. When parents place unrealistic demands to perform on the child, or have a lack of concern for the well-being of the child, concern is needed. The parent who appears unduly distrustful and suspicious of school personnel, or is aggressive and abusive when approached about concerns regarding his or her child, may also indicate a situation of child abuse or neglect.

Advice to the Teacher

When a case of neglect or abuse is suspected, the teacher should:

a. review the appropriate child welfare legislation for the province of employment;

b. consult school jurisdiction policy;

c. if unsure, consult the school principal or superintendent for advice;

d. not interview the child, or in any way attempt to prove the suspicion; and

e. contact Social Services.

The Needs of Abused Children

After the teacher has reported a case of suspected neglect or abuse, and after the teacher has handled his/her own concerns (insecurity, perhaps even guilt), the teacher must work with the child in the classroom setting. Only in the most severe cases is the child removed from the home.

alleviate guilt

The biggest job will be to alleviate guilt, and raise self-esteem. The student needs to know that he/she is *well*. The student needs age-appropriate guidance and to be taught age-appropriate social and peer behavior and be provided with positive adult interactions. Abused children must establish trust in other people. They may need to re-establish affectionate behavior. They will be required to

self-esteem

establish appropriate coping behaviors including ways to vent and deal with their anger, and will need help in asserting their right to control over their own person.

The Youth Justice System

In 1984 the federal government enacted the much heralded substitute for the old *Juvenile Delinquents Act* (first passed in 1908), and proclaimed the *Young Offenders Act*. This Act deals with young persons who are twelve years of age but not yet eighteen years of age who have been accused of violating specific federal or provincial statutes, municipal by-laws or of sexual immorality or similar forms of vice. Several amendments were proclaimed into law in 1986. The purpose of the new act was to have young persons bear responsibility for their own criminal actions – to hold them accountable. The act recognized that young people have special needs and require assistance; that the public needs protection from the offences committed by youth, but that young people have certain guaranteed rights and freedoms.

At Time of Offence

At the time the young person has or is about to commit an offence, the police officer has three options: (1) issue a warning and speak to the parents; (2) refer the youth to a program of community help; or (3) take formal action in either arresting and taking the young person to the police station or issuing a summons to appear in court later.

options

If formal action is to be taken, the police are required by the act to notify the person of his/her rights to silence, to consultation, and to warning about the use of statements as evidence. (See Section 56 of the Act contained in Chapter 7.) In summary they state that:

a. the young person is under no obligation to give a statement;

b. any statement given by the young person may be used in court;

c. the young person has a right to consult another adult person; and

d. the person selected as consultant may be present when the young person provides his or her statement.

If the young person is being held for a substantial period of time, or detained, the parents must be notified. The young person must be finger-printed and photographed but if acquitted, these must be destroyed. Where the young person is to be detained, he/she must be apart from adults unless there is no other place for detention, or detention with another youth could result in the accused being harmed by the other youth.

notify parents

At the time of trial, the *Act* guarantees, as it has from the beginning of the process, the right to legal counsel provided for by the youth, the parents, or legal aid. Crown Counsel has the responsibility of deciding what action should be taken after screening the case. Upon consideration of the needs of the youth and of society, Crown Counsel may recommend (even with sufficient evidence) that the youth be sent to the Alternative Measures Division, if this is considered appropriate and the young person agrees to participate.

legal counsel

alternative measures

Alternative measures programs are handled by the Solicitor General's Department (provincial). Alternative measures include an apology, hours of community service, restitution to the victim, involvement in counselling, or a combination of the above. Alternative measures are available if the offence is, for example:

a. break and entry under $1 000 (if not a private home);

b. theft under $1 000;

c. possession of stolen property under $1 000;

d. mischief and vandalism under $1 000;

e. causing a disturbance;

f. joyriding;

g. simple possession of cannabis and its products.

Youth Court

legal counsel

In youth court the young person has an absolute right to legal counsel. The trial is usually open to the public with a media publish or broadcast ban to protect the youth's identity, and an encouragement (sometimes requirement) that the parent(s) attend. At the first appearance, the charges are read, a plea taken, and if a *guilty* plea is entered, a conviction and disposition (sentence) is made, usually after adjournment in order that a predisposition report be received. If the pleas is *not guilty*, the judge will set a trial date. Usually the youth is released awaiting trial unless detention is necessary to ensure court attendance, or for the protection and safety of the public – not for the youth's protection, for shock effect, or because of lack of residence.

options

At the trial, the judge will make the best decision possible, based upon evidence heard. The options open to the judge are:

a. absolute discharge;

b. fine up to $1 000 depending on ability to pay;

c. compensation to the victim (work to pay debt);

d. restitution (replace);

e. compensation to innocent third party (property sold to third party);

f. community service (not to exceed 240 hours);

g. probation up to two years (maybe treatment order);

h. open custody; and

i. secure custody.

Types of Offences

The Parliament of Canada has exclusive jurisdiction to enact laws relating to criminal offences. The provincial governments may however create laws and offences relating to property and civil rights. Young offenders, i.e., children between the ages of twelve and seventeen, inclusive, are almost always students attending school classrooms who may be charged with a great range of *criminal* offences including the following.

criminal offenses

1. Theft – the fraudulent taking of the property of another with the intent to deprive that person . . . of the property (Section 283 *Criminal Code*).

2. Possession or trafficking in drugs – "to have in his personal possession or knowingly has it in the actual possession of another person" (or group of persons) and to traffic to "manufacture, sell, give, administer, transport, send, delivery or distribute or . . ." (Sections 3(4) and 4(11) of *Narcotics Control Act*). Drugs under the aegis of the Act include opium, heroin, morphine, cocaine, and cannabis. Youth may also become involved with drugs under the *Food and Drug Act* (controlled) drugs.

3. Assault and sexual assault – "A person commits an assault when (a) without the consent of another person, he applies force intentional to that other person, directly or indirectly . . . and includes sexual assault, actions usually defined as sexual harassment, sexual assault with a weapon, and aggravated sexual assault (wounds, maims, disfigures or endangers life). (Section 244 *Criminal code*.)

4. Vandalism – willful damage of property (Section 287 *Criminal code*).

5. Fire-related Offences – willfully setting fire to a building or structure (Section 389 *Criminal Code*).

6. Liquor Offences (*Liquor Control Act*).

7. Abduction of Females and Children – without lawful authority, takes or causes to be taken any unmarried person under the age of sixteen out of the possession and against the will of the parent or guardian . . . (guardian is a person who has in law or in fact the custody and control of that person.)

8. Obscenity – makes, prints, publishes, distributes, circulates, or has in his/her possession for the purpose of publication, circulation or distribution any obscene written matter, picture, model, photograph, record . . . or crime comic. (Section 59 *Criminal code*)

9. Party to a criminal offence – aiding and abetting, accessory after the fact, counselling the commission of the crime. (Sections 21(1), 23(1) and 22 of the *Criminal Code*)

Probation

Probation refers to the period of time during which the young offender is under court-ordered supervision. This normally occurs under the control of a probation officer or youth worker and may include the young person's atten-

publishing names

dance at school or other place of training (sentenced to school). It is with this specific order that the teacher and the education system face at least two distinct problems. First, Section 38, *Young Offenders' Act* prohibits the publishing of the name (identity) of the young person who has or is alleged to have committed a crime. This has a considerable impact upon the keeping and circulation of the student's school records and upon the destruction of certain records when the probation order has been satisfied. Second, actions such as student expulsion almost always results, when school attendance is a term of the probation order, in the school board *forcing* the student to violate a court order, and necessitating a denial of the *publication* ban. In some instances the court ordered probation period can in effect limit the range of disciplinary actions which the school may take. The teacher is urged to exercise extreme caution with respect to administrative procedures concerning students on probation, especially moves to expel the student from school attendance and the keeping of probation-related records.

Summary

In summarizing this chapter, the reader should be able to identify the legislation which imposes a legal requirement upon the professional shoulders of the teacher with respect to cases of suspected child abuse and the criminal violations of young offenders. The teacher should be able to define child abuse; should know the reporting requirements; and should be able to assist the child with some coping activities. It is suggested that teachers familiarize themselves with local school jurisdiction and school-level policies designed to guide the administration of child abuse identification and remediation programs. The reader should also understand the requirements of the *Young Offenders' Act* with respect to the legal rights of young persons between the ages of 12 and 18 and the distinction between the requirements of the civil authority (police) and the school teacher (in *loco parentis*).

10

Copyright and the Educator

Copyright, literally, the right to copy . . .

> Copyright Law
>
> Protection for Producer and Public
>
> Penalties
>
> Revisions to the Statute
>
> Guidelines

Introduction

The presence of copying machines in every school and the requirement for extensive instructional materials entice many teachers to copy copyrighted materials. Many contend that copyright infringement is the most common form of criminal action in Canada. copying machines

The professional teacher uses materials and ideas from a wide range of sources. The process of *internalization* and *absorption* is always present in the teacher's preparations to increase the effectiveness of instruction. Therefore, it is not expected that every word, every idea and every statement of fact is original to the teacher. Also, the teacher increases the instruction-learning process by the judicious use of materials placed in the hands of the students. The question which surfaces constantly is whether the materials are used fairly and legally, that is, whether such use is permitted by the *Copyright Act*. Further, the teacher is a model as well as an instructor, and therefore must be aware constantly of the moral and ethical considerations, in addition to the legal considerations, of the use of copyrighted materials. Ignorance of the law and the press of daily teaching assignments frequently cause the teacher to violate both legal and moral obligations. internalization absorption teacher as model

Consider the writer who has spent hundreds of hours of time, and hundreds (perhaps thousands) of dollars of his/her own money to produce a book or other work which is useful to teachers and their students. Consider further, another person, not associated with the author, who then determines the commercial possibilities of the work, proceeds to reprint and sell or distribute the work with no financial benefit to the original author. Consider further, a third person, realizing the educational value of the work for his students, who proceeds to reproduce it on the school-owned copying machine, with no financial consideration for the original author. The unfairness of these situations becomes obvious. Consider a salesperson who drops off a copy of a recently-published mathematics workbook for school inspection, and who later returns to the financial consideration school to check up on teacher acceptance, only to see a neat pile of copies of the workbook sitting on the school office counter with a note from a teacher requesting the secretary to make sufficient copies for his/her class. Teachers who would not consider stealing a colleague's car are sometimes not as law-abiding with respect to written works. There is a parallel between these two situations, but theft of creative work is a less easily defined type of theft. The objectives of the Canadian copyright laws include the protection of authors from those who would deprive them of their just rewards for efforts. On the other hand, once a work has been published, the public has a right to *just* and *lawful* use of that work, a protection also ensured by the copyright laws.

theft

Copyright Law

intellectual property

Copyright laws refer to intellectual property in a physical form, and include items such as books, computer programs, plays, poetry, paintings, music and lyrical arrangements. The word sequences and diagrams and figures contained in a book may be copyrighted but the ideas, theme, and plot may not. The musical score and lyrics of a song can be copyrighted but the topic *prison walls* cannot. Limited and restricted similar sequences of notes and words are permitted, but not the notes and words *per se*. Unlike patents, trademarks, and industrial designs, copyright does not prevent others from using or copying the ideas, information and/or facts contained in a specific work.

In early Roman law, for example, the proper reward for an author was not money, but fame and therefore legislative protection for the author was not as necessary. Also, the absence of today's technology made copying extremely difficult, a situation which inadvertently gave added protection to the author and the owner of the work. With the development of the printing press came increased awareness of the need for author protection from indiscriminate, unauthorized copying. As technology in this field developed further – off-set presses, radio, television, duplicators, cameras, audio and video tapes and word processors, for example – governments in most countries developed copyright laws to protect both the authors and the public.

author and public protection

federal jurisdiction

Courts in pre-confederation Canada used the reasoning found in English common law (the basis, until recently, of Canadian law in general). The passage of the *Constitution Act*, 1867 gave the federal government exclusive jurisdiction over copyright; however it was not until 1924 (the effective date of the 1921 legislation) that the tie to the United Kingdom copyright law was severed and the Canadian courts were empowered to adjudicate copyright disputes on the basis of Canadian statutory law. Since 1924 the common law basis for determining copyright disputes became ineffective, leaving only statutory law to provide the necessary protection.

international conventions

Canadian copyright law is associated with international copyright conventions. In this regard it must be noted that international copyright provisions are not the basis for judicial decisions regarding Canadian copyright. Rather, Canadian copyright law embodies the agreements of the international treaty but it is the Canadian statutory law which is supreme in this area. International copyright, as it affects Canadian citizens and/or Canadian residents, is encoded in the 1886 *Convention of Berne* (modified in Berlin in 1908, Berne in 1914, Rome in 1928, Brussels in 1948, Stockholm in 1967 and Paris in 1971). Fifty countries ascribe to these international convention agreements. This means that Canadian copyright provisions are effective relative to these fifty countries only; however these countries include the United Kingdom and the United States.

Subject to certain requirements (being a Canadian citizen and/or a Canadian resident and/or being a resident of a subscribing country) the *Copyright Act* of Canada encompasses *every original literary, dramatic, musical and artistic work*. Both published and unpublished works are protected. *Original* means that the work originates from the author, and that his/her talent and skills have been used in producing the work. Work copied from another work or work that is in the public domain is not considered *original*. For example, a book may enjoy copyright even though there is a chapter in it copied from the original works of Plato. This copied chapter of public domain material would not enjoy copyright protection in that anyone else could also copy the material from the original source. Further, copyright does not extend to works that are "of an immoral, obscene or scandalous character, that deceive the public or are blasphemous or fraudulent." *[original works]*

Copyright implies an ownership, but contained in the terminology is a more difficult definition of the meaning of the word *ownership* than the one associated, for instance, with owning a car. The latter is a *corporeal* ownership whereas the former is *incorporeal*. A person may purchase a book in a bookstore and therefore becomes the owner of the book. The owner may burn the book, give it to friends, or use it for decoration on a shelf, because the purchaser owns the physical book. However, that person has not purchased the right to make copies of the book, or parts thereof – that act would involve violating the incorporeal (in law, without material existence, for example a franchise) ownership rights retained by the owner of the copyright. *[ownership]*

There are no formalities involved – the author automatically has first copyright. However, as with the owner of a car, it is wise to place a lock on the vehicle to notify others of ownership. Even though there is no lock on a car, the taking of the car without permission is still theft. If a car has a lock, and the lock is used, theft of the car becomes more difficult. The copyright symbol serves this same purpose. Because of the international aspect of copyright law and because different countries have different copyright laws (even though based on agreed-upon conventions), the proper symbolic notification of ownership of copyright should be considered as important. This lock has the format of an encircled c followed by the year and the name of the owner at that time, of the copyright. For this book, for example, this notification, normally found on the reverse title page, could read: *[no formalities]*

© 1994 by T.E. Giles and A.J. Proudfoot

There are provisions, of course, for registering the ownership of a copyright but essentially this does nothing except serve further notice of the copyrighted ownership.

Notice, however, that on the reverse title page of this book the notification of the copyright reads:

© 1994 by Detselig Enterprises Ltd.

ownership

T.E. Giles and A.J. Proudfoot, being the authors of this book, automatically owned the copyright. As with physical commodities, the right of ownership can be given, bartered or sold. The inference in this example is that there must have been some agreement between the authors and the publishing company so that ownership of the copyright has *changed hands*. And although the title page indicates that Detselig Enterprises Limited owns the copyright, this may not necessarily be true. Subsequent to the publication of this book, Detselig Enterprises Limited could sell the copyright to someone else. The statement of ownership (at least) gives the reader a basis for determining ownership at a particular time. Normally, in books where it is indicated that the author owns the copyright, the publisher would have, in the contract, made provision for limiting the author from publishing *not authorized* other copies; in other words, the authors retain ownership without full ownership rights (perhaps comparable to a caveat placed on a piece of property).

Protection for Producer and Public

public
protection

The provisions for copyright not only protect the copyright owner but they protect the general public as well. That is, once a work is published, the public has a right to acquire access to it. If the publisher fails to provide copies, then a license to publish by someone else (with limitations) may be obtained – after paying royalty fees to the publisher. Remember this procedure is not possible while the publisher continues to offer copies for sale to the public. Note also that copyright is not forfeited merely by allowing the material to remain out of print.

term of
copyright

The term during which copyright on a published work can be held is limited. For unpublished works the copyright never expires (the copyright on that love letter you received remains with the writer and the mere act of sending the letter is not considered publication). For published works the term length for which a copyright may be held is for the life of the author, plus fifty years. (After a time span of twenty-five years, a license to publish may be obtained providing a royalty is paid.) For joint authorship, the fifty years relates to the age of the last-living author. For previously unpublished works which become published after the death of the author, the term is fifty years from publication date. In general, the copyright expiry date for photographs, reproduction by *mechanical contrivances*, and government prepared material is fifty years.

death of
author

ideas

Ideas cannot be copyrighted as such nor can materials produced in the future. Thus, two people could each author a document on the same topic, and even use the same title, without infringing on each other's copyright. There is no copyright in news as such but the labor and skill expended in reporting the news may import some personal quality or aspect which would place the material under copyright provisions. Titles of books normally cannot be copyrighted (but sometimes a certain distinctiveness or length may make a title more protected).

A distinction needs to be made between copyrights and patents. A patent protects the inventor of a device from the effects of having the same device developed by another person, whether or not the second person copied, or developed the device quite independently of the first development. Basically this means the first person to register the unique device receives *patent* protection. In copyright a second person is not precluded from copyright protection merely because someone else finished a work first.

patents

The following excerpts from Canada's copyright legislation should prove useful in guiding teachers through the important decisions they must make. Section 3(1) of the *Copyright Act* lists the rights the copyright holder enjoys.

> For the purpose of this Act, copyright means the sole right to produce or reproduce the work or any substantial part thereof in any material form whatever, to perform, or in the case of a lecture to deliver, the work or any substantial part thereof in public; if the work is unpublished, to publish the work or any substantial part thereof; and includes the sole right:

defined

sole right

> 1. to produce, reproduce, perform or publish any translation of the work;
>
> 2. in the case of a dramatic work, to convert it into a novel or other non-dramatic work;
>
> 3. in the case of a novel or other nondramatic work, or of an artistic work, to convert it into a dramatic work, by way of performance in public or otherwise;
>
> 4. in the case of a literary, dramatic, or musical work, to make any record, perforated roll, cinematographic film, or other contrivance by means of which the work may be mechanically performed or delivered;
>
> 5. in the case of any literary, dramatic, musical or artistic work, to reproduce, adapt and publicly present such work by cinematograph, if the author has given such work an original character; but if such original character is absent the cinematography reproduction shall be protected as a photograph;
>
> 6. in the case of any literary, dramatic, musical or artistic work, to broadcast by radio communication; and to authorize any such acts as aforesaid.

Section 17(1) of the *Copyright Act* notes that copyright in a work is:

> deemed to be infringed by any person who, without the consent of the owner of the copyright, does anything that, by this Act, only the owner of the copyright has the right to do.

This normally means copying from a work which is protected by copyright. There are some situations which do not violate this provision. For example,

> Any fair dealing with any work for the purposes of private study, research, criticism, review or newspaper summary

is not a violation. Neither is:

> the publication in a collection mainly composed of non-copyrighted matter, bona fide intended for the use of schools, the title and in any advertisements issued by the publisher, of short passages from published literary works not themselves published for the use of schools in which copyright subsists, if not more than two such passages from works by the same author are published by the same publisher within five years, and the source from which such passages are taken is acknowledged.

Another exclusion is:

> the reading or recitation in public by one person of any reasonable extract from any published word.

In the area of performance of any musical work the following exclusion is pertinent to schools (Section 17(3)).

> No church, college or school and no religious, charitable or fraternal organization shall be held liable to pay any compensation to the owner of any musical work or to any person claiming through him by reason of the public performance of any musical work in furtherance of a religious, educational or charitable object.

immunity
Complete immunity, however, is not intended, so be careful of interpretation of this section.

In another chapter in this book, "Legal Liability of Teachers," the master-servant relationship was central to many of the court considerations. These master-servant cases illustrate the master-servant relationship between the school board and the teacher. In court rulings in cases involving copyright it has generally been held that the relationship of the teacher to the board is essentially a *contract of service* which is a master-servant relationship, as opposed to a *contract for service*, which is not. The importance of this distinction is shown by the wording of Section 12(3) of the *Copyright Act*.

> Where the author was in the employment of some other person under a contract of service or apprenticeship and the work was made in the course of his employment by that person, the person by whom the author was employed shall, in the absence of any agreement to the contrary, be the first owner of the copyright;

This means that a teacher does not necessarily become the owner of the copyright for material authored while functioning as an employee of the school board. Most contracts with teachers are silent on the matter of copyright, which in-and-of itself may express agreement that the school board becomes first owner of copyright. However, if the teacher produces a work during other than usual hours or work, utilizing facilities that are not owned or rented by the school board, and the work is not a direct preparation for class instruction, the copyright ownership would probably accrue to the teacher. The best arrange-

written agreement
ment rests with a written agreement between the teacher and the board. Remember that copyright cannot be transferred except by an agreement in writing.

Teachers who are preparing materials for sale (workbooks, textbooks, etc.) are urged to remember that most students do not have the legal capacity to give permission for the use of their work in any capacity, for example, in an anthology to display student-produced works (exhibition rights), or to perform a student-authored play (public performance rights). Performances are not protected by copyright, unless they are *stored* in some way. It is advisable to seek student, parental or guardian permission before proceeding.

stored

In addition to moral and ethical considerations relative to copyright violations, the legal considerations are also important. Unfortunately some educators often assume the following position: how great can the violation be without risking legal action? This is equivalent to saying, "How much can I steal from my neighbor before he calls the police?" Any violation is theft, even though the terminology embodied in copyright laws does not use the term *theft*.

theft

Penalties

Creators are entitled to seek an injunction (to get all copies back), to demand compensation in dollars for the sale of copyrighted materials, or to demand compensation for cheating the holder out of money which would be due from the sale of the item. The criminal process can be initiated by anyone, not just the copyright holder. The maximum penalty for a serious offense is a fine up to $1 000 000 and/or two years in jail and for less serious crimes, a fine of up to $25 000 and/or six months in jail. The persons who can be held liable are those who carry out the infringing act and those who authorized the making of the copy. In foreign litigation, this was found to be the university which supplied a copying machine in a library. The university was found to be responsible since it appeared to authorize breaches. (*Moorhouse v. University of New South Wales* (1974) 23 FLR 112.) In the milieu of the classroom teacher, the results of this decision would probably be translated to mean the teacher and the school board as employer. Infringement is doing something which only the copyright holder is entitled to do. But, in the reported cases of copyright violations in Canada a pattern of criminal penalties is not readily determinable.

injunction

criminal
penalties

Educators should consider copyright violation as being serious, not only from the viewpoint of upholding the law as a model to the students but also as a violation of the rights of other people.

violation
serious

General guidelines to follow are difficult to establish, other than to say "do not violate copyright law." However, the educator works daily with copyright material and thus needs some guidance. Readers are aware that Canada's copyright legislation is old (some would say ancient). However, a number of studies have been made and recommendations received by the government. Major revisions which will modernize the act are under way, and some of the changes are discussed later in this chapter. Notably, the penalties have been increased, but the changes of most importance to teachers are the provisions for copying instructional materials. The old exemption provisions, even the *fair dealings* clause which stated that anyone could make a print copy for private

fair
dealing

study, research, review or summary, were extremely narrow. The person was required to make the copy himself/herself, unless the other person was given a signed permission to exercise his/her individually-held right.

Revisions to the Statute

Bill C60 which carried the proposed revisions to our statute was drafted in two phases. Phase I was passed in June, 1988. Phase II proposes changes of importance to those who do teaching or research in educational institutions. For example, live or literary performances such as the recital of a poem, or the performance of a play will be provided for under the *fair dealing* clause. Use of news and public affairs programs will be permitted, if destroyed within 120 days. Copyright holders will be encouraged to join what are termed *collectives* in order that school systems can negotiate licenses to use materials and royalty payment amounts with groups of creators. Some computer software companies will grant *site* licenses, for a fee, so that a site (school/school jurisdiction) can make as many copies as necessary. This is a very valuable innovation to the computer and computer-assisted instruction ventures which are current in many schools.

site licenses

Bill C-316, when passed into law, offers several benefits to the teacher. In general intent, it provides for the repealing of the *fair dealings* provisions by introducing *fair use* terminology of the type entrenched in American copyright law. By doing this it seems reasonable to expect that Canadian courts would "cast an eye" towards United States jurisprudence for guidance in cases of alleged copyright violation.

fair use

The Bill proposes the addition of a separate *fair use* section and the repeal of paragraphs 27(2)a and 27(2)d of the current act (these refer to the present education exemptions and fair dealing provisions).

Bill C-316 reads:

> 28.1 (Fair use). For the purposes of section 28.2 and 28.5 "copyright works" means a work in which copyright subsists but does not include a work that is included
> (a) in the lists of a society, association or corporation referred to in section 67; or
> (b) in the repertoire of a licensing body referred to in section 70.1.

> 28.2(1) The fair use of a copyright work, for purposes of, without limiting the generality of the foregoing, teaching, review, legislative or judicial proceedings, research, criticism, comment or newspaper summary, does not constitute an infringement of copyright or the moral rights of the author of that work.

> (2) The fair use of a copyrighted work includes fair use by the reproduction of the work by any means.

> (3) For teaching purposes, the reproduction by any means of multiple copies of the work for instruction constitutes fair use of that work.

28.3 For the purposes of this Act, the factors to be considered in determining whether the use made of a copyrighted work is a fair use, shall include:
(a) the purpose and character of the use, including whether the use is for non-profit purposes;
(b) the nature of the work;
(c) in a case where only part of the work is reproduced, the amount and substantiality of the part used in relation to the whole work; and
(d) the effect of the use upon the potential market for, or value of, the work.

28.4(1) Where a person reproduces a copyrighted work that is broadcast by any means and the reproduction constitutes fair use of the work, the person shall destroy the reproduction within one hundred and twenty (120) days from the day it is made, except if the reproduction is made for teaching purposes (for instruction) and represents less than ten (10) percent of the entire work.

(2) Copyright in a work shall be deemed to be infringed by any person who contravenes subsection (1).

28.5 No royalties may be recovered in respect of a copyrighted work where there is a fair use of that work.

Subsections 28.2(3) and 28.4(1) are of dramatic and direct benefit to teachers. Subsection 28.2(3) deems that the reproduction of copyrighted works for instructional purpose is *fair use* of such works – without qualification. Subsection 28.4(1) allows educators to retain reproductions made of copyrighted works that have been broadcast, so long as the reproduction is made for instruction, constitutes less than ten percent of the work, and of course is deemed a fair use of the work. Taking the effects of subsection 28.2(3) it seems reasonable to assume that the *fair use* requirements of subsection 28.4(1) will be satisfied in every case where the reproduction is made for instructional purposes.

reproductions

The teacher should note that the *fair use* provisions of the Bill apply only to *copyrighted* works as defined in subsection 28.1. These provisions exclude work that is included in the list of performing right societies and licensing bodies of copyrighted works.

performing rights societies

Bill S-8 proposals by the federal government are also of importance to teachers. Bill S-8 was designed to amend Section 27 of the Act by adding subsection (7) which states:

(7) When a licence for the reproduction, communication by television performance or exhibition of a published work is not obtainable on reasonable terms and conditions by an educational organization recognized as such by a provincial or municipal government or any agent thereof, it is not an infringement of the copyright in the published work if it is, without motive of gain,

(a) reproduced,

(b) communicated by telecommunication to the public,

(c) performed in public, or

(d) exhibited at a public exhibition other than a trade exhibition, for educational purposes, by or on behalf of the educational organization or a person giving or taking instruction at the educational organization or doing research in accordance with any requirements of the educational organization.

Observations respecting this Bill are that it allows educators and students to make certain use of published copyrighted works without the necessity of obtaining a license to do so. There are certain precautions which must be taken.

1. The work must be a *published* work (copies of the work must have been issued to the public).

2. The licence must be *not obtainable* on reasonable terms and conditions. (Reasonable will be specific to the special circumstances, user, and work, thus no definitions were included.)

3. Attempts must be made to obtain the license before the protection is afforded to the user.

4. It is the educational organization which is responsible for making the attempt.

5. The organization must be recognized by a provincial or municipal government. (All *approved* schools would, by definition, be included.)

6. The words *without motive of gain* will have to be determined in each specific circumstance. (A drama production at which admission tickets were sold would have to demonstrate that the proceeds were used to defray costs of production or were used for a *bona fide* educational purpose.)

7. The work must be used for educational purposes. (Administrative purposes, although conducted in support of an educational purpose would probably not comply with the Bill's intent. Educational means *educational.*)

8. The words "by or on behalf of the educational organization, or the person giving or taking instruction ... or doing research" does not state, for example, that the teacher, student, or researcher, must physically do the copying. If the reasons are valid, it would seem that a secretary, commercial firm, or the centralized duplicating services of an educational organization are afforded protection. When Bill S-8 becomes law, the standard disclaimers by the employer respecting duplication will no longer be required. (When a teacher states that consent has been obtained, or that reasonable attempts to obtain approval from the copyright holder have been attempted, the duplication can proceed.)

Computer Software

Computer software is a copyrighted work, however the impact of the revisions outlined probably would not apply. All computer software is obtained by consumers by way of a license which spells out certain terms and conditions. Since *these* conditions are in that sense part of a private contractual set of rights and obligations and the software producer can sue on the basis of the terms and conditions specified.

license

Guidelines

The authors suggest the following guidelines as being reasonable (some use discretion copyright owners may not agree, so use discretion).

1. For the purpose of study and research the educator may make one copy of material for private use. (A reasonable expectation would be a limitation of one chapter.)

2. Multiple copies of reasonable length materials may be duplicated for class use. (Normally this would not exceed a paragraph or two – certainly never an entire article or chapter.) Exercises from workbooks, even less than a page in length, must never be duplicated for class use without permission.

3. When the school arranges the performance of a play or musical for *educational purposes*, it is still expected that the school will purchase sufficient copies of the music or play for the individual actors/singers. (Never photocopy to produce these.) Also be warned that when a school states that the performance is for educational purposes, the law may not necessarily agree.

4. Obtain permission in writing before duplicating copyrighted material, whether this material is from a book, a periodical, or a television program. Sometimes the concept of urgency may appear paramount – for example, the article in today's daily newspaper is particularly pertinent for tomorrow's class. Using discretion, the teacher may duplicate this for the class but certainly a year later the same material should not be duplicated without permission.

5. Normally, requests to duplicate copyrighted material should be sent to the publisher. Indicate precisely what material is being considered, how many copies are to be made, how many times, and what audience will use the material. Provide a simple statement at the end of the letter for the signature of the publisher when granting permission. (For routine requests the publisher does not wish to take the time to formulate a letter of reply.) Send two copies of your letter so the publisher can retain one for its own files.

6. Be reasonable. Perhaps the owners of the copyright feel the same way about their materials as you do about your car. Should you be expected to loan your car to numerous strangers, for vague reasons?

7. Authors would have a difficult time in getting material published unless the publisher could expect some recompense to enable the payment of reasonable royalties. Is your misuse of copyright material preventing the copyright owner from receiving payment?

8. As a writer, composer, creator, be sure to establish copyright ownership with your employer. Most universities waive these rights but many school boards do not have written policies covering these matters. Unless there is agreement to the contrary, copyright ownership will rest with the employer in a master-servant relationship. Obtain this waiver in writing.

9. Do not duplicate numerous copies of any letter you receive. First, the letter you receive is normally *not* in the public domain (usually the author of the letter has not published the letter). Second, remember that where the letter was considered to be *published*, the writer of the letter has copyright protection.

10. Do not audio-tape or video-tape copyright material for use in your classroom, without permission.

11. Even when permission is obtained for classroom use of copyright material, be sure to acknowledge the source of the copied material (consider academic honesty as well as legal responsibility).

12. Consider buying the instructional material you need rather than, in a sense, stealing it.

Summary

become
literate

Professional teachers are advised to become familiar with the requirements of copyright legislation and the ways in which they can avoid committing a violation. Since public bodies such as school jurisdictions and universities have become more sensitive to the issues of violations by employees, probably because of the easy availability of good quality duplicating equipment, computers in schools, the rising costs of published materials, and limited school budgets for instructional materials, most make available seminars and printed materials on the topic. Through reading and seminar attendance, the teacher can become literate in copyright law as well as family and tort law.

Part Three

Administration in Canadian Schools

The Teacher's Work Place

The professional need not be a scientist, but he should be sophisticated enough to make competent use of scientific knowledge . . .
Douglas McGregor, The Human Side of Enterprise

Defined

Structure as a Framework

Goals as a Framework

Models

Formal and Informal Relationships

Organizational Culture

Cultural Leadership

Introduction

Much stress would be alleviated if school leaders would,

> treat their workers as their most important asset, demonstrate faith in their abilities, and show a tough-minded respect for the individual, demonstrate the willingness to train his/her *practical autonomy* in order to prepare them to step out and contribute directly to the job (Peters & Waterman, 1982: 239).

Administrators must behave in a way which fosters the trust relationship and conveys a message of caring for their teachers' socio-emotional needs. They must allow for the free expression of ideas. There must be an acceptance of the fact that teachers are able to identify those issues in the school system which are problematic, and they ought to be given an open forum in which to discuss them, and be given an opportunity to mutually resolve those which can be resolved. Administrators should provide opportunities for teachers to set up networks of support and assistance among themselves. The importance of social events and other regular opportunities for staff members to make contact with fellow teachers cannot be over-emphasized. *(message of caring)* *(networks of support)*

Much of teachers' stress (see Chapter 19) results from expectations which are not clear about policy and performance standards, from perceptions of unfair treatment or from feeling they lack control over their destinies. To alleviate these stresses, there are a number of things which astute, sensitive school leaders can do. They can find ways to communicate expectations both formally and informally; provide ongoing feedback to staff members, and give constructive suggestions and direct help when required. More time should be spent conducting consistent and useful formative and summative evaluations *(stress)* of the teacher's work and assisting teachers in career planning. Paying attention to tiny details when planning staffing assignment schedules, or implementing changes can prevent much of the interpersonal conflict and misunderstanding which so often occur when simple errors are perceived by staff members as examples of preferential treatment or as acts of deliberate malice.

communication   Ongoing, informal, face-to-face communication is vital in a people-oriented profession like teaching. Skills in mediating conflict, conferencing, managing group processes, handling bureaucratic procedures, as examples, are not only skills which administrators should have, but are skills which should also be taught to teachers through professional development programs. Opportunities should be provided for teachers to collaborate in decision making and to take leadership control of group projects which would, for example, formulate discipline policies, organize class assignments, or even interview and hire new staff. Mentoring systems or team-teaching situations provide support and encouragement for inexperienced teachers.

obsessed with listening   As Peters states (Peters & Waterman, 1982), supervisors must become "obsessed with listening." Like Peters' exemplary managers, they must "wander around," experience the front line and keep the door open to listen and respond to teachers' concerns. Through these actions they become sensitized to potential problems and the demands placed upon teachers. They are often able to resolve problems early, before they become serious sources of stress and dissatisfaction. Administrators should also make every attempt to become informed about teachers' professional activities and students' accomplishments in order to recognize and *celebrate* them publicly .

The teaching profession does extraordinarily well at utilizing effective management practices *with students*; in finding ways to increase student autonomy and self-esteem; and in providing positive feedback and strong student social networks, while still exerting disciplinary control. It is time that teachers practiced those same principles with their colleagues as well, for the increased satisfaction of everyone involved.

larger social system   Although teaching occurs largely within the confines of a classroom, it also occurs in the larger social system of the school. Thus when one is developing a comprehensive view of the role of the teacher it is necessary first to examine and study the *organizational* context of teaching and administrative activities. What are the major elements of the school organization which influence classroom behavior? What are the opportunities and restraints produced by organizational forces and pressures? To what extent is the school a bureaucracy? What is legitimate authority, and what is its converse? How do different structures, and the different applications of authority affect the teacher? What are the *actual* patterns of organization called the school, and what do we know about the *informal* organization which grows out of the formal structure as the workers apply their skills and personalities to the work place?

social needs   Although organizations are usually considered to be mechanisms for satisfying social needs and for providing a way to advance the human condition, they may actually produce *stricture* rather than structure, and *demean* rather than empower. There are a number of reasons why the study of organizational theory is important to the teacher. First, there appears to be some confusion about the appropriate role of the teacher within the school setting. Second, the school itself is an important part of the network of institutions and organizations which serve society. Third, formal educational organizations are assessed in terms of their goals, their operating structure, and their effectiveness. Fourth, all of us spend much of our lives working with a formal organization (often estimated to be at least 30 percent of our waking lives).

A survey of the literature on organizations shows five paths: the structure of organizations; the functioning of organizations; the management of organizations; people in organizations; and organizations in society. This chapter will attempt to provide a sample of some of the literature in only two of the five areas: (1) structure of organizations, and (2) people in organizations. Of these two, *people in organizations* will receive more attention, but this text will present only a very limited survey of some of the available thought.

five paths

The fundamental purpose of any organization is to accomplish work that cannot be accomplished by one person working alone. Volumes have been written on this topic. The text which follows will attempt to draw from the original sources as much as possible, in order to get at the control ideas.

Definition

In its simplest definition, an organization is a scheme for getting things done (Alfonso, Firt & Neville, 1981).

Many scholars have considered the concept *organization* and have thus been driven to formulate definitions. Two extensive but useful definitions are found in the works of Talcott Parsons and Amitai Etzioni, writers who are senior scholars in this branch of study.

organization
definition

Talcott Parsons (1960) wrote:

> An organization is a system which, as the attainment of its goal, *produces* an identifiable something which can be utilized in some way by another system; that is, the output of the organization is for some other system, an input. In the case of an organization with economic primacy, this output may be a class of goods or services which are either consumable or serve as instruments for a further phase of the production process by other organizations. In the case of a government agency, the output may be a class of regulatory decisions; in that of an educational organization it may be a certain type of *trained capacity* on the part of the students who have been subjected to its influence.

Parsons

Etzioni (1961) offers this description:

> Organizations are social units (or human groupings) deliberately constructed and reconstructed to seek specific goals. Corporations, armies, schools, hospitals, churches, and prisons are included; tribes, classes, ethnic groups, friendship groups, and families are excluded. Organizations are characterized by: (a)

Etzioni

divisions of labor, power, and communication responsibilities, divisions which are not random or traditionally patterned, but deliberately planned to enhance the realization of specific goals; (b) the presence of one or more power centres which control the concerted efforts of the organization and direct them toward its goals; these power centres also must review continuously the organization's performance and re-pattern its structure, where necessary, to increase its efficiency; (c) substitution of personnel, i.e., unsatisfactory persons can be removed and others assigned their tasks. The organization can also recombine its personnel through transfer and promotion.

This word of caution is offered by R. Jean Hills, in a text entitled *Toward a Science of Organization* (Hills, 1968, pp. 1-2).

Hills

Although there has been a vast amount of research done in organizations, and about organizations, there has been little study of *organization* as such. We study leadership, morale, decision making, communication, bureaucracy, and role conflict, but not organization. More frequently than not, a particular role, e.g., that of superintendent of schools, has been studied in isolation. It is as though the chemist selected a single element of a compound for examination and never got around to investigating how that element interacted with other elements *to form the compound.* In the field of educational organization and administration we have had innumerable studies of the roles of superintendent, principal, teacher, trustee, etc., but we know very little about *organization.* We cannot even say, in any precise way, what there is about an educational organization that makes it different from a business firm.

Current writers of textbooks on organization have not changed these definitive statements.

How are Institutions Organized?

There are two sets of theories about the way institutions are organized. One set deals with *structure* and how the parts are coordinated and controlled, while the other concerns itself with the *goals* of the organization and how the structure has evolved around a need.

goals

Structure as a Framework for Analysis

Weber

Much of the thinking about organizational structure and function originates with the work of Max Weber and the bureaucratic model which was formulated during the time of the Industrial Revolution, when managers were accused, among other things, of nepotism, cruelty, and whimsical judgments. A series of charismatic leaders often caused many (and sometimes radical) changes in direction, thus the need for order became apparent to Weber. The purpose of the bureaucratic model was to provide a useful framework for organizational structuring.

structure

Bureaucracy calls for the following.

1. A rigorous chain of command (usually in the shape of a pyramid).

2. A high degree of specialization and division of work in all task areas.

3. A set of rules (standard operating procedures) to guide employee actions in all situations in the work activities.

4. Employees are selected and promoted on the basis of technical competency.

5. General level of impersonality with respect to human relations.

In the designs which follow it can be seen what Weber's response is to the situation described.

Max Weber's model led to the development of well-defined functional specialization and control through a formal hierarchy and authority mechanism and a rigid structure which promotes efficiency. For example, it proved for: advantages

a. effective discipline;

b. control of routine procedures;

c. strong management which could respond quickly; and

d. effective control over large numbers of people.

However, there were also disadvantages. Bureaucratic organizations tended   disadvantages
to:

a. limit the organization;s ability to meet changing conditions because the structure lacked flexibility and adaptability;

b. reduce innovation and creativity;

c. develop functional specialists who may become isolated and thus not make effective contributions to the achievement of organizational goals;

d. increase non-productivity (*downtime*) because workers are often required to wait for decisions to be passed down from the top;

e. have a depressing effect on the *human spirit* (Jay, 1967, p. 70);

f. produce rigidity . . .

> The hierarchical system enshrines and sanctifies the qualities that brought that success in the past, and continues to search for and promote men with those qualities even when circumstances have changed and different qualities are needed (Jay, 1967, p. 70); and to

g. neglect the informal organization.

Following upon the work of Max Weber, Richard Hall developed a school   school operating
operating inventory (SOI) which he used to characterize the two rational   inventory
organizational patterns in schools: bureaucratic and professional. Hall's inventory consisted of six scales: (1) hierarchy of authority, (2) rules for incumbents, (3) procedural specifications, (4) impersonality, (5) technical competence, and (6) specialization.

By placing the result of the hierarchy of authority, rules for incumbents, procedural specifications, and impersonality scales (bureaucratic) on one axis and the results of the technical competence and specialization scales (professional) on the other, Hall was able to conclude there are in fact four types of possible school organizational structures. They are:

Type I: High Bureaucratic/High Professional (Weberian)

Type II: High Bureacratic/Low Professional (Authoritarian)

Type III: Low Bureacratic/High Professional (Professional)

Type IV: Low Bureaucratic/Low Professional (Chaotic)

(Hoy & Forsyth, p. 85; Hoy & Miskel, p. 123)

Mintzberg

identifying
the parts

Mintzberg (1979), a frequently quoted writer in the field of organizational behavior, directed his attention to developing a framework that identified the parts of the organization and how they were coordinated. The parts which he identified are:

a. the operating core (those who perform the basic work; produce the essential output);

b. the strategic apex (the top administrators; the superintendent and his/her assistants);

c. the middle line (those administrators such as school principals who connect the *apex* to the operating core; they direct or coordinate);

d. the technostructure (the administrative component with delegated responsibility for planning; they design, plan and train – perhaps the supervisors and instructional leaders) and;

e. the support staff (outside the basic work flow, but supportive to the organizational output – the caretakers, payroll people, cafeteria workers, etc.).

From this analysis, Mintzberg provided us with a very useful way of viewing the organizational context of the teacher's work. He isolates five prototypic organizational structures.

prototypical
structures

1. *Simple structure* organizations in which the strategic apex is the key part, and *direct* supervision is the device for coordinating efforts.

2. *Machine bureaucracy* types of organizations in which the technostructure (planning) is the central part and standardization of work processes is the major device for coordination.

3. *Professional bureaucracies* are organizations in which the operating core (teachers) is the key unit. Standardization of skills is the major device for coordinating work.

4. *Divisionalized* forms of organizations place the middle line people in key positions. Standardization of *output* is central to coordination.

5. *Adhocracy* is the type of organization in which the support staff have become the key parts. Mutual adjustments produce coordination.

Since there exist no pure types, the school organizational context facing the teacher will probably be a combination of the above; however Mintzberg's work does contribute to our insights and may produce a useful starting point for observing and adjusting to the school's organizational structure.

Goals as a Framework for Analysis

The work of Weick (1979) was chosen to represent the group of *loose coupling* theorists who contended that in schools, for example, there is loose control over how well the work is done. As a consequence, school systems evolved into systems which invoke a *logic of confidence* in which the administration and the school board introduce policies and procedures they then assume teachers will follow. Schools are frequently regarded as organizations with ambiguous goals, technologies which are not clear, fluid participation patterns, uncoordinated activities, and loosely connected structural elements. Many contend that the bureaucratic ideals of standardization and control simply do not adequately explain the operations of a school. Theories which consider *goals* rather than structure are contended to hold more promise in explaining what is happening.

Weick

Talcott Parsons (1960) bases his typology of organizations upon what he calls *social* functions. Parsons states that, in general, there are four problems facing all social systems:

Parsons

1. Adaptation (how to obtain resources).

2. Goal achievement (how to define and implement them).

3. Integration (how to maintain solidarity of purpose).

4. Latency (the problem of how to maintain and renew motivational and cultural patterns).

Parsons' contention is that the organizational goals of an organization will reflect the issues that society values the most. He contends that in the United States the acquisition of wealth (adaptation) is most important. In India it is speculated that religious order (latency) is most important. It is interesting to speculate as to which of Parson's four problems is most important to Canada. The thesis of Parson's work is that those institutions that set goals consistent with the values of society will be supported by society. Talcott Parsons has a message!

Blau and Scott (1962), other writers in this same area, maintain that organizations are structured around the answer to the question, "Who is benefited?" This is termed the *prime beneficiary* typology. They suggest four identifiable groups of beneficiaries.

Blau and Scott

1. The members or the *rank and file* participants in what they call mutual benefit associations such as political parties, associations of professionals, the members of clubs and the adherents of religious sects. Since the problem is often membership apathy, the prime problem of these organizations is to maintain control over the membership. Blau and Scott refer to this as the

prime beneficiary typology

problems of oligarchy. For example, to win a teacher strike vote and the larger cause, democratic procedures may have to be set aside.

2. *Business concerns* such as industrial firms, retail stores and banks, i.e., those whose primary goal is profit.

3. *Commonwealth interests* in that the public is the primary beneficiary. Examples include the military, police and fire-fighting services. The primary concern is a balance of control between efficiency and public interest.

4. *Service organizations* whose prime beneficiary is the public itself. In addition to schools, this cluster of organizations includes hospitals, social work agencies, prisoner assistance societies, and mental health clinics. The central problem for schools for example, is to maintain the client (student) as the prime beneficiary. Administrators and teachers must not lose sight of the student's welfare because of pre-occupation with their own status (mutual benefit), or by becoming pre-occupied with immediate problems.

Carlson

select clients

Carlson (1964) and others introduce a new twist by focusing upon service organizations and addressing the matter of the organization's ability to select clients, and the client's ability to select organizations. Carlson uses a two dimensional grid. The result is four organizational types.

1. The organization chooses and the client chooses.

2. The organization chooses but the client does not.

3. The organization does not choose, but the client does.

4. The organization does not choose the client and the client does not choose the organization.

bad or good students

Carlson states that most public schools are of type four, so the clients (students) and the organization (school) must develop adaptive behaviors to deal with their inability to choose. Segregating *bad* and *good* students is but one example of how schools deal with non-chosen students. Private schools or home schooling are examples of how parents deal with *bad* schools.

Etzioni

Etzioni (1964) bases his theory of organizational structure upon the three types of power used within the organization in order to force organization members to comply with organizational goals: coercive power is applied through physical sanctions; remunerative power is applied through material rewards; and normative (symbolic) power results from the application of symbolic rewards and sanctions. Etzioni contends that subordinates have three ways in which to react: they can react by *calculation*, i.e., adopt a wait-and-see stance. He then placed these six observations on a grid to produce three distinct types of organizations.

1. Coercive organizations (coercive power and worker alienation, perhaps withdrawal).

2. Utilitarian organizations (remunerative power and worker calculation – wait and see).

3. Normative organizations (normative power – the use of symbolic power to obtain worker commitment).

Schools typically use normative or coercive power to make students and teachers comply – marks for students and pats on the back or threats of termination for teachers. Sometimes students face various forms of *discipline* and teachers face *instructions* or job sanctions. The organizational goals of the school will dictate the compliance structure (methods) to be applied by teacher, administrator, or supervisor to students and teachers.

Models of Organizational Behavior

Keith Davis (1967, p. 480) grouped organizational behavior under four broad headings. They are autocratic, custodial, supportive and collegial. The autocratic model, which has its roots in history (Industrial Revolution for example), depend upon power; those who are in command have the power to demand. The employee is oriented toward obedience and performance results were minimum. custodial models arise when it was discovered that although employees do not talk back they certainly *think back.* Employers attempt to increase employee satisfaction, usually through money. Employees are oriented toward security and benefits programs. The employer receives passive cooperation because employees seek security. The supportive model, whose roots lie with the work of Renis Likert, depends upon leadership support rather than power or money to obtain job performance. The employee's needs are met through status and recognition. Employees have a feeling of *participation.* A useful extension of the supportive model of organizational behavior is the collegial model which has its basis in a partnership. Management is oriented toward teamwork; the employee is oriented toward responsible behavior; self discipline is the psychological orientation of the employee; the employee's needs are met through *self* actualization; and the result is enthusiasm (moderate, not excessive) for the work to be done.

To this point, the text of this chapter has reviewed a small portion of the literature on organizational context; however, since schools are social systems, some attention must also be given to the formal and informal relationships within the system, to *ethics* and to the *culture* of the organization.

Formal and Informal Relationships

Authority is initially vested in the formal (status) leader of the organization. This implies control from the top. However, the key flaw in Weberian (Bureaucracy) formulations was the failure to note that there exists in all organizations an informal structure – a social organization which could direct the behavior of the workers by the application of powerfully-felt sanctions and rewards. Blau and Scott (Hoy & Forsyth, p. 98 and Hoy & Mitzel, p. 218) use two dimensions to divide social organizations.

1. Social structure (the network of relations based upon group status); and

2. Culture (shared valued, norms, role responsibilities, and privileges).

power of
social group

When the school administrator (leader) taps into the power of the social group it can become a source of personal power – subordinate loyalty – the informal power of an administrator.

Homan

Homan (Hoy & Forsyth, p. 100-104) describes how informal structures are formed. He identifies three social behaviors: (1) what people do (activity); (2) the effect of an action on another (interaction); and (3) the internal emotional, physiological and cognitive states (sentiment). Through shared activities, people form groups in which they interact. The environment of the organization will either stimulate or place limits on informal group behavior and will stimulate the formation of shared sentiments. Within the larger work group, smaller social units will develop to meet individual needs. How these smaller groups evolve will depend upon the frequency, duration, initiative of the workers, and the degree of reciprocity of interactions (Hoy & Miskel, p. 100).

sentiment

Affiliations build informal status structures. Frequently administrators attempt to insert the *sentiment* of the formal organization into the social fabric of the work situation. The success of these administrative overtures depends upon many factors, some of which are found in the responses to the problems which are being encountered in the formal organizations, for example, work group dysfunctions, goal and outcome conflicts, problems with environmental relationships, poor internal and external feedback loops, morale levels, leadership styles and the problems associated with bureaucratic socialization (Hoy & Miskel, p. 220-221). As an illustration of one such area, Hoy and Miskel (p. 78-80) note ten possible areas of conflict between an employee and the organization.

1. Role conflict (between formal expectations and the person's expectations).

2. Personality conflict (basic incompatibilities).

3. Norm conflict (personal norms conflict with informal group norms).

4. Goal conflict (which direction? what purpose?).

5. Role-norm conflict (between formal and informal norms).

6. Role-goal conflict (bureaucratic expectations conflict with organizational goals).

7. Role-personality conflict (role not personally suited).

8. Norm-personality conflict (norms not personally suited).

9. Norm-goal (informal norms undermine official goals).

10. Goal-personality conflict (individual teachers may not comply with organizational goals – not in teacher's best interest, not psychologically equipped, or the goals of the school, or the needs and the motives of teacher are unrealistic).

informal
communications

Communication networks provide another excellent example. Again from Hoy and Miskel (1987, p. 221):

> Formal systems of communication in schools are typically not sufficient and are inevitably supplemented with informal ones. One finding that has been

repeatedly demonstrated by researchers is that informal communications exist in all organizations regardless of how elaborate the system of formal communication. Communications flow quickly and freely through the grapevine. These informal patterns of communication in schools are built around social relationships among school members; informal channels arise for such simple reasons as common classroom areas, shared lunch hours, car pools, and friendships. Teachers, like other organizational members, have a need to know what is happening and why; in fact, need for such communications and understanding may be one of the basic reasons for the existence of small, informal groups.

Informal structure provides a channel for circumventing formally prescribed rules and procedures that may have positive or negative effects. Charles Pages' study of informal structure demonstrates that pressing problems develop for which efficient solutions or communications are not possible within the formal framework; hence, the informal structure assumes increased importance. Similarly, Laurence Iannaccone's study also confirmed that when the formal organization of a school does not respond to up-to-line communications from teachers in a satisfactory way, then the informal system is used in an attempt to obtain a satisfactory response. In schools, knowledgeable and flexible administrators can use the informal system to avoid the bureaucratic frustrations and impediments of the formal system. As a communication vehicle, the grapevine provides efficient machinery, provided that administrators recognize its importance, understand its structure and functioning, and are able and willing to use it.

grapevine

Culture

Timm and Peterson (1986, p. 105) describe culture within organizations as "that which includes the whole set of pervasive values, norms and attitudes within the organization." They emphasize the importance for all who work within an organization to learn the culture – *the way things are done around here;* the unwritten rules (not found in a policy manual); and the values and norms which are predominant. Peters and Waterman in *In Search of Excellence* (1982) refer extensively to what they call *company* culture. Their research found that all of the excellent companies they studied had recognizable cultures – no matter what the industry. In whatever successful business that was being studied, the company was doing things to make sure that all employees were buying into the company's culture – or opting out! Most of the recent literature on *corporate culture* supports and extends the findings of Peters and Waterman on the significance of the culture to the goal of excellence.

culture

unwritten rules

corporate culture

Thus, in its broadest context, culture refers to an organization's history, the events that shaped the organization, the dreams, ambitions, values held by its leaders and members, the relationships and motivation of its members – all that *folksy* background of the organization and its way of doing things, responding to demands, approaching problems, and dealing with change, innovation, failure and success. Nevi (1988, p. 61) refers to culture as "the activities, attainments and values of a group of people." Hofsted (1980) found (Sergiovanni & Corbally, 1987, p. 59) culture defined as "the collective

collective programming

programming of the mind that distinguishes the members of one school from another." Sergiovanni and Corbally (1987, p. viii) add that:

> ... the stuff of culture includes customs and traditions, historical accounts be they mythical or actual, tacit understandings, habits, norms and expectations, common meanings associated with fixed objects and established rites, shared assumptions and inter-subjective meanings.

Anthropologists refer to it as the collective manifestation of a people's core values.

school
culture

Within the school culture is, in much the same way, the external manifestation of the shared meanings and values held by teachers and students. It is their visible enactment of what they stand for, and what they attend to, and what they feel to be important. It includes the attitudes and beliefs which nurture the organization and the shared view of what is meant by school success. It is dress codes, hoopla, rituals, attendance policies, songs, and trophies and all those things which say a great deal about the school's integrating philosophy. It is image-conscious. It is the *real thing*. Slogans like Ford's, "Quality is Job 1" exhort commitment. Organizational stories (how Lee Iacocca emptied the Chrysler board room) are not just stories; they become legends, they contribute to the culture of, in this example, the Chrysler Corporation.

Cultural Leadership

A very important aspect of the principal's work is to act as cultural leader. The principal articulates the school's purpose and mission. As cultural leader the principal socializes new teachers and other employees to the school, and helps to develop and display symbols which reflect the goals and values of the

symbols

school and school jurisdiction. Through the actions of the school's cultural leaders (principals and other support staff), members are provided with the opportunity to enjoy a special sense of personal importance and significance. Essentially this is a school/community-building venture. But in order to do this, the leader must provide a great deal of freedom to teachers, students, and others but especially to the teachers to permit them to decide how to honor and realize the school culture's core of values.

Most of what is being described above is akin to *ethos* in the *effective school's* movement spearheaded by Mortimer and others (1979) or the more

effective
school

mundane topic, school spirit. The *effective schools* movement will be part of the material presented in Chapter 12. The point is that the nature of the school's culture and the degree of involvement in it are essential to the teacher, the school, and its clients, the students. The teacher must fit, and to be successful the incoming administrator must work within existing bounds, before moving toward change. The notion of school culture and cultural leadership are very useful concepts in the thrust toward excellence.

Functionality of Organizational Structure

The following elements are important parts of a visible school organization.

1. Work is managed against goals.

2. The organizational structure is developed to follow function.

3. Decisions are made near the source of information.

4. Communications contain little distortion.

5. There is a high degree of collaboration and a low degree of competition internally.

6. Conflict situations are managed.

7. A feeling of ownership is maintained.

8. The team is the basic unit of work.

9. There exists a built-in, continuous improvement mechanism.

Summary

Teachers and teaching are influenced by the larger social system of the school. Organizational studies have taken at least five distinct routes: studies or organizational structure, organizational functioning, the management of people, and the relationship of organizations to the larger social milieu. This chapter has provided a sample of findings drawn from studies into the structure of organizations, with reference specifically to the school as an organization. Studies were grouped into framework-oriented and goal-oriented analyses. The findings of some of the works of Weber, Hall, Mintzberg, Weick, Parsons, Blau and Scott, Carlson, and Etzioni were reviewed. Keith Davis' model of organizational behavior was outlined. Culture, as a way of describing an organization, was defined and related to the emerging concept of school culture and cultural leadership as important aspects in the organizational life of a school.

12

Authority and Role of School Administrators

The very choice of the principal as school *administrator* often stands in the way of the right choice. To administer an enterprise is to keep it running as smoothly and effectively as possible. This is no small task and certainly an essential one. But it is not the top priority. What ultimately makes the difference is leadership. Administration can be learned; leadership is an inherent strength. A principal who is a leader can leave many of the administrative tasks to others: A principal who is an administrator, even if a good one, cannot expect others to lead.

Fred M. Hechinger, President
New York Times Foundation

The Management Process

Role of the Principal

Educational Leadership

Introduction

Part One of this text set the structural framework within which the work of the teacher is set. Chapter 4 directed attention to the local setting of school districts, school boards and local schools. The functions and responsibilities of major players within this structure were highlighted. Also Chapter 17 will elaborate upon some of the administrative duties of the school teacher. The purpose of this chapter is to set forward the responsibilities of school level administrators and specifically the role and responsibility of the school principal. This chapter, in order to avoid duplication and perhaps confusion, assigns the roles to be performed and the skills required of the school principal in the knowledge that in an operational sense many of the tasks are delegated (sometimes by policy but often by operational procedures) to other members of the administrative team such as assistant (vice) principals, department heads, team leaders and teams of teachers.

role and responsibility

The Management process in organizations, with any minimal level of complexity, can be divided and described at a number of different levels. The descriptive materials which follow first set the management process in a total framework for attaining results, then builds upon the basic elements of: (1) ideas, (2) things, and (3) people through task and function areas, to (4) a description of the more evident of the *activities* areas involved.

The Management Process in Its Total Framework

basic elements   The management process has three basic elements: ideas, things, and people.

1. Ideas – the management task is to do conceptual *thinking* for the purpose of formulating notions/alternative plans.

2. Things – the task is to *administer* or manage the affairs of the organization.

3. People – the task is to influence people to accomplish the desired goals by providing *leadership*. ("Influences" herein used is defined as the capacity to produce effects on others by *intangible* or *indirect* means and differs from power which, according to Kanter (1977), "is the ability to get things done by being able to *mobilize* resources . . . as well as (having) *control* over conditions that make action possible.")

management process   The management process has three continuous functions: analysis of problems, decision making, and communicating alternatives.

1. Analysis of problems (gathering facts, ascertaining causes, developing alternative solutions).

2. Decision making (arriving at conclusions and judgments).

3. Communicating (ensuring understanding by employees and others).

functions   The process undertakes a number of functions which are sequential in nature.

1. Planning – predetermining a course of action. (What is needed? What should be done?)

   a. Forecasting in order to determine where the present course of action will lead.

   b. Setting objectives, i.e., determining the desired end results (goals).

   c. Developing strategies, i.e., determining how and when to achieve desired results.

   d. Programming in order to establish the priority sequence and timing of steps.

   e. Budgeting to allocate resources.

   f. Setting procedures (methods).

   g. Developing policies to assist decision making on important recurring matters. (Results in policies, procedures, methods).

2. Organizing – arranging and regulating work in order to accomplish effectively agreed upon objectives. (Where? Who?)

   a. Establishing an organizational structure and drawing up organizational charts to show formal relationships.

   b. Describing relationships (roles, in order to define liaisons which are directed toward promoting coordination of effort).

   c. Creating position descriptions in order to define the scope of the job relationships with others, as well as authority and responsibility areas.

    d. Establishing position qualifications, i.e., defining the qualifications for persons in each position (results in work division, work assignment, utilizing authority, providing work place).

3. Staffing – choosing competent people for positions in the organization (Who? How?).

    a. Selecting – recruiting and bringing qualified people into each position.

    b. Orienting – familiarizing new people (and transferred employees) with the job.

    c. Training – making all employees proficient through instruction and practice.

    d. Developing – helping improve knowledge, attitudes and skills and preparation for career advancement. (Results in personnel policies).

4. Directing – bringing about purposeful action toward the desired objectives or goals. (Getting it done.)

    a. Delegating – assigning responsibilities and accountability for results.

    b. Motivating – inspiring and persuading people to take desired actions.

    c. Coordinating – relating the efforts of employees into an effective team.

    d. Managing differences – encouraging independent thought, and managing conflicts which may arise.

    e. Managing change – stimulating creativity and innovations which are goal directed (results in administrative procedures).

5. Controlling – ensuring that progress is directed toward objectives, and according to plan (are actions according to plan?).

    a. Establishing a reporting system by determining what critical data is needed, and when and how.

    b. Determining performance standards in order to set the conditions that will exist when responsibilities have been performed satisfactorily.

    c. Measuring results – to ascertain how much deviation from goals exists in the organization.

    d. Taking corrective action by making adjustments, repeating actions, or replanning.

    e. Rewarding – praising, remunerating, and disciplining where necessary (results in quality and quantity reports, evaluations, audits).

Role of the Principal

In order for the teacher to understand his or her administrative and instructional roles, it is advisable for the teacher to understand and appreciate the roles of significant others in the educational enterprise. The basic roles of the school board and superintendent were presented in Chapter 4. The principal is the on-site administrator.

roles of significant others

The importance of the principalship in creating an effective school has always been accepted. Recently Madeline Hunter affirmed and documented the influence of the principalship.

> The principal has a unique professional obligation and opportunity in that he or she is an administrator whose primary function concerns the education of each student, but who must work through the skills of teachers. Consequently, enhancement of those teaching skills becomes the principal's primary concern. To nurture, develop and escalate instructional excellence is the single most important function of the principal . . . (Hunter, 1984, p. 183).

Sergiovani

Sergiovani has stated, "Principals are important! Indeed, no other school position has greater potential for maintaining and improving quality schools" (1987, p. 149). Lovell and Wiles (1983, p. 46) suggest that, "the focus of the supervisor's role is . . . to facilitate the release of the human potential of organizational members that makes available a more competent staff to conduct the human interaction that is called education." Thus, the task of providing supervision becomes the most important role of the principal in the revitalization of personnel toward the achievement of the instructional plan.

Lovell and Wiles

Lovell and Wiles (1983) have done much to describe and elaborate upon the responsibilities of the school principal. The list which follows is illustrative of the range of responsibilities attributed to the principal.

1. Officially designated leader.

2. Key communicator.

3. Chief instructional leader.

4. Facilities manager.

5. Facilitates staff selection, support, and facilitate professional growth.

6. Coordinates supervisory activities.

7. Communicates the system's goals and objectives.

8. Coordinates efforts to define and evaluate school goals.

9. Plans, implements and evaluates school programs.

10. Evaluates and coordinates the work of staff.

11. Facilitates change.

12. Coordinates the provision of adequate materials, equipment, and facilities.

Other lists of school principal duties look something like this.

1. Supervision of instruction.

2. Plan and implement curriculum programs.

3. Evaluate programming and seek improvement.

4. Maintain and direct public relations.

5. Plan and supervise extra-curricular activities.

6. Develop and plan the school budget.

7. Establish and maintain a good climate.

8. Involve staff in decision making.

9. Conduct regular staff meetings.

10. Ensure effective discipline.

11. Encourage in-service programs.

12. Assure adequate support staff.

13. Schedule regular supervision.

14. Welcome and orient staff.

15. Obtain substitute teachers when necessary.

A large urban school system enunciated the following sixteen responsibilities for their school principals.

Role

Under the direction of the Associate Superintendent, and within the Policies and Regulations of the Board, and the provisions of the *Alberta School Act*, the principal shall, with input from staff, students and community, direct and have total responsibility for instructional leadership and supervision of all aspects of organization, management, discipline and the safety of students and staff in the assigned school.

role

Responsibility

Within the scope and expectations of this role, the responsibilities of the principal (school administrative team) shall include the following list of activities.

responsibilities

1. Developing the philosophical base (mission) and direction for the school.

2. The planning, developing and reporting of programs that reflect provincial, system and local community expectations, and which are tailored to the specific needs of the students.

3. Promoting positive attitudes in students and staff toward self, others, school and learning.

4. The establishment of a program of staff development to ensure the growth and performance of all school-based staff.

5. The formal assessment of all school-based staff according to system expectations.

6. Involvement in determining the suitability of all school-based staff placements.

7. Deployment of school-based staff through consultation, to meet the educational needs of students.

8. Determining the administrative structure and school organization through consultation with their Superintendent and the school community.

9. Communicating the educational program to the community, seeking input from the community, representing to the greatest possible extent the aspirations of the community for its children.

10. Communicating sensitively with parents, students and staff and obtaining their support and commitment regarding the school's philosophy and direction.

11. The development of positive attitudes of parents and community toward the school, the district and its programs.

12. The planning and control of expenditures of funds both allocated and generated by the school.

13. Assessing the condition of the grounds, building and contents.

14. To have direct input and to facilitate as required *community use* of schools, in accordance with Board Policy.

15. Being concerned for the safety, welfare and conduct of students who are participating in school programs.

16. Being aware and knowledgeable of the regulations, directives and other communications issued under the authority of the Board, the Minister of Education, and making them available to staff members.

(Calgary Board of Education, 1983)

The reader's attention is drawn to Exhibit 12-1, The Principalship.

The principalship today is a complex and demanding educational leadership position made up of the responsibilities suggested and outlined in the lists previously provided. Another way of looking at the job of the chief administrator at the school level is to consider two broad bands of functions – (1) Educational administration functions, and (2) School development functions.

Performance of these functions calls forward two types of leadership.

1. Management Leadership

management leadership

Management leadership requires that principals have competence in a number of areas:

a. knowledge of the power and influence structure of the school community;

b. capacity to conceptualize the change processes useful at the school level;

c. control over the pacing and timing of school development activities;

d. access to resources and the ability to distribute them effectively;

e. ability to deploy effectively staff in support of quality educational activities;

f. skills to develop effectively the school budget and school class schedules; and

g. facilitating effective communication throughout the school, with the central office, with the community, especially the parents.

2. Instructional Leadership

instructional leadership

Instructional leadership is a many-faceted concept that combines the skills and attributes of a good leader with the ongoing instructional activities particular to a school. Leadership activities require that the principal can work effectively with others in the school setting. The principal must be proficient at: (1) team building, (2) conflict resolution, (3) motivation;, and (4) staff empowerment. Principals need to be effective in both oral and written communication as well as having a clear vision for their schools. Knowledge and understanding of curriculum and the instructional process are required. All the above requirements must be supplemented by an individual who possesses a strong commitment to education, has the physical energy to carry out the job, can analyze situations and can develop alternative solutions. Just as management and leadership work hand-in-hand, supervision, evaluation and staff

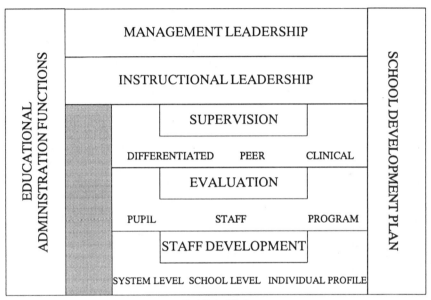

Exhibit 12-1
The Principalship

development are essential to effective instructional leadership. All three of these activities must be addressed with equal vigor by the principal and none can be forgotten. The final result will be an effective school development plan which will enhance the long-term as well as short-term educational activities for the individual school.

The reader will note that in Exhibit 12-1, The Principalship, the left band, involves teacher supervision, evaluation, and staff development. (See Chapter 14 and Exhibit 14-1 for a more complete explanation of this part of the principal's role.)

The *educational administration plan*, which is the left band of Exhibit 12-1 would follow the *design of the management process* as described at the beginning of this chapter – the ideas, things, and people of the organization.

The attention of the reader is now directed toward the common thread for both management and school development plans – leadership. Also, the matter

leadership
plan

of leadership skills is central to both the teacher's teaching activities as well as his/her administrative role.

James Olivero stated:

> Without leaders, any dream is likely to fade in and out of focus. For today's education, the principal – more than any other person – is keeper of the dream. The principal realizes upward mobility for students in the school is possible when individuals possess the skills, attitudes and knowledge that accrue from a quality education . . . (1976, p. 197)

Educational Leadership

new vision

Leaders demonstrate the skill and ability to pull others toward them by creating a *new* vision. Teachers want to be part of an organization that has a vision which is larger than reality. When a leader is able to share his or her power with others and get them committed to it, it is said their vision *engages* others.

acceptance

Effective leadership depends as much upon acceptance of directions by the followers as it does upon the leader's ability to give them. Power and influence are concepts central to the leader's job. The sources of the leader's power are summarized in the following.

1. Legitimate power. (Teachers do something because the leader has the right to request them to do it, and they have an obligation to comply.)

2. Reward power. (Teachers may do something in order to receive rewards that the leader controls – promotions, pay raises, better assignments.)

3. Coercive power. (Teachers may do something in order to avoid negative rewards – punishment.)

4. Referent power. (Teachers may do something because they admire the leader, want to be like the leader, and want the leader's approval.)

5. Expert power. (Teachers may do something because they believe the leader has special knowledge and expertise and knows what is required to accomplish the task.)

followers

Recently we have begun to realize that not only do schools need leaders who can lead, they need followers who can follow. What are the characteristics of effective followers?

1. They manage themselves well – able to think and work independently without close supervision.

2. They are committed to purposes outside themselves – a cause, a product, a work group, a calling.

3. They build their competence and focus their efforts.

4. They are courageous, honest, and credible; they are independent critical thinkers whose knowledge and judgment can be trusted.

(Stephen Robbins, *Organizational Behavior*, p. 382.)

Bennis and Manus (1985), authors of *Leaders: The Strategies for Taking* Bennis and Manus
Charge, make an interesting distinction between managers and leaders. They
describe managers as people who do things right, and leaders as people who do
the right things. They exhort their readers to manage themselves and lead others.
We join them in their exhortation.

Within the field of education, there is ample opportunity to take on a
leadership role. Being a teacher puts one in the position of being a leader since
leadership is described as the process of helping individuals and groups work
toward common goals or purposes. Many theorists and practitioners today feel
that every teacher is a leader and every leader is a teacher. The process of
leadership could be viewed as a series of activities that contribute to individual
satisfaction and group cohesiveness. Leadership allows the job to be done while
enhancing group feelings of comfort and ease. Leadership provides the setting,
the clear definition of objectives and it supports the group cooperatively
working toward these ends (Michael and Dolores Giammatteo, 1981). One
should not limit one's view of who is a leader within education to just the school
administrators and superintendents. Classroom teachers effectively fill this role
on a daily basis, not only with students but also with colleagues and parents.

One of the most striking and universal facts about groups is that they always leader
have a leader. Studies indicate that virtually all animals that live in groups
appear to have leaders (for example: cows, chickens, monkeys, wolves).
Human groups are not the exception.

Some psychologists have been interested in studying how a leader becomes
a leader, and what behaviors a leader exhibits which are different from those
of other group members. From that research, two theories regarding the
emergence of group leaders have been presented.

The first theory suggests that some individuals are *born leaders.* There is born leader
the phrase – *he is a born leader.* In other words, an individual emerges as a
leader because of some innate personal characteristics which influence his/her
behavior toward leadership activities. Proponents of this theory would suggest
that individuals like Jesus Christ, John F. Kennedy, or Joan of Arc became
leaders because of the personality characteristics they possessed. That is, these
individuals would be leaders in any situation.

The second theory of leadership suggests that individuals become leaders
because of the social situation in which they are interacting. According to this situational
leader
theory, leadership is a *role behavior,* and if individuals are required to play a
leadership role, then they become leaders (if they assume the role). If, however,
that same person is involved in a different situation and is not required to play
the leadership role, then he or she will not behave as a leader. Thus, for
proponents of this theory, leadership occurs because of the demands of a
situation, not because of certain inborn tendencies. An individual who is a
leader in one group may not be a leader in another group because of the different
types of behaviors required in the two groups. It is quite likely, therefore, that
everyone assumes a leadership role in some group (even if it is only for a short

period of time). An individual may not see himself or herself as a leader, but consider the times of interaction with younger individuals. The assumption of leadership during many of these interactions is quite likely.

Most of the recent research on leadership indicates that leaders do arise in response to the needs of a group at a particular time (situational leadership). Thus, the research tends to be more supportive of the second theory regarding leadership, i.e., leadership is a role behavior. There are some characteristics of individuals, however, which probably make them *leadership prone*. That is, some people have certain personal characteristics which make it more likely they will be accepted as a leader by the group than do some other individuals. The literature suggests the following five features are likely to make individuals *leadership prone*.

1. *Some Social Distance from Other Group Members.*
   Leaders must be objective in making group decisions. If they can maintain some social distance from the group members, it will be easier for them to maintain objectivity. Objectivity allows them to discern differences in kind and level of contribution among group members. Often this is important to the group's overall effectiveness.

2. *Acceptability to the Group.*
   The individual cannot be too *far out*. Behaviors, while they may be distinctive, will probably not be accepted by the group members if they differ substantially from the behavior of the rest of the group. For example, it is not very likely that an individual who does not share the same values or interests as his/her peers would become a leader of the peer group. They may be seen as too *traditional,* too *goody-goody*, too *freaky* – too different.

3. *Empathy and Awareness of the Needs of Others.*
   To be a leader an individual must be able to perceive and, to some degree, *feel* how other members are feeling. In order that a leader can involve everyone in the group, the leader must be able to perceive the needs and feelings of the members. This requires a certain amount of empathy on the part of the group leader.

4. *Centrality or Availability.*
   While interacting in the group, the leader will probably assume a central position. In this way, he or she can interact with (or communicate to) all of the group members with equal ease. If the leader is not available to all group members, sub-grouping (splinter-grouping) has a greater chance of developing.

5. *A Relatively High Level of Intelligence.*
   Research does not support the idea that high intelligence is necessary for leadership. In some groups a leader may be the one who is the strongest, who can drink the most, or who can tell the best jokes. On the average, however, the individual who assumes leadership usually has a relatively high degree of intelligence. This does not mean that the individual is a genius,

but at least the individual is able to evaluate group functioning and make decisions on the basis of that evaluation.

Formal and Informal Leaders

Sometimes the individual in a group who has been designated as leader was not the leader at all. In other words, there may have been an official, or *formal* leader, but that leadership was not respected or accepted by other group members. This would be an example of where an individual has been assigned or elected to the leadership role but is not able to carry out the leadership activities required by that role. Individuals occupying positions of formal leadership (chairmen, presidents, supervisors, principals) are expected to behave as a leader. If they are unable to assume the leadership role effectively, subgroups and/or informal leaders will usually arise.

formal
leader

The *informal* leader emerges not from a formal election, or a promotion to the role of leadership, but rather from the influence that the person's behavior has upon group members. Their personality and ability to make popular decisions may be more acceptable to the group than those of the formal leader. In many groups, informal leaders are supportive of the formal leader. On the other hand, they can also sabotage the plans or efforts of the formal leader (and perhaps even of the group).

informal
leader

Leadership Styles

The writers in the field usually separate leadership styles into three groupings: autocratic, laissez-faire, and democratic. Research has been conducted where the performance and member satisfaction of three groups, each having a different leadership style, were compared. The group climate varied with leadership style. Three styles of leadership were used.

1. The first style was an *autocratic* style where the leader was very authoritarian. The group structure was very rigid; individuals were told how and when to complete their tasks. There was no room for individual decisions or individual responsibility.

autocratic

2. The second style of leadership was *laissez-faire*. In this group, the leader was very non-involved. There was very little initiative taken as to what the members should do, when they should do it, or how they should do it. The leader merely indicated a task was to be done and then left the individuals on their own.

lsissez-faire

3. The third style of leadership was *democratic*. In this situation, the leader indicated the task to be done and then the group discussed the possible procedures for accomplishing it. Group members voted in order that each had a share in group decisions.

democratic

Results showed that behavior patterns in the groups varied in accordance with the kind of climate the leader created. Autocratic leadership climates produced a great deal of work-oriented behavior but there was a low degree of personal involvement on the part of the members because when the leader left the room, the members tended to abandon their tasks and to become involved in horseplay and other kinds of behavior that were not task-oriented. They also became more dependent on the leader, less able to make decisions for themselves, less able to work together cooperatively, more easily discouraged, and more inclined to behave aggressively toward weaker members of the group.

Under a democratic climate, the individuals did not work quite so hard, but they showed a higher degree of involvement in their tasks. When the leader left the room, for example, they were more likely to continue with their tasks and to resist attempts to distract them. The democratic climate also appeared to encourage a greater degree of communication and cooperation among the members, and there was no appearance of the tendencies to victimize weaker members that characterized the autocratic climate.

Under the laissez-faire leadership climate and style, morale and group output were both low and irresponsibility ran high. However, laissez-faire groups were somewhat less distractible when the leader was out of the room because task involvement had been self-initiated.

influence

The central attribute of leadership is *influence*. Whether the leadership is formal or informal, or whether the climate in which it occurs is autocratic or democratic, the leader is generally the person in the group who has the most influence upon the activities and beliefs of other members. The leader is the one who initiates action, makes decisions, makes judgments, dispenses approval or disapproval, serves as inspiration, and generally is in the forefront of any activity.

Giammatteo

Michael and Dolores Giammatteo (1981), in their monograph *Forces and Leadership*, state that leadership is both an art and a science. It is a science when we learn the scientific principles and theory supporting effective leadership and an art when we use finesse and apply theory to practice in an effective manner. Good leadership usually involves change, and change usually results in an alteration of behavior. The literature suggests that the mixture of science and art is not driven by a formula, but is frequently *situation specific*.

The following are some of the leadership skills that are important to learn and to practice.

1. Skills of Personal Behavior. The effective leader:

   a. is sensitive to feelings of the group;

   b. identifies self with the needs of the group;

   c. learns to listen attentively;

   d. refrains from criticizing or ridiculing members' suggestions;

   e. helps each member feel important and needed; and

   f. avoids arguing.

2. Skills of communication. The effective leader:

   a. makes sure that everyone understands not only what is needed but why it is needed; and

b. makes good communication interactions with the group a routine part of the job.

3. Skills in Equality. The effective leader recognizes that:

a. everyone is important;

b. leadership is to be shared and is not a monopoly; and that

c. leadership improves when leadership functions are dispersed.

4. Skills of Organization. The effective leader helps the group:

a. develop long-range and short-range objectives;

b. break big problems into small ones:

c. share opportunities and responsibilities; and

d. plan, act, follow up, and evaluate.

5. Skill of Self Examination. The effective leader:

a. is aware of motivations that guide actions;

b. is aware of members' feelings of hostility and tolerance so that appropriate counter-measures are taken;

c. is aware of their fact-finding behavior; and

d. helps the group to become aware of their own strengths, attitudes, and values.

Hersey and Blanchard (1988), in their text *Management of Organizational Behavior: Utilizing Human Resources*, differentiate between leadership and management. They feel that *leadership* is a much more all-encompassing concept than is *management*. Management is action that directs its attention toward achieving organization goals. Leadership, on the other hand, attempts to influence individual and group behavior. The resultant action may not necessarily be directed toward the achievement of organization goals, it may be directed toward personal goals.

Hersey and Blanchard

There are four levels of change we must be aware of when providing leadership.

1. Knowledge Changes – this type of change takes minimal time and minimal effort.

2. Attitudinal changes – change in this area takes a little more time and more effort than when we are dealing with knowledge change.

3. Behavior Changes – changes in this area take extensive time and effort when compared to attitudinal and knowledge changes.

4. Group or Organizational Performance Changes – take maximum time and effort.

Our ability to lead effectively could be influenced by our understanding of how individuals in groups react to these four levels of change. Indeed it is much easier and involves less time to impact new knowledge than it is to alter group behavior.

Theory X	Theory Y
1. The average human being has an inherent dislike of work and will avoid it, if possible.	1. The expenditure of physical and mental effort in work is as natural as play or rest and commitment to objectives is a function of the rewards associated with their achievement.
2. Because of these human characteristics (dislike of work) most people must be coerced, controlled, directed, and threatened with punishment to get them to put forth adequate effort toward the achievement of organization objectives.	2. People will exercise self-direction and self-control in attainment of objectives to which they are committed.
3. The average human being prefers to be directed, wishes to avoid responsibility, has relatively little ambition, and wants security above all else.	3. The average person under the proper conditions learns to accept and seek responsibility.
4. The capacity to exercise a high degree of imagination, ingenuity, and creativity in the solution of organizational problems is narrowly distributed within the working population.	4. The capacity to exercise a high degree of imagination, ingenuity, and creativity in the solution of organizational problems is widely distributed within the working population.
5. The intellectual potential of the worker is only partially utilized and cannot be enhanced.	5. Under the conditions of modern organizational life, the intellectual potentialities of the average person are only partially utilized but through effective leadership this situation can be effectively addressed. (McGregor, 1960)

Exhibit 12-2
Theory X and Theory Y

McGregor

Douglas McGregor (1960) became concerned about the traditional management view of the worker. Management felt that employees were not motivated to achieve and that they required direction. As a result, organizations were structured in such a way as to centralize the control in the hands of the management. Workers had little or no say in the direction of their lives. McGregor felt that managers/leaders needed to structure their organizations around more up-to-date and accurate research in regard to motivation and human nature. As a result, McGregor developed a continuum of assumptions about the human nature of employees. Theory X describes the end of the continuum which viewed people as requiring strong direction and centralized control. The Theory Y assumption supported giving more control to the worker through decentralization because most people, when properly motivated, are self-directed and motivated to achieve. If indeed there is a continuum moving from Theory X to Theory Y, then it is possible that individual manager's/leader's views on what makes workers work effectively will fall at varying points along that continuum depending on the leader's understanding and beliefs about human nature.

Theory X

Theory Y

Theory Z by William Ouchi (1981) suggests that much could be learned from studying Japanese management styles. In his book Ouchi builds upon the concepts developed by McGregor to stress that leadership should be found at all locations within the organization (business), and that leadership is based upon the use of influences in a *trusting* relationship. If judicially used, leadership results in a commitment of energy and loyalty. Ouchi stresses that performance levels are limited only by the composite capacity of the work group. The three key factors in Theory Z are trust, subtlety (organization and individual values and objectives are openly discussed and decisions are considered against them), and intimacy, wherein feelings have a value and a place in the organization.

Theory Z

As the job of providing leadership became more complex, so did the ways of viewing leadership as a process as well as an activity. Blake and Mouton (1964) developed the *Managerial Grid* which provided a way of looking at the relationship between concern for people and concern for production (see Exhibit 12-3).

managerial grid

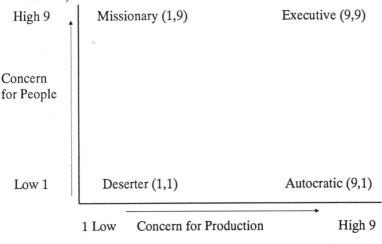

Exhibit 12-3
Management Styles

Blake and Moutan

<table>
<tr><td>Blake and
Mouton</td><td>

Blake and Mouton placed a value on each managerial style and suggested that the *executive type* was the most effective style. The *autocratic type* of leader is highly production-oriented while the *missionary type* is very people-oriented. The 1/9 Type could also be referred to as *country club* management. The *compromiser type* is the manager who will try to maintain a balanced style and live with the status quo. The *deserter type* is considered by Blake and Moutan to be the least effective leadership style that one could utilize. The 1/1 Type has also been referred to as the *impoverished* style of leadership.

</td></tr>
<tr><td>Hersey and
Blanchard</td><td>

Hersey and Blanchard have subsequently extended the Managerial Grid along a third dimension and have removed any inference of a value being given to any of the management/leadership styles. They now believe that at the appropriate time and under the right conditions any one of their four leadership styles should be utilized. Some types of leadership previously thought to be desirable may prove to be dysfunctional in certain situations. The original plan highlighted certain principles, but these principles are now considered to lack universality.

</td></tr>
<tr><td>zone of
tolerance</td><td>

Some individuals and groups at a particular point in their work life require strong direction and less concern for human relations, i.e., their *zone of tolerance* has shifted. This situation usually occurs early in the change process. As individuals or groups become more knowledgeable about the situation, more concern for relationship can occur. As individuals and groups continue to mature gradually, the leader can be less concerned with the task and concentrate more fully upon relationships. Since this is a developmental process, the leader may eventually withdraw concern for both relationship and task because the individual or group is now ready to operate on their own for a period of time.

</td></tr>
</table>

In general terms:

A leader knows who he/she is. The process of reflection, study and constant thinking about the experiences of leadership and the building of a theoretical base of leadership give the reflective leader a reservoir of insights directed toward the leadership challenge. Leaders have a *foundation* (emotional, intellectual, spiritual) that gives them the *presence* leadership demands.

A leader does not see the practical world of work and professional interaction in absolute terms. Flexibility is part of the leader's makeup; yet, where matters concerning professional ethics and group goals are concerned, the leader will stand on principle.

Leadership is communication. A leader must constantly be in the flow of organizational communication and thus part of the constant process of discussion, dialogue, and decision making. The leader cannot remain apart from this process.

A leader knows that delegation is essential. The leader cannot do everything. However, leadership, either formal or informal, must exist at key points in the group's activities.

A leader is an excellent listener. Leaders must be aware of the common listening problems. Leaders listen for more than words. They remember the words of Carl Rogers: "If I can listen to what he tells me, if I can understand how it seems to him, if I can sense the emotional flavor which it has for him, then I will be releasing potent forces of change within him."

Leaders know that sincere and ongoing dialogue is at the heart of the resolution of most problems; sincere dialogue results in the best planning.

A leader knows that, generally, people do not always trust each other especially in situations where serious problems are to be dealt with. It is in the handling of the situation that leadership skills are tested.

Conflict, disagreement and argument are part of the group process, at least to some degree; once a climate of open, honest, non-competitive communication is established, the best strategy is to have all conflict and disagreements explicit (see Theory Z).

A leader understands that abusive power has no place in the collegial environment.

A leader understands Maslow's basic principles (individual needs hierarchy), never forgetting, however, that each individual is unique and thus has unique personal needs as well.

A leader understands that the use of anger is destructive. Great joy and emotion may be shown. Anger should never be displayed publicly

A leader is not self-serving.

A leader must be able to make decisions. Even when leaders see the decision making process as a collegial one, group members know and accept that leaders will have to make some decisions in isolation.

A leader knows that any matter of personal evaluation must be dealt with in a sensitive, professional manner. Clear criteria must be established. Confidentiality must be observed. Individuals who are being evaluated must know and feel that they are part of the evaluation process.

Leaders articulate what is expected from the group and its members.

Any leader in an educational supervisory/administrative capacity must first focus on a teacher's strengths before working toward a developmental process that accentuates even the smallest weakness.

A leader understands that timing is an essential aspect of working with individuals who may need developmental assistance. Where intervention is necessary, every care must be taken to ensure that the group or person is *ready* to be helped. Diplomacy – careful, sensitive intervention – is an essential part of the leader's work.

A leader must develop a system of organization that helps manage his or her group's work more easily and more effectively.

A leader is honest and ethical.

A leader understands the value of the personal involvement and of group pressure.

A leader understands that humor is an essential part of life.

A leader is an excellent teacher.

The leader knows that change is a gradual process, not a quickly-realized product.

A leader helps group members form a complete perspective (mental picture) thereby preventing them from drawing rash conclusions or leaping to premature decisions.

A leader knows how to bring out an individual's feelings so that issues can be approached in a more objective manner.

A leader takes the initiative to change the essential nature of group relationships.

A leader must not make assumptions that there is but one appropriate or correct format for what constitutes good achievement.

A leader must not pass judgment on any issue too early.

A leader helps others to make choices for themselves; wherever possible, he/she resists the temptation to tell others what to do.

Summary

requirements

In summary, evidence indicates that effective school administrators (principals, vice principals, department heads, team leaders) in addition to possessing a clear understanding of the requirements for leadership and appropriate leadership styles, tend to be actively involved in their school's instructional program in a number of ways. Specifically they:

a. become knowledgeable about instruction, especially in relation to basic skills;

b. set clear goals for the school's instructional program and announce these goals to students, teachers, and community;

c. set high expectations for the behavior and achievement of students;

d. emphasize the importance of basic skills;

e. set expectations for collegiality and continuous improvement;

f. participate with teachers in staff development activities;

g. use sanctions advisedly and only to further school goals;

h. buffer the staff from undue pressures, either community or central office;

i. insist upon giving priority to instructional concerns by, for example, concentrating time and effort on instructional time, and effort on instructional matters, and delegating to others as many non-instructional tasks as possible; and

j. make instruction and its improvement the central concern of the school.

School administrators are expected by their staffs to display the following ompetencies competencies in order that they can foster an appropriate learning environment.

1. A thorough knowledge of students' growth and development patterns.

2. A knowledge and ability to put into practice, or help others put into practice, effective classroom management techniques.

3. A knowledge of learning theories and practices.

4. A knowledge of subject matter to such a degree that he/she can assist, or find others to assist, teachers in organizing content for the most effective instruction.

5. An ability to observe in classrooms and provide constructive help and support to the teaching staff.

6. An ability to evaluate staff performance in a responsible and reliable manner.

7. A knowledge of pertinent legal and fiscal matters that will permit himself or herself to expedite school decisions.

8. A knowledge of where to find answers or people to assist with all educational tasks.

Coach P. Bryant of college football fame is reported to have said:

> If anything goes bad, I did it. If anything goes semi-good, then we did it. If anything goes real good, then you did it. That's all it takes to get people to win football games for you.

Some Concepts
Basic to Administration

Some schools work and more can.
                R.R. Edmonds, *Social Policy*, 1979

Decision Making
Strategic Planning
Mediating Conflict
Line and Staff
Useful Management Terms
Effective Schools
Communication
Values
School climate
Innovation
Mandated Change
Ethics
Trust
Administrative Monitoring

Introduction

The previous chapter presented a brief summary of some of the literature respecting the management and leadership roles of the school principal. This chapter will bring together, perhaps in a more isolated and less holistic fashion than desirable, a number of concepts and ideas which impinge directly upon the efficiency and effectiveness of the teacher in his or her administrative role and duties within the context of the school environment. Selections have had to be made, and of course the content has been summarized severely. What is hoped for is that the reader will sense the importance of these concepts and consider future study of them as part of a personal development plan.

personal development plan

Decision Making

Decision making is a pivotal process in the life of the school. Who does it and how it is done will determine the way teachers perceive the school environment. Some principals and department heads look upon their jobs as the centre of all decision making in their area of responsibility. They seem to think that failing to make each and every decision amounts to shrinking from their administrative responsibilities. The classroom analogy is obvious. But, as in the classroom, this is not the way that decisions are reached in most schools. The teacher has a principle role in the decision making process, especially respecting the instructional program.

group
decisiion

The participation of group members in setting goals and reaching decisions has been extensively researched, and the overwhelming conclusion is that decisions made by the group are more effective than decisions made external to the group. Status leaders such as principals may sometimes believe, or indeed possess, superior knowledge; however the leader's decision is not likely to be effective, until the *decision* becomes a group decision. Participation increases the rate of output and the quality of the product. However, if time is of the essence, unilateral decision making is quicker. Obviously some types of decisions do not merit or require group decision making activities.

The literature on decision making is extensive since the process is central to the administration of an organization.

1. The Classical Models. (Optimizing Strategy)

optimizing

These models direct their efforts toward complete rationality. They employ what is called the *optimizing* strategy because they seek the best possible alternative in order to realize the achievement of goals and objectives. The process looks like this:

a. a problem is identified;
b. goals/objectives are formulated;
c. *all* possible alternatives are generated;
d. the consequence of each alternative is studied;
e. all alternatives are evaluated in terms of goal/objective attainment;
f. the *best* alternative is selected; and finally
g. the decision is implemented and evaluated.

end-means
analysis

Decision making is an end-means analysis. First the ends are established and then the means to achieve them are sought. There tends to be a heavy reliance on theory and policy.

2. Administrative Model. (Satisficing Strategy)

This model rests upon the following assumptions (Hay and Miskel, pp. 317-320):

a. decision making is a cycle of events which include identification and diagnosis of a difficulty, the *reflective* development of a plan, the initiation of the plan and the evaluation of its success;

b. *administration* is the performance of the decision making process (individual or group) within the organizational context;

c. complete rationality is impossible, therefore the administrator or group seeks an acceptable solution (satisfice) because they lack full knowledge, ability, or capacity to maximize the process;

d. the basic administrative function is to provide each subordinate with a suitable *internal* environment (within the organization) for as much personal and organizational rationality as possible;

e. the decision making process becomes a generalized pattern for action for all major functional and task areas – for example, curriculum development, assignment of physical facilities, student personnel policies, and public relations; and

f. the decision making process happens in substantially the same generalized format each time; recognition and definition of problems, analysis of the difficulties (classify problems, collect data, specify problem), establish the criteria for problem solution, develop a plan or strategy (probable alternatives – possible consequences – deliberation – selection of course of action), and initiate the plan (program steps – communicate – monitor and appraise).

3. The Incremental Model. (Successive Limited comparisons).

Charles Lindblom, in a paper entitled *The Science of Muddling Through* (Hoy & Miskel, pp. 329-332), first introduced the incremental model as the only feasible approach. The process is based upon the successive limited comparisons of possible alternatives in order to find the best outcome. He contended that when dealing with a complex problem there exists only a narrow range of existing similar situations for comparison. Setting objectives and generating alternatives are intertwined. Means and ends are not separable as assumed in other models, thus the means-ends analysis is not appropriate. The test of a good decision is when the decision makers can agree upon an alternative without having to agree that it is the *best* decision. The focus is upon alternatives similar to the existing state, so many alternatives may be ignored. There is, because of the limited range, little need for decision making theories.

incremental model

best decision

4. Conflict Theory

This theory, also called the Janis-Mann Model, identifies five patterns for coping with stress which is often the antecedent of a decision. Hoy and Miskell (p. 322) state:

Janis-Mann Model

> There is no question that errors in decision making are a result of many causes, including poor analysis, ignorance, bias, impulsiveness, time constraints, and organizational policies. But another major reason for many poorly conceived and implemented decisions is related to the motivational consequences of conflict – in particular, attempts to overcome stress produced by extremely difficult choices on vital decisions.

Janis and Mann describe five basic *coping* mechanisms employed by decision makers. These are:

coping mechanisms

a. conflicted adherence – decision maker ignores information and continues;

b. unconflicted change – decision maker uncritically accepts the most salient or popular course of action;

c. defensive avoidance – decision maker evades conflict by procrastinating or shifting responsibility elsewhere;

d. hypervigilance – decision maker panics and searches frantically, vacillates between alternatives, and then seizes upon a hastily-formulated decision; and

e. vigilance – the decision maker searches carefully and reflects upon the alternatives before making a decision.

5. Who to Involve?

zone of acceptance

Since decisions are not made in isolation, the question of when to involve teachers becomes critical to the administrator and to the teacher. Studies by Edwin Bridges and others (Hoy & Miskel, pp. 338-344) formulated the concept of the *zone of acceptance* in order to attempt an answer to the question stated above. He postulated that when the administrator involves teachers in decisions within the teacher's zone of acceptance, participation will be low and less effective. (Zone of acceptance refers to the willingness of the teacher to accept the directives of the principal.) There are three basic categories of zones:

a. organizational maintenance – administrative routine;

b. personal – very personal or that have little relevance for the organization; and

c. professional – dealing with school issues which call for professional judgment.

two tests

It is quite obvious in which zone teachers are least likely to accept the directives of the school principal or senior administrators. Bridges proposed two tests that were useful in defining what decisions would fall within, and which without, the teachers' zone of acceptance. The two tests were:

a. the test of relevance, i.e., Do the subordinates have a *high personal stake in the decision?* and

b. the test of expertise, i.e., To what extent are the teachers *qualified* to make useful contributions to the decision making process?

shared decision making

When the teachers believe they have a high personal stake and the knowledge base to make a useful contribution, they are less likely to accept administrative directives. The following quotations from the works of Hoy and Miskel are based upon the research of Victor Vroom and Arthur Yetton (1973), and serve to provide a good summary of the process of shared decision making.

1. Keep the model simple. If subordinates have a personal stake (high relevance) in the decision and have the requisite knowledge to make a useful contribution (high expertise), then the decision clearly falls outside of their zone of acceptance, and subordinates should be involved in the decision making process.

2. Hoy and Miskel (p. 339) also note that the involvement of teachers in decision making which falls within the teacher's zone of acceptance (of directives) will likely produce resentment (wasting my time).

The following three sets of rules, enunciated by Victor Vroom and Phillip Yetton (1973) provide excellent advice to teachers and principals involved in, or considering, shared decision making.

Victor Vroom
Phillip Yetton

The quality can be enhanced by following the rules listed below.

1. *The information rule.* If the quality of the decision is important and if the superior does not possess sufficient information and expertise to solve the problem alone, then a unilateral decision is inappropriate; in fact, its use risks a low-quality decision.

2. *The trust rule.* If the quality of the decision is important and if the subordinates cannot be trusted to decide on the basis of the organizational goals, then decision through group consensus is inappropriate. Indeed, the superior's lack of control over the decision may jeopardize its quality.

3. *The unstructured problem rule.* Given an important decision, if the superior lacks information or expertise and if the problem is unstructured, then the method chosen to solve the problem should include sufficient procedures for collecting information. The participation of knowledgeable subordinates should improve the quality of the decision.

(Hoy & Miskel, pp. 344-345)

To enhance acceptance the following rules are appropriate.

1. *The acceptance rule.* If subordinate acceptance of the decision is critical for effective implementation and if it is not certain that an autocratic decision would be accepted, then some sharing of the situation and participation of others are necessary. To deny any participation in the decision making risks the necessary acceptance.

acceptance
rule

2. *The conflict rule.* If acceptance of the decision is critical and if an autocratic decision is not certain to be accepted, then the decision making process should be structured to enable those in disagreement to resolve their differences with full knowledge of the problem. Thus group participation is necessary; all subordinates would have an opportunity to resolve any differences.

conflict rule

3. *The fairness rule.* If the quality of the decision is not important, but its acceptance is critical and problematic, then a group decision should be made. A group decision will likely generate more acceptance and commitment than a hierarchical one.

fairness
rule

4. *The acceptance priority rule.* If acceptance is critical, not assured by an autocratic decision, and if subordinates can be trusted, only group decision making is appropriate. Any other method provides the unnecessary risk that the decision will not be fully accepted or receive the necessary subordinate commitment.

acceptance
priority rule

(Hoy and Miskel, p. 345)

Strategic Planning

Peter Druker   In the mid 1950s Peter Druker, one of the leading writers in administrative literature noted that:

> Only a clear definition of the mission and purpose of the business makes possible clear and realistic objectives . . . Strategy determines what the key activities are and strategy requires knowing what our business is, and what it should be.

strategic planning   Strategic planning involves:

a. decisions made by top administration (for the teacher these are the school principal and often the central office staff);

b. allocating large amounts of resources – money, labor (for the school, this would mean the entire effort of the school – teachers, support staff, material and equipment resources, etc.);

c. planning which has a significant long term impact; and

d. focusing on the organization's interaction with the external environment (for the school, usually the first visible manifestations of strategic planning is the school's mission statement – a statement of what the school intends to do.)

The literature suggests there are two areas of advantage to strategic planning. First, it improves performance and second it brings with it a number of behavioral benefits.

1. Strategic planning should enhance the problem-prevention capabilities of the school, for example. Because it is planning oriented, the staff pay attention to planning. Problems tend to be identified earlier, and thus the school principal is in a position to initiate problem solution actions.

2. Group based decisions are almost always better able to consider the available alternatives.

3. Teacher motivation improves when they are able to participate in developing a plan.

4. Participation in strategic planning activities points to gaps and overlaps because it is *responsibility* oriented.

5. Resistance to change is reduced because uncertainty is reduced respecting the personal ramifications of the plan. Future consequences of today's decisions and actions are better understood.

components   There are six components to the strategic planning process (see Exhibit 13-2).

mission statement   The mission statement for the school is a clear and concise expression of purpose, function, and uniqueness in its services to students and community. It identifies the school's reason for existence. Six helpful questions are presented.

1. Who are we?

2. In general, what are the basic social and political needs we exist to fulfill?

3. In general, how do we want to respond to these needs?

4. How should we respond to our key shareholders?

5. What is our philosophy, and what are our core values?

6. What makes us distinctive or unique?

Strategic Planning Involves:	Strategic Implementation Involves:
a. defining the school's mission;	e. implementing the strategy;
b. establishing objectives;	f. follow-up and evaluation.
c. identifying strategic alternatives;	
d. formulating a strategy;	

Exhibit 13-2
Strategic Planning Process

While the mission statement acknowledges reality and also aspires toward the ideal, it forms the basis for the entire plan – the other five parts enunciated follow. School mission statements are usually clearly displayed on banners, on school stationery, and are included in school newsletters and other school-based publications. The goal is to have every student, teacher, secretary, caretaker, and parent know and accept the mission statement.

Exhibit 13-3 presents a framework for viewing the strategic planning process.

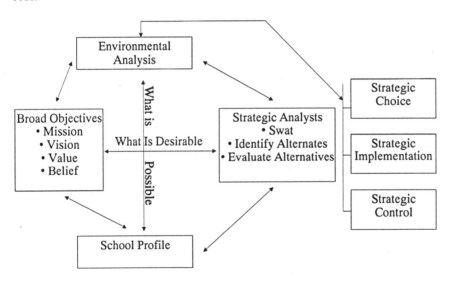

Exhibit 13-3
A Framework for the Strategic Planning Process

Mission has been defined earlier in this section.

vision
statement

Vision is a statement of what might be, what could be. It is a description of the future, not as it is, but what it could be. The vision statement of the school staff is a description of what the mission statement would be like when it is put into action. It describes the chosen future. Warren Bennis in *The Principalship*, p. 107, notes that, "Compelling vision is the key ingredient of leadership among heads of highly successful organization." The path finding function of the vision is very important.

core value
statement

Core value statements refer to what is regarded as being intrinsically desirable. Core values are the principles that determine our beliefs. They are the ideals toward which we strive. A core value has a richness of meaning based upon the past, cast into a promise and potential for the future. Successful schools, for example, usually have only a few key values and teachers are given room to set goals which support these values. Teachers are urged to remember that too many goals lead to confusion and lack of success in most instances.

Beliefs drawn from the core values are the states of mind or habits in which confidence or reliance is placed. Commonly held beliefs are the same as a school's vision from which goals, planning instruction and evaluation practices are derived.

environmental
analysis

Environmental analysis refers to the systematic assessment of information about the school's external environment – especially major threats, problems or other impediments and challenges.

school
profile

The *school profile* refers to a careful assessment of the school's resources and skills. Thoughtful matching of the school's profile with the environmental analysis generates appropriate strategic options.

Strategic analysis refers to that point where the school personnel (sometimes selected parents) have completed the environmental analysis and school profile and are now in a position to make decisions. This phase consists of the following.

1. SWOT, an acronym for identifying strengths, weaknesses, opportunities, and threats.

2. Identifying strategic alternatives. The first step is to look at existing strategies and perform what is called *gap analysis*. Here the school team determines

gap
analysis

whether a *gap* exists between their existing strategy and what they realistically could expect to accomplish. If there is no gap, the current strategy is appropriate. Where serious gaps exist, the team concentrates upon identifying promising alternatives for closing the gap.

The next stage of the strategic planning process is the point where the team applies the following four criteria in order to systematically select option. These criteria are often enunciated in the form of questions.

1. Is the option compatible with our broad objectives, purpose, value, mission, or will it necessitate a major departure from current practices?

2. Does the option focus upon and exploit key opportunities?

3. Does the option take advantage of our internal strengths, and minimize our weaknesses (deficits)?

4. Is this option realistic in the light of the above? Will it work?

When the new strategy has been incorporated into the daily activities of the school, the implementation phase has been achieved. This will require the development of short-term plans to provide immediate guidelines. Also, short-term objectives must be developed for each part (program) of the school.

Strategic Control requires the principal (or team) to monitor changes – gap reductions. Critical milestones, critical stages are points for control. Three questions are central. First, is the strategy being implemented as planned? Second, are the critical assumptions upon which the strategy was based, still valid? Third, is the strategy achieving the desired results?

monitor changes

Conflict

Most writers in the area of organizational management conclude that in organizations where there is little disagreement, the organization will fail in competitive environments. Members are often either too homogeneous and therefore ill equipped to adapt, or they are too complacent to see the need to improve (Whetton & Cameron). Also, school administrators, for example, often view interpersonal conflict as being the result of personality defects – the *trouble-makers*, the *bad apples*. The way to handle the situation is to dismiss or transfer the offending individuals. Again, most writers in organization theory conclude these actions are taken in error.

The exhibit which follows sets forward the four most common sources of interpersonal conflict, and suggests where the focus of the conflict will be. In one's daily role as a teacher, the ability to mediate conflict not only in the classroom, but also in the staffroom, in person to person interactions, and at formal meetings becomes an extremely important function.

interpersonal conflict

Sources of Conflict	*Focus of Conflict*
1. Environmental stress	Resource scarcity and/or uncertainty
2. Information deficiency	Misinformation and misrepresentation
3. Personal differences	Perceptions and expectations
4. Role incompatability	Goals and responsibilities

Exhibit 13-4
Sources, and Focus of Conflict

Environmental stress, especially when enduced by tight budgets, can lead to disputes over resource requests, lowering of trust, increased egocentrism, and often reduced participation – ideal incubators for interpersonal conflict. Uncer-

environmental stress

tain environments also foster conflict. This is especially true when co-workers are experieincing difficulty in predicting what is going to happen. Often this state, frustration/conflict, arises from rapid changes in task assignments, school philosophy, lines of authority, and procedures for increasing accountability. This type of conflict, although intensive, dissipates quickly when the changes become routinized. Information (misinformation, misrepresentation) deficiencies lead to interpersonal conflict which is less emotional than other sources of conflict since they tend to be more factual. Rewording messages, reconciling contradictory data, or redistributing lost messages are usually sufficient to ameliorate the problem.

personal
differences

Since educators bring different backgrounds to their roles in the educational enterprise, personal differences types of conflict may result if not managed carefully. Values and needs are shaped by socialization processes which are dependent upon cultural and family traditions, breadth of experience, level of education, which in turn influence interpretations of events and expectations about relationships with others (perceptions and expectations). Differences can become highly emotional and often take on moral overtones. Disagreements can easily become bitter arguments over what is *morally* right. Left wing – right wing, liberal – conservative, ethnic, color and gender-based conflict are to be found in this source of conflict.

incompatible
roles

A potential source of conflict within the education setting results from a setting in which tasks are interdependant but roles can be incompatible. The classic example is the frequent conflict between administration and teachers. Both groups frequently have different responsibilities and different priorities. This potential for conflict, placed in the current setting of scarcity of resources, can result in heightened tensions. Often mediation by a common superior (the superintendent, for example), is required to achieve resolution. Survival of the school depends upon the interdependance of roles. Interdependency can be the trigger. Lack of agreement on goals and responsibilities will be the cause.

basic
approaches

Ruble and Thomas (*Organizational Behavior and Human Performance,* 1976) state there are five basic approaches to managing conflict.

1. Forcing. A person predominates by stating *what's right.* The person believes that it is better to cause a few hard feelings than to abandon the issues to which commitments have been made.

2. Avoiding. The objective is to avoid the conflict situation, usually by stating, "I'm neutral on that issue." It is believed disagreements are inherently bad, or at least not worth the effort because they create tension.

3. Compromising. This is reading an agreement quickly. The conversation goes something like this, "Lets search for a solution we both can live with, and get on with our work." It is believed that conflict, at least prolonged conflict, distracts people from their work and creates bitterness.

4. Accommodating. The attitude is to not upset others. The basic position is that the incumbent's position is not sufficiently important to risk bad feelings. Maintaining harmony is the goal.

5. Collaborating. This is solving the problem together. "This is my position, what is yours?" "What do the data suggest?" Collaborating requires that the position of both parties are accepted as equally important, but not necessarily equally valued. Fairness in the decision making process is essential. Some appropriate strategies include:

a. establishing superordinate goals;

b. separating people from the problem;

c. focusing on interests, not positions;

d. inventing options for mutual gain;

e. using objective criteria; and

f. defining success in terms of gains, not losses.

Conflict is a difficult topic to face. Our culture gives the term negative connotations, and places a high value upon getting along with others and being kind. Teachers understand intellectually the value of conflict but they frequently feel uncomfortable when confronted with it. Much of the discomfort results from a lack of understanding of the process and a lack of training in ways to handle interpersonal conflict. There exists a substantial literature on this topic. Perhaps as part of personal self-supervision and self-development, activities can be undertaken to further exploration of the topic. negaative connotations

The following *rule of thumb* list of advice is presented in summary.

1. Collect information at the source of the conflict. Four sources are suggested in the previous exhibit.

2. Utilize the collaborative approach.

3. Use the *forcing* approach only when the issue is *extremely* important or where a high sense of urgency exists.

4. Use the accommodating approach only when the issue is not as important, or where a close on-going relationship with the other party is critical.

5. Use the compromise approach in issues which are very complex and of moderate importance to both parties.

6. Use the avoiding approach only when the issue is not important, the relationship is not critical, and time is not a factor.

Conflict Mediation

In summary, the advice most often given to those who are involved in mediating conflict are contained in the following five suggestions.

1. Acknowledge the conflict exists, select an apppropriate setting (one-on-one, small group, etc.) for coaching and fact finding, and propose a problem solving approach.

2. Maintain a neutral posture. Become a facilitator, not a judge. Do not belittle the problem or berate the parties. Be impartial. If correction is necessary, do it in private.

3. Manage the discussion to ensure that fairness exists. Focus the issue. Keep the discussion issue oriented, not personality oriented. Do not permit some to dominate the discussion. Use a direct questioning approach.

4. Explore options by focusing on issues behind the stated positions. Explore the "whys?" Help parties see commonalities and use these commonalities to generate alternatives. In this maintain a non-judgmental manner.

5. Ensure that all parties support the agreed-upon solution. Verify understandings of, and committment to, specific actions. Establish a mechanism for follow-up. (See also p. 255)

Line and Staff

line
position

staff
position

A useful distinction can be made with respect to the various positions within the educational organization on the basis of the terms *line position* and *staff position*. In simple terms line officials have formal authority to commit resources and are held responsible to implement actions. They have direct authority over the organization's primary output; they are in charge of the organization's decisions. Power, authority, and responsibility are directly delegated from the *superordinate* governing level. Power comes from above and reporting is made to the superior (directly above) level. On the other hand, staff positions furnish specialized and/or technical advice to the appropriate line officials. Staff authority resides in the specialized knowledge or skills which individuals possess.

The reader's attention is drawn to the organizational chart of a typical school district (page 80). Although the difference between line and staff positions is not as easy to distinguish in practice as it is in theory, the appropriate responses to be made by a teacher will vary, in part, upon the basis of the *line* and *staff* position of other members of the organization to whom the response is directed.

In exhibit 4-1 the line relationship emanates from the school board to the superintendent (as chief executive officer), to the school principals, to department heads, and then to the teachers. Formal communications (downward and upward), formal reporting channels and accountability will follow the alignment of line relationships. In the exhibit, examples of staff (advisory) positions would be found in the assistant superintendents who assist the superintendent in carrying forward the range of chief executive officer duties; and in the business manager (treasurer, superintendent of finance) who assist with budgeting, payroll, purchasing and the full range of treasurer duties. Supervisors in areas such as special services, curriculum, and transportation provide knowledgeable advice to the superintendents and sometimes to school principals. At the principalship level, individuals such as vice-principals, secretaries, custodians, advise the principal on policy decisions and carry out important in-school functions. Staff officers report to the appropriate line officer rather than to the superordinate body.

Formal organizational charts such as exhibit 4-1 however, rarely describe the full story. At other points in the text, mention has been made about informal groups and informal communication channels. Some writers use a system of overlays placed upon the official (formal) organizational chart to indicate that a fuller description of the organization can be obtained, for example, by placing an overlay of informal communication patterns to describe who actually talks to whom, a sociological overlay to depict who visits with whom, and a power overlay to describe who actually holds the power, i.e., who can get things done? These may not be obvious at first, but careful observations over time will permit the teacher to more fully understand how things are *actually* done "around here." formal organizational charts

Some Useful Management Terms

1. *Single Executive.* Within Canadian school jurisdictions there exists a difference of opinion as to whether a single executive or a dual executive structure is most advantageous. The single executive structure sees the superintendent, as chief executive officer, reporting directly to the school board on behalf of the total enterprise. The dual structure on the other hand has the school superintendent and the chief business officer (usually the secretary treasurer) holding positions of equal rank, with the superintendent reporting on and administering the educational enterprise and the business officer reporting on and administering the business/financial segment of the school board's business. Counties which combined educational and municipal functions in one structure often experience problems with acceptance of their unique structure by educators; when the school superintendent is named chief *education* officer; the assistant manager of the county as the chief *municipal* officer with both officials reporting to the county Manager who is then held accountable to the County Council for the overall administration of the county. In this plan, the county manager (almost always not an educator) is named chief executive officer. In the former illustration the coordination necessary for goal achievement is performed by an educator; in the latter the coordination is performed by (with very few exceptions) a business manager. single-dual executive

2. *Unity of Purpose.* This administrative term refers to the necessity for clearly defined goals and purposes in order to eliminate the debilitating effects upon the organization brought about by conflicting objectives and by personal conflicts between and among operatives. School-level mission or goal statements usually serve this purpose within the school setting.

3. *Unity of Command.* The effectiveness of the school organization is enhanced when every person in the organization knows to whom he/she is responsible. Numerous problems are created when workers are called upon to serve *two* or more masters. The school teacher reports to the school principal (department head). The school handbook should state this clearly.

MBWA

4. *MBWA* (Management by Walking Around). Sometimes this phenomenon is called *visible management* or *hands on management*. Sergiovanni calls it informal supervision. The essential features are that it helps teachers to stay in touch with students, or principals to stay in touch with teachers and students. It is generally concluded that MBWA serves at least five purposes.

1. The management becomes accessible.

2. The management is able to keep people informed.

3. The management can model the vision.

4. It builds rapport.

5. It is fun and it reduces stress.

span of
control

4. *Span of Control.* This principle of administrative theory states that an administrator should not be assigned to a greater number of persons than he or she can effectively supervise. There is extensive literature on the topic, but in general, the principle often leads to a heightening of the organizational pyramid on one hand, or, on the other hand, to a situation where effective supervision is hampered by excessive numbers of persons to be supervised. Often in professional-dominated organizations the span is exceeded either in order to reduce the direct impact of the supervisor, or in order to cause the first line workers (teachers) to become more independent, and less dependent upon control by principals, department heads, or other supervisory personnel within the district.

Effective Schools

effective
schools

Of the number of *movements* which have swept through the educational milieu, the effective schools movement has had a considerable impact upon Canadian schools at all levels, but especially at the secondary school level. The movement began more or less simultaneously in Britain and the United States, especially with the work of Rutter and his colleagues in England, and with scholars such as Edmonds and Goodlad, in the U.S. This short section will deal only with the British study done by Rutter, Maughan, Mortimore, and Ouston entitled *Fifteen Thousand Hours* (1979).

Observers concerned with the London, England school system noted a number of unfavorable characteristics about the system, a school jurisdiction which incidentally enjoyed a good level of educational financing.

First, secondary schools in inner London differed markedly in the behavior and educational attainments shown by their pupils. The evidence was found in the children's behavior while in school (reported by teachers and pupils themselves); the regularity of pupil attendance; the proportions of students staying in school beyond legal age requirements; the rate of student success on *public* examinations; and their rate of delinquency behavior. Second, although the schools differed in the proportion of behaviorally difficult and low achieving children that they admitted, these differing rates did not account for the variations between schools in the student's later achievements and behavior.

Even when comparisons were made on the basis of matching family, economic backgrounds, and personal characteristics, marked school performance variations remained. In short, students were more likely to show good behavior and good scholastic attainment if they attended some schools than if they attended others. Third, the variations between schools in terms of consistency of *outcomes* was found to be reasonably stable over a period of four or five years. Fourth, schools tended to perform similarly (high or low) on the various measures of favorable and unfavorable outcomes. Those schools which did better than average in terms of student behavior also tended to do better than average in terms of examination results, pupil retention, and delinquency rates. (There were some exceptions, but in general, success or lack of it, pervaded all factors measured.) Fifth, the differences in outcomes were found not to relate to physical factors such as size of school, age of buildings, and amount of space available. Some schools were found to be obtaining good outcomes in spite of their poorer quality in school premises, and it should be noted also that these good results happened within the context of somewhat differing school-level administrative arrangements.

The results of the research confirmed that the differences between schools in outcome *were* systematically related to their characteristics as social institutions, and to their ethos – the attitudes, values and other behaviors exhibited by teachers, students, and administration. Factors as varied as degree of academic emphasis, teacher actions during lessons, the availability of incentives and rewards, the presence of good conditions for students, and the extent to which students were able to take personal responsibility were all significantly associated with *outcome* differences among schools.

characteristics and ethos

Rutter, Naught, Mortimore, Ouston, pp. 177-178

The researchers noted that almost all these factors studied were open to modification by the teachers and administrators. None were fixed external constraints.

The results of research into effective schools, and the available literature on the topic tend to isolate the following seven factors presented below, as providing a summary of the essential areas (most influential features) of effective schools.

1. Use of rewards and praise.

2. Instructional emphasis.

3. The level of student expectations that teacher behavior sets.

4. The level of student participation.

5. Appearance and comfort of the school environment.

6. School organization and teacher skills.

7. Firm leadership by the principal and teacher involvement in decision-making.

Following are some teacher-oriented observations regarding the seven areas noted – some from Rutter's work and some from other scholars, such as Goodlad and Edmonds.

Use of Rewards and Praise

formal
prizes

Formal prizes are relatively ineffective in providing incentives toward higher achievement. In fact, when material rewards are given for intrinsically interesting activities, the result may indeed be a decline in motivation. Rewards are, however, valuable in providing a public demonstration of the value placed by the school upon *good achievement*.

An important factor in formal prize-giving is the proportion of students who received prizes. (They are usually only given to a few so that the discouragement felt by the majority is often as important as the benefits that accrue to the minority). Schools can do things to counter the effects of contra-school – peer group influence, for example, by increasing the rewards and satisfaction open to less able or problem students in the school, thus in that way ensuring that *their* particular needs are met.

The effects of positive classroom praise are stronger than the association held between prizes and good outcomes.

It is important to organize things so that most students are able to succeed most of the time, while providing a gradient of difficulty in order that there will be a steady progress in achievement.

Rewards come not only from praise and prizes, but also from the successful accomplishment of a job well done (intrinsic rewards).

Teachers tend to persist more with students who are identified as high achievers. They give them more clues, more rephrasing, and allow them longer to respond.

balance

The right balance is required between praise and punishment.

Particular rules and approaches may be less important than the existence of some generally recognized and accepted set of standards. For example, keep rules to a minimum.

– Treat every person with respect for their dignity, their welfare, and their material goods.

– Know that everyone has the right to learn. No one has the right to interfere.

A clear, concise reward system is used by effective teachers and effective schools. Students should know, however, exactly what they are being rewarded for. This should be specific as to what is being rewarded and then proceed to set progressively higher goals, i.e., raise expectations. Encouragement and praise work only when teachers are *significant others* in the lives of the students.

Instructional Emphasis

In effective schools it is imperative that instruction for students, at all levels, be designed to employ all of the ways we learn – by hearing, seeing, moving, acting, tasting, smelling, constructing, and touching.

It was found that students had better academic success in schools where homework was regularly set and marked. The research findings did not show how or why homework is associated with better outcomes, but the researchers *speculated* that, in addition to consolidating the learning of work introduced in the school, it was of symbolic importance in emphasizing the school's concern for academic progress.

Students had better academic success in schools where the teachers expressed expectations that a high proportion would do well, also achievement data was used to change and improve the curricula and/or teaching strategies on a regular basis.

In effective schools when questionnaires were given to students, parents, teachers, caretakers, secretarial staff, and para-professionals, the most frequent response was that the school cared most about instruction. The school clearly had a *mission* or *purpose* that was obvious to everyone.

Schools that are *effectively* teaching poor students do not separate them according to ability.

In lower achieving schools, a disproportionate number of students are either placed in slow or remedial groups where low academic *expectations* prevailed. Observations offered by teachers in ineffective schools suggested that they were willing to accept the slightest improvement in achievement as sufficient evidence they were fulfilling their obligations, even when achievement was well below grade level.

Higher achieving schools spend a larger proportion of class time in instructional activities. The proportion of instructional time during which students received academic feedback was high. Schools with high achievement are likely to use more teaching games in which groups of students are competing as teams rather than as individuals.

Student's sense of futility accounts for more of the difference in achievement than does socioeconomic status, racial composition, or other school climate variables. It would appear that the *sense of futility* developed, as measured by the students' perception of their lack of control over those factors in the school environment that affect their achievement. For achievement motivation to be maintained, it is necessary that students believe they personally influence their academic outcomes. High achieving students, especially, believe that *effort* produces academic outcomes.

The Level of Student Expectations that Teacher Behavior Sets

While specific actions on the part of teachers transmit expectations, so does the general attitudes in the school. Teaching performance is a function of the school environment as well as of personal qualities. For example, a staff which

Margin notes: ways we learn · homework · class time · sense of futility displays high regard for its own punctuality can expect punctuality from the students.

staff
interaction

In effective schools students were influenced by the way staff interacted with one another and the opinions which they held about the school. This is important since children have a strong tendency to copy the behavior of other people, especially people in positions of authority if they like and respect them.

The willingness of teachers to see students about problems at any time provides a positive model. General conditions for (and staff attitudes toward) students demonstrate teacher concern.

good morale

It appeared that an efficient school within which teachers worked harmoniously towards agreed-upon goals, was conducive to both good morale and effective teaching. People work and behave better when they are well served and feel those in charge understand and respond to their personal needs.

In effective schools teachers must demonstrate they expect all students can learn, and all students need to know their teachers believe in their personal ability to learn.

There are numerous specific teacher behaviors which clearly demonstrate the level of teachers' expectations.

Level of Student Participation

Giving students responsibility for looking after their school books and papers conveys the teacher's expectations that they will behave responsibly and that they will take good care of the school property. Schools which expected students to care for their own resources had better behavior, better attendance, and less delinquency.

student
responsibility

Providing students with positions or tasks of responsibility was associated with better student behavior. The findings suggested there are likely to be benefits in ensuring a higher proportion of students have the opportunity to hold some kind of post or position of responsibility.

shared
activities

Shared activities between staff and students outside the classroom helped both groups to appreciate the other better. Many began to share some of the same goals.

As students are able to take responsible roles, and achieve satisfaction from them, they will also become more prone to identify with school goals.

success

In effective senior schools students are active representatives on policy making councils such as the *administrative council*. Student involvement appears to enable students to accept more responsibility for policies, procedures and discipline. *Success* should not be measured merely in terms of specific task skills or paper accomplishments, even across a wide range of activities, since the taking of responsibility in the school is also most important for success.

Appearance and Comfort of School Environment

physical
factors

Differences in student outcome were *not* due to such physical factors as the size of the school, the age of the building, or the space available. Schools can obtain good outcomes in spite of initially having rather unpromising and unprepossessing school premises. Behavior and academic attainment tended to be better when the school was clean and tidy, with attractive pictures and plants. Access to telephone, availability of refreshments and being allowed in the building during breaks were important factors.

People work and behave better when they are well looked after and feel those in charge understand and respond to their personal needs. A school that is clean and in good decorative condition provides a positive model.

clean school

The schools should be physically secure and provide a satisfactory environment. The question should not be, "Why is the window broken?" but "How long has the window been broken?" This is an expression that those in charge, *care.*

secure

The researchers found that schools which displayed a lot of students' work on the classroom walls had better academic customs. This could influence students in several ways:

students' work

a. by stressing the academic side of school;
b. by encouraging students to work well and rewarding them by displaying their work; and
c. by making the school more visually attractive.

They also found an *inverse* relationship between the amount of students' work and other materials displayed, and the amount of graffiti observed in the building.

graffiti

School Organization and Teacher Skills

The overall ethos (personality) of the school seemed to provide support and a context which facilitated good teaching. Lessons are prepared in advance. Teachers arrived on time, which provided modelling, an expression of the school's values, and also maximum instructional time. Students are *kept actively* engaged in productive activities, rather than waiting for something to happen. Behavior was better when there was a high proportion of *topic* time per lesson as opposed to time spent setting up equipment, handing out materials, and performing other administrative chores. Smooth transitions between planned activities assisted successful teaching. If a student was not learning the way the teachers are teaching, then the teachers need to teach in a way that their students can learn.

role model

Frequent disciplinary interventions are linked directly to the amount of disruptive behavior. Quiet reprimands are more effective than loud ones.

quiet reprimands

Teachers in higher achieving schools exhibit more concern for and commitment to their students' achievement and expressed this concern through interaction with their students.

Effective teachers hold high expectations for their students.

Schools in which a high proportion of students had remained in the same student grouping tended to have lower rates of delinquency.

student responsibility

In effective schools teachers make rules, consequences, and procedures clear on the first day of the school year. They establish a system of student responsibility and accountability for work.

rreinforcement

In high achieving schools, the general practice was for teachers to make immediate correction of work and provide reinstruction when students fail to give the correct response. Teachers should reinforce even the smallest steps towards the desired level of achievement, but at the same time make it clear to the student what further improvement should be made.

Firm Leadership by Principal and Teacher Involvement in Decision Making

principal involvement

Consistent attention was given by principals as to whether or not instructional behaviors of teachers contributed to student learning. This was accomplished by visiting classes, by being knowledgeable about what was happening, and by principals giving support and guidance to their staffs. Principals responded to teacher needs, i.e., they were able to suggest a repertoire of ways for teachers to overcome a problem and thus the principal became an instructor and creditable resource for the teacher. Getting rid of unreasonably high expectations by the principal was noted by the schools as being a critical leadership factor. the principal maintained an ongoing, effective staff development program, knowing that his/her staff regularly requires new skills and knowledge in order to achieve and maintain excellence.

In schools with good outcomes, decisions tended to be made by the administration team after considering the views of the staff. Teachers and school administrators agreed that the combined effect of the school is much more powerful than any one individual teacher's efforts in fostering student academic achievement.

atmosphere

The atmosphere of any particular school will be greatly influenced by the degree to which it functions as a coherent whole, with agreed upon ways of *doing things*, ways which are consistent throughout the school and which have the general support of the entire staff.

group planning

Group planning provides opportunities for teachers to encourage and support one another. In effective schools, planning was a group matter, generally based in departments with joint curriculum planning at the school level as well. In less effective schools, teachers worked on their own to a much greater extent with the obvious consequence that often there was little coordination between the work of teachers even within the same department.

The greater the group agreement on crucial issues, the greater the tolerance which is possible for individuality and idiosyncrasy on other matters.

school expectations

Examination successes were more frequent and delinquency less common in schools where discipline was based upon general expectations set by the school, rather than those set by individual teachers. Discipline was easier to maintain where the students appreciated that it related to generally accepted approaches and did not simply represent the whims of the individual teacher.

Teachers need the opportunity to take responsibility in, to feel rewarded by, and to identify with, the school.

Another significant positive feature in teacher morale was the provision of adequate clerical help. This was taken to reflect the extent to which the school had taken teachers' needs seriously.

clerical
help

Communication

Teachers in their administrative and supervisory endeavors, as well as in their classroom work, must be good communicators of both feelings and ideas. The socio-psychological theory of communication proposes that the *communication*, (written, verbal, or non-verbal) is to be found in the meaning which people attach to the message they receive, not necessarily in the intended content of the sender. Put simply, in the conversational setting, the message *sender* has an idea, perception, or feeling which he or she *encodes* (converts) into language (symbols), either body or speech. The *receiver* hears or sees it and *decodes* (interprets) the message thus giving it meaning in the context of the receiver's *perception* of both the sender and the situation. The receiver then formulates a response which is encoded and sent. The conversation (communication) continues. during the encoding, decoding, and transmission stages of message sending, there is always *noise*. This consists of internal and external factors such as physical and perceptual *distractors* within and among the situations and the people involved. the original sender intends that certain activities, for example, will be performed by the receiver. In a face-to-face communication situation (usually the most effective kind) one person can, through dialogue, assess the accuracy of the other person's message in order to be sure that they are both *heading* in the same direction, so to speak, and at the same rate. This requires not only being articulate, but also being an active listener who is picking up verbal and non-verbal cues (Hoy & Miskel, p. 360).

good
communications

encodes

decodes

disstractors

In organizations the formal lines of communication (verbal or written) often convey the content, but the informal ones (non-verbal, previous perceptions, etc.) convey the true intent. The teacher must learn to deal openly and honestly with such subtleties in a search for true meanings.

informal
communication

A very important part of the communications process is listening. Webster defines listening as "to hear with thoughtful attention." Listening is often described as being a process involving four interrelated steps. Listening is receiving, interpreting, analyzing, and retaining certain sound stimuli in the receiver's environment. Other definitions describe listening as involving four distinct but interrelated processes – attention, hearing, understanding, and remembering.

listening

1. In the *attention* process the receiver focuses conscious awareness on certain specific stimuli. Distractions are filtered out.

2. In the *hearing* process the receiver (listener) undergoes the automatic physical action of receiving aural stimuli.

3. In the *understanding* process, meaning is assigned to that which is heard.

4. In the *remembering* process, the receiver (listener) retains some of what is heard.

content
retention

It is estimated that most people are able to retain 50 percent of the content immediately after listening; and up to 25 percent of the original content for upwards of 48 hours (Costely & Todd, p. 177).

The tree main *listening* roles which we perform are:

1. as a subordinate – where we listen for instructions, in order to get the facts and become an informed processor;

2. as a peer – where we share information for the purpose of reaching mutual decisions in a cooperative problem solving setting; and

3. as a superior – where we gather feedback to understand problems, evaluate progress, formulate plans, hear the speaker out, and listen critically to what is being said and to what is *not* being said.

better
listeners

Peters and Waterman in their text, *In Search of Excellence*, (1981, p. 193) maintain "The excellent companies are better listeners." They get *close to the customer* by being better listeners. Tom Peters contends that the highest form of courtesy is listening.

It seems self-evident that listening is a highly-valued skill. Yet as Costley and Todd (1987) point out:

> No communication skill has been more neglected in the education system than listening behavior. Most individuals are continually taught the skills of reading, writing, and speaking throughout the educational process. Rarely are individuals taught to listen effectively. (p. 117)

Some interesting statistics: approximately 50 percent of a student's time is spent listening, and 65 percent of this time is spent listening to the teacher. The average person spends 40-50 percent of his or her waking time in listening, but the accuracy and efficiency level is believed to range somewhere between 25 and 50 percent.

barriers

Some barriers to effective listening include:

1. *daydreaming* or creating distractions – pretending to pay attention while thinking of something else;

2. mentally *arguing* with the speaker – reacting strongly and thus blocking receptivity;

3. *desire* to talk – rehearsing what the listener wants to say next;

4. *indifference* and lack of interest – tuning out; and

5. *negative reactions* to the speaker's appearance, speaking style, personality – that is, missing the message.

In order to improve listening skills, the listener should:

1. *stop* talking;

2. *emphathize* with the speaker;

3. *ask* questions;

4. *concentrate*;

5. *show* the speaker that he or she wants to listen – look interested using face, eyes, body;

6. *control* the emotions;

7. get rid of *distractions* – keep eye contact with the speaker remembering there is a lot of *spare time* since most people speak at 100-150 words per minute, but can listen at 400-500 words per minute.

8. *look* for areas of agreement;

9. *avoid* jumping to conclusions;

10. *listen* for main points; and

11. don't become too *preoccupied* with oneself.

(Costley and Todd, pp. 117-120)

Values

Timm and Peterson, in their book *People at Work* (1986) define a personal value as being, "an idea of something that is intrinsically desirable to you." personal value

Peters and Waterman in *In Search of Excellence* (1982) contend that the excellent companies are driven by coherent value systems, and these values are of paramount importance in the companies' day-to-day operations. "The value-shaping leader is concerned with soaring, lofty visions that will generate excitement and enthusiasm." The leader "instills values through deeds rather than words: no opportunity is too small." The same would hold true for school principals and schools. coherent value systems

In his book, *Leadership and Administration* (1957) Philip Selznick states "the institutional leader is primarily an expert in the promotion and protection of values." Selznick believes values are not usually transmitted through formal written procedures but through the stories, myths, legends, and metaphors of the organization. Effective value systems are known to inspire people at all levels of the organization. Selznick

In a study of company values, Peters and Waterman (1982, p. 285) concluded that all the better performing companies had a well-defined set of guiding beliefs. These basic values were identified as: basic values

1. a belief in being the *best*;

2. a belief in the importance of *people* as individuals;

3. a belief in superior *quality* and service;

4. a belief in the importance of *innovation* and the willingness to support failure;

5. a belief in *informality* to enhance communications;

6. a belief in the importance of *economic* growth and profits; and

7. a belief in the importance of the *details* of execution (doing a job well and efficiently).

value systems

Value systems are also inherent in schools in the form of a set of beliefs held by the staff, and perpetuated by their actions.

personal perceptions

The difficulty arises when one realizes that values are based upon *personal* perceptions, and thus are certainly widely varied according to past experience. This makes the formulation of group values a challenging task indeed for the school staff, and where success occurs, it is most often attributable to the strength of the leader.

Values can be seen from varying perspectives. Each teacher will have a set of values which he or she brings to the school. As professionals, teachers will have developed their own beliefs regarding teaching, learning, and the nature of students. Administrators may share these perceptions as former teachers, but they may also have another set of beliefs about other teachers and about the school system. And, of course, teachers will also have a set of preconceived ideas about administrators and the school system, which could be diametrically opposed to the views of other colleagues.

value clarification

In recent years there has been a shift in thinking toward bringing together a *value system* which the staff will accept and work toward. Administrators now encourage staff members to explore and clarify values and beliefs, both personally and professionally. Personal value clarification has become an important aspect of individual growth plans for teachers.

Professional values for teachers might include beliefs held about children as learners and as social entities. For example, if one has an identified belief that children learn best by involvement, then one would work toward child-centred, hands-on learning activities. If one believes that social growth is a very important aspect of child development then one must inquire as to how the school will address that belief. Clarification and melding of values requires time and team building. Often, in groups, school goal-setting activities provide a useful procedure.

School Climate

value clarification

Organizational *culture* refers to the predominant values of the organization (Costley & Todd, p. 13). Organizational *climate* refers to the "feeling, tone, spirit, or degree of voluntary cooperation found in organizations (Costley & Todd, p. 562). School climate is a general synthesizing concept that is directly influenced by the conduct and leadership styles of principals and supervisors, which in turn affects the motivational level of teachers and students. Some general statements which can be made with respect to the state of the school's climate includes the following.

special environment

1. Teachers teach best and students learn and enjoy more in a positive, vital, and robust learning environment. Teaching and learning can become exciting, challenging and even rewarding. Create a special environment by, for example, "sprucing up" the physical setting, exuding enthusiasm, promoting fun, empha-

sizing growth, setting and maintaining standards, being inventive and creative, helping and supporting colleagues, and championing respect and acceptance.

2. Great schools and great teachers make an effort to be close to students. Each decision taken and activity conducted emanates from the central question: *"What is best for the children?"* Teachers can stay close to and be children-centred by including students in decision making, by promoting active learning, by providing variety, and by allowing for student differences.

3. Research tells us that we get what we expect. Beliefs and attitudes about others including how we treat them (which in turn influences their attitudes, behavior and performance) can create a positive *self-fulfilling* prophecy. Expect the best from students, send positive messages, model high standards, *catch others succeeding*, watch the praise, and being candid but positive, and have sound guidelines.

self-fulfilling
prophecy

4. Rewards are tangible, visible symbols of success. Perpetuate the winning attitude by, for example, applauding pacesetters, using multiple and varied awards systems, and *showcasing* academic performance.

rewards

5. A great school resembles the best families; its members support and help each other in ways such as: peer support programs, high teacher turn-out at school activities, being involved in, for example, staff meetings which can become *pulling together* sessions, and by being able to acknowledge and deal with conflict, should it arise.

6. Parents and community members should expect and demand quality education. Schools can develop a closeness with parents and communities through conversations with parents, showcasing the school, inviting feedback, and working toward *customer satisfaction.*

7. Keep communication lines open and the flow positive, by keeping others posted, being an active listener oneself, by choosing words carefully, and especially by communicating positive student progress to student and parent.

8. Great schools are driven by pride. To get that special feeling, it is helpful to set and track personal goals, set and track classroom goals, set and track school building goals, and *find achievement.*

pride

9. trust (reliance upon the integrity, strength, ability, etc., of a person); confidence and openness are the essential elements in building bonds between people. Where trust exists, leaders can lead, teachers can teach, and learners can learn in a positive school climate.

Innovation

Innovation is the process of bringing a new idea or new application into general use. Although innovation is commonly thought of as the development of new products, the term has a more general application including the introduction of new skills or policies. Lee Iaccoca's autobiography (1984) offers many examples to support the argument that modern organizations must be innovative. He stresses the importance of flexibility and adaptation to change.

Iaccoca

When discussing his role as president of Ford, he said, "I had to think of the big picture. Where was the company going to be five years from now? What were the major trends we had to pay attention to?" (p. 106)

predictability
Traditionally, the main concern of most organizations has been to maintain current operations. Tom Peters (Peters & Waterman, 1982) maintains this leads to "a conservative bias," "an abstract heartless philosophy," a "negativity" and a "rigidity." Peters, in his recent book, *Thriving on chaos* (1987) stresses that the world is no longer predictable and that today's leaders will confront a chaotic world of "shattering and accelerating change."

innovate
In educational organizations, the ability to innovate and respond to external changes is equally as important. Although we are not market driven as is business, there is ample evidence that reforms are necessary in curricula, academic standards, teacher preparation, teacher evaluation, and many other areas in order to educate the children for a change-oriented, future-oriented society.

Every innovation must be accompanied by opportunities for experiential learning, within a climate of openness and trust, which provides rewards for success, and encouragement of risk-taking, and provides for direct assistance when it is needed.

Mandated Change

The job of the teacher is, with a limited number of exceptions, not to choose what to teach (the curriculum) but to choose how to teach. This does require, however, a fundamental understanding of the curriculum in order that the teacher becomes able to plan, implement, and evaluate a program of instruction. The curriculum is in a state of constant flux in its effort to adjust to changing societal and political demands. Teachers, through their *technical expertise*,
technical expertise
translate curriculum objectives and prescribed resources into meaningful sets of activities for the students. A problem, however, is that the teacher's interpretative and commitment levels to a set of externally-imposed directives can vary significantly.

program change
Educators are frequently required to facilitate the adoption of a mandated program change. The first point to remember is that the forces that motivate individuals to participate in change occur when individuals view the change as beneficial, when they perceive opportunities for professional growth within the change, and when they see opportunities to participate in leadership roles, in group decision making, and in collegial networking. Second, the potential sources of resistance to change are: a lack of information about the purpose or implementation of the change, a feeling off excessive work pressure, and/or an anxiety about failure, and perhaps loss of status or security. Third, use effective strategies such as permitting participants to *stand out*, and finding ways to promote consensual decision making, interaction effectiveness, and staff commitment. Fourth, methods to maintain the change and sustain the actual use of the new practice in the classroom may be found in developing local materials,

providing for in-classroom assistance, permitting peer classroom observations, ensuring regular communications about *practical* concerns, and by providing for specific training.

Inherent in the idea of *pro-active change* is an appreciation of the empowering force to be found in collaborative relationships which are generated through mutual determination of goals within a spirit of open and diagnostic inquiry.

pro-active
change

Ethics

Ethics are established in the early stages of development and are "... strongly influenced by the values of our parents and by our environment." They consist of "... personal values of correct and incorrect behavior, societal values of honesty, truthfulness, fairness, and equity." (Costley & Todd, 1987, pp. 505-506).

Along with establishing a *value* system, an organization such as a school also establishes a set of rules of acceptable behavior for the members of the organization. In some instances, the proper behaviors or ethics are clearly defined in the form of a written *code of conduct*; a definition of how one is expected to behave as a member of the group. In other instances the code of conduct is inferred in the way that organizational members conduct themselves as they go about their work and leisure. The behaviors of members will in fact, reflect the ethics of the organization – especially in unguarded moments. In some cases, ethical behavior not only refers to conduct on the job, but may also include how one *should* behave in all aspects of life.

code of
conduct

In education, teachers are governed by codes of professional conduct and codes of ethics. These codes describe universally acceptable behavior with respect to such matters as student relationships, relations with school administrators and colleagues, and with the profession as a governing body. Chapter 18 provides a fuller description of the codes which govern the professional teacher. However, the ethical stance of the school as an organization will become *visible* through the ways that teachers, students, and administrators conduct themselves as they administer and teach and relate to each other.

Trust

In their text, *People at Work*, (1986) Timm and Peterson discuss the five components necessary to build a positive climate in an organization. They are:

1. the degree to which management is supportive of the employee's efforts;

2. the extent of participatory decision making;

3. the *degree of trust* employees have for management;

4. the freedom to communicate openly; and

5. the amount that performance goals are emphasized. The authors state that the single most important ingredient of good organizational climate is trust among organizational members.

trust

Costley and Todd (1987) also discuss the term *trust*. They write about it with reference to the term "psychological contracts." The degree of trust and confidence employees and managers have in each other depends upon whether each believes the other is supporting the psychological contract. If employees seem unwilling to follow established rules and procedures or to not perform as well as the manager knows they can, the contract may appear to be broken and the manager may no longer *trust* the employee to complete assigned tasks. Managers who are perceived by the employees as being unfair, insincere, incompetent, or unwilling to listen and respond also break the psychological contract and therefore may not be trusted by employees. Without mutual trust, the primary conditions of an effective psychological contract are broken and performance deteriorates. Eventually the organization may not only suffer losses in productivity levels, but may also develop a strong adversarial relationship between managers and employees. Failure of the trust relationship between and among professional people is frequently at the root of school failure.

Administrative Monitoring

monitoring

Glatthorn (1984) defines *administrative monitoring* as "a process by which the administrator monitors the work of the staff, making brief and unannounced visits simply to ensure that the staff are carrying out assignments and responsibilities in a professional manner." (p. 5)

Administrative monitoring is a quality control mechanism rather than an employee improvement activity – to many administrators it is *Management By Walking Around* (MBWA) which has become a very successful practice for business leaders. (Peters & Austin, 1984)

The inclusion of an administrative monitoring component in school supervision has sent a symbolic message to teachers. According to Sergiovanni (1987), the supervisor is saying:

... you are important; I am interested in teaching and learning, these areas constitute the most important part of my job; I communicate this message to you by my actions ... by spending time with you and your students involved in teaching and learning (p. 111).

In the school context, administrative monitoring is normally conducted as a purely informal process with feedback (positive and perhaps negative) coming to the teachers through conversations and sometimes informal notes.

Administrative monitoring will become, according to Sergiovanni (1987, p. 11) a normal part of school life since "the principal, as principal teacher, has a right and a responsibility to be part of all teaching that takes place in the school.

Mediating Conflict

Human history is, generally, a recording of the continuous struggle to learn   conflict
how to live and work productively and constructively with others. Conflict
within organizations, if unchecked, can lead to frustration, worry, backbiting,
blaming, rumors, cliques, complaints, a decrease in commitment and an increase in anger, hate, intolerance and aggression. Also conflict may lead to
information distortion and therefore a low quality of decision making. The
essence of conflict is disagreement or incompatibility. It comes in several basic
forms:

1. goal conflict wherein the desired end-states, or preferred outcomes appear
   to be incompatible;

2. cognitive conflict in which ideas or thoughts are perceived as being incompatible;

3. affective conflict in which feelings or emotions are incompatible; and

4. procedural conflict wherein the conflicting groups or persons differ on the
   process to be used, often on the procedures to be used to resolve the conflict.

The converse of the damage-oriented view above suggests that conflict
within the organization (school) may have a positive affect and lead to an
increase in motivation and energy, innovativeness, diversity, healthy competition, as well as increased understanding of one's role and position within the
organization. Conflict may simply be a sign of dynamic relationships which
lead to positive change. Too little conflict can be detrimental by leading to
lethargy, decreased sharing of controversial information and on unwillingness
to challenge tradition. Conflict can contribute to a group's performance, but
most groups try to avoid it.

It must be recognized there are two basic groupings of conflict : intrapersonal   intrapersonal
and interpersonal. Intrapersonal conflict is conflict within the individual. Inter-   conflict
personal conflict involves two or more individuals who perceive themselves as
being in opposition to each other over preferred outcomes and/or attitudes,
values or behavior. Intragroup conflict refers to clashes among some or all of   interpersonal
the members of a group. These conflicts can affect the group processes and   conflict
effectiveness. Intergroup conflict refers to opposition and clashes between two
or more groups. Union-management conflict provides a classic example.

Vertical conflict refers to clashes between levels in an organization, for   vertical
example, when subordinates resist superior's attempts to control them, espe-   conflict
cially when the control is thought to be autocratic – too tight. Horizontal
conflict, as the name suggests, refer to clashes between groups of employees
at the same hierarchical level. It usually occurs when each department of   horizontal
division strives for its own goals while disregarding the goals of others.   conflict
Line-staff conflict results from clashes over authority relationships. In another
section of this chapter, the line-staff relationship is defined, but in general *line*
personnel who have responsibility for some process or division of the organization (the school for example) and the authority to perform the function find

themselves in conflict with staff personnel, those whose authority rests in specific knowledge and/or skills.

conflict
stages

Most writers on conflict suggest there are at least four distinct, but interrelated stages in the conflict process. Recognition of the phases is essential to conflict mediation. Stage one (potential) denotes the presence of conditions that create opportunities for conflict to arise. Stage two (personalization) happens when the conditions cited in stage one generate frustration. The potential for opposition is actualized. Stage three (behavior) is described as the stage where members engage in actions that frustrate the attainment of another's goals or prevents the other from furthering own interests. Stage four (outcomes) is the phase in which the overt conflict behavior and the conflict-handling behaviors result in consequences. This is the stage for the five management styles listed below. Among the barriers to conflict mediation are:

1. refusal to listen;

2. stubbornness;

3. determination not to compromise;

4. impatience;

5. suspicion;

6. lack of compassion; and

7. differences on deeply held values.

management
styles

The literature on interperson and its variation, intergroup, conflict suggests five management styles:

1. avoiding (uncooperative and unassertive);

2. forcing (uncooperative and assertive);

3. collaborating (cooperative and assertive);

4. accommodating (cooperative and unassertive); and

5. compromising (intermediate level of cooperation and assertion).

There are a number of methods for managing intergroup relations.

1. Rules and procedures. This method is simple and inexpensive. A set of formalized rules and procedures specify how group members are to interact with each other – standard operating procedures (SOP).

2. Hierarchy. Coordination is achieved by referring problems (conflicts) to a common superior higher in the organization. This is another low-cost solution but may lead to vertical conflict.

3. Planning. Through the planning process each work group has specific goals for which it is held responsible. Each group knows what it is supposed to do. Intergroup problems are resolved in terms of goals, expectations, and contributions.

4. Liaison roles. This procedure assigns liaison roles to individuals who then facilitate communication between interdependent work units.

5. Task forces. A task force is a temporarily established group made up of representatives from a number of departments, for example. They exist only long enough to solve the problem.

6. Teams. Often tasks are very complex and the traditional coordinating procedures are not sufficient. Decisions are delayed. Communications become extended. Top management is required to spend more and more time on day-to-day operations. Teams are typically formed around frequently recurring problems. Team membership is more lasting than for task forces. Members maintain responsibility to their primary functional department and to the team.

7. Integrating departments. This is the next most permanent and costly procedure for conflict resolution. Where rules, hierarchy, planning, liaison roles, task forces and team fail, a permanent structure, the integrating department, will be formed and assigned the task of integration between two or more groups.

8. Negotiations on conflict mediation, a procedure of a different order (not structural), is placed here since it is used frequently. Negotiations is defined as a process in which two or more parties, both having common and conflicting goals state and discuss proposals concerning the specific terms of a possible agreement. Negotiations involve compromise, collaboration, some cooperation and some forcing.

The literature on negotiations points to at least four basic types which are described briefly as follows.

1. Distributive negotiations. This is the traditional win-lose, fixed pie situation where one party gains and another party loses. Distributive negotiations most often occur over economic issues.

2. Integrative negotiations. The focus of this process is to use joint problem solving to achieve a solution in which both parties gain. The parties (a) identify mutual problems, (b) identify and assess alternatives, (c) openly express preferences, and (d) jointly reach an acceptable solution.

3. Attitudinal structuring. Some parties throughout negotiations exhibit relationship patterns (hostility, friendliness, competitiveness, cooperation). This type of negotiations attempts to structure the process by which the parties establish desirable attitudes and relationships.

4. Interorganizational negotiations. In interorganizational negotiations the key players on each side attempt to build a concensus for agreement within their side. This process is especially necessary in situations wherein each group employs agents for their group. The agents may reach agreement but there remains the necessity for them to build agreement within their constituents.

5. SBS model (Savage, Blair, Sorenseon). The SBS model is based upon the assumption there is not a strategy which will work for all situations, and therefore Savage, Blair, and Sorenson concluded that strategy depends upon desired *substantive* and *relationship* outcomes. They contend that the crucial context for any negotiation is the individual's current *and* desired relationship outcome (feelings and attitude) with the other party. While attempting to secure the best *substantive* outcome (issues and goals) they may overlook the impact of the negotiations on their relationships. This oversight is thought to hurt relationships and hamper current and future substantive outcomes. Since many negotiations are not win-win or win-lose situations, but combinations of both negotiations require both collaboration and competition. This situation, SBS contends, is difficult for most people to handle. the relationships that exist prior to negotiations, the relationships which unfold during negotiations, and the relationships which are desired often influence whether each party will share the pie, grab it all, give it away, or re-create it.

SBS model

The two central questions at the beginning of SBS are:

1. is the substantive outcome in terms of goals or issues at stake very important; and

2. is the relationship outcome (feelings and attitudes between the parties) very important?

Hellriegel, Slocum and Woodman in *Organizational Behavior* (6th edition) note that four unilateral strategies emerge.

1. Trusting Collaboration – both relationship and substantive outcomes are important.

2. Open Subordination – where individuals are more concerned with establishing a positive relationship with the other party than with making substantive gains.

3. Firm Competition – substantive issues are important, but relationship issues are not.

4. Active Avoidance – where neither the relationship issues, or the substantive issues are important, the individual should actively avoid negotiations. Refusing to negotiate is the most direct way to show avoidance. The action will usually negatively affect relationships.

The competent negotiation will not only assess their position with respect to these four strategies, but also attempt to assess the other party's position respecting strategies.

The teacher who is interested in conflict mediation through negotiations should spend time researching the considerable literature available on the topic. The presentation here is intended only to point some directions. The four strategies discussed can be focused or softened. The literature provides descriptions and advice.

14

The Supervisory Process

I asked my supervisor why he was visiting me. He said, "Because the school board rules say I have to."

"What do you do with your notes?" I asked (as though I didn't know).

"They go into your file, but don't worry, they're complimentary enough," he replied.

I guess my file is more important than I am. Strange world, isn't it?

A Classroom Teacher – Doll, p. 1

Supervision and Administration

Background

Trends

Purposes

Personal Performance

Improvement Plan

Types of Supervision

Staff Development

Introduction

An effective growth program for the staff in any school system should encompass supervision, evaluation, and staff development activities. These three processes must be supported by insightful, decisive, creative, and caring leadership provided by superintendents, school principals, department heads or team leaders (where appropriate) and by colleagues, of course. Supervision is a formative process for helping employees do their job better. It is a process of observing, listening, clarifying, encouraging, presenting, problem solving, negotiating, demonstrating, directing, standardizing, and enforcing. Supervisors endeavor to identify employee needs and operationalize an effective improvement plan at the work site. Closely associated is the term *staff development* which is a planned change process leading to the achievement of identifiable goals (personal, work site, and/or school system). Within this chapter staff development materials will emphasize the process at the personal level. Also closely associated with supervision is the term *evaluation* which is herein defined as the formal appraisal of an individual's performance. Sometimes the term used in the literature is *summative evaluation*. Reports are usually written and placed in the employee's file. Employment status decisions may be made. The importance of supervision is well recognized as a crucial

supervision
evaluation
staff development

aspect of organized school life. As a result, superintendents, principals and others who have specific supervisory assignments are expected to have insight and skill in helping employees to function effectively. Many advanced level courses at universities are directed toward theory and research in these skill areas.

supervision
responsibility

Today, in most schools, teacher supervision is primarily the responsibility of the school principal. Yet it has been established, in both theory and practice, that effective teacher improvement programs require teachers to assume responsibility for their *own* growth and development, and for helping colleagues grow as well.

inspection

Inspection of teacher performance (often considered as being synonymous with supervision) has in the past done much to strike fear into the hearts and minds of teachers, and has done little to improve or *revitalize* teaching and learning.

A strong supervisory program should include the following elements.

1. It should be continuous and ongoing in nature with on-site coaching being utilized.

2. The process should include the opportunity for face-to-face contact between the supervisor and staff member, when appropriate, as well as the opportunity for joint identification of areas to be supervised.

3. Policies should be cooperatively developed and clearly understood by all staff.

4. Policies should be adhered to by supervisors.

5. Supervisors should understand how effective supervision is provided and should have the necessary skills to carry out the function.

6. Within the process, staff should know who is providing supervisory assistance to them as well as being an active partner.

7. The supervisory program should result in improved performance and a feeling of being (empowerment) valued as a member of the staff of a particular organization.

8. Adequate time and financial resources should be allocated to support this function.

Exhibit 12-1 of Chapter 12 illustrated diagrammatically that the educational administration function of the principalship exists at three levels: (1) differentiated, (2) peer, and (3) clinical, and that evaluation activities are both formative (directed toward helping), and summative (directed toward decision making). The staff development program should be operative at the system and school level as well as at the individual teacher level. Supervision, and evaluation of staff development activities are a part of the overall school development plan; a plan headed by the school principal as instructional leader, but planned and implemented by the total staff.

Supervision and Administration

Writers such as Hoy and Forsyth (Hoy & Forsyth, 1986), distinguish the role of the school administrator (the principal) from the role of a supervisor as follows:

> Administrators face day-to-day problems of running a school . . . engaging in organizational maintenance activities. Supervisors, by contrast, have the duty of improving teaching and learning in the classroom, a complex task that is planned and conceived in terms of months and years. (1986, p. 8)

Thus, it appears they believe the two activities, supervision (instructional leadership) and administration (management leadership), are mutually exclusive and, by implication, are therefore suggesting the same person has difficulty fulfilling both roles. They contend the supervisory role is orientated toward change; innovation is the expectation. The supervisor expects change to take a long time with well-ordered steps and feedback at strategic points along the way. Hoy and forsyth seem to believe the supervisor is responsible for instructional change and that the principal is responsible for creating the climate/environment conducive to that change. The principal, through positional authority provides personal, professional, financial, and personnel support to teachers and their instructional supervisors. The *staff* (see Chapter 13) position of the supervisor carries with it little formal authority: "authority is primarily informal and earned – arising from the supervisor's expertise and personal skills" (p. 9).

Although this view of the distinction between administration and supervision enjoys support, this text has taken the position that *instructional leadership*, of which supervision is a part, and *management leadership* can be, and are normally performed by the same person, the school principal. Supervision is a process. To suggest otherwise would be, in our view, like proclaiming that supervisory activities could not take place in small schools or in jurisdictions that employ few specialized personnel. Many of the management functions of the school principal are specified by statute and school board policy and therefore must be performed as his/her first priority. But perhaps even more in smaller than in larger schools, the principal must attend to the instructional leadership needs of the staff – varied instructional loads, multi-graded classrooms, curriculum changes and new expectations, such as the addition of instructional units on the subject of human sexuality to the Health Program.

Definitions of Supervision

Wiles (1955) defines supervision as "the procedure by which a school system improves the curriculum and instruction. . .." John T. Lovell defines instructional supervision as, "a behavior system formally provided by the organization for the purpose of interacting with the teaching behavior system in such a way as to maintain, change, and improve the design and articulation of learning opportunities for students" (Lovell & Wiles, p. 6).

(margin notes) Hoy and Forsyth · instructioanl leadership · management leadership · statute · pollicy · Wiles · Lovell

Doll

Doll states that:

> The fundamental purpose of educational supervision is to increase the confidence and improve the competence of teachers in elementary and secondary schools. (Doll, 1983, p. ix)

Oliva

Oliva defines supervision as "a means of offering to teachers specialized help in improving instruction" (Oliva, 1976, p. 7), while Pfieffer and Dunlop consider supervision to be:

Pfieffer and Dunlop

> A process of interaction in which an individual or individuals work with teachers to improve instruction. The ultimate goal is better student learning. The achievement of this goal may involve changing teacher behavior, modifying curriculum, and/or restructuring the learning environment. (1982, p. 5)

The common elements in definitions of supervision in schools were found to be improved teaching and improved instruction.

Background of Supervision

Beach and Reinhartz

Beach and Reinhartz (1989, p. 27) note that various views of supervision have evolved on the continent, over time. Historically, the schools reflect the values and attitudes of each generation. Beach and Reinhartz label the phases as:

1. the colonial period (1600-1865);

2. the state and national period (1865-1910);

3. the scientific and organizational period (1910-1920);

4. the professional and bureaucratic period (1920-1935);

5. the progressive and cooperative period (1935-1955);

6. the *change* oriented period (1955-1970);

7. the clinical and accountability period (1970-1980); and

8. the managerial period (1980 to the present).

The literature indicates that supervision of instruction began with the visits by *lay* people (and later visits by professional superintendents) for the purpose of *inspection*. Doll notes that, "educational supervision began with inspecting teachers and the classrooms they managed" (1983, p. 3). Inspections were authoritarian and performed solely for *summative evaluation* purposes, that is, for *reporting* purposes. Traditionally, school inspectors saw little need for formal professional management policies and *participative* management practices. One of the major problems with inspection is that:

summative evaluation

> ... nothing is done subsequent to it to aid the development of the teacher in service. Ratings and descriptions go into teachers' personnel files ... (and teachers) see no profit in it except that it adds potentially complementary materials to their personal files. (Davis & Newstrom, p. 738)

traditional

This traditional mode of supervision by inspection has been rejected in the light of advances in understanding human motivation and behavior in a participatory work setting, coupled with the growing professionalism on the part of all teachers. Thus evolved the presently accepted concept of supervision as being for the improvement of instruction, with an emphasis upon staff development. Of course, formal teacher evaluation activities remain as part of the supervisory program (see later section) since decisions on permanent employment, promotion, and termination must still be made, but summative teacher evaluation no longer holds the central place that it once did. However, school principals will still be required to make decisions regarding the future of unwilling or unable staff; the reassignment of personnel; or as another example, decisions regarding the reduction in staff complement when school down-sizing is required. This latter point is a major issue in the current economic situations wherein governments and school boards struggle to cope with reduced revenues.

Current Trends in Supervision

The shift in focus from traditional supervisory roles based on authority and inspection designed to determine, or declare an employee's traits, deficiencies and abilities for the purposes of determining retention, rewards, and/or promotions to a focus on teacher vitalization has almost been completed. The current philosophy stresses employee participation in setting future professional goals. The 1970s and 1980s have witnessed an increased emphasis upon staff development activities as the way to improve teacher performance. Parents are demanding better schools, and school officials are seeking better systems designed to motivate personnel to constantly seek higher levels of performance (Castetter, 1981). Research and practice-sound procedures are being implemented in response to the demand.

employee participation

Recent theory of supervision indicates the classroom teacher in any district must play an integral part in the supervisory program. Neagley and Evans note (1980) that:

> (The teacher) must have opportunities to participate in evaluation of the district instructional program, curriculum development and revision, and analysis of their own teaching-learning situations. In other words, the professional integrity of the school principal and the classroom teacher are basic to any effective program of supervision in the modern public school. (p. 12)

The policies, guidelines and procedures of supervision should outline the premises upon which the program is based, the purposes of supervision, the criteria to be employed in decision making, the timelines, and the budget; in general, the directions which the supervisory program will take; the plan – a supervisory plan.

Purposes of Supervision

As noted earlier, supervision and evaluation policies have often been ritualistic and conducted as a matter of routine. Changes have been called for. Many teachers and administrators are tired of one-shot inconsistent practices. They assert that supervision must be developmental; that it must be a process, not

ritualistic

simply an exercise; that it must result in the improvement of instruction; and that there must be a plan to guide the process.

need

The need for supervision of teaching and teachers has appeared consistently in the literature on teaching and learning. Madeline Hunter (1976, 1982) for example, declared the fundamental purpose of all supervision is to provide feedback on performance in order to facilitate development toward improved teaching and learning. Hunter's contention is that staff development is essential for a number of reasons. First, the climate of a school must be positive and conducive to excellence in teaching and learning if teachers are to be successful in their own classrooms. Second, instructional competence is an essential part of educational excellence. Third, staff development (in the form of professional growth programs) provides the opportunity for teachers to share and develop

student
growth

expertise together. The principal as instructional leader is the key person in the supervision of teaching. The role of the principal is to assist teachers in designing and implementing effective instruction which will increase the probability that all students will learn. A basic assumption stated by Sergiovanni and Carver (1982) is that growth and development goals for students are best achieved by teachers who are committed to the goals of developing awareness, creativity, respect, sensitivity, responsibility, a desire for learning, a spirit of inquiry and a capacity for love, not only for students, but for themselves. The human dimension therefore takes on a new importance. Goldhammer et al. (1980) strongly believe that of the things that educators do, the things that promote professional growth of teachers and the improvement of the teaching and learning situation are the most important. They support both formal and informal approaches to professional growth and they advocate patterns of instruction which encourage teachers to plan and work together as teams.

mentoring

Recent literature on teacher supervision adds a new dimension. The focus still requires the leadership of an effective principal, but it recognizes that effective development requires that teachers also assume responsibility for their *own* growth and development and that of their colleagues, Teachers can meet their own growth and development needs by forming, for example, mentoring relationships. Mentoring is the process by which a trusted and experienced person takes a personal and professional interest in the growth and development of new or less experienced teachers (Krupp, 1987). Mentors for example, can provide assistance with such things as helping others to adjust to a new school or grade level, classroom management, instructional planning, teaching strategies, and personal relationship issues. Mentoring presents an opportunity to provide a mode of supervision which can overcome many of the difficulties faced by administrators. There ar, of course, many other ways in which mutual help can be given.

Personal Performance Improvement Plan

Exhibit 14-1 and the pages which follow provide one illustration of how a plan for supervision at the district and school levels can be translated into a personal performance improvement plan for the individual teacher.

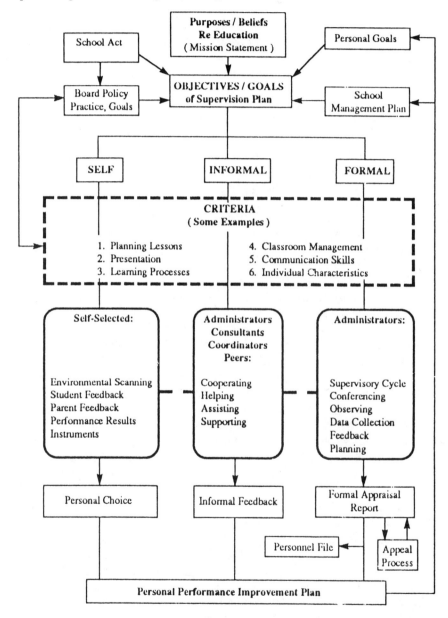

Exhibit 14-1
A Supervisory Plan

Objectives/Goals of the Supervision Plan

The objectives and goals of the supervision plan are the focal point upon which all components of teacher supervision are based. School districts or schools develop their supervision plan based on the following: (Refer to Exhibit 14-1)

values

1. *Purposes and Beliefs of Education.* The mission of a school district and/or a school reflects the values that the school organization hold to be important in the education of its students. In order to fulfill its missions, a school or school district must focus all actions toward achieving the mission. Goal-directed activities are central. Leadership directed towards these purposes and beliefs becomes the role of each individual within the organization. Goal-oriented traditions become part of the daily rituals of the school or school district. All programs and plans draw focus from the *mission statement.*

natural
justice

2. *The School Act and Natural Justice.* First, the school act (education act) and the accompanying regulations are the statutes of the province which set out the legal requirements for the operation of schools. Included in the school act are rules and regulations that identify educational requirements for teachers, and the specific duties that teachers, administrators, and parents are required to perform. They also identify educational requirements that schools must provide to their students, and the means by which educational concerns are addressed. Supervision plans therefore must be in harmony with school legislation. Second, natural justice is a legal concept which basically means that anyone in a position of authority must act and proceed in a judicial and reasonable manner, and have legally justifiable reasons for acting in a specific way. In relation to supervision, natural justice means: the conduct and expectations required of teachers are reasonable and known by the teacher; the teacher understands that failure to fulfill the expected behaviors are objectively investigated and specific data recorded to verify the situation; any disciplinary action reflects a position that is consistent with the seriousness and nature of the inappropriate behavior; the teacher's previous record must also be considered and the disciplinary treatment that he or she receives is consistent with that received by others who have been disciplined for the same of similar actions. In short, natural justice ensures there is *just reason* for any corrective action, and there is consistency in the way leaders act.

policies

3. *School Board Policy, Practice and Goals.* Each school district is required to develop and implement policies governing educational and financial practices within the school jurisdiction: policies governing teacher, program, and school evaluations, as well as policies on school district programs and operations evaluations. The outcomes of these evaluations are directed toward the improvement of teaching and learning in the schools and within the school district. A complete evaluation plan will have criteria established which can be applied in the analysis of teaching and learning

personal
goals

4. *Personal Goals.* Each person who is employed in a school has unique gifts and talents to offer in the process of educating children; however one cannot presume teachers and support staff devote all their time and energy toward education and teaching. Personal goals are an integral part of a staff member's life and wherever possible, these goals should be considered in the supervision plan. The feedback from the supervision plan, in the form of a *personal improvement plan,* becomes part of the input in the constant review and revision of the supervision plan. Individual teacher's personal goals, the goals of other staff members, and the school's plans are brought together to generate a school management plan and a parallel school supervision plan.

5. *School Management Plan.* The school management plan is the leadership plan that is developed annually to best utilize the resources available to lead the school and/or school district towards its goals and mission. Some of the components of the School management plan consist of a set of (1) annual goals, (2) a school improvement plan, (3) a professional development plan, (4) a budget plan, and (5) an instructional plan. These plans are a description of the organizational strategies which have been designed to promote progress toward the desired goals. The supervision plan provides progress and development information and feedback in relation to the overall school management plan.

leadership plan

The objectives and goals of the supervision plan represent a collection of many of the goals and objectives of all other areas of school, and of the school district's operations. The overarching purpose of the supervision plan is to improve the effectiveness of the educational service to students through continuous development and growth. Some specific purposes of a supervision plan are as follows.

purposes

1. To improve the delivery of all school and school district services.

2. To improve the instructional program.

3. To motivate employees to more nearly attain their potential, and to improve their performance.

4. To provide information on the strengths and weaknesses of individual employees with the purpose of providing assistance, developing in-service and job upgrading programs to strengthen the individual in his/her area of need, and to identify special interests, aptitudes, and special abilities which can be added to the *pool* of human resources available.

5. To provide a variety of input information for the purpose of making wise administrative decisions in regard to the total staff, groups of employees and the individual employee.

6. To provide a basis for tenure decisions, permanent appointments, and promotions.

mutual trust

The supervision plan is based upon the principle that each member of the organization shall promote and maintain a strong relationship of mutual trust, confidence and respect among all members of the organization. This also requires that all individuals in the organization conduct themselves with integrity and honesty.

Criteria

For the purposes of this model, six criteria which represent the range of performance activities and criteria, have been selected. While the following list is not exhaustive of all the criteria that could be applied when measuring effective teaching, it is intended only to illustrate the range of performance criteria that may be applied to the supervision of teaching. No attempt has been made here to place criteria in any order of importance, since a decision on degree of importance is *situational* to specific teaching and learning situations.

planning

1. *Planning.* Effective teaching is built upon a set of plans that are prescribed by the province, the local school board, the school and the teacher offering the course. Effective planning requires that a teacher be knowledgeable about the program of studies, and be able to translate the objectives of the program into meaningful learning episodes. Planning involves being prepared for each class. Long range, yearly or unit planning forms the basis for the daily instructional plans – an act of being prepared for each class.

process of teaching

2. *Presentation of Learning Activities.* This refers to the *process* of teaching. It addresses the area of how students are presented with new learning, how they are motivated to learn, and how the subject matter is developed, and related to other learnings. Questions are asked here, such as, "Is the new learning student centred?" Follow-up exercises and evaluation of new learning are also parts of this criteria area.

learning process

3. *Learning Process.* The criteria addressed in the *learning process* are centred on questions such as, "Does the teacher establish reasonable, but challenging expectations for students?" Interactions between student and teacher are examined to determine whether objectives are accomplished; whether the curriculum is organized effectively for optimal learning, and whether the teacher evaluates students' curricular competence effectively. Included in this set of criteria are the personalizing of the teaching process and the maintenance of an appropriate classroom learning atmosphere.

classroom management

4. *Classroom Management.* Classroom management refers not only to the organization and structure of the classroom, but also to whether students are aware of their responsibilities and are willing to do their part to ensure that optimal learning occurs in the classroom. Teachers must, among other things, use resourceful discipline techniques, encourage regular attendance, sustain student attention and interest in learning, and make efficient use of learning time – time on task.

communication

5. *Communication.* Teaching *is* communication. Teachers must communicate and work effectively with students, other teachers, parents, support staff, administrators, and community members. Teachers must in their communi-

cations demonstrate respect for students, treat them fairly and objectively, be sensitive to their feelings, and provide them with opportunities for success whenever possible. (See also Chapter 13.)

6. *Individual Characteristics.* A very important, yet difficult area to assess and provide supervision in is apparent in the area of *personal* characteristics. Each teacher is a unique individual, yet there are certain expectations placed on everyone who becomes a teacher. There are certain expectations regarding appearance, voice, manner, poise, confidence and initiative. Teachers are expected to be personally involved in their teaching assignments, to be committed and supportive of the principles and purposes of education, and to be punctual and dependable, for example. Teachers are also expected to assume responsibilities outside the classroom, both in the school and in the community. Teachers are expected to let their uniqueness *shine* through but they must always act as exemplars (models) to their students.

performance
criteria

The purpose of defining performance criteria is not to mold every teacher by the same die, but to establish benchmarks against which teachers may measure their own performances, and to set out the expectations in as clear a manner as possible so that supervisors are measuring teachers against theoretically and practically achievable goals. In this model it is stated the criteria are determined by board policy, acceptable practice, and attainable goals. This is not to say they are fixed and unchangeable. Throughout the process of supervision, it is important to have feedback loops in order for appropriate change to be made to improve the supervision cycle.

Types of Supervision

Supervision and assessment of performance is a process-oriented task; therefore a supervision plan must be continuous, and contain self-directed, informal and formal supervision procedures. In self-directed supervision, it is the responsibility of the individual staff member to engage in the practice of continuous self-evaluation and development. This is the central part of being a professional person. *Informal* refers to those procedures where the teacher, the administrator or the supervisor assesses performance and makes decisions related to teaching, but does not prepare a written report which is descriptive and summative of overall performance. *Formal* refers to the procedures where the appraisal statements are recorded and discussed with the teacher or staff member. These activities are intended to be formal in outcome, the results of which are placed in a personnel file. Now for a more detailed examination of each form of supervision.

informal

formal

1. *Self-Supervision.* Self-supervision is the process that every *reflective* person goes through in trying to improve his or her own performance. Informal discussions with other teachers, reading professional literature, membership in specialist instruction and general educational teacher councils, and attending workshops, institutes, in-service sessions, conventions, and visitations to the classrooms of colleagues are but a few routes toward self-development. *Envi-*

self
supervision

ronmental scanning is a useful tool in the hands of a reflective practitioner. Environmental scanning is the process of gathering all the data possible from the surroundings, such as job demands, characteristics of the leadership, school organizational styles and traditions, and situational variables such as population growth, population shifts, family transiency, and changing expectations of parents. The important step for the teacher in environmental scanning is in selecting the data which is meaningful to the task and useful for interpretation and application in problem solving. Another source of information and data is student feedback on a specific teaching unit, for example, and on the student's level of satisfaction respecting the teacher's performance and/or student assignments. (Students leave many clues for a teacher to read and hear.) Parent feedback is another important source of information for teachers. Parents are often eager to share their expectations for their own children, and thus become an important source of information. Performance results from both teacher and students can be utilized as another means in the process of self supervision. Student examinations can be an excellent tool to determine the effectiveness of a teaching style or instructional plan. Teacher performance appraisals are key documents for teacher self-supervision, since they reflect an *observer's* assessment of teaching skills. There are also many other useful self-assessment instruments available for teachers. Some examples of these are personality inventories, leadership style questionnaires, and time management scales.

environment scanning

2. *Informal Supervision.* Informal supervision involve the day-to-day contact and discussions with other staff, administrators, supervisors and/or consultants which teachers have. It also involves having teachers work with each other in a *peer* relationship, toward the improvement of instruction. These are situations which facilitate a sharing of expertise, knowledge and skills. Key processes in informal supervision are cooperating, helping, assisting and supporting. Some examples of these key processes are listed below.

informal supervision

a.. *Goal Setting.* Teachers can be assisted in establishing and clarifying what is expected of them.

b. *Instructional Input.* This refers to the information and knowledge which the student receives in relation to a particular content or skill. Teachers can be helped in developing skills in the planning and use of textbooks, audio-visual resources, visual support materials, and the use of other teaching materials.

c. *Modelling.* Modelling allows the teacher to observe examples of teaching performance that exemplify key teaching behaviors and skills. There are many ways that a teacher can be involved with modelling – through opportunities to visit and observe classrooms of effective teachers, demonstrations of teaching in the teacher's own classroom by experts or area specialists, and by team teaching assignments with other capable staff members.

d. *Practice.* Practice refers to the opportunity given to a teacher to try out new teaching behavior or skill in a sheltered environment before attempting to incorporate the practice in his or her own classroom. Role playing often provides an excellent opportunity for teachers to try out a new skill, without risk. Sometimes the practice is accomplished by predictive exercises in which the teacher *visualizes* what probably will happen in the lesson and with specific students. Lots of self-talk is often involved in the exercise.

e. *Feedback.* Feedback is information about past behavior that is presented to the person who performed that behavior. Feedback may be presented to the teacher in connection with opportunities provided for practice, or in connection with observations of another teacher's performance.

f. *Reinforcement.* Reinforcement is anything that is directed toward strengthening or maintaining the frequency or duration of an appropriate behavior. Supporting a teacher may be provided through reinforcing a positive performance by words and actions.

g. *Counselling.* Professional assistance may be made available to teachers to assist them in dealing with crisis situations (classroom or home) and personal problems which may interfere with their teaching performance.

h. *Environmental Change.* This refers to modifications that are made in the situational context in which a teacher works. Environmental change may be necessary if a class group develops behavior patterns which are contrary to the process of good teaching and learning. Assistance may be given through reassignment, transfer or provision of greater resources to deal with the problem.

Informal supervision is a continuous process that sometimes happens on a scheduled basis, sometimes on an unscheduled basis. The duration and frequency of assistance is situation specific, and depends largely upon the individual teacher. It should be considered usual, appropriate, and valuable for informal visits and discussions to occur between colleagues, administrators, supervisors, consultants, and teachers.

3. *Formal Supervision.* Formal supervision is designed to be structured in nature and in outcome. This means that a plan for supervision is established between the administrator and teacher. In this example (suggested by exhibit 13-1) the process is called a *supervisory cycle*. In the model, formal supervision is carried out by a person who has administrative responsibility for the teacher. The administrator with formal responsibility for the supervision of teachers is usually the principal of the school. In large schools, or in schools with special needs, for example French immersion schools where the supervisor must be bilingual or where the content is advanced, the school principal may delegate responsibility for supervision to other administrators such as assistant principals or department heads. It is expected however that this delegation would be formalized in writing to the teacher and to the superintendent of schools where it is not already specifically enunciated in policies or formal role descriptions. In some provinces, school legislation designates who is responsible, and the procedures to be followed in doing formal supervisory activities.

formal supervision

Also, legal (statutory) procedures may specify the routes of appeal open to the employee when actions to terminate, transfer, or suspend are initiated.

role of principal The role of the principal or designate, as educational leader, is to:

a. set the climate that stimulates the improvement of performance and the quality of instruction;

b. promote communication and cooperation between administrators, teachers and others involved in the teaching and learning process;

c. determine specific competencies and interests among staff members;

d. determine strengths and/or weaknesses in teaching performance (formal appraisal) for the purpose of praising good performance and/or providing assistance where it is needed by the less able;

e. maintain records of pertinent information pertaining to teaching performance; and to

f. assist in the administrative decisions in regard to staffing, continuing contracts, and teacher placement.

supervisory cycle To accomplish these objectives, the administrator must engage in a process of formal supervision herein labelled a *supervisory cycle*, which contains the following elements.

a. *Conferencing.* formal conference(s) are arranged between the administrator and the teacher to plan the supervisory cycle. Information is shared and a plan for visitations and feedback is developed. Specific information may be shared regarding lesson objectives, proposed teaching strategies, anticipated problems, and areas for evaluation to occur.

b. *Observations and Data Collection.* Formal observations are conducted by the supervisor and observed data is recorded. A review of planning and record keeping may be useful in clarifying the content of observations. The purpose of classroom visits is to identify teacher performance – strengths and/or weaknesses – and to witness first-hand the process of teaching and learning in the classroom or instructional setting. Additional data may be collected from any appropriate source that yields useful additional information on teaching and learning. Examples of such data are parent feedback, test and evaluation results, examples of student assignments, samples of student-produced work, and demonstrated skills.

c. *Feedback.* The supervisor is bound by *natural justice* to provide feedback as soon as possible to the teacher. It is advisable to share all written feedback with the teacher as a source of information for improvement, and to develop a trust relationship with the teacher. This feedback can be the source of direction for future planning or assistance.

d. *Planning.* The fourth element of a supervisory cycle is planning. Planning is essential so that appropriate praise can follow good performance and offers of assistance can follow marginal performances. Where serious problems exist, careful planning is essential in order for the supervisor to support the teacher' efforts at improvement. Good planning includes clear statements of expectations, performance improvement targets, and deadline dates for accomplishment. Plans should be in written form so that communication is clear, understood, and recorded.

Formal Appraisal (Summative Teacher Evaluation/Teacher Evaluation)

Supervisory cycles may be repeated as often as deemed necessary by either the teacher, the administrator, or both. The end product of the supervisory cycles is a formal written appraisal report prepared by the administrator who is held responsible for the supervisory cycles. The formal appraisal report consists of a summative analysis of teaching performance over a set period of time, which is usually a school year. This report contains observations, recommendations, commentary and signatures. It addresses strengths, skills, weaknesses, suggested areas of improvement, and, if necessary, mandatory requirements for the teacher. Teachers with identified serious problems must, in this report, be directed to specific remediation and/or assistance, because if not set forward in policy, these steps *will* be demanded by the legal system if the teacher elects to appeal the ruling of the supervisor.

report on teaching

The formal appraisal report must follow the criteria established by the board for the supervisory process so that consistency is maintained throughout the supervisory plan. The formal appraisal report is discussed with the teacher, and the teacher should have an opportunity to respond with any comments, if he or she so wishes. Often the formal report is signed by the teacher as well as the supervisor and a copy placed in the teacher's personnel file.

formal appraisal

Where the teacher feels misrepresented by the report, or feels the report is in error, he or she should have the opportunity to appeal the formal appraisal report. The appeal process consists of a set of procedures implemented according to a timed schedule, for officials of the school district, such as superintendents, to review the teacher-expressed concerns, to review the written data on teacher performance, and to carefully assess the contents of the formal appraisal report. The superintendent, by virtue of school legislation is usually the person empowered to verify, alter or destroy the contents of the formal appraisal report. The findings of the local appeal process are final and are submitted to the teacher. If the teacher wishes to further challenge the report he or she may file the case with a Board of Reference (or similarly titled quasi-judicial body), as set out in appropriate school legislation. Teachers are urged to become familiar with the procedures appropriate in the province of employment. The professional association is an excellent source of help.

appeal

There are linkages between all three components of the supervisory plan. Information should be shared in a professional manner between all individuals who participate in the supervisory plan. This factor is represented by a dotted line in the figure. The guiding principle that directs this sharing process is that the individual teacher must be made aware of the information that is being shared. Failure to do so in most provinces would constitute a violation of the professional association's code of ethics. All teachers must be aware of the

linkages

codes which govern their conduct (see Chapter 18). Consideration is now given to the outcomes of supervision.

Personal Performance Plan

The final component of this proposed supervisory plan is for the teacher to develop a plan for improving personal performance. The personal performance improvement plan represents the teacher's commitment to grow *as a teacher*. The teacher is charged with the responsibility of collecting all the data presented in the three components of the model (self, informal, formal) and developing a personal improvement plan which should be shared with the school administrators in order that the critical components which require assistance and resources can be identified for priority effort in the ensuring time frame. Teacher ownership of the improvement plan is critical to its success. In the *self-supervision* component, teachers are free to choose the components and instruments that best suit their own improvement needs. The individual teacher chooses the components from this section to carry on into the personal performance plan.

self
supervision

informal
feedback

Informal feedback from individuals in the organization charged with supervisory or program responsibilities (consultants, coordinators, peers, administrators) is the second component chosen to become part of the personal improvement plan. the informal feedback is essential to the personal improvement plan. The formal appraisal report also becomes an important component because it contains the formalized recommendations for improvement of teaching performance. The personal goals outlined in the personal improvement plan are carried forth to join with the personal goals of all the other staff members to have input to the ensuing *supervision plan* and *school management plan*. Thus the supervision plan is complete, with a self-renewing process built into it.

Musella

According to Musella (1988) common supervisory procedures for all levels of personnel serves no useful purpose other than to communicate that *sameness* is valued over individual needs. Each must be as unique as is the teacher.

Staff Development

One of the current administrative and policy issues confronting school boards and administrators is how to effect changes within the professional teaching staff – changes which are directed toward staff/school improvement. These policies are usually fashioned into a plan for staff development. Staff development is defined as the totality of educational and personal experiences that contribute toward an individual becoming more competent and satisfied in the assigned work-related role. The term is also used to describe school or unit-wide programs. Further, staff development can also be referred to as the procedures and processes through which teachers develop and improve their skills. Staff development can be further defined as "any activity or set of activities designed to enhance an institution through the promotion of the personal/professional growth of the administrative and/or instructional staff of that institution" (Caldwell & Marshall, 1982, p. 26). It is implementing a plan for performance improvement. As Joyce, Hersh, and McKibbon state:

> If the education profession is to flourish and if schools are to be a vital force in society, it is necessary to rebuild the school into a lifelong learning laboratory not only for children but for teachers as well. The improvement of staff development is a matter of generating a rich environment in which every educator becomes a student of education and works continuously to improve his/her skills. If schools are not being improved, they atrophy. The environment of the school must regenerate the relationship between teachers, learners, and community members or the school will lose its vitality. (Joyce et al., 1983, p. 149)

Research indicates the role of the principal is the key to providing an effective staff development program (Killion, Huddelson & Caspell, 1989). The principal as instructional leader as well as manager of an effective school, has the responsibility to initiate and maintain teacher renewal for school improvement, (Rallis & Highsmith, 1987; Killion et al., 1989), or staff development plans.

staff developmnt plans

Research in the area of the *effective schools* movement has shown that effective schools share many characteristics in common. These include:

1. presence of a comprehensive needs assessment program;
2. staff involvement in the selection of goals and in the planning, implementation, and evaluation of the school program in all its aspects;
3. congruency among personal and system goals;
4. ongoing evaluation, feedback, and adjustment;
5. attention given to the principles of adult learning;
6. school system support by way of written policies, adequate time, incentives, and resources;
7. awareness of *change theory*;
8. continuous support given to teachers; and
9. active participation of the school principal.
(Thompson & Cooley, 1986; Orlick, 1983; Van Voorhees, 1984; Gleave, 1983)

The Principal and the Vision

Principals forget to realize that, in their eagerness to provide a vision for staff development, the vision and the staff development program must not only address system-wide (sometimes even province-wide) needs, but also the needs of individual schools and individual teachers. Effective change can only be attained by addressing the specific concerns of the school (Wood et al., 1982), and the teachers. The *doers* must communicate their needs to the *planners*.

purposes

Vision is necessary to:

1. relate program to mission statement (goals);

2. overcome *the smorgasbord syndrome* wherein staff development programs appear to be a series of unrelated presentations;

3. help staff set priorities and refine focus;

4. set new directions;

5. share directions and coordinated growth; and

6. help overcome a possible sense of frustration and pressure.

methods

A recent study of school principal effectiveness identified six ways in which principals appear to exercise instructional leadership through staff development. They were:

1. informing teachers of professional development opportunities;

2. disseminating professional and curriculum materials;

3. focusing staff attention on a specific theme;

4. soliciting teachers' opinions;

5. encouraging experimentation; and

6. recognizing teacher achievement.

(McEvoy, 1987, p. 73)

further
training

In order to do this, school principals are, through further training (workshops), professional reading, university courses, peer exchange and support, and other upgrading activities, being advised to provide instructional leadership through school-based staff development programs. In overall terms, the principal is being advised by these sources that his or her actions can promote or impede the progress of the staff development activities which could lead to desired change and that initial and continuing support of the teacher's efforts is critical (Albrecht, 1988). Without the facilitating behaviors of the principal, the whole program could grind to a halt (Wood et al., 1982). Their support should occur through allocation of time and resources; formal and casual conversations; and observations and suggestions that assist teachers in their daily efforts to improve. The goals of the program should be set collaboratively by all staff members, who then design and implement the activities of the school necessary to achieve these goals (Gleave, 1983). The school principals are told the principal is the institutional leader who facilitates staff development through managerial and leadership skills. The teacher should expect to become a part of the instructional team, in a true sense of the work team.

Principals are expected to model behaviors that are conducive to staff development, thus reinforcing the concept of legitimacy for all staff members. Through continued participation and commitment to the staff development activities, the whole program will develop a long-term perspective (Doggett, 1987). The principal must continue to remove barriers to goal achievement, to provide conditions supportive of interaction and self-reflection, and to prevent teacher isolation. School principals are expected to be *educational facilitators* who support and encourage the type of activities capable of nurturing and maintaining necessary strategies. "The effective principal creates an environment in which procedural obstacles to innovation are removed, an environment in which teachers are treated as professionals who can themselves improve instruction" (Rallis & Highsmith, 1987, p. 21).

educational facilitators

In short, just as teachers are expected to upgrade and remain up-to-date, principals must also assume a similar responsibility by preparing themselves for management and instructional leadership roles.

Summary

An effective growth program should encompass supervision, evaluation, and staff development activities. The supervision program should grow from the mission or purpose statements of the school jurisdiction. Recognition must be given to school law, school board policy, and teacher goals in order to develop a sound school management plan. Supervision has three stems: self, informal, and formal. Teachers, in developing their own personalized performance improvement plan, will usually use a combination of personal choice, informal feedback from administrators, consultants, coordinators and peers, coupled with administrator-initiated formal appraisals of their achievements.

effective growth program

When the plan has been developed, the teachers in conjunction with their instructional leaders (usually principals, but in larger schools at the second school level, assistant principals for instruction, team leaders, or department heads) will proceed to put in place a school-based staff development plan which has both individual and group aspects. There are but two keys: teacher willingness and principal capabilities.

Part Four

Organizing the Schools

15
Longitudinal Organization

To find one plan of . . . organization that can be executed by all teachers with all children is as difficult as finding a word to rhyme with orange.

Emmett A. Betts

> Grades
>
> Levels
>
> Continuous Progress
>
> Semestering

Introduction

Each provincial government has designated specific age limits within which every child (with certain minor exceptions) must attend school. These legal age limits tend to be from six years of age to fifteen or sixteen years of age. Societal pressures, exerted mainly through educational prerequisites to jobs and positions, encourage most students to continue beyond the legal school leaving age. Thus the nine or ten years spent in the only compulsory occupation, attending school, becomes semi-compulsory for another two or three years. Because of this compulsory nature of education, the school authorities, including teachers, have an even greater moral and legal responsibility to each and every student within the system than would otherwise exist. The focus of this chapter is the division of this compulsory and semi-compulsory sojourn in school into organizational time frames. This is the longitudinal view of school organization.

compulsory occupation

Throughout discussions on longitudinal organization, some fairly basic philosophical decisions need to be made. On the one hand there is the school of thought which believes that there is a certain body of content matter and skill development which needs to be mastered. When the student has demonstrated this to a satisfactory degree he/she has finished the usual twelve grades in school. This stand would mean that more capable and more highly motivated students should be able to complete the required sequence in less than twelve years while other students may require thirteen or fourteen (or more) years to achieve the same result. On the other hand is the concept that the child is placed in the school for twelve years of attention and that the school is to provide the fullest and richest educational program possible for those twelve years. The first view connotes a content commitment; the second view connotes a time

longitudinal organization

commitment. The adherents of the content-based philosophy have differing opinions of appropriate time frames for school organization from those who adhere to a time base. The most appropriate structures are those which give consideration to both points of view – with the most appropriate mix being very difficult to determine (and administratively very difficult to accomplish in an orderly fashion).

These questions are evident in several ways in the school. For example, many schools have basic or core subjects and subjects which are not so designated (exploratory, options, electives). The core subjects are usually English, Social Studies, Mathematics and Science, whereas the non-core subjects (even though sometimes compulsory) are subjects such as Physical Education, Art, Dramatics and Music. The distinction is sometimes made in an unobtrusive manner, for example: to calculate honors, only the core subjects are considered; or if some instructional time must be lost, *the core subjects must not suffer;* or final examinations in non-core subjects must not interfere with core examinations. This can be rationalized through the importance attached by society to certain subjects but it is also a reflection of the content versus time question, where the core subjects reflect an expectation of time allotment. Historically, the core subjects were those which were required to make a living and the non-core were extras, usually aimed towards leisure time and the well-educated person. Of course, all this is an over-simplification since there are other factors at work, but perhaps this illustrates that the organization of schools, from a longitudinal viewpoint, does hinge to a considerable extent upon the viewpoints of these two dimensions.

Progression by Grades

From a time standpoint the educational program is traditionally divided into school years, with eleven or twelve years considered as the usual requirement for pre-college or pre-university education. A quality control (or administrative convenience) is normally injected into this plan and thus the result is grades (forms, standards, and whatever). These grades become hurdles during each time frame, usually a school year. Some students master the content and skill development faster than other students and, therefore, provision is sometimes made for such students to move through more than one hurdle during a particular time frame (acceleration). On the other hand, provision is sometimes made for the retention of students in a particular time frame when the quality of their work falls below the required standards (failure).

Administratively, various combinations of grades are structured together as a unit. The more common of these combinations are the elementary school (grades one to six), junior high school (grades seven to nine) and senior high school (grades ten to twelve). There are numerous reasons for these various combinations of grades, administrative convenience being only one. For example, senior high schools, in order to offer a substantial program (as measured by numbers of subjects available), need a larger student base than does the elementary school. Socially, it is preferable to group together students with

core

electives

quality control

acceleration

retention

somewhat similar social development and stage of maturity, thus segregating the younger from the older. Teacher interests in the various age levels vary – dividing the student population into two or three major organizational patterns permits this greater concentration of teacher interests and expertise. Although busing students to school has become commonplace, the majority of students still walk, ride a bicycle or use the public transport. Older students are more capable of travelling further to school resulting in the concept of the elementary school being in the immediate neighborhood, the junior high being a little further afield, and the senior high serving a number of neighborhoods, often a considerable distance away. Another reason is that the different age groups require variations in the physical plant – the senior high requiring a basketball court sized gymnasium, the elementary requiring lower blackboards and wash basins, as examples. Lastly, however, it is not possible to ignore the emphasis on the activity commitment for the younger students as compared to content commitment for the senior students.

age
segregation

activity

content

Although combinations of grade organization vary, the concept of a three-level system has become deeply imbedded subsequent to the establishment of grades as used in the Quincy Grammar School in Boston in 1848. These three levels are the elementary school, with its emphasis on skill development, the junior high school, to serve the special needs of the adolescent, and the senior high school with its emphasis on preparation for occupational training and further education. From time to time educators, in particular, become concerned about the insularity which they feel develops in the separation of the educational program into the three categories. This spurs the attempts at *vertical integration,* the integrating of the program from kindergarten to grade twelve. Most efforts to achieve this integration are only moderately successful. This circumstance is due in large measure not to a lack of will, but due to the historical divisions which have been present in the organization and administration of schools.

Quincey
Grammar
School

vertical
integration

The graded program has long been a favorite target of both the educational critic and the educational innovator. Much of the reasoning for advocating the abolition of the graded system stems from inadequacies in the educational system itself rather than from the use of grades in particular. The caution to the beginning teacher is not to *throw the baby out with the bath water.* There are problems associated with the use of grades, but how successful have the alternatives to the graded system been in alleviating these particular difficulties? In other words, the strengths of the graded systems should be preserved while developing other systems which will overcome the inadequacies of the graded system. In time, the graded system, as it is now known, may very well disappear but the proven alternatives must supplant what currently exists. (The teacher as member of the administrative team and as pedagogical expert will have much to say in these decisions.)

alternatives

strengths
of grades

expectations

competition

administratively
feasible

inadequacies
of grades

self-competition

The educational literature attributes the following as strengths of the graded system. First, it is an organized system which is readily understood by the general public, the parents and the students. Second, orderly progression through the school years is achieved. The curriculum content can be divided on the basis of normal expectations of twelve years as being reasonable for completion of the program, assisting in a more structured approach to curriculum development. Third, the expectations for the student are relatively clear. Students normally work according to expectations held for them, and by them; the graded program attempts to set the hurdles at the appropriate height and encourages the students to master these hurdles accordingly. Fourth, competition is a fact of life. Used judiciously, competition is helpful in the learning process and is an inherent component of the graded system. Fifth, the graded program provides a more organized, structured and understood basis for evaluation of students' progress. Sixth, administrative feasibility should be considered. Although no program should be developed with only administrative convenience in mind, the corollary is important; any educational program if it is to succeed, must be administratively feasible. Administratively feasible applies to the teacher as well as to the principal – the graded system provides a ready framework which saves the teacher countless hours in preparation and planning. Or, more positively, the graded system permits the teacher more time to plan lessons and for student assistance because less time is needed for the planning of the structure. Lastly, the graded system can be considered more student time-oriented and less content-oriented. If the basic philosophy is to provide the best possible educational program for the twelve years during which the student is in school, the structure of the graded system can enhance this possibility.

On the obverse side are a number of inadequacies generally attributed to the graded program, foremost of which is the concern about rigidity. Students are individuals who learn at different rates and have differing interests and motives. The graded system is inclined to treat students as if they were all the same. Second, teachers are professional people, possessing professional expertise which can be utilized more extensively when they are unfettered by the rigid structure imposed by grades. Third, while recognizing the importance of competition, the emphasis should be placed on self-competition, a concept which is more difficult in a graded program. A fourth weakness is the treatment given to students who fail a grade. In the subsequent year the student normally starts at the beginning of the grade regardless of what has been learned in the preceding year, thus inviting boredom and frustration.

The beginning teacher should consider these strengths and weaknesses as points of emphases only, since much can be done to transfer the strengths of a graded system to other types of organization. Also, some of the weaknesses often attributed to graded organization can be overcome within the working mechanisms which really are not as rigid and inflexible as they may appear on the surface. A graded organization, or any other type of organization, will only be as successful as the teachers want it to be.

Grades Divided Into Levels

Rather than having a student repeat the work of an entire school year, some systems utilize a *levels* system whereby the pass-fail hurdle is considered at the mid-way point in each school year and again at the end of the school year. Basically this is a graded system with twice as many grades but with each grade constituting half the time and content. Each of these "half-grades" is called a level, making fourteen levels to the end of grade six (levels one and two are normally reserved for the kindergarten period). The levels system is essentially a phenomenon of the elementary school. At the junior and senior high grades a somewhat similar arrangement, that of semestering, is utilized. The emphasis of semestering is sufficiently different to warrant a separate discussion on its structure and utility.

Although the levels system is, in reality, a graded system, there are a number of advantages which teachers may wish to consider. First, a student who is unsuccessful in passing a pass-fail hurdle faces the prospect of repeating four or five months rather than an entire school year, a situation which is more palatable to the student. Repeating half a year is not likely to be much more successful a procedure than repeating a full year, since research indicates that repeating generally does not produce the expected gain. Nevertheless, repeating, even though not as common now as it was a decade ago, is likely to remain part of the educational scene. Frequently the alternative to repeating a grade is what is often called the social promotion. Second, while teachers continually assess the progress of their students, extra effort is applied at the decision point of passing or not passing. Making this decision twice a year instead of once forces the teacher to give greater attention to evaluation of the students' progress. Third, utilizing levels facilitates a double entry system for kindergarten and grade one students. Rather than having to wait an entire extra year to enter school, if a child just misses the deadline for entrance, the wait will be only a half year. Thus if a levels system is utilized throughout an entire school system, students will be finishing a "grade" in the middle of the school year, eventually resulting in two graduation times per year for grade twelve. These *middle of the year graduates* would numerically correspond to middle of the year grade one entrants, making no extra demands on the school system.

Fourth, various forms of semesters have been relatively common at the senior high level in Canada, extending as well into the junior high school. There are common aspects between the levels system and semestering so that the levels system is sometimes thought of as a downward extension of semestering. Fifth, the levels system can be an aid to grouping students more effectively. True, regrouping could be done at any time of the school year but usually the grouping for distribution of students (according to teacher and available space) is normally done once a year. Many changes take place within the span of a ten-month school year and thus the levels system, where grouping consideration is activated twice a year, is more apt to achieve grouping in accordance with the purpose for which it was intended. Sixth, grading, according to some

half-grades

semestering

levels

social promotions

educators and some segments of the public, has become synonymous with *tradition, rigidity,* and *bureaucracy.* This is not a justifiable combination of terminology but it does exist and therefore the utilizing of levels instead of grades may provide a more acceptable structure, administratively speaking. (It is interesting to note that even the meaning of the word *bureaucracy* has undergone a metamorphosis since Max Weber first used the term at about the turn of the century.)

Thus the levels system is really a graded system but with twice the number of grades where each level requires half the time span of a grade. Some of the advantages of levels system would indicate that perhaps even shorter promotion periods could be used effectively: a quarter-year system with four decision levels, for example. This reasoning could then be stretched to develop a monthly promotional period, then a weekly period, and finally, promotion on a daily basis. As more and more decision points are developed throughout the school year, the idea of "grades" becomes less and less distinct. Working this idea to its extreme, the decision points become continuous. The repetition resulting from incomplete learning becomes repetition of very small segments of education indeed. It is at this point that repetition is not really noticeable and we have arrived at what is now commonly called continuous progress.

Continuous Progress

Before discussing continuous progress in detail, we need to define three terms which are commonly, but mistakenly, understood as being synonymous. These terms are "nongraded" (or ungraded), "continuous progress" and "individualized instruction" (or individually prescribed instruction). It is difficult to determine what the term *nongraded* really means. To some it indicates a steady, individual progression through the subject matter at school; to others it merely means that the term "grades" is not used – levels perhaps, or even units, terms or sections, but not grades. That is, nongrading should not be taken to imply any particular kind of organization of the students; a nongraded arrangement can be rigid or flexible; it can emphasize groups or individuals; it can be found in old *traditional* schools or in modern innovative schools. Therefore, "nongrading" in this book will be taken to mean the disuse of the term "grades" and nothing more. *Continuous progress* and *individualized instruction* are separate and discrete terms. They are commonly found in association with one another but the meanings of the terms are quite different. Briefly, individualized instruction is the aiming of the instruction and concomitant learning activities at the individual student whereas continuous progress is the constant progression of learning activities geared to the level of the learners. Further, there can be both continuous progress and individualized instruction within the graded system.

nongraded

individualized instruction

continuous progress

Students should learn within their range of abilities. In the organization of materials for continuous progress time, as such, becomes a secondary factor – that is, the relationship between performance and credit is continued but the relationship between time and credit becomes subsidiary. The graded system assumes a certain body of material as being equivalent to one school year's work, with students who are able to assimilate more or less than that amount having to adjust to meet the demands of the yearly allotment. This overstates the actual situation; on the surface it appears that every student begins the material at the beginning of the school year and must finish it exactly at the end of the year (in the same manner that the toast and jam must somehow come out even at the breakfast table). In actual practice the rigidity implied in the graded system is usually not there, for example: the grade three teacher determines *where the students are* in reading and proceeds from there. Thus an element of continuous progress is injected into the graded system.

Continuous progress is based on achieving success and eliminating failure. From a practical standpoint it is not true to say that failure is eliminated but rather that failure makes its appearance in much smaller packages and, there-fore, does not appear to be failure. The repetition may only involve the material of that last thirty minute period. There is no repetition in the sense of having to repeat a whole grade (however, keep in mind that failing a grade does not have to mean the exact repetition of the material of a whole grade).

repetition

In any organizational structure for instruction, attention must be focussed on the individual. Above all, any group is merely a special collection of individuals. The continuous progress organization is no exception to this. No organization will force every student to learn at the very same rate since this is impossible, but some organizational patterns take greater cognizance of this reality than others.

Consider then, the following situation illustrated by the diagram. Assume the concept to be learned has been shown through previous experience of the teachers to take five class periods for the average child (remembering that the time length is subsidiary to the prime issue which is the mastering of the concept).

<u>Time Required to Master the Concept</u>

STUDENT A <u>Day 1</u>	<u>Day 2</u>	<u>Day 3</u>	<u>Day 4</u>	<u>Day 5</u>
STUDENT B <u>Day 1</u>	<u>Day 2</u>	<u>Day 3</u>		
STUDENT C		Day 1	Day 2	<u>Days 3, 4 and 5</u>
STUDENT D <u>Day 1</u>				

Exhibit 15-1
Concept Mastering – Four Individual Students

In this diagram the lines represent that portion of the concept mastered. Thus Student A has mastered one-fifth of the concept in each of the five days, probably within the regular period time frame. Student B has mastered the enrichment

concept in three periods – which now leaves the question of what to do with Student B during the time the student would normally be expected to be in that class for the fourth and fifth periods. There are several possibilities: the student may spend the fourth and fifth period helping Student C master the concept; the student could go home and do nothing for the two periods (not usually an acceptable alternative); the student might explore that concept further through investigation of practical applications (enrichment); or Student B may spend periods four and five on some other subject – perhaps more time is required to master another concept in another subject; or perhaps the student will use the time reading or experimenting in areas not necessarily tied directly to any concepts in regular school studies.

Student C has not progressed very far in the first three periods in the mastery of the concept. A possibility for days four and five would be an extension of time beyond the normal period allotment and, therefore, still permit the mastering of the concept by the end of the fifth period. Or it may be that Student C was not feeling well during the first three days, did not work well and could not pay attention, but compensated for this on the fourth and fifth days (perhaps with the inclusion of some home study time).

Student D mastered most of the concept during the first period (or perhaps has mastered most of the concept before the concept was introduced to this class). The student could, like Student B, pursue other activities during days two, three and four, but return to this concept on day five for investigation of practical applications of the concept and for evaluation.

independent study

These four examples do not exhaust the possibilities but do illustrate the idea of continuous progress, even within a highly structured situation. Continuous progress must not be confused with individualized learning programs or independent study; elements of these are useful in any meaningfully organized school program but in and of themselves are not continuous progress.

Continuous progress still involves teaching and all the aspects associated with teaching: motivation, instruction and explanation, discussion, elaboration, consultation, and evaluation. Continuous progress can be organized on a group basis, on an individual basis, or on some combination of both.

element of success

Continuous progress can be organized within a graded structure or in a school which does not use *grades* as such. However, the element of success must be present, and failure, other than in very small pieces, cannot be considered. This means that students require constant grouping and regrouping, and the teachers will need to be perceptive in determining the needs of the student. Continuous progress can be teacher-dominated and directed or the teacher may play a more passive, consultative role, but preferably some combination of the two will exist.

Semestering

Semestering is an administrative arrangement whereby the school year is divided into two distinct halves. This is a relatively common arrangement at the senior high level but is less often found in the junior high schools. The term itself has a number of meanings attached to it but basic to any of the definitions is the concept of a school year divided into two halves. The levels system (discussed in a previous section) is in reality a type of semester system but the connotation of semestering is a concept which first started at the university and college level, then gradually worked its way through senior high school and now is found in some of the junior high schools.

In general, there are two methods of dividing a school year. One way, more common in the United States, is to take the subject arrangement of the school, find a halfway point in the school year and make the boundary sharp and distinct at that point. Consider then what happens to the grade ten English course, as an example. Where formerly the course would start in September and end in June, with the final evaluation of the entire year's work in that course being made in June, but in the semester system the English course would be divided into two halves on the basis of an equivalent coverage of content in each half. Each half then becomes a course in its own right, half the length of the original course, and the final evaluation to take place at the end of the first five months for the first half, and in June for the other half.

The other general method, which is more distinctively Canadian, is to divide the school year in half, and then compress full year courses into halves. Using the same example of the grade ten English course – where formerly the students would take approximately three hours of instruction per week for the entire school year, they would now take six hours of instruction for half the year. The result then becomes not the dividing of subjects into halves but rather doubling the time per subject and completing the subject in half the school year, thereby necessitating the undertaking of half the number of subjects in each half of the year.

half year

The strengths of dividing each course into two half courses (in the American manner) parallel the strengths of the levels organization, with perhaps greater motivational pressure because of the immediacy of the final examinations in each course. With the inclination toward content emphasis in the upper grades, a course for a full year can appear to be a formidable barrier to overcome, whereas a half course, even in a dreaded subject, is more palatable.

half course

It is rare for an elementary student to have a choice of subjects but the further a student progresses through school, the more choices the student will have. In a large senior high school a student is able to choose from four or five times as many courses as he/she would have time to undertake. Some courses become compulsory because of their prerequisite nature to other courses and to admission in post-secondary institutions; others become compulsory because of administrative concerns. Even so, students have some opportunity to explore their interest in certain areas. The "exploration" risk of a half-course is worth taking, but the gamble of a full year, unknown course can be harmful to a student's program.

The half courses permit students who did not finish their high school in the *one grade per year* pattern to complete courses in which they were deficient without being committed to an entire extra year. Also, the student who works hard and is a high achiever can finish schooling a half year sooner. Without the semestering arrangement, the saving of one half year in the high school program would not be possible.

The other type of semestering, utilizing the compressed course principle, bears further discussion as to its advantages and disadvantages. Some of these advantages and disadvantages are unique to the compressed course semester system but others are common to both types of semestering.

One advantage is the degree of concentration on the subject matter which is made possible. The student is taking half as many courses at any one time and thus is able to concentrate on fewer subjects. The student becomes immersed in a subject for longer periods of time on a daily basis, reducing retention loss from period to period. Reviewing becomes less essential because of the shorter time span, and the reviewing time thus saved can be utilized in extending the content coverage or delving deeper into the concepts, understandings and skills relative to the subject.

immediacy
of goals

From the time a student starts the course, the end is in sight. The immediacy of the goals is a strong motivational force which encourages the student to concentrate on the subject immediately, eliminating the introductory time lag that is common for full year courses.

The student realizes that extra concentration is needed and, therefore, is less apt to miss classes or be involved in disciplinary problems. The teacher, because of the extended daily contact period, is better able to know each student as an individual. This not only is an asset to reducing discipline and attendance problems but also encourages, and permits, more individual attention. The student is better able to work on the material or problems in class time, where help is available when needed. Without the extended class periods, the student is not as likely to be able to work on the assignments until he or she is at home. Then even a small misunderstood point in the assignment can negate much of the value of the assignment.

If a student is unsuccessful in a course, the student can enrol in the same course the next semester. What the student failed to learn in the first semester happened not more than half a year earlier, thus the positive benefits of repetition are on a much firmer base which increases the chances of success. Former drop-outs are encouraged to return and try again.

fewer
preparations

The teacher has half as many classes and is able to concentrate more on fewer classes. This means fewer preparations (and logically better preparations) per day. The extended time permits laboratory exercises and more effective group projects, which means the teacher is able to organize a more effective course. The teacher is also under pressure because of the concentration of the course and will be more conscious of eliminating unproductive activities.

From the negative viewpoint, the concentration becomes a serious handicap should the student, or the teacher, be absent for only a few days. Each absence is equivalent to two absences under other circumstances. Teachers sometimes complain about the very long period not being as effective as more short periods for certain subjects, such as modern languages. The length of the period can lead to boredom unless suitable variety and initiative are exercised. From the administrative viewpoint, there is much more work involved with two registration periods per year instead of one. Also, the balancing of a teaching load is more difficult so that during one half of the year the teacher may have no preparation time but in the other half of the year may have more preparation time than necessary.

absences

The time lag between sequential courses is the most common complaint relative to semestering. A student may take, for example, the grade ten Mathematics course during the first half of this year and the grade eleven course during the last half of the next year, leaving an entire year during which the student does not study Mathematics at all.

time lag

Surveys by the hundreds have been conducted and invariably the surveyed populations – the students, teachers, administrators, and the parents – are in favor of semestering at the senior high level. Junior high school survey results are not as conclusive but do encourage some semestering at that level as well. With careful planning, and a dedicated staff, semestering is found to be a very suitable type of organization for instruction.

The material for chapters 15 and 16 appeared originally in Braun & Giles, *Strategies for Instruction and Organization,* Detselig Enterprises Ltd., 1976. Revisions have been made for this publication.

16
Cross-Sectional Organization

The organizational context of the school is a set of contracts and opportunities
that form the environment in which each individual classroom operates.
Hoy and Forsyth, p. 150

> Homogeneous Grouping
>
> Heterogeneous Grouping

Introduction

Organization skills are part of the administrative process. When a mechanic
has a certain job to do, an appropriate tool is selected. Probably several different
tools could be used, but from experience and training, an optimum selection is
made. Like the mechanic, the teacher should consider various organizational
patterns as tools. By doing this, the emphasis will be on the purposes for which
organization takes place rather than on the organization itself. The purpose of
this section, however, is to examine the tools of cross-sectional organization.

At opposite ends of a continuum are the cross-sectional organizational
concepts of homogeneous and heterogeneous grouping. The basis for homogeneous grouping is an effort to homogenize, or make as alike as possible, the
constituent members of the group. This is done on the premise that a group of
similar constituents enhances the teaching-learning situation. The basis for
heterogeneous grouping is that it really does not matter whether the constituent
group members are similar because the teaching-learning styles can be adjusted
to meet the situation. The following discussion focuses first on homogeneous
grouping and then on heterogeneous grouping.

homogeneous heterogeneous grouping

Homogeneous Organization

Assume the lesson to be undertaken is finding what percent one number is
of another. Then consider the difficulty of teaching this lesson to a group of
students in which one student has just learned how to count, another student is
able to add but is having difficulty in multiplying, another student works with
percentages every day in his father's store, and yet another student is at the
stage of differential calculus. Perhaps each of these students will receive some
benefit from the percent lesson but more success could be achieved working
with a group of students who had mastered adding, subtracting, multiplying,
dividing whole numbers and fractions (to a reasonable degree) and had a
working knowledge of ratios.

On a broad basis, the placement of students in grades homogenizes, to a
limited extent, those with somewhat similar backgrounds. For instance, at least

293

limiting
the variance

in a very rough way, it can be assumed that the commonalty of background for grade three students would be greater than would the commonalty of background for a group of students whose grade placements normally would be grade one, grade three, and grade eleven. That is, keeping the same grade level students within an instructional unit, in addition to being a convenient administrative device, does provide a certain degree of homogeneity within the group being taught.

In most schools, basketball skills are not taught to groups containing grade three and grade twelve students at the same time but rather to groups within (or close to) the same grade level. This gives a certain degree of homogeneity of size, strength and endurance, recognizing of course the differences that exist. Most swimming classes are organized according to certain levels of accomplishment – beginners, junior, intermediate, senior, for example. within each class, there are differences of ability in swimming but at least the range of differences within one group is less than if no basis was used for grouping. Boys' physical education classes and girls' physical education classes illustrate another effort toward providing a degree of homogeneity – this time on the basis of sex.

Other examples of grouping to provide homogeneity on at least one basis are readily available in the educational scene. Suffice it to say, at this point, that various bases are used to limit the range of particular factors within each kind of grouping: age; sex; achievement; ability; and other specific characteristics. Rightly or wrongly, there appears to be a basic belief in our schools that limiting the variance within a group enhances the teaching and learning situation.

how to limit
variance

The main controversial points relative to organizing classes to achieve some degree of homogeneity are usually not whether the students should be in a certain grade (although this, too, raises many spirited discussions) but rather *how* to organize the number of students who have been assigned to a grade. To examine this basic concern, consider a situation with one hundred grade six students, and a teaching complement of four teachers. For the school that wishes to utilize homogeneous grouping, there are several possibilities. One possibility is to homogenize on the basis of sex, likely two rooms of boys and two rooms of girls; or perhaps on weight, or height, or even ethnic origin. Presumable these, and a number of other factors, are not normally used as viable bases for dividing students into groups. To most educators, homogeneity means using either ability or achievement (or both) as bases.

ability grouping

To homogenize these one hundred students on the basis of ability would mean the rank ordering of the students on the basis of intelligence rating, such ratings to be determined by means of intelligence tests. The students would be ranked from the highest to the lowest, with the top quartile forming one class, the second quartile the next class, the third quartile another class, and the fourth quartile forming the last class. This would result in four "homogeneous" classes based on ability. With assumed comparable abilities within each class, the teachers would then adjust their teaching and plans accordingly. A word of caution is in order here – this organizational pattern does not produce the degree of *ability* homogeneity one might expect, a point which will be discussed later in this section.

The other common basis is grouping by achievement. With our one hundred students we would place the top achievers in one class, the next-to-the-top achievers in another class, and so on for the third and fourth classes. Each teacher would then, presumably, be able to plan and teach without the concern of whether the lesson was too easy for some students while being incomprehensible for others. Various bases can be used for sorting students according to achievement. For example, a composite ranking according to report card marks from the previous June, or from the final examinations which may have been used, in part, to determine those end-of-year gradings, could be used. Another possibility is the use of a recognized standardized achievement test, such as the Canadian Tests of Basic Skills or the Iowa Tests of Basic Skills. Using the composite score from the standardized tests, students might be ranked and sorted into the various classes in much the same way as was described for ability grouping.

achievement grouping

Achievement and ability are not synonymous in spite of positive correlations existing between them. Using achievement only, the range of ability within a class is considerable, but using ability only produces a wide range of achievement within a class. A combination of ability and achievement probably is most appropriate if homogeneous grouping is desired, but the appropriate mix is difficult to achieve.

For example, if homogeneity is desired, the students would be grouped on a reading basis for reading instruction, and so on through the various subject areas. Although administratively more awkward, this is a more defensible position for homogeneous grouping. Homogeneous grouping provides the teacher with a better opportunity to use the materials and methods most appropriate for the student with whom he or she is working. Unless the teacher takes full advantage of this opportunity, the strengths of homogeneous grouping are lost and the advantages of heterogeneous grouping surface. Even when this happens within subject areas, questions concerning the advisability of homogeneous grouping will arise.

apppropriate materials and methods

Heterogeneous Organization

Efforts by teachers to utilize grouping practices designed to narrow the range of abilities and/or achievement within each group are normally only partially successful. Even where achieved to the satisfaction of the staff, constant vigilance and regrouping is necessary to maintain effective learning conditions. Too often schools are inclined to group students on one criterion only, such as an intelligence test, an achievement test or a reading test, and then retain these same groups for all subjects for the entire school year, or sometimes for two or three years. The effect of this is to reduce the beneficial effects which can be

regrouping

obtained through homogeneous grouping and to violate the vary bases on which the decision was made to group in this manner.

At the other end of the continuum is heterogeneous grouping, where groups are formed more or less on a random basis. For example, one hundred grade eight students could be divided into four groups by assigning every fourth name to one, group, the next name after each of these to the next group, and likewise for the third and fourth groups. The intent of the following discussion is not to castigate teachers who support homogeneous grouping, which can be an effective method of grouping, but rather to explain a few ways in which heterogeneous grouping can be more effective.

First, heterogeneous grouping avoids the administrative and educational
avoids administrative problems
problems associated with attempts to make groups sufficiently homogeneous to capitalize on narrower ranges within the groups. Questions can be raised about random selection for heterogeneous grouping, for example, once selected does the selection mean permanent placement within a group or should there be regrouping on a random basis at frequent intervals. No grouping should ignore all extenuating circumstances and, therefore, some changes should be expected, or even encouraged. However, some of the strength of a heterogeneous group is obtained when the students work together for an extended time
mutual assistance (such as a school year) and thus get to know one another, increasing the opportunity of mutual assistance.

One of the most serious handicaps to homogeneous grouping is the unintended discriminatory practices which can, and often do, result. No educator would support grouping students by race or by origins for example: placing all the new immigrants in one class, all the Indian or Black students in another, and the Anglo-saxons in a third; or perhaps inner city students in one group and the suburban students in another. Yet this is precisely what tends to occur. Where the student has not yet acquired fluent use of English, his standardized intelligence and achievement tests are likely to place him or her in the lowest group. Cultural deprivation and cultural differences will also be reflected in testing. Placing these students in one group reduces their contact with the wide mixture of all students and, therefore, denies them the profits of inter-race, inter-denominational, inter-cultural contacts. Canadian society does not tolerate discriminatory segregation practices, and the schools in particular must avoid such practices, even where unintentional.

A less noticeable discriminatory practice is for more boys to be assigned to lower groups and to remedial classes. Again, this is not intentional but is fairly commonplace. Boys tend to be rougher and more disruptive; they tend to have more sloppy writing and work that is less neat; they are less likely to conform. All of these factors will tend to place more boys than girls in groups for lower achievers, not an educationally sound practice.

Growth rates vary – whether they be for maturation, physical size, social maturation, or learning. Too often students who are properly placed in a
maturation particular homogeneous class will suddenly vary their rate of development on

the particular criterion that was used to determine the grouping and thus, within a short span of time find themselves in the "wrong" group. Constant regrouping will overcome this to a certain degree, but heterogeneous grouping alleviates the problem. There if greater opportunity in heterogeneous classes to maximize for the individual the advantages associated with varying developmental rates.

Recognizing teacher influence of expectations, is important. Students tend to gravitate toward the expectations held for them, at least as they perceive those expectations. In a heterogeneous class it is true that the slower students are not expected to compare with the *faster* students but at the same time they are expected to compete with the majority of the students. Those more capable than the slower students influence the slower students, thus effecting a higher level of achievement. If all the slower students are segregated into one class, the general expectation held by the students is inclined to be, "We are the dumb ones who are not capable of much," and therefore they achieve accordingly. This is a feeling which is difficult to overcome (not impossible, however) in homogeneous groupings, particularly for the slower groups. Further, it must never be assumed that all learning will take place via the teacher; students do learn from each other and therefore the faster students help the slower students, either directly or indirectly.

expections held

Being assigned to a low-achievement or low-ability group is a stigma which must be borne by the students so assigned. Even if their achievement is not greater when placed in a heterogeneous group, the stigma is less and is easier to bear. Teaching strategies for the higher groups are more inclined to be stimulating, something which lower-group students particularly need, but may miss in homogeneous situations.

stigma

Differentiated staffing, use of teacher assistance, team teaching, continuous progress, individualized instruction, and other techniques are becoming increasingly popular, and there is evidence that these innovations can benefit all students. As a result of these techniques, the need to homogenize groups becomes less because the teacher is more able to personalize the instruction for each student.

differentiated staffing

Homogeneous grouping will likely always be part of the educational scene, perhaps not to the same extent as at present. There are certain groups which may need to be segregated, even for part of the school day: the blind, the deaf, those in the lowest mental ranges. Some educators would suggest that the very gifted as need some special homogeneous grouping as well, particularly at the senior high school level, where some of the courses are sequential in nature. The student who does not pass the prerequisite grade ten mathematics course will not appear in the grade eleven course. That is, at the high school level, students will sort themselves into programs and courses on the basis of achievement. The resultant groups are somewhat homogeneous in nature. The choice of programs and courses at the senior high level permits students to become homogenized on the basis of interest and skill, as well as on the basis of achievement.

sorting on the basis of achievement

Teacher Duties

I am presumed to know, but I am not the only one in the situation to have relevant and important knowledge. My uncertain ties may be a source of learning for me and for them.

Schön, 1983

Attendance	Evaluation of Exceptional Students
Detentions	Parent-Teacher Interviews
Suspensions, Expulsion	Report Cards
Student Progress Records	Defamation
Duty Schedule	Use of Volunteers
Educational Malpractice	Special Services
Substitute Teachers	Helping Professionals
Student Control	Staff Meetings

Introduction

The technical function of the school is teaching. The teaching professional makes decisions, in part on what to teach, and almost totally on how to teach. Classroom teachers, with the help of school principals, team leaders, and department heads decide upon instructional goals, diagnose learner needs, and select suitable instructional objectives and strategies, instruct, and apply evaluation procedures. For some, this simplistic description is all that there is to teaching. Of course this is not true. There is more.

teaching technical function

Budgets for:

Supplies
Services
Equipment purchase and repairs
a. audio visual
b. office
Library/resource centre
Computers
Staff resources
Substitute teachers
Professional development activities
(Sometimes) professional and support staff

Communications
(What must, what may, and what may not)

Equipment
Repair
Replacements
Utilization
Inventory
Storage

Learning Environment
Lighting
Ventilation
Heating
Seating
Handicapped

Learning Materials (permanent)
Quantity
Quality
Suitability
Utilization
Storage
Inventory
Student deposits

Learning Materials (borrowed)
Ordering
Utilizing
Sharing

Physical Facilities
Adequacy
Timetabling use

Shared Resources
Scientific and other displays
Computers
Software

Time
Lesson and unit planning
Curriculum development
Professional development
Staff meetings
School timelines
Field trips
Staff planning
Substitute teachers
Program reviews and evaluation
Working with others

Security

Tests and exams, funds, equipment, building
Children, custody, kidnapping, self-inflicted injury

Copyright

Student and Staff Safety
Operating machinery and equipment
Using chemicals
Storing chemicals
Occupational health and safety legislation
Out-of-school activities
General safety

Student Records

Attendance and latest test results
Report cards
Interviews
Promotion

Exhibit 17-1
What Has to be Organized and Managed

In Supervision for Better Schools (Knoll, 1987), Knoll suggests a useful summary of the range of skills required to do the job.

CLASSROOM ENVIRONMENT

Physical Arrangement	1. Furniture is arranged to provide easy and safe movement of students.
	2. Furniture is arranged to match instructional objectives.
	3. The classroom is neat and clean.
Materials Arrangement	1. Learning materials are organized, easily available, and neat.
	2. Room displays reflect current student work.
Atmosphere	1. Student ideas are accepted.
	2. Teacher's physical appearance is positive.

PREPARATION FOR INSTRUCTION

Determination of needs	1. Student needs are diagnosed.
	2. Students are individually assessed.
	3. Progress is monitored.
Organization of Subject Matter	1. The specified curriculum is taught.
	2. Content presentation is sequential.

Instructional Plan	1. Time is appropriately allocated.
	2. Individual differences are addressed.
	3. Skill gaps are addressed.
	4. Provision is made for teacher absence.
Use of Resources	1. Provides for variety in instruction.
	2. Considers individual learning styles.
	3. Seeks outside resources.
	4. Operates equipment effectively and safely.

INTERACTION WITH STUDENTS

Use of Student Responses	1. Responses are valued.
	2. Responses are clarified.
	3. Responses are related and extended.
	4. Responses are used to summarize.
	5. Deals with incorrect responses.
Types of Questions Asked	1. Lower-level questions.
	2. Higher-level questions.
	3. Open questions.
Motivation Techniques	1. Uses student experiences.
	2. Uses past knowledge.
	3. Clarifies importance.
Variety of Instructional Approaches	1. Lecture.
	2. Discussion.
	3. Hands-on involvement.
	4. Independent work.
Variety of Instructional Groups.	1. Whole class.
	2. Groups.
	3. One-to-one.
	4. Peer instruction.
	5. Self-directed.

MANAGEMENT OF THE LEARNING ENVIRONMENT

Record Keeping	1. Daily interaction.
	2. Participation in classroom activities.
	3. Completion of homework.
	4. Production of products.
	5. Test results.
Established Routines	1. Use of the classroom.
	2. Leaving/entering the classroom.
	3. Completing work.
Discipline Guidelines	1. Noise control.
	2. Deals with complaints.
	3. Controls student friction.

4. Students respond to a request for order.
5. Students attentive to the lesson.

PROFESSIONALISM

Relationship with Colleagues
1. Cordial and friendly interaction.
2. Helpful and encouraging interaction.

Self-Development Activities
1. Stays current with the field.
2. Involved in staff development activities.
3. Seeks and shares ideas/information.
4. Committee involvement.
5. Engages in self-evaluation.

School Policy
1. Aware of procedures.
2. Follows guidelines.
3. Participates in evaluation.
4. Participates in the development of a new policy.

PARENT/COMMUNITY INTERACTION

Holds Conferences with Individual Parents
1. Is available.
2. Is interested.
3. Is helpful.
4. Is confidential.

Interprets Educational Information
1. Test results.
2. Student involvement in particular programs.

Encourages Involvement
1. Invites parents to visit.
2. Seeks community interaction.
3. Supports community efforts.

The purpose of this chapter is to isolate and comment upon a number of teacher duties which, although not viewed by many as being essential or central to the teacher's role, are nevertheless a part of the administrative tasks of the classroom teacher. In several instances there are legal and/or policy requirements to be fulfilled, in others there are tasks to be performed which are adjunct to the central function, or which are supportive of school goals. *adjunct tasks*

Attendance

Teachers are required by law to keep accurate records of pupil attendance and lateness. How does the teacher report student absences? This is normally accomplished through a central record-keeping system aided by a computer. The teacher is required to provide information accurately and promptly. Student absences must be noted. The teacher is required to make a decision as to whether the absence is excused or unexcused. From our own personal background, this requirement may not seem to be an important issue, but the number of children with unexcused or irregular attendance (attendance problems) is alarmingly high. Children are guaranteed a right to an education. Parents and guardians are required by provincial statutes (school acts) to ensure that the children attend. *right to an educattion*

One of our jobs as educators is to keep accurate records and assist in enforcing the law. We are permitted very little individual freedom. For example, the Alberta School Act states with respect to compulsory school attendance and permissible exemptions:

compulsory
school
attendance

8(1) An individual who
    (a) is eligible to be enrolled in a school,
    (b) at September 1 in a year is 6 years of age or older, and
    (c) is younger than 16 years of age,
shall attend school.

(2) A resident student of a board, unless otherwise permitted under this Act or by the board, shall attend the school that the board directs the student to attend.

(3) Notwithstanding subsection (1), a student is excused from attending school on a day on which the school is open if

(a) the student is unable to attend by reason of sickness or other unavoidable cause,

(b) the day is recognized as a religious holiday by the religious denomination to which the student belongs,

(c) the principal of the school has suspended the student from school and the suspension is still in effect,

(d) the student has been expelled from a school and has not been given permission to enroll in another school, or

(e) the board or, if the student is enrolled in a private school or resides in an unorganized territory, the Minister

(i) determines that the parent of the student has shown sufficient cause as to why the student should not be required to attend school, and
(ii) excuses the student from attending school for a prescribed period of time.
(4) Where a student is excused from attendance at school under subsection (3)(e), that student is excused from attendance at school only during the period of time prescribed by the board or the Minister, as the case may be.

(Alberta School Act, 1988)

In addition to local provisions, the Alberta legislature has, because of the considered seriousness of non-attendance, made provisions for attendance problems referred by local authorities to be heard by a Provincial Attendance Board composed of community members. The duties of the attendance board are as follows:

Attendance
Board

(108) An Attendance Board shall hear all matters referred to it under this Act with respect to the failure of a student to attend school.

(Alberta School Act, 1988)

The Board has the right to serve notice, summon and compel witnesses and documents, and is governed by the rules of evidence and natural justice, and to make orders following adequate hearings. The range of options available to the Board are to:

110(1) On hearing a matter referred to it, the Attendance Board may, subject to any terms or conditions that the Attendance Board considers proper in the circumstances, make an order doing one or more of the following:

(a) directing the student to attend school;
(b) directing the parents of a student to send the student to school;
(c) subject to sections 23, 29 and 30, directing the student to take an education program, course or student program set out in the order;
(d) reporting the matter to a director under the Child Welfare Act;
(e) imposing on the student's parent a monetary penalty not exceeding $100 per day up to a maximum of $1000 to be paid to the Crown for each day that the student does not attend school;

(f) giving such other direction not referred to in clauses (a) to (e) as the Attendance Board considers appropriate in the circumstances.

(2) A copy of an order of the Attendance Board may be filed with the clerk of the Court of Queen's Bench in the judicial district in which the cause of the proceedings before the Attendance Board arose.

(3) On the filing of a copy of an order with the clerk of the Court of Queen's Bench pursuant to subsection (2), the order of the Attendance Board has the same force and effect as if the order were an order of that Court.

The teacher must also become conversant with school and school district policies and procedures respecting student attendance. Although the classroom teacher is not required to attend personally, the members of the attendance tribunal base many of their decisions upon written evidence prepared initially by the teacher. The purpose of the Attendance Board is not punitive. It is to ensure that the child receives an adequate education. Special educational provisions are frequently a part of the Board's orders. Almost always, the classroom teacher is involved in providing the instruction. What are the school's policies regarding parents who ask to take their children out of school for reasons other than those prescribed legally? What about excuse notes?

school policies

The instructional side of the issue also arises when the teacher has to make special provisions for students who are absent due to illness, religious holidays and special family activities.

Detention, Suspension, Expulsion from Class or School

What special supervision problems are imposed upon the teacher who detains a student after school hours? What are the school bus arriving and departing times? Are there special bus runs scheduled for children involved in the activities program which could be utilized for children involved in homework or behavior problems? The answers to these questions are probably school specific; however it is the teacher's duty to become informed, prior to the first problem.

How do suspensions and expulsions work? Most teachers have little first-hand experience to call upon so it is necessary to fully understand the statutory and local school board policies in this area. This is essential since, in a sense, what is being denied is a right to education. In general terms, the teacher is usually permitted to suspend the student from a class period, the principal is permitted to suspend the student from one or more class periods, the school or school bus, and only the school board is permitted to expel the student from school.

teacher
suspensions

principal
suspensions

Student suspensions, for the reason mentioned earlier (denial of education), are almost always subject to strict legal requirements such as parent notification, the means of parent notification, time limits and procedures for lifting the suspension. Consult the School Act in the province of employment. Student expulsions by the board are subject to even more rigorous legal requirements, usually including a requirement for appeals and the Minister of Education notification, with reasons. The Minister has the right to overrule the local authorities.

legal
requirements

Categories and Requirements (Drawn from Calgary Board of Education, mid-1980s policies and intended only to be illustrative of the extent of local policies and regulation.)

1. Suspension from Class

(a) A "suspension from class" is the removal of a student from class by the teacher to an approved supervised location in the school (Brief exclusion from class is not included.)

(b) The purpose of a suspension from class is to provide the teacher with time to consult with the principal and to consider an appropriate resolution of the discipline problem.

(c) Suspensions from class must meet the following requirements:

(i) Immediate notification to the principal.
(ii) Resolution of the problem by the teacher and student in accordance with school policy.
(iii) Notification of the parent.
(iv) Return of the student to class as quickly as possible (usually overnight or weekend).
(v) Documentation.
(d) The principal has authority to reinstate the student.
2. In-School Suspension

(a) An "in-school suspension" is the temporary removal of a student by the principal from class to another learning centre located in that or another school.

(b) The purpose of an in-school suspension is to bring the effect of exclusion from regular classroom activity to bear upon the discipline problem.

(c) In-school suspensions must meet the following criteria:

(i) Approval of the principal of the school.
(ii) Notification of an consultation with the parent.
(iii) Provision of an alternate program of instruction.

(iv) Return of the student to regular classes when appropriate.

(v) Documentation.

3. Informal Suspension

(a) An "informal suspension" is the temporary relocation of a student from the school to the custody of the parent pending resolution of a discipline problem through consultation between the school and the parent.

(b) The purpose of an informal suspension is to bring the effect of being excluded from school to bear upon the resolution of a discipline concern and to provide time for discussion involving the student, the parent, and school personnel regarding future action.

(c) Informal suspensions must meet the following requirements:

(i) Approval of the principal.

(ii) Prompt notification of the parent, providing the reason for the suspension, made known to the parent in writing provided also that when a student of less than 16 years of age is sent home during school hours, notice must be given to a parent.

(iii) Involvement of the parent in discussion concerning future action relative to the suspension.

(iv) Duration must be no longer than five school days.

(v) Documentation.

(d) Resolution of the suspension will be decided by the principal in consultation with the student, the parent, and staff.

(e) Advice to parents who express dissatisfaction with the school's action of their right of appeal to the superintendent.

4. Counselled Withdrawal

(a) Definition

A "counselled withdrawal" is the withdrawal of a student from school by agreement of the student, an administrator, and a parent.

(b) Purpose

A "counselled withdrawal" gives recognition to the agreement of all concerned that the continued attendance of the student in the current semester or school year will not serve his/her best interests.

(c) Criteria

A "counselled withdrawal" may be implemented subject to the following understandings:

(i) The student has reached age 16 years.

(ii) The student will return to the same school at commencement of the next semester or school year for placement by the school in a program or in another school.

(iii) The measure is endorsed by the student and the parent.

(iv) The measure is documented.

5. Administrative Student Transfer

(a) Definition

An "administrative student transfer" is the transfer of a student from one school to another by arrangement.

(b) The purpose of an "administrative student transfer" is to give the student an opportunity to continue his/her education in a new school setting.

(c) Criteria

(i) Administrative student transfers for disciplinary reasons may be arranged by principals of schools subject to the following conditions:

. approval of the parent;
. filing of required documentation.

(ii) The sending school retains responsibility for the student should the terms of his/her placement not be honored during the period of probation specified.

6. Formal Suspension

(a) A "formal suspension" is the relocation of the student from the school to the custody of the parent.

(b) The purpose of a *formal suspension* is to engage the parent and student in the solution of a discipline problem.

(c) Imposition of a formal suspension requires observance of the following:

(i) Immediate notification of the parent by telephone or personal contact.

(ii) Immediate notification of the superintendent's office.

(iii) Prompt filing of the prescribed suspension documents.

(d) Having received notice of formal suspension of student of school age, the superintendent's office is required to ensure that action is taken to resolve the suspension.

(e) While the student is under suspension, he/she is to be retained on the school's attendance register.

(f) The superintendent must take one of the following steps within five school days of the date in which written notice of the suspension was received from the school:

(i) reinstatement;
(ii) transfer;
(iii) counselled withdrawal;
(iv) exemption; or
(v) expulsion.

(g) The superintendent must consult with the student, parent, and appropriate school or district resource staff prior to determining the course of action to be taken.

(h) The student and parent must be given prompt advice regarding the course of action decided upon.

7. Expulsion

(a) An *expulsion* is exclusion of a student from any program operated by the board for a specified period of time.

(b) Resort to *expulsion* is made by the superintendent when the other alternatives listed in items 6 (f) above, are deemed to be inappropriate.

(c) Expulsion requires adherence to the following:

(i) Notification of the student and/or parent of the superintendent's decision within five school days of receipt of a school's written report.

(ii) Notification of the student and/or parent of their right to appeal to the board.

(iii) Notification of the student and/or parent that immediate written application for a board hearing must be submitted.

(iv) Submission to the board by the superintendent of a report recommending the student's expulsion together with a copy of the letter which has been sent to the student and/or parent.

(v) Provision of a hearing by the board. (Usually the student, the parent(s), and the school principal participate).

(vi) Notification to the student and/or parent of the board's decision. If the expulsion is confirmed, this notification is to include advice of the right of the student and/or parent to appeal it to the Minister of Education.

(d) Reinstatement to school program following an expulsion must be under the supervision of the central administration.

Duty Schedules

Teacher duty roster obligations fall into clusters; student safety supervision (halls, playgrounds, etcetera), student study supervision (study halls, detention rooms), student co-curricular and social activities (dances, basketball games, parties), assisting with field trips for outdoor education, teacher social and activity events, and professional association obligations. We don't just teach classes. Extra-curricular duties are also part of our role; the point being to suggest the scope of personal involvement, to urge involvement, and to request that teachers fulfill their scheduled duty obligations diligently and promptly. Often maximum time limitations are placed upon the assignment of duties other than instruction-related duties, usually through the collective agreement between the teachers of the school board, but voluntary involvement is always the teacher's business.

duty roster

Educational Malpractice

Teachers play a central role in the lives of the children of our country. Previous pages have addressed, at least in part, the many duties of the school teacher. Part Two of this text presented a number of ideas, principles, and definitions respecting the teacher and the law, legal liability and family law. But teachers must protect the children educationally as carefully as they protect them physically and legally.

failure to teach

failure to place
appropriately

Children are sent to school to learn. That is the purpose of the whole thing, but sometimes children do not learn. Suits for educational malpractice may follow wherein it is contended that the teacher has failed to teach, or has failed to place the child in a proper program of studies. Charges of educational malpractice are but one more legal risk of practising in our chosen field. There is no question that teachers and school administrators are increasingly concerned about the risk of legal suits. These concerns need not reach the level of "preoccupation" if certain cautions are heeded. Doctors are not amused by malpractice suits. Neither, for that matter, are lawyers.

reasons for
civil litigation

The trends toward civil litigations similar to those noted in Chapters 7 to 10, and actions claiming malpractice are due to at least five factors working within our society:

1. A trend toward a reduction of individual self-reliance and a concomitant increase in reliance upon the state.

2. Large impersonal institutions that dominate much of our lives. (Provincial government and local school boards are of this type.)

3. Increased urbanization and the crowding which results in increased personal pressure for *space*, *rights*, control of our own lives.

4. Our mobile population. (We come into contact with many more people and institutions, which we do not know *personally*.)

5. An increased awareness of the presence of large amounts of liability insurance protecting these impersonal and unknown institutions.

6. Our professional status as teacher. (We have reached professional status and are thus expected to play by the same rules as do doctors, lawyers, architects, and engineers.)

Consider what it was like thirty or forty years ago. More of us knew the teachers of our children. Schools were usually smaller and more personal, or so it seemed. There exists a natural disinclination to sue our neighbors. We are now less inclined to accept the argument of the unavoidable and unfortunate accident. There must always be blame. Someone must be legally responsible, and it that someone is an unknown school board or person working for the board, it is more likely that body or person will be charged with blame.

student
placement
tribunals

Suits charging educational malpractice are uncommon. To date there are no Canadian cases directed toward school personnel and only a small number which have gone to court in the United States. This does not mean that charges have not been made by parents on behalf of their children. Provincial and locally appointed *student placement* tribunals have relieved some of the pressure by making remedial recommendations to school boards. But it is only a matter of time. The United States Educational malpractice suits have centred upon either failure to teach properly, failure to use proper methodology, or failure to properly diagnose learning difficulties and thus failure to place children in appropriate programs.

Every person who enters into a learned profession undertakes to bring to the exercise of it a reasonable degree of care and skill . . . There may be persons who have high education and greater advantages . . . but he undertakes to bring a fair, reasonable, and competent degree of skill.

Lamphier v. Phipos (1838, Britain)

Parents have had limited success, we believe, not because parents have been unable to meet the tort of negligence tests of duty, standard, failure, and loss, but because the courts have been hesitant to open the floodgate of litigation, or are unable to find a causal link, or believe that educational malpractice is not an actionable tort.

Teachers and school boards, however, should not count upon continued stances of non-interference. It is only a matter of time. The best defense in the future is the same as it is now – act as a prudent teacher would act. Be as mindful of the children's educational safety as you are of their physical safety. Apply the principles of the case law surrounding the tort of negligence and the teacher acting in loco parentis.

Preparing for Substitute Teachers

Classroom teachers also have a responsibility to make provisions for the instruction of their students on days and at times when they are unable to be in the classroom because of personal or family illness and other personal absences due perhaps to participation in other activities.

In order that the substitute teacher will have the best possible chance to provide worthwhile learning, the regular teacher should make provisions to leave:

what to leave

a. a seating plan;

b. a timetable for the day(s) of planned absence;

c. notes on classroom procedures such as attendance taking, opening exercises, and collecting forms, homework, etcetera;

d. lesson plans and if detailing is impossible, at minimum notations on the topics to be covered, exercises to be completed, and supplementary activities to be undertaken. Often a copy of the unit plan is advisable since it will assist the substitute in determining the learning goals which are anticipated; and

(e) information on students with special needs.

Student Control/Classroom Management

Donald Schön (Schön, 1983) proposed a fundamental reorganization of the ways in which we think about professional practice and the relationship between theory and practice. Through the concept labelled reflective practice, Schön stresses the idea of practical professional knowledge – he calls it knowledge in action. He stresses the value of permitting the practitioner the opportunity to identify and redefine the problems of practice – to say what is

reflective practitioner

wrong and what directions need to be changed. Perhaps nowhere are the ideas contained in *reflective practice* more apropos than in the topical area, classroom management wherein the teacher is required to organize for a steady flow of learning experiences. Attention must be given to the management of materials and to disruptive students.

As the teacher grows in experience, he/she grows in ability to manage student conduct. Indeed problems of managing students rank high on the list of issues faced by teachers. Everyone – parents, principals, and one's colleagues – has different views on how things *should be done.* Careful study of child growth and development literature and discipline research will be useful, but a posture of reflective practice will probably be most useful since classroom management, like many other parts of the school's work, is teacher and class specific. What is presented here are a number of suggestions and comments *designed to highlight the issue.*

teacher
class specific

self-discipline

Student self-discipline is the ultimate goal of good classroom management (discipline). In order to accomplish this goal (to promote self-discipline) a number of policies, regulations and practices should be put in place by the teacher, the administration, and the school board.

Expectations for Students

Education statutes over the years have been reasonably consistent in requiring that students:

(a) diligently pursue their studies;

(b) comply with the reasonable rules of the school;

(c) attend regularly and punctually;

(d) respect and cooperate with their teachers and principals;

(e) depending upon age, display accountability for their own actions;

(f) respect the rights of others;

(g) be courteous;

(h) be respectful of the property of others.

Expectations for the School

It is expected that the management practices of the school will meet the following minimal set of criteria:

(a) will have been developed by the principal in consultation with staff, students and parents;

(b) will be consistent with the policies and regulations of the board on such matters as purposes and appropriate practices;

(c) will be consistent with provincial legislation;

(d) will be communicated through handbooks, newsletter, brochures which are made known to students, parents, and staff;

e. will be reviewed regularly in view of changing circumstances.

Expectations for the Teacher

Classroom discipline practices should be:

a. developed by the teacher in consultation with the principal and the students;

b. consistent with school and school district and provincial policy – the teacher's freedom is frequently rather limited. For example, some jurisdictions and the provinces prohibit the use of corporal punishment; and

c. understood by the students, and perhaps published in the classroom.

Features

As a minimum classroom discipline, classroom management practices should align themselves with the following features. (Calgary Board of Education regulations, modified.) The practices should:

a. be fair, objective, consistent, and reasonable;

b. betypical of the discipline exercised by a kind, firm, and judicious parent;

c. provide for appeal to other levels of discipline authority;

d. avoid threats, enticements, or coercion;

e. provide for early detection and attention to avoid the necessity for severe and punitive measures;

f. involve other helping professionals such as counsellors and resource personnel;

g. provide for early consultation with parents regarding potential and actual discipline measures to be taken;

h. provide for prompt action;

i. encourage positive school practices and effective teaching as a means of discouraging student misbehavior;

j. complete documentation.

Response to Misconduct

Some useful responses include:

a. assignment of an alternative activity;

b. use of sufficient force to restrain a student from carrying out a destructive act;

c. withdrawal of privileges;

d. detention;

e. exemption (students under 16 years of age);

f. counselled withdrawal (students 16 years of age and over).

g. administrative student transfer;

h. corporal punishment;

i. suspension; and

j. expulsion.

Student transfers, suspension, or expulsion are usually not considered suitable courses of action until the following procedures have been tried:

a. counselling by teacher, resource teacher, school or district counsellor and perhaps other referral agencies

b. consultation with parents or guardians;

c. use of milder discipline measures; and

d. advice to the student and parent respecting possible future disciplinary actions.

Detentions

1. The end result of a detention should be corrective.

2. The length of a detention on any school day shall not exceed, for example, the following:
   (i). thirty minutes in the case of elementary students;
   (ii). sixty minutes in the case of secondary students.

3. Detained students must always be supervised by a staff member.

4. No student may be denied lunch or recess for the purpose of serving a detention. In the case of students (at least from the elementary school level) who are transported to the school by chartered bus, arrangements for alternative transportation must be established with the parent as a condition of requiring the student to serve a detention at the end of the school day.

Prohibited Measures

Most school discipline policies will prohibit the use of the following procedures:

a. physical threats or attacks;

b. mass detention and mass punishment;

c. the use of verbal attacks such as sarcasm or racial or personal references;

d. deliberate humiliation; and/or

e. depending upon local or provincial policy, perhaps the use of corporal punishment, and only as a last resort, under strict supervision with advice to the parents, and careful documentation of the circumstances, witnesses, and offense.

Safety Precautions

Part of the administrative role of the teacher relates to the framework and classification of matters relating to school safety. The following list used by the Ontario Ministry of Education is useful in categorizing and describing the areas of teacher involvement.

1. School Premises:
    (a) gymnasia and general purpose rooms, laboratories, technical shops including industrial arts rooms, visual arts and family studies;
    (b) general areas and standard classrooms:
    (c) stairs and hallways;
    (d) cafeterias and lunchrooms;
    (e) washrooms, change rooms;
    (f) library resource centres;
    (g) swimming pools.

2. School Grounds:
    (a) playing areas (elementary and secondary);
    (b) playground equipment;
    (c) parking lots;
    (d) general school grounds;
    (e) outdoor education centres and bush areas, and bodies of water;
    (f) bus loading zones.

3. School Transportation:
    (a) field trips;
    (b) discipline on buses;
    (c) articles carried on buses;
    (d) personal forms of pupil transportation

4. School Emergencies:
    (a) fire;
    (b) bus accidents;
    (c) persons with weapons;
    (d) bomb threats;
    (e) injured or impaired students;
    (f) hostage taking;
    (g) attempted suicides;
    (h) local industrial hazards.

5. School Environment:
    (a) administration of medication;
    (b) health care procedures;
    (c) absenteeism (safe arrival);
    (d) sound, lighting, and ventilation;
    (e) foreign substances

Staff Meetings

One of the administrative requirements of the teacher is to attend staff meetings. There is usually a legally-constituted minimum number of meetings, held with published agenda, and under proper rules of order. These are the business meetings of the school. Normally they are collegially structured, and

business meetings

problem-solution oriented. They provide the teacher, especially the young teacher, with an opportunity for involvement and with many answers to day-to-day questions.

Student Progress Records.

In addition to the teacher's obligation to keep attendance records, he/she is required to maintain systematic records of evaluations of student progress, test results, measurements of aptitude and ability, and anecdotal records.

student records

Effective evaluation procedures and adequate records are first, essential to successful teaching, but second particularly important to parent-teacher interviews and student report cards. Many interviews with parents are unscheduled so accuracy and currency are essential. Third, when student evaluation records procedures are good, teachers are provided with a useful source of data on the impact of their own teaching skills.

Each province has developed its own procedures respecting the parent's (and sometimes older students) right to inspect and sometimes alter student records. The teacher is advised again to consult local policies and the laws which exist in the province of employment to ensure that a thorough grasp of existing policy exists. No longer are student records for teacher eyes only. Often professional interpretation must be supplied. for example, one province requires:

18(1) A board shall establish and maintain pursuant to the regulations a student record for each student enrolled in its schools.

(2) Subject to subsection (3),

(a) if a student is younger than 16 years of age, his parent,
(b) if a student is 16 years of age or older, his parent and the student, or
(c) if an individual has access to the student under an order made under the Divorce Act (Canada), that individual
may review the student record maintained in respect of that student.

(3) Where a student record contains

(a) a test, a test result or an evaluation of a student that is given by a person who has a recognized expertise or training in respect of that test or evaluation, or
(b) information relating to a test, test result or evaluation referred to in clause (a)
the individuals referred to in subsection (2) are entitled, subject to subsection (4), to review these records.

(4) An individual referred to in subsection (2) is entitled to review the test, test result, evaluation or information referred to in subsection (3) only at a time when a person who is competent to explain and interpret the test, test result, evaluation or information is available to provide him with an explanation and interpretation of that test, test result, evaluation or information.

(5) A board, as soon as practicable after it receives a request from an individual referred to in subsection (2) for an opportunity to review a record to which subsection (3) applies, shall ensure that a person who is competent to explain

and interpret the test, test result, evaluation or information is available to provide an explanation and interpretation of that test, test result, evaluation or information.

(Alberta School Act, 1988)

Those individuals, (the teacher, for example), who supply information for the records are shielded from legal action provided that they:

a. acted in good faith;

b. acted within the scope of his/her duties and responsibilities; and

c. did not act in a negligent manner.

Where information is inaccurate or incomplete, the person (parent or student) may require the school to rectify the record.

Student Evaluation

The keeping of student progress records and promotion practices are based upon a foundation of appropriate student evaluation practices since teachers are required by statute to "regularly evaluate students." It seems useful to review the basic requirements of student evaluation systems. Evaluation in this context is taken to include all available methods of obtaining information regarding what the students are learning and how effective has been the teaching. Much evaluation in the classroom is casual in nature; that is, the teacher observes behavior and makes evaluations, and this is important. However, in order to carry forward this function there must be a close relationship between teaching objectives and student evaluation. Sound, clearly-defined objectives are essential to clear judgment. A clear plan is equally as important.

basic requirements

Types of student evaluation. When planning a whole school year, the teacher should include three different types of student evaluation. First, diagnostic evaluation, (which is designed to assess skills, interests, abilities, difficulties and level of achievement, or to determine the underlying causes of learning difficulties, and which is used to make decisions about program modifications done informally and continually) has an important place in anecdotal reporting, but should not become part of a student's mark. Second, formative evaluation is conducted continually throughout the year or semester or unit. It keeps teacher and student aware of the objectives to be achieved. Three clusters of purposes and procedures appear evident.

diagnostic evaluation

formative evaluation

Teacher-conducted Evaluation.

a. to measure individual and class growth;

b. to provide information to student, class, or teacher on progress toward objectives;

c. to indicate which skills are at a satisfactory level and which need improvement;

d. to evaluate the effectiveness of a program with reference to its content, methods, sequence and pace;

e. to provide records as part of the summative evaluation program.

Student Self-evaluation.

Student self-evaluation is useful in that it helps:

a. to develop students' sense of responsibility for their own learning;

b. to add to their awareness of the course objectives;

c. to help them learn to evaluate their own work;

d. to help the teacher gauge student reactions to the lesson or course.

Student Peer Evaluation.

Peer evaluation is useful in that it helps:

a. to provide a response to student work which does not come from the teacher;

b. to create situations where students compare their work to that of others;

c. to provide additional records to be considered as part of summative evaluation.

summative evaluation

Third, summative evaluation occurs at the end of a unit, activity, course, term, or program. It, along with formative evaluation practices, permit the teacher to determine student achievement and program effectiveness. Summative evaluation has as its purposes:

a. to measure student achievement;

b. to grant or withhold credit or promotion;

c. to report to parents, students and the school administration;

d. to monitor overall student performance;

e. to provide data on needed program modifications or changes.

evaluative program

An effective evaluation program normally has the following characteristics:

1. There must be an obvious connection between objectives and evaluation procedures.

2. There must be an obvious connection between the learning process and the methods of evaluation.

3. There must be a variety of evaluation approaches to measure student strengths and weaknesses.

4. Informal as well as formal evaluation procedures must be used.

5. The evaluation plan should cover the whole year or semester and must be made available to parents and students.

6. Evaluation plans must offer opportunities for higher level thinking and learning during the evaluation process.

7. Evaluation approaches should provide practical (useful) information.

8. Provisions should be made for both group and individual procedures in order to judge the growth of/or development of the individual.

9. Students should understand procedures regarding distribution of marks, grade distribution, bonus marks, re-writes, time restrictions, open-book examinations, optional assignments, provision of relevant formulae, etc.

When designing a student evaluation system and the accompanying records, the teacher would probably ask the following questions:

accompanying records

1. What are the purposes of the evaluation program?

2. Who should be involved?

3. What techniques should be used?

4. Do certain students need alternative evaluation techniques?

5. How will students prepare?

6. When will students be informed of evaluation techniques?

7. How will students receive their results?

8. How often should evaluation occur?

9. For what purpose will the evaluation results be used?

10. What information will be collected, and what will be recorded?

Evaluation and Recording for Exceptional Students

Because evaluation is closely linked to the course objectives, because evaluation is an integral part of the education process, and not merely a testing of the end product, and because teaching methods are under constant evaluation by the professional teacher, it is essential that the services and programs be modified. This is especially true for exceptional students. Evaluation practices are not an exception. Practices must be modified for children who have the following exceptional characteristics.

modified practices

1. Communication exceptionality – learning disability – autism, learning impairment – language impairment – speech impairment.

2. Behavior exceptionality – emotional disturbance – social maladjustment;

3. Intellectual exceptionality – giftedness – slow learner – trainable retardation.

4. Physical exceptionality – orthopedic, visual or physical handicaps.

5. Multiple handicapped.

Parent-Teacher Interviews

The parent-teacher interview normally follows the issuing of report cards, or perhaps is done in conjunction with report-card day. It is suggested that teachers prepare for interviews by:

preparations for interviews

1. re-examining the student's record;

2. having the student's record available for the interview;

3. collecting samples of the student's work from the beginning of the year;

4. having a complete record of marks and attendance and class lates;

5. having available a statement of the course objectives;

6. having an account of the course modifications that have been made for the specific student;

7. arranging for a congenial interviewing situation and privacy;

8. deciding whether or not the student will be present;

9. deciding whether other colleagues who teach the child or administrators will also be present (team interviews).

During the interview the teacher should, as a minimum, follow the eight suggestions below.

1. Begin and end on a positive note. Remember parents are on your territory.

2. Don't do all the talking.

3. Show by example how the course/program has been modified for the student.

4. Suggest how the modifications have affected the student's progress.

5. Identify areas in which the parent and teacher could work cooperatively toward the desired goal.

6. Be sure to have more to say than "I have no problems."

7. Summarize points covered.

8. Try to have the parent leave the interview situation with a positive attitude and confidence in the child.

Report Cards

parent
language

Assessment of the student's progress should be submitted to the student and parent in a clearly-written format. Use honest, positive feedback. Be descriptive. Do not use general statements such as "doing well." Use *parent* language. Provide motivation to learn. Many jurisdictions make use of charts, graphs, checklists, and short notes to indicate progress.

Provisions must also be made for different levels of student ability and course difficulty, for example: basic, general, and advanced.

Teacher recording practices should be designed to dove-tail with the format of the report card and interview design. School newsletters are a useful adjunct to report cards, not for individual students, but for class or school activities in which the students are involved.

Defamation

Teachers and administrators are required to communicate information concerning the abilities, personal and moral qualities, and the private and personal reputations of others. The task breaks down into three processes: (1) maintaining the custody of records, (2) receiving and recording information, and (3) transmitting information to other persons. The nature of some of the information can be damaging to another's reputation. In tort law a person is entitled to *honor* and *reputation*. Every person has the right to a reputation unaffected by false statements. In common law defamation can be communicated in two forms: slander is defamation communicated by spoken words, significant sounds, looks, or gestures; libel is the permanent form of defamation in the form of written or printed word. The law does not provide a remedy to the plaintiff for the *mere utterance* of defamatory materials. The law is activated when the defamatory utterance is *published*. To utter and to publish are tortious acts. For example, if the statement goes directly to the person about whom it is written, there is no publication. In the case of slander, the words must be uttered in the *hearing* of a third person.

honor and reputation

There are two defenses in cases of defamation. First, *truth* is a defence, but only if it can be strictly proven. This strict guideline makes defence very difficult. The second defence is *occasions of privilege.* That is, a defamatory statement having been duly published can be made without adverse legal liability provided that the circumstances or occasion are *privileged* by law. There exists in law two types of privilege: qualified and absolute. Since absolute privilege cannot be seen to apply to school teachers and administrators, the topic will be dropped. Qualified privilege, on the other hand, is clearly relevant. Qualified privilege is determined on a case-by-case basis but in general the pleadings will be based upon the allegation that:

defences: truth & privilege

a. the statement was made in compliance with a duty to communicate;

b. the statement was made in the protection of an interest; and/or

c. the statement was made in certain classes of reports.

For a duty to communicate to exist there must also exist a reciprocal duty to receive. The duty does not necessarily have to be legal; it can exist morally and socially as well.

As noted in *Earnest v. College of Physicians and Surgeons of Saskatchewan* (1954) C.C.P. 538,

> A privileged occasion (qualified) is an occasion where the person who makes a communication has an interest or legal duty, social or moral, to make it to the person to whom it is made and the person to whom it is made has a corresponding interest to receive it.

Information may be given in reply to a query and the communicator may be a recipient of the benefit of qualified privilege.

legitimate
inquiry

The best advice is to provide information as part of a legal duty or in answer to a legitimate inquiry.

An educational case illustrating the protection of private interests is that of *Mallet v. Clark* (1968) 70 D.L.O. 67. Mallet has attended a vocational school in British Columbia for the purpose of learning hairdressing. He subsequently had been expelled by the principal of the school. Mallet complained to the local newspaper about the alleged injustice of his expulsion. The news reporter on telephoning the principal (Clark) had been informed that the former student, Mallet, had been "terminated permanently for conduct detrimental to his class and his customers . . . and that he lacked the tact and adaptability for his chosen profession."

The student claimed he had been defamed. The words were held by the court to have been both defamatory in nature and published to a third party.

private interest

The principal was held to be protected from the consequences because he we replying to an attack and defending a private interest – his personal reputation.

The educational administrator or teacher may well find himself/herself in the position of hearing a complaint about staff activities by one who claims to provide such information on the basis that the public interest is being affected by such activity. When one is advised of the intemperate habits of staff the complaint usually justifies the allegations on the basis of protecting a public interest. Merely uttering that a statement is made in the public interest does not make it so. Teachers should guard against the tendency to use this defense, without careful thought.

Student Promotions

criteria

Students and their parents should be adequately informed on school and classroom level policies and regulations governing student evaluation and promotion, including criteria upon which the decision will be made, and the possible uses of school-wide, system-wide, or provincial tests. Criteria usually includes results in compulsory core programs, optional courses, co-curricular activities and clubs and sports. Adjustments are usually made for students with learning difficulties, the gifted and talented, non-English (French) speaking students, those with eyesight or hearing difficulties, and those who spend a portion of (or entire) school day in program activities in locations beyond the school. Often chronological age becomes a factor. Student behavior may be considered. To do an adequate job the teacher must maintain good student records which are carefully annotated respecting special circumstances or conditions. Just before the first reporting period is too late for designing grading procedures and data collection. Careful monitoring is essential. No one should be lost in the *system*.

learning
difficulties

promotion
policies

Thus the teacher should become thoroughly conversant with the school system's *promotion* policies. Are decisions based upon academic achievement, social factors, or both, or others? Will students be promoted annually, or semi-annually? What are the policies regarding retaining a child in the same grade and/or accelerating him/her? What criteria are used? What kind of evidence must be collected? What symbols are used for grade-recording purposes? Are there district-wide, or school—wide, or province-wide tests which will have an impact upon judged student achievement?

Use of Volunteers

Due in large measure to the increased emphasis placed upon community-based education, the *volunteer* has become an integral part of the teacher's work life. Perhaps in a few isolated instances, the community volunteer has been viewed as cheap help, but it is to be hoped that, in most instances, the volunteer has been brought to the school and the classroom in order to further the goals which the school has set for itself. since the teacher is the professional, the teacher is the person who is required to plan and organize the situation in order that student learning will be maximized.

volunteers

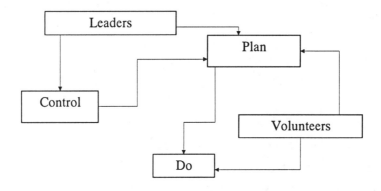

Exhibit 17-2

Key Components in the Organization and Administration
of a Parent/Volunteer Involvement Program

The Alberta Teachers' Association lists the following activities as being suitable for the in-classroom volunteer to perform.

a. Listen to students read orally.

b. Dictate spelling and arithmetic drills.

c. Read stories.

d. Make teaching aids, such as charts, diagrams, games, pictures, under the instruction of the teacher.

e. Arrange displays.

f. Check homework and tests for which answers can be provided (not for those requiring subjective and professional judgments).

g. Make arrangements for special activities, such as field trips, guest lecturers in the classroom, under the direction of the teacher.

h. Assist in preparing for activities, such as art (mix paints, spread papers, etcetera), music (check instruments), science (set up lab equipment).

i. Assist in supervising play areas, lunch rooms, cloakrooms, etc.

j. Write assignments on the blackboard, prepare for audiovisual presentations (setting up overhead projectors and television, filing slides and video-tapes, etc.).

k. Assist in the preparation of duplicated and laminated materials.

(Alberta Teachers Association *Your First Year,* 1988)

guest
speakers

Other classroom assignments could include volunteer guest speakers and instructional assistance, and, or course, school-wide assistance in preparing materials, duplication activities, supervising lunch rooms, filing non-confidential materials, and book re-shelving.

The key components of a parent/volunteer involvement program include the following:

a. Positive attitudes, positive climate,

b. Clearly-defined policy and objectives,

c. Centralized administration,

d. A written plan,

e. Provisions for both groups and for individuals,

f. specific jobs and duties which can be assigned,

g. Organized recruitment efforts,

h. Procedures for interviewing and placing parents,

i. Procedures for preparing parents and paid staff,

j. Procedures for supervision,

k. Regular evaluation,

l. Provision for recognition, promotion, and job rotation, and

m. Accurate record keeping.

Management Roles and Responsibilities

The responsibilities include:

a. Planning;

b. Job development;

c. Recruitment;

d. Selection, developing skills bank;

e. Orientation;

f. Placement;

g. Training (preservice and inservice);

h. Supervision on the job;

i. Record keeping;

j. Evaluation; and

k. Recognition (formal and informal).

Recruitment

The recruitment of the volunteers should be well planned to ensure that the volunteers needed to do the jobs are available. Recruitment is made easier by the development and maintenance of a good volunteer program with *meaningful jobs* for volunteers. recruitment

1. The organization should have well designed jobs before recruitment begins.
    a. consider the components of good job design before a recruitment plan is developed.
    b. Planning – why do we need parent/volunteer involvement anyway?
    c. Leadership Style – what will be delegated to volunteers, how will participants be supervised?
    d. Organizational Climate – will volunteers want to be here?
2. The development or design of job descriptions should include the following consideration:
    a. The range of tasks or jobs that schools ask parents/volunteers to complete should be flexible enough to include different levels of commitment and responsibility.
    b. The job description for a *more* responsible job should be defined in very broad terms and there should exist the authority and freedom to decide 'how' to do the job.
    c. The *less* responsible jobs should have more specific detailed description of tasks to be complete and thus will have *less authority and freedom.*
    d. The organization of jobs should (along with feedback gained and given) enable individuals to move along a personal growth continuum from the more specific tasks with less authority to the less specific tasks and more authority.
    e. It is important that records be kept to ensure that personal growth and development of individuals can be captured for the participants themselves as well as the organization.
    f. along with offering participants a well-constructed position, one needs to outline carefully benefits that will accrue as a result of *their* involvement in the program.

Recruitment Methods

1. Word of mouth.

2. Newsletters projected into the general community.

3. *Target* recruitment.

4. Aim at the new as well as tried and true.

5. Use *benefits to children* point of view.

6. Inviting *guests.*

7. Friends and relatives are a good resource.

8. Through children themselves.

Selection

Interviewing volunteers is vital to ensure the proper placement of individuals so they are as *suited* to the task(s) as possible. The school and the potential volunteers need an opportunity to discuss whether the job to be done and the potential volunteer are suited to each other.

It is necessary to build into the volunteer selection process procedures for ensuring suitability, appropriateness and quality control. The school/teacher must screen out those clearly unsuited for certain jobs and redirect them to other appropriate placements, if possible. This is essential because:

a. Children must be protected. They must be helped, not hindered, by volunteer involvement;

b. The organization's reputation is greatly affected by the people who work there;

c. Morale declines when inappropriate or poor placements occur;

d. The parents/volunteers, and teachers themselves suffer when misplaced. People responsible for selecting volunteers must be genuinely interested in that person: as a person first; as a person who can do the job second. When it is apparent that the school really does care, real communication becomes possible and with it the possibility of making a good match is increased.

An application form should contain all the statistical; and pertinent data so that interviewer can utilize non-directive questions. The interview should help identify the person's attitudes, values, interpersonal skills, emotional stability and motivations.

Listening to what the potential volunteer is saying is important. Use the silences effectively – to reflect and to restate the ideas and observations of the interviewee. A good listener needs to be genuinely interested, allow enough time for a good exchange, build from one comment to another, and stay alert.

Potential volunteers should know at the close of the interview or shortly thereafter, whether they are accepted or not and what the next steps are.

Preparing Parents and Teachers

The way that potential volunteers (or already accepted volunteer) will perform is largely influenced by the 'orientation' they receive.

The content for the orientation session can be determined by a group of organizational leaders brain-storming or otherwise determining the answers to the question: "What does a person need to know about this organization to do the task successfully?" The *orientation* is that part of the introduction to your school that sets the stage for volunteers to determine if they are interested in volunteering with and for you.

The potential volunteer can be aided to a personal decision to become involved or not.

The orientation step is so important that it should be conducted by the organizations' *key leaders* (volunteers or staff).

1. It is crucial that the leaders for this activity are able to speak for the organization as well as embody the school's spirit and climate.

2. Their enthusiasm and genuine dedication to assisting potential volunteers to make a good personal decision should be part of their fabric and not *just* an assignment.

The content and methods incorporated into an orientation process are the basis on which the involvement of volunteers is based. The supervision, evaluation, reassignment, etc., steps are all linked back to the stage that is set at the orientation.

The methods used in orientation for potential volunteers need to be planned around good learning principles. Each type of group, (i.e., adults, parents, seniors, teachers) need to know what to expect and how they will learn.

In addition to consideration being given to effective methods of sharing factual information and of creating a receptive climate, we need to remind ourselves that the orientation session should assist potential volunteers to determine whether they would see themselves as making a commitment to the organization.

Placement

It is necessary at the this point to match the skills and interests (obtained through recruitment) to the jobs to be done.

placement

Volunteer Inservice Preparation and Training

Here are nine guidelines for improving volunteer training programs.

1. All volunteers need orientation to the school. Plan to do this before they start work, either collectively (in a large training session), or individually. The school may also wish to invite other volunteers to lead orientation sessions.

2. Seek advice and input from professionals on what to include in the volunteer training. The school may want to form an advisory committee of experts to help design or evaluate a training plan.

3. Seek advice and input from the staff who have worked with parents. Ask them what should be included in the training.

4. Analyze the job volunteers will be trained to do. Ask, "What are the key tasks my volunteers will have to perform?" Then design simulated role-playing exercises for each task.

5. List inappropriate behaviors in a volunteer, and design training exercises to test for those behaviors. In this way volunteers can be screened curing training.

6. Provide feedback after each training session. Tell the volunteer what they did well and where they need improvement but more of the former, please.

7. Assess your volunteers after six months and after a year. In these review meetings, find out what they found most helpful in your training.

8. Provide informal on-the-job training.

9. Where possible, have skilled volunteers participate as trainers of others.

Developing Job Descriptions

1. List the skills that the participants need in order to do the assigned tasks.
   i. knowledge.
   ii. attitudes.
   iii. skills.

2. What training will be provided?
   i. pre-training?
   ii. on-going?

3. Which resource people will be used – teachers, principals, other parents?

Supervision

Volunteers, like all workers, obtain substantial satisfaction from knowing their efforts are considered meaningful. Supervision, wisely understood to involve factors and principles essential to creative learning, is often a primary way for volunteers to measure the importance attached to their participation.

The following definitions of supervision are applicable to the administration of volunteer programs:

a. Supervision is the function of assuring that work is being done in accordance with plans and instructions;

b. Supervision is a relationship between a supervisor and supervised in which the supervisor helps the supervised perform their assignment;

c. Supervision is getting things done through other people;

d. Supervision is a process through which workers are helped to learn, according to their needs, and to make the best use of their knowledge and skills so as to perform more effectively with increasing satisfaction to themselves; and

e. Supervision is the guiding of human and physical resources into dynamic organizational units that attain their objectives to the satisfaction of those served, and with a high degree of morale and sense of attainment on the part of those render the service.

The above statements mention different factors, reflect various purposes or objectives, and suggest certain roles and relationships, all of which are relevant to the operation of a volunteer program.

Volunteers must see the value of supervision. Two major purposes emerge from careful analysis of the definitions of supervision:

a. Getting the job done in the best possible fashion; and

b. Helping the person experience personal development and satisfaction.

Frequently, one or the other of these purposes receives greater emphasis. The teacher should guard against a distorted emphasis on one side or the other.

Maintaining Involvement

Organizations spend a lot of time, energy, and (in some cases) money, to enable volunteers to carry out the business of the organization. The retention of a percentage of these volunteers from year to year is desirable and should be planned.

maintain involvement

A volunteer who becomes involved in an organization can take a considerable amount of time to become very comfortable in their role. The typical volunteer is a part-time participant and therefore, since it is usually not his/her main focus, it takes many more hours and varieties of contact to establish the same degree of familiarity as would be the case for a full-time staff member.

Volunteerism, as a movement, understands that there is a tendency for people to volunteer for short-term projects.

These two situations accentuate the need for organizations to work at retaining at least some volunteers to ensure continuity and to hand on the mission and history to newcomers. The best way to retain volunteers is not to ask them for several years of commitment but to *ensure that they are satisfied*. Volunteers must feel that their services are needed and valued by the school. A volunteer's job needs to be both enjoyable and challenging. The organizational climate created by the structure and enhanced by the leadership, will ensure that parent involvement is year-to-year and that some are involved in different roles for many years.

Utilizing special Services

Teachers are required, because of their professional commitment, to make use of all available special services in support of the student. This requires that the teacher become informed and maintain an updated resource file. The teacher's goal is to make recommendations and referrals to appropriate other helping professionals. This requires that the teacher understand student growth and behavior patterns, and the signs of atypical behavior, or the presence of special needs.

What are the district's facilities for special schools or classrooms for the exceptional child, including the gifted, the mentally handicapped, autistically handicapped, visually impaired, orthopedically handicapped, neurologically handicapped, aphasic, cerebral palsied, and emotionally disturbed? The teacher must also know what services are available to young people in trouble with the law. Also, teachers should be acquainted with the provisions for health examinations and innoculations.

The teacher must not only be able to recognize students in need of special services, but he or she must also be able to make referrals in an efficient and informative manner.

Working with Other Helping Professionals

It has been said many times that schooling is a complex business, and it is. Driven by societal changes, the needs of young people have changed to the point where professional teachers cannot perform well without considerable *networking* activities with other helping professionals. How to do this effectively is a vexing problem since we, as teachers, and the institutions within which we work have tended toward an independent stance. To meet with others on an *ad hoc* basis, while effective for some issues, leaves too much to chance. The teacher and the school must also make provisions for planned procedures. The scope of this text does not permit a full discussion of the shared responsibilities of helping professionals. There are other sources available, and the section on volunteers in this chapter will provide some ideas for personal initial planning to work cooperatively in the best interest of the students.

Other Duties

The administrative duties of the typical classroom teacher are legion. Below is a list of other administrative concerns.

1. Handling keys and key security.
2. Obtaining instructional materials – texts, supplementary class sets, equipment, apparatus, computers, calculators and paper supplies.
3. Duplicating and typing – who does it? What are the timelines?
4. Using of the library/resource centre – bookings and procedures.
5. Procedures for taking field excursions.
6. Obtaining use of community facilities.
7. Making parent contacts and scheduling interviews.
8. Providing student counselling.
9. Requisitioning special materials and equipment.
10. Having procedures for handling activity and special funds – recording, depositing, etcetera.
11. Involvement in community school and parent advisory council activities.

Part Five

Teaching as a Profession

The Professional Teacher

What the Teacher Believes

No printed work nor spoken plea can teach young minds what man should be,
not all the books on all the shelves, but what the teachers are themselves.

Anonymous

> Characteristics
>
> Teaching – A Profession
>
> Codes of Ethics
>
> Union and Profession
>
> Services
>
> Teachers' Associations

Introduction

Being a *professional* took its meaning from medieval times when an individual took *vows* in order to be received into a religious community. It was the act of openly declaring or publicly *professing* a belief or faith. Over the centuries, the word began to mean a *calling* requiring specialized knowledge and the pursuit of high standards.

belief or faith

Is teaching a profession? The answer to this question is not a simple *yes* or *no* but rather an impression, a feeling, a belief. The answer does not lie strictly within the collection of facts or opinions on the matter. Rather, it is something more personal, and it is somewhat emotional. The purpose of this chapter is not to provide a definite answer to this evasive question, but rather to discuss the measuring sticks which may assist the individual in deliberating upon the matter. In making a decision, we are assisted by a knowledge of the generally acceptable criteria used by others. The question is a central one because the way teaching is considered influences how teaching is done. That is, there is an emotional involvement which affects the teacher's expectations of others, and in turn, the referent groups' expectations held for the teacher.

Teaching can be, and in some parts of the world is, considered as *labor*. That is, it is rationally planned, programmed, routinized, and is guided by a set of standard operating procedures. Others view teaching in the nature of a *craft*. Crafts can be described as consisting of a repertoire of specialized techniques. Knowledge of techniques includes a set of generalized rules for their application. The craftsman carries out the work without detailed instructions or close supervision. When teaching is regarded as a *profession*, the practitioner is expected to have command of a body of theoretical knowledge and to exercise judgment in the application of his/her knowledge. When teaching is considered

nature of teaching

to be an *art*, the techniques and their application may be novel. The work is personalized, not standardized. The teacher uses intuition, creativity, and improvisation. When teaching is viewed as a *science*, the teacher will apply verified and generalizable research results.

How do we know whether teaching is a profession? One measuring stick frequently used is to compare teaching to other occupations which have received common acceptance as being professional. There may be some question in peoples' minds as to whether occupations such as mechanical engineering, optometry, accounting and paleontology are in fact professions, but there seems to be little hesitancy in recognizing medicine, law, and the ministry as professions. Therefore, much of the literature regarding professions focuses almost exclusively upon these three occupations. Writers have attempted to analyze the accepted professions in order to determine what these groups have in common and what they have that other groups of people do not have, the assumption being that the differences between these groups (i.e., doctors, lawyers, ministers, and other similar work groups) can be used to describe the characteristics of a profession.

medicine
law
ministry

This type of reasoning is similar to that used in much of the leadership research, particularly in the earlier leadership studies. The basis of study was first to determine who was accepted as being an effective leader, and then to ascertain the main traits of these leaders. The assumption was that if other people could somehow develop these same traits, then they too would become effective leaders. While there is little doubt these trait studies furthered our knowledge about leadership, it must be accepted that this type of reasoning was not totally adequate. Therefore, this type of converse thinking may assist us with the problem of defining a profession, but we should not accept at face value the results of such research, expecting it to have universal application, or that it will provide us with the full answer.

raits theory

Characteristics of Occupations Recognized as Professions

The following discussion emphasizes some of the features of occupational groups which, by general consensus, are considered professional. It does not necessarily follow that if an occupational group acquired a similar listing of characteristics, it would automatically be considered as a profession. No doubt this would help somewhat in the professionalism process, but it is not a method which would guarantee results. There is more to being a profession than meeting the requirements of a list of characteristics.

The earlier recognitions of professionalism involved a degree of mysticism. The professional (for example, the medicine-man) was the intermediary between man and unfathomable mysteries of nature. This early type of professional activity gradually divided into two categories or occupational groups: one the mystical healer of physical ills and the other, the intervener of the spirits for the good of man. Later, other groups of people such as those whose duty it was to interpret the vagaries of institutionalized regulations and laws, to the usually uneducated individual, began to be accepted as professions.

mystical healer

intervener

As one reads the literature regarding teaching as a profession, or the more general literature on professions, three terms emerge: profession, professionalism, and professionalization. It is useful to draw a distinction among the three and thus gain a better understanding of the fluidity of the topic of this chapter.

The term *profession* refers to an ideal condition (type of organized occupation) which does not exist in reality; it is one that serves as a model state or goal toward which some people feel compelled to strive. *Professionalism* is the ideology which induces or compels people to seek the ideal state (profession) and *professionalization* is the term used to describe the processes which a person, or any occupational group, have used in striving toward the goal of having the occupation regarded as a profession.

profession

professionalism

professionalization

In 1915 Abraham Flexner stated that a profession was based mainly on six criteria. The first of these was that a profession was intellectual. Second, it was learned; that is, a profession was based on a substantial body of knowledge which developed over a long period of time and which was transmissible to students through a lengthy training program. Third, a profession was practical in that its knowledge could be used to solve problems in important recurring situations, such as birth, death and marriage. Fourth, a profession had skills or techniques that could be taught to others. Fifth, a profession was organized into associations which regulated entrance into the association and guided the further education for its members. Sixth, a profession was guided by altruism; that is, a desire to serve mankind.

Corwin, in *A Sociology of Education* (Corwin, 1965), defines the ideal structure of a profession as consisting of a legal monopoly over the application of theoretical knowledge to the solution of a social problem, and as having a structure which provides for legal control over the actions of the membership of that profession. This control would include control over licensing standards and would also provide for a code of ethics sanctioned by law. In another publication (Carver & Sergiovanni, 1969), Corwin notes that the professional can be characterized by his/her orientation and attitude toward (1) the client, (2) colleagues, (3) participation in decision-making, and (4) monopoly over certain skills and knowledge.

legal monopoly

client

Ryan and Cooper (1980, p. 372-3) point out that before an occupation can claim professional status, it must meet the following criteria.

criteria

1. It renders a unique, finite, and essential social service.
2. It relies upon intellectual skills in the performance of its service.
3. It has a long period of specialized training.
4. Both individual members and the professional group enjoy an extended degree of autonomy and decision-making powers.
5. It requires its members to accept personal responsibility for their actions and decisions.
6. It emphasizes rendering of services more than personal financial rewards.

7. Its members accept and are governed by a code of ethics.

8. It is self-governing and accepts responsibility for controlling the conduct of its members.

The Alberta Teachers' Association (1965) provides this description:

self-directed

self-disciplined

> It is a self-selected, self-disciplined group of individuals who hold themselves out to the public as possessing a special skill derived from education and training and who are prepared to exercise that skill in the service of others.

Traditionally, professional people belong to tightly organized and exclusive groups designed to maintain and improve the standards of entrance to the profession, to improve professional practice, to widen the field of knowledge of members, to protect the public from malpractice through ethical codes and self-disciplines, and finally to protect the economic interest of the members.

vital personal
relationships

The professional task is distinguishable from others because it required the practitioner and deal directly with the delicate and private functioning of lives of individuals, . . . vital and highly personal relationships . . . The value judgments which the practitioner makes must be subject to the highest ethical precepts to which there must be at all times complete dedication.

Many other descriptions of the characteristics of occupational groups considered as professions have been developed. There are variations due mainly to differences of opinion as to which occupational groups are indeed professions. Generally, however, the characteristics can be summarized as follows.

1. A profession serves a unique, essential service to mankind.

2. A profession is based on a body of knowledge which has taken a long period of time to develop, and upon an active, planned effort to understand this knowledge and to further it for the betterment of mankind.

3. Members of a profession undertake a long training period; often added to this is an internship period before the candidate is recognized by his/her particular association, and the public, as being competent to practice.

4. The public accepts and respects the opinions and practices of the members of the profession.

5. The lifestyle of the members of the profession reflect an above-average standard educationally and culturally. Usually, this is accompanied by an above-average monetary entitlement.

6. Members of professions organize into closed shop associations which protect the public from *unprofessional* practices and protects the profession from unscrupulous members of the public.

mysticism

There still exists a certain mysticism about the professions. The lay public is awed by the amount of knowledge and skill possessed by professionals. Invariably, this is accompanied by a technical language indigenous to the profession and not readily understood by other groups of people – adding to the impression that the group is in possession of a great wealth of knowledge. What the professional does is usually not completely understood by the public.

The public or clients must place their faith in the judgment of the professional – even life and death decisions. For this kind of confidence, the public readily pays comparatively high fees, usually without questioning the validity of the fee. The public accepts a closed shop arrangement whereby the members admit new members to the profession, police their own members, and provide insulation between the lay public and the individual professional members – all with the acceptance of the public. All members of the professions are not necessarily rich, but there is usually the acceptance that professional people should be able to enjoy the finer things in life. Often the opinions of professional people are respected above those of other people in matters which are not necessarily related to the particular profession. That is, the trust placed in the hands of the professional people extends well beyond necessary professional competencies possessed by the group.

In order to police their own members and to provide a degree of protection from the public, a profession, through its professional association, develops a code of ethics which reflects expected ethical behavior of its members and sets the framework for standards of professional work. An example of a code of ethics from a recognized profession, medicine, follows.

protection to public

The Canadian Medical Association Code of Ethics

Principles of Ethical Behavior for all physicians, including those who may not be engaged directly in clinical practice.

1. Consider first the well-being of the patient.
2. Honor your profession and its traditions.
3. Recognize your limitations and the special skills of others in the prevention and treatment of disease.
4. Protect the patient's secrets.
5. Teach and be taught.
6. Remember that integrity and professional ability should be your only advertisement.
7. Be responsible in setting a value on your services.

The medical professional also developed a guide to the ethical behavior of physicians. This guide operationalizes the code of ethics in that the responsibilities of doctors are enumerated in a more specific manner (for example, "An ethical physician ... will recognize that he has a responsibility to render medical service to any person regardless of color, religion or political belief.") The guide specifies the ethical physician's responsibilities to the patient, to the profession, and to society.

Writers such as Hellriegel, Slocum and Woodman (1992), who write in the field of organizational behavior and business management, express deep concern for the frequency of unethical behavior found in the market place. They stress that the prudent act is to have codes of ethics and whistle-blowing procedures in place within company policy in order that all employees and management will understand the standard of conduct expected in the work place and board rooms. Their purposes are the same as the purposes of professional associations – to define and enforce a standard of public conduct and performance.

feel
professional

Teaching – A Profession

However, no matter how important the various characteristics commonly accepted as being professional-based are, it appears that acceptance is the most important criterion. That is, do the individuals within the occupational group readily accept themselves as professionals, and do the general public and the clients also accord them the same acceptance? If teachers wish to be professionals, they will need to do more than simply attempt to meet the standards of measurement which reflect already established professions. Teachers will need to *feel* professional and to gain public acceptance of professional status, both of which are difficult tasks but ones on which much progress has been made in Canada.

In order for teachers to arrive at professional status, one of the first requirements is to analyze where they stand on the characteristics of accepted professions. As fallacious as this method may be, the self-image of the teacher needs to be measured. Teachers must have confidences in themselves as a profession or they never will become one. These measuring sticks are vague and ethereal, but at least they are something to start with. As Giustic and Hogg (1973, p. 16) state:

> The only service which the teacher provides that entitles him/her to be classified as a professional is his/her skill in causing children to learn.

Teaching provides a service that is somewhat unique. However, every member of the public has had the experience of going to school. This makes it

no mystique

more difficult to incorporate an aura of mystique comparable to that of other accepted professions. The general public appears to believe that there is nothing special about teaching spelling – anyone can do that. The teaching of arithmetic facts can also be done without training – at least in the eyes of many of the public. Many other phases of teaching fall into the same realm. The present movement toward individualized instruction, often misunderstood, coupled with greater teacher visibility, has not helped the situation much. Non-professional people – the teacher aide, the parent, the school secretary – often observe teachers at work because of the open-area school concept. Too often the public sees a teacher as a person sitting at a desk giving instructions to the students – "do pages seven and eight, if you have any difficulty, see me." When students seek help, they are often told to find out for themselves. The impression given by the misuse of an important instructional concept, *individualized instruction,* or many other important instructional concepts which emphasize to teachers, and to the public, that there is very little that is unique about teaching. Our present teaching methods are more open to public scrutiny than ever before – the uniqueness is sought more and is more difficult to attain.

Education is an essential service to mankind. However, its essential nature is frequently determined in the long-term sense. The public may agree with the essential aspect of the job, but they are also quick to point out there is much which a teacher does that is non-essential.

The training period for teachers has increased considerably since the early settlement days of Canada. Most provinces now require teachers to have four years of formal training (university) before they receive initial certification. Compared with medicine, law and other professions, however, the years of training possessed by many teachers presently teaching in Canada seems quite inadequate for the task to be performed and for development of a scholastic-academic image of the practitioner. — training needed

Practice teaching is invariably a part of the training program but to date internship has not become a basic requirement for certification. Teacher training programs are gradually including more school-related experiences in their programs. Teacher internships are being discussed at senior levels. Perhaps they will become an integral part of the preparation program for teachers. — practice teaching

The base of knowledge for teachers has taken a long time to develop. Efforts are being made continuously to analyze, understand and further this knowledge. The lag between research and practice in education is overly long, but sound research is becoming more acceptable as a basis upon which knowledge is furthered. Since it is only recently that increased periods of training for certification have been required, most of the teaching force in past years has had insufficient background upon which to utilize, to the fullest advantage, the knowledge base which has developed. — base of knowledge

There appears to be some difference of opinion as to the degree of acceptance and respect given to teachers by the public. This may be, in part, because the general level of education of the general public has increased faster, comparatively, than that of the teaching force.

With these qualifications in mind, it appears teachers are at least holding their own on the *acceptance and respect* scale.

The lifestyle of teachers has not been above-average educationally or culturally. Their lifestyle reflects a lower middle class perspective – one which is shared by many non-professionals. In the past, the professional person had a lifestyle which was considerably better than the majority of the people. Today other groups of people (those who in the past had not been considered as professionals and who are not now so considered) are developing lifestyles analogous to the professional person. Thus, the improvement in the relative lifestyle of teachers is not as obvious as it once might have been. That is, teachers have been required to struggle simply to maintain their comparative palace, let alone increase it noticeably. — lifestyle

Finally, teachers are organized into associations, most of which are closed shops. There have developed codes of ethics and standards of professional onduct. *The Code of Professional Conduct* of the Alberta Teachers' Association (1986) exemplify the ethical bases which provincial associations hold for their memberships.

Code of Professional Conduct

The Code of Professional Conduct stipulates minimum standards of professional conduct of teachers but is not an exhaustive list of such standards. Unless exempted by legislation, any member of the Alberta Teachers' Association who is alleged to have violated the standards of the profession, including the provisions of the Code, may be subject to a charge of unprofessional conduct under the Discipline Bylaws of the Association.

In relation to pupils:

1. The teacher teaches in a manner that respects the dignity and rights of all persons without prejudice as to race, religious beliefs, color, sex, physical characteristics, age, ancestry or place of origin.

2. (a) The teacher is responsible for diagnosing educational needs, prescribing and implementing instructional programs and evaluating progress of pupils.

(b) The teacher may not delegate these responsibilities to any person who is not a teacher.

3. The teacher may delegate specific and limited aspects of instructional programs and evaluating progress of pupils.

4. The teacher treats pupils with dignity and respect and is considerate of their circumstances.

5. The teacher may not divulge information about a pupil received in confidence or in the course of professional duties except as required by law or where, in the judgment of the teacher, to do so is in the best interest of the pupil.

6. The teacher may not accept pay for tutoring a pupil in any subjects in which the teacher is responsible for giving classroom instruction to that pupil.

7. The teacher may not take advantage of a professional position to profit from the sale of goods or services to or for pupils in the teacher's charge.

In relation to school authorities:

8. The teacher protests the assignment of duties for which the teacher is not qualified or conditions which make it difficult to render professional service.

9. The teacher fulfills contractual obligations to the employer until released by mutual consent or according to law.

10. The teacher provides as much notice as possible of a decision to terminate employment.

11. The teacher adheres to agreements negotiated on the teacher's behalf by the Association.

In relation to colleagues:

12. The teacher does not undermine the confidence of pupils in other teachers.

13. The teacher criticizes the professional competence or professional reputation of another teacher only in confidence to proper officials and after the other teacher has been informed of the criticism.

14. The teacher, when making a report on the professional performance of another teacher, does so in good faith and, prior to submitting the report, provides the teacher with a copy of the report.

15. The teacher does not take, because of animosity or for personal advantage, any steps to secure the dismissal of another teacher.

16. The teacher recognizes the duty to protest through proper channels administrative policies and practices which the teacher cannot in conscience accept; and further recognizes that if administration by consent fails, the administrator must adopt a position of authority.

17. The teacher as an administrator provides opportunities for staff members to express their opinions and to bring forth suggestions regarding the administration of the school.

In relation to the profession:

18. The teacher acts in a manner which maintains the honor and dignity of the profession.

19. The teacher does not engage in activities which adversely affect the quality of the teacher's professional service.

20. The teacher submits to the Association disputes arising from professional relationships with other teachers which cannot be resolved by personal discussion.

21. The teacher makes representations on behalf of the Association of members thereof only when authorized to do so.

22. The teacher accepts that service to the Association is a professional responsibility.

Other Canadian teacher associations have similar codes and statements of professional competency levels which are intended to guard their membership from the unprofessional conduct of others and to protect the public from the educational malpractice of their own membership.

Those who believe themselves to be professional teachers have not only a legal but a moral responsibility to uphold the code of their associations, and where changes seem warranted, to proceed under the democratic procedures provided for in their association's by-laws.

moral responsibility

Union and Profession

The lack of compatibility between union and professional activities is now regarded as being more acceptable than it was even a few years ago. It is now recognized that some of the forces employed by professions such as medicine

unionism

are the same forces used by unions. The medical doctors' strikes or withholding of all but emergency services, for example, demonstrates clearly that many professional groups will use union tactics when it is necessary for self-preservation. There are numerous examples of professionals working on negotiated salary schedules rather than on a fee-for-service contract. The closed shop of the professional organizations resembles that of unions; the control and discipline unions have over their members are often as strict as those which professional organizations have over their members. Thus, it is not easy to separate *professionalism* from *unionism* on the basis of organizational structure. Teachers' associations often are associated with other labor unions due in large measure to their inclusion under the provisions of provincial labor legislation. Teachers' associations themselves maintain that union tactics are often necessary in order to upgrade teaching by obtaining a better standard of living and working conditions that are commensurate with other professions. In so doing, it is held that the climate is provided within which professionalism can operate.

Services Provided to Members

Provincial associations provide extensive services to their own membership and toward improvements to education generally. Individual members can anticipate: help toward professional growth; advice (sometimes legal) on contractual rights, pending dismissal or termination actions by the employer; advice and assistance with salary grievances, unemployment insurance and pensions; professional assistance through seminars, conferences, workshops; and professional library services.

professional
development

Local groups of teachers are offered assistance with: locally operated professional development programs; communications to membership, the public, and the media; and economic (negotiation) matters and grievances regarding pay and working conditions.

Provincial teachers' associations work with departments (ministries) of education on such matters as curriculum policy and development, special student services, and proposed legislation. They also become actively involved with faculties of education in policies regarding the professional preparation for teaching.

lobbying

Government and MLA lobbying regarding educational enactments and regulations, school financing and labor legislation are central, and frequently not very visible, activities of all teachers' associations.

In summary, in order that teaching will be considered a profession, the individual teachers must personally feel they are professional and must be able to gain the respect and acceptance by the public, that has marked the growth of other professions.

Teachers' Associations in Canada

Concerning the beginning of teachers' associations, we were not able to pin-point a particular date in Canadian history as being the date of organization of the first Canadian teachers' association. Groups of workers tended to form, and dissolve, to form organizations – both formal and informal; however to pin-point the time when the formation of a group becomes the formation of an association is mainly an exercise in semantics. Often the passage of a statute will fix a specific date and mark the formalization of the process. From the earliest times in Canadian history, teachers naturally formed interest groups comparable to those formed by other groups of workers. For example, the mathematics teachers in a certain geographical area, or perhaps, the teachers who taught in a certain parish school, may have formed a group or association. The purpose of this section is to provide a brief review of those teachers' associations which bore some resemblance to the provincial organizations now common in Canada, and in particular, to highlight those associations which contributed substantially to the development and protection of teaching as a profession.

early interest groups

One of the first of the more formal teacher organizations, which had many of the attributes of a professional teacher's association, was the Teachers' Association of Canada West which was formed in 1861 (from 1867, called the Ontario Teachers' Association). However, this organization would best be described as a group of people (some lay) who were interested in education, rather than being an organization of teachers interested in themselves for welfare purposes as well as professional growth and development. The Provincial Association of Protestant Teachers of Quebec, founded in 1864, and continuing under the same name today, came closest to being what today we would call a professional teachers' organization or association. They obtained a provincial charter in 1889, the first in Canada.

first professional association

Other teacher organizations subsequent to this time were founded and dissolved, two examples being the Ontario Teachers' Alliance of 1908, and the Educational Society of Ontario in 1886. This latter organization aimed "to combine the advantages of a labor union and of a fraternal benevolent society." Early substantive beginnings of the organized teacher movement included the Nova Scotia Teachers' Union in 1895, the Newfoundland Teachers' Association in 1890, the New Brunswick Teachers' Association in 1902, the Territorial Teachers' Association before 1907, the Alberta Teachers' Alliance in 1917, and the Manitoba Teachers' Federation in 1919.

Even though the movement toward the formation of professional organizations began early in Canadian history, it was not until after World War I that substantial results were obtained in developing basic organizational structures which could become more professional in nature. Prior to the war, the teachers were not strongly organized, nor did they generally have clear aims regarding

post WWI

professional recognition. Many of the organizations were educational in nature but usually not professional in nature; that is, they did not concentrate on becoming a profession. Undoubtedly, the comparatively low salaries and poor working conditions experienced by teachers in the early 1900s spurred the development of teachers' associations (unions).

Today, there are provincial teachers' associations or organizations in each of the provinces, as well as in the Yukon and North West Territories. For most provinces, there is one association representing the teachers of that province; however, Ontario, Quebec and New Brunswick have multiple associations.

bureaucratic system

Many writers argue that a school is a bureaucratic organization and that this design in itself creates a fundamental conflict between the administration and the professional classroom teacher. The organization's need may run counter to the response patterns of the professional. Some professionals behave as though any organizational or administrative requirement constitutes an unwarranted imposition. Some administrators believe that they are heading an organization peopled by *prima donnas* and *impractical academics*.

In the middle groups there is some evidence to suggest that some tension exists between the organization and the teacher. The typical organization and certainly a public organization is a bureaucracy. Organizations (schools and school systems) often see things quite differently. These differences can produce tensions. The Max Weber enunciated dimensions of a bureaucracy are as follows.

1. The organization sees authority resting in the position; the professional sees it existing in skills and knowledge.

2. The organization is designed upon a division of labor; the professional views the central component as the individual student (whole person).

3. The organization expects a set of specified behaviors to be followed; the professional teacher sees a range of behavior alternatives.

4. The organization operates on the basis of defined procedures; the professional values adaptability.

5. The organization tends to impersonality; the professional feeds on interpersonal relations.

6. The organization values competency; the professional values competency (see also, chapter 19).

In summary, in a school organization there are two different behavior systems at work – a bureaucratic system and a professional system. In order to avoid or minimize conflict and maximize agreement, skillful administration and teacher cooperation are required.

19

Quality of the Teacher's Work Life

When organizations have addressed the issue of the quality of working life, they have always achieved great productivity breakthroughs.

Jerome M. Roscow

The Concept

Job Enrichment

Natural Work Teams

New Trend Management

Deteriorating Quality of Work Life

Professionals and Bureaucracies

Causes of Stress

Worker Alienation

Introduction

Later in this section, material will be presented on teacher salaries and rewards. The purpose of this chapter is to explore a number of other job-related aspects of the meaningfulness of work in the life of the teacher – quality of the teacher's work life issues.

Several major trends hold promise in influencing modern organizations. Among them, a significant trend labelled *quality of the work life* sets forward a number of factors which contribute to employee productivity and to conditions that foster personally satisfying work experiences. It is not based upon a definite theory, technique or system, but rather is a movement that is concerned with working toward a *climate of mutual respect,* for example, between principals and teachers. Chapter 18 concluded with a brief description of the potential conflict between administrators who are working through a bureaucratic model and teachers whose response patterns often are professional in nature. Traditional work designs have tended to extract high human costs. Workers become alienated. What is being sought is a user-friendly work environment. *(trends)*

The concept is not linear; it is cyclical. How the teacher approaches life and how the teacher approaches the job are intertwined. What is done outside of school affects what is done in school and vice versa. What is done in schools and what the teacher feels about school life affects the children and also the teachers' colleagues. Approximately 30 percent of the teacher's working years *(the concept)* are spent in the schools. What happens or fails to happen there has, of course, an impact upon the school but the quality of the teacher's work life may also have a substantial impact upon the teacher.

early stages   In its early stages, the elements of a typical quality of the work-life program included items such as open communication, equitable reward systems, a concern for employee job security, and *participation* in job design. Several projects focused on job enrichment in the belief that classical administrative (management) styles gave inadequate attention to human needs, and indeed *job enrichment* almost became a distinct trend in itself.

Other early experiments in modifying the quality of the industrial work life in plants such as General Foods (USA) included:

a. reducing the distinction between technical specialists and workers;

b. providing operators with the same kind of decision-making information as previously only managers received;

c. enlarging jobs and mechanizing routine work;

d. providing team-controlled redistribution of tasks when other members were absent; and

e. team counseling of members who failed to meet team standards.

Traditionally management had solved its worker problems by:

a. leaving the job as it is, and employing only workers who like rigid environments and routine specialization – some workers do, or were thought to value this type of work;

b. leaving the job as it is, but paying workers more so that they will more readily accept the situation; or

c. mechanizing the routine jobs – industrial robots replace people for routine work.

As will be illustrated later, the theoretical bases have been expanded to include psychological elements and leadership styles as well as expanding the concept of *employee* beyond assembly line and other industrial workers to now include professional (knowledge worker) persons as well.

The Concept

salary envelope   The theory wherein management considers these parts of the work life of the worker that go beyond the *salary envelope* is not new; in fact the basic pieces
motivation   have existed for a long time and were found in administrative textbooks under
worker alienation the titles *motivation* or *worker alienation.*

It appears that the trend of considering the quality of the workers' work life as part of the compensation package began in a General Motors Corporation (Tarrytown) automobile plant in the United States. The plant experienced innumerable work stoppages, work slowdowns, and *wildcat* strikes, sufficient to demonstrate there existed a high level of worker dissatisfaction. Plant management, using pay hikes and traditional (but not outdated) management practices, were unable to rectify the problem. Union leadership discovered by the prevalence of non-union organized work stoppage and from the discussions at union-sponsored meetings with the workers, that they were no longer in a position to control large numbers of their own membership. Management and union leadership concluded that they must address other worker concerns not previously addressed. The quality of work life movement spread through the automobile and other industries and into the public service domain.

Guest (1979) defines quality of the work life (Q.L.W.) as covering a person's feelings about every dimension of work including economic rewards and benefits, job security, working conditions, organizational and interpersonal relationships, work's intrinsic meaning in a person's life, and the process by which an organization attempts to unlock the creative potential of its people. Other writers express the definition of the movement as being the degree to which work permits an individual to satisfy a wide variety of personal needs such as security, satisfying interaction with others, a sense of personal usefulness, and a recognition for achievements. Some use a non-specific definition such as favorableness or unfavorableness of the job environment. Doll, writing in the field of teacher supervision (Doll, p. 256) summarizes the *stimulators* to able teachers as being: — Q.W.L. defined — higher level needs

a. a sense of achievement;

b. a sense of being recognized for specific achievements;

c. a sense of participating in significant work;

d. a sense of having worthwhile responsibility; and

e. a sense of being properly advanced in the school system.

The roots of the issue are to be found in the adverse effects of job specialization (promoted by the proponents of scientific management) and the nature of the modern (new breed) of workers who expect work to meet more than their basic physiological needs. They are seeking satisfaction on the job.

Exhibit 19-1
Maslow's Needs Hierarchy

Abraham Maslow (1954) theorized that human needs were both physiological and psychological and that needs existed at a number of levels. He contended that lower level needs must be met first before the person moved on to higher level needs. He believed that needs moved upward in order from food and shelter needs, to needs for safety and security, to needs to belong and be loved, then to needs for esteem and status, self respect, power achievement, prestige, recognition (ego), to needs for self-actualization (self-fulfillment).

Job Enrichment

dissatisfiers

satisfiers

Frederick Hertzberg (1959), following the findings of his own research and that of others, concluded that there are basically two types of factors at work: *dissatisfiers* and *satisfiers*. *Dissatisfiers* are those elements such as job security, quality of administrative performance, relations with subordinates, peer relations, quality of supervision received, and company policy. Hertzberg concluded that the prime satisfiers were feelings of achievement, recognition, responsibility, advancement, and the nature of the work itself. If the *dissatisfiers* were absent or adverse, they caused job dissatisfaction but when they were present or judged adequate they were helpful but they tended to be taken for granted. Hertzberg labelled these elements as *hygiene factors* (preventative or environmental). They provide a neutral state when satisfied. *Motivational factors,* Hertzberg's *satisfiers,* provided job satisfaction and thus improved the quality of the working life, and caused better performance.

core of job
enrichment

Other writers (Hackman & Oldman, 1975) use a job enrichment approach to the issue of quality of the work life. They conclude that the core dimensions of job enrichment are:

a. task variety, wherein the worker performs a number of different operations. Jobs which are high in the variety of different skills required are seen as being more challenging. This also relieves monotony;

b. task identity, in that the worker works with a complete piece of work. Often workers were required to work on such small parts of the whole that they were unable to identify a product with results of their efforts;

c. task significance, that is, the work appears important. The essential point for the workers is that they are doing something of significance for the organization and for society;

d. autonomy, in that the workers have some control over their own work. Perhaps this is an additional step in the Maslow's Needs Hierarchy. (See the section on powerlessness later in this chapter.); and

e. feedback, whereby the worker receives positive strokes. Since workers are investing a substantial part of their lives into work, they want to know how they are doing.

The Variables Affecting Quality of the Work Life

1. Compensation
   a. Does the income from full-time employment meet socially determined standards of sufficiency or the subjective standard of the recipient?
   b. Does the pay received for certain work bear an appropriate relationship to the pay received for other work?

   My raise. His raise

   My effort. His effort.

2. Safety and Health
   a. Are there reasonable working hours and rules which are enforced by a standardized normal work period, beyond which premium pay is required?
   b. Are physical working conditions present that minimize risk of illness, stress and injury?

3. Use and Development of Human Capacities
   a. Does the job allow for substantial autonomy and self-control relative to external controls?
   b. Does the job permit the learning and exercise of a wider range of skills and abilities, rather than a repetitive application of narrow skills?

Natural Work Teams

Natural work teams grow out of the concept of a *natural work module*. When jobs are designed to be performed in a complete cycle of work in order to make a whole product (or major sub unit), then the employee is performing a natural work module – the job flows naturally from start to finish. The worker feels *task identity* and *significance*. In the same way, work can be designed so that a group of employees (*natural work team*) performs an entire unit of work. People who work together learn from each other, satisfy mutual (often non-job related) needs, and develop team-work. <small>natural work team</small>

Some workers may not like to be members of a natural work team. This is especially true:

a.   if they are unable to tolerate increased responsibility;

b.   if they dislike more complex duties;

c.   if they are uncomfortable with group work;

d.   if they dislike relearning;

e.   if they prefer security and stability;

f.   if they are comfortable with supervisory authority; and

g.   if their skills are not adaptable.

New Trend Management

In his text, *Management in the Third Wave,* Alan Raymond (1986) notes that some organizations have transformed themselves into what Raymond terms *organic organizations.* These are organizations which have at least these four common characteristics.

1. Innovation and creativity are highly prized values. Their development is encouraged and sought after.

2. Bureaucratic practices are avoided. Practices are simple, clearly communicated, and effective.

3. Organic organizations see their employees as members rather than as employees. Managers genuinely want and expect employees to contribute more than skills. Employees are expected to believe that the organization is theirs and that its success or failure is dependent on the employees' actions and decisions.

4. Flexibility and responsiveness to change is also a common element of third-wave organizations, which consciously seem to meet the demands of the future.

Theory Z

The quality of the work life and third-wave organic management movements have a great deal in common. Both stress people, involvement in the work place, and human relations built upon mutual trust, confidence, and performance expectations. William Ourchi, author of *Theory Z* (1981), expressed a similar idea when he noted that innovation, care for people, and concern for the overall health of the organization are essential to keeping the management posture positive, the workers satisfied, and the venture successful.

Consequences of Poor or Deteriorating Quality of Work Life

Many historians question whether adventurer Frederick Cook fabricated his claim of being the first person to reach the North Pole in 1908, but few question the authenticity of his description of the isolation and bleakness of the area he visited:

> Beyond the 83rd parallel, life is devoid of pleasure. The intense objective impressions of cold and hunger assailing the body rob even the mind of inspiration. Even the best day of sun and gentle wind offers no balm.
>
> (Frederick Cook, *My Attainment of the Pole.*)

stress

eustress
distress
hypostress

hyperstress

When the quality of the work life is poor, the stress level of the employee will generally increase. The reader is reminded that there are four basic types of stress: *eustress* which is a positive and usually pleasant degree of stress; *distress* which is unpleasant and disease producing; *hypostress* (under stressed) which results in lack of self-realization, boredom, sometimes physical immobility and sensory deprivation; and *hyperstress* (overstress) in which an individual's limits are exceeded. This chapter is directed toward the causes and consequences of distress and especially hyperstress.

Professionals and Bureaucracy

Our society has become highly bureaucratized. Governments have become increasingly involved in attempting to address many of the personal and persistent needs of the community such as social welfare, child care, education, and health care. As this movement intensifies, many of the givers of service have had an increased interface with bureaucratic structures. The issues involved have generated a considerable amount of literature on the topic, the professional and the bureaucracy. McKay (Carver & Sergiovanni, 1969) among others, has attempted to bring structure to the issue. He points out that the professional employee:

professional
beliefs

a. stresses the uniqueness of the client's (child's) problem;

b. stresses continued research and change;

c. considers rules as *alternatives;*

d. places emphasis upon the achievement of client (child) oriented goals;

e. considers that his/her own skills are based upon a monopoly of knowledge;

f. expects to make decisions concerning policy in professional matters depending upon the uniqueness of the problem;

g. considers that rules governing conduct should be legally sanctioned by the members of the professional grouping;

h. has loyalty to the professional association and the clients rather than the local administrative structure; and

i. believes that his/her authority grows out of professional competence rather than status or rank, or role.

But, on the other hand, the bureaucratic structure is governed by essential beliefs such as:

bureaucratic
beliefs

1. authority lies in the position (the role) of the incumbent;

2. division of labor and specialization are necessary for efficiency, and

3. there should be specified behavior (rules) for each situation.

In summary, conflict results because the two groups of workers tend to be directed in different directions.

The Organization	The Professional
1. Authority is in the position.	1. Knowledge is authority.
2. Division of labor is important.	2. The client (student) is seen as a whole.
3. Specific behavior is appropriate for specified situations.	3. Behavior alternatives are available for specified situations.
4. Defined procedures are to be followed.	4. New problems require new ideas, and new methods – adaptability is essential.

| 5. Roles not persons are central. | 5. Interpersonal relations are central. |
| 6. Competency is the desired goal. | 6. Competency is *the* goal. |

Exhibit 19-2
Professional/Organizational Conflict

Stress

A vast literature exists which attempts to define stress, characterize its manifestations and prescribe stress-management techniques. Stress is herein defined (in its negative connotation) as the phenomenon of anxiety, dissatisfaction, tension or frustration which results in low morale and impaired job performance. Job-related stress involves a set of complicated interactions between an individual and the work environment. When work (environment) demands (stressors) are perceived as being more than can be tolerated, (some use the metaphore *permanent white water*),the individual will use a variety of *coping* tactics, many of which are ineffective, resulting in an escalating cycle of dysfunction.

coping tactics

symptoms

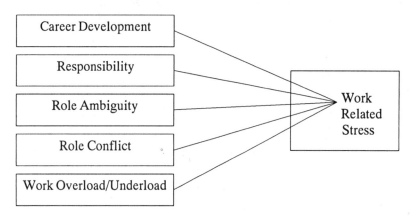

Exhibit 19-3
Sources of Work-Related Stress

A teacher's perception of his or her career status and progress can cause *career* development stress. This is especially true during the current times of employment uncertainty.

Increased responsibilities can be a positive force in our lives, but where teachers meet excessive parent, community and administration expectations, or classes of very divergent student characteristics (integration), the burden can become so great that the teacher is unable to cope adequately.

Role ambiguity refers to a lack of clarity about the work the person is expected to do. This is often a problem for the young teacher.

Role conflict causes stress when there is an incompatability between the role behavior which is normally expected to be associated with teaching, for example, and the role of being a spouse, parent, or community leader. In another form, role conflict may be induced in the teacher when he or she is expected to be supportive and caring of students, and at the same time disciplining and controling their behavior.

An optimum amount of stress is helpful for good performance. When the quantitative and qualitative demands placed upon the teacher are more than he or she can handle, *stress* results. Underload, the opposite of overload, can be equally stressful because it often leads to boredom, depression, frustration, and a feeling of being *trapped* in the job. Employees often attempt to relieve this kind of job stress by utilizing on-the-job distractions, such as reading paperbacks, filing nails, or visiting at the waterfountain.

Symptoms of stress include moodiness, unexplained fatigue, forgetfulness and physical ailments such as high blood pressure, stomach problems, sleep disturbances, or increased dependency on alcohol, drugs or tobacco. As stressors increase, the person may exhibit impaired decision-making and information-processing abilities, social withdrawal, a tendency to get sidetracked, irritability, cynicism, or in extreme cases, depression or severe psychotic responses. Organizational performance suffers from the resultant absenteeism, impaired performance and relationship problems such as low morale, lack of trust, and negative attitudes (Truch, 1980).

Behavior effect	drug and alcohol abuse, eating disorders, emotional outbursts, grinding teeth, nervous laughter, proneness to accidents, ticks, trembling.
Cognitive effects	unexplained forgetfulness, inability to concentrate, mental blocks, overly sensitive, especially to criticism.
Organizational effects	greater than usual absenteeism, job dissatisfaction, low productiviity, lower job commitment, poor relations with management.
Psychological effects	aggression, anxiety, boredom, depression, fatigue, general irritability, guilt, loneliness, nervousness.
Physiological effects	persistent chest pains, headaches, increased heart rate and blood pressure, low-grade fevers, lower back pains, muscle contractions, tightness in neck and shoulders

Exhibit 19-4
Consequences of Stress

It has been recognized for some time that teachers are faced with some unique school-related stressors.

student
discipline

Blase and Matthews (1986) report that student discipline is a primary source of stress for teachers and that school leaders directly contribute to stress by inconsistently enforcing student discipline policies. Supervisors contribute to teacher stress when they lack knowledge of both curriculum and students, provide inadequate information about standards and goals, make unreasonable demands for extra duties, conduct arbitrary and unclear teacher evaluations, fail to provide adequate resources or psychological support, or fail to allow teacher input into decisions.

management's
practices

Thus the management practices of school administrators do much to add stress to the teacher's working environment. Often school administrators are so beset by budgets, politics, bureaucratic rules on today's memo from central office, that they lose sight of the crucial focus on people, and the importance of giving them meaning, security, and a feeling they are doing something of value.

work
relationships

Sparks and Mannon, in *Managing Teacher Burnout*, contend that the prime cause of job-related stress for teachers is the poor quality of the work relationships that exist in many educational organizations.

The following are some examples of problem work-related situations.

1. Teachers are forced to teach a curriculum and execute school policies without being significantly involved in the decision-making process.

2. Teachers have little or no control over the work environment.

3. Teachers are required to meet numerous and varied demands.

4. Teachers often are required to conform to unreasonable and illogical procedures.

5. Teachers as a group often suffer public criticism and perhaps a feeling of powerlessness, and, at best, they experience non-support.

School-based Causes of Teacher Stress

The causes of teacher stress are frequently grouped under three categories of variables: time, students, and school climate (Kratzman, 1981).

time

Time variables include the following.

1. Total hours of work assigned per week.

2. Hours assigned to formal instruction (class time).

3. Hours assigned to essential instruction-related activities (preparation, evaluation, counselling, tutoring, consulting).

4. Hours assigned to extra-instructional optional school activities (clubs, teams, cultural events, literary activities and the like).

5. Hours assigned to non-instructional essential school responsibilities (administrative/clerical activities, supervision of study halls, grounds, building corridors, lunch rooms, social activities, sports events, etc.); and

6. Time allotted to required continuing professional development.

The two major dimensions of the student variable are: student variables

a. their number (class size of the number of students for whom the teacher is responsible); and

b. their profiles (range of students' educational, behavioral and physical conditions and their social characteristics).

School climate is, according to Rutter (1979), the set of values, attitudes, and behaviors (the *ethos*) which characterizes the school as a whole. Some refer to school climate as something akin to school personality. Climate variables include: school climate

a. the quality and commitment of colleagues;

b. levels of teacher and student morale and satisfaction;

c. the nature and quality of administrative leadership provided;

d. presence and absence of factors which induce stress, and;

e. quality of the relationships which the staff has with the school board and central office personnel.

There are also a number of less controversial and less directly related variables that may affect the quality of the work life of teachers. These variables are: school size; school type (primary, elementary, junior high, senior high); school organization (grade/subject/class structure, length of school day, length of sequencing of class periods, number of school days in the school year); numbers and characteristics of school-based professional personnel (administrators, counsellors, librarians, resource teachers, nurses); number of school-based non-professional personnel (teacher aides, secretaries, caretakers, laboratory assistants, volunteers); specific school-system personnel (individual school trustees, administrators, consultants); resources available (instructional/learning materials and technology, supplies, equipment, specific facilities); and opportunities or lack of opportunities for continuing professional development at school, district, provincial, and/or professional association levels. other variables

Worker Alienation

Frequently writers in business, industrial, and sometimes educational administration will use the term *worker alienation* to describe the condition akin to those herein labelled as poor quality of the work life. The dimensions of worker alienation are usually described as being feelings of: alienation dimensions

a. powerlessness, in that workers feel they have no control over things which are significant to them in the workplace;

2. meaninglessness, where the worker is unable to devise a cognitive map to help predict the results or outcomes of his/her own acts;

3. normlessness, in that the workers use illegal or non-legal means to satisfy their own goals;

4. isolation, where the worker isolates himself/herself from the means and ends of the organization. Slavish conformity to rules is prevalent for many individuals who fall into this category; or

5. self-estrangement, in that the worker loses all interest and involvement in work. Strangely, he/she may still be on the job.

routes for
alienated

There are a number of routes alienated workers can take. The following five are the most frequently listed reactions.

1. Conformity, whereby the individual finds a balance and conforms to the means and the ends of the organization.

2. Innovation, the most frequent route is for the worker is to accept the ends or goals of the organization, but to change the means by which they will be reached.

3. Ritualism, where the worker accepts the means but rejects or refuses to accept the ends or purposes of the organization.

4. Retreatism, a form of avoidance behavior whereby the worker rejects both the means and the ends but may continue to work in order to earn money to finance off-the-job fulfillment.

5. Rebellion, often characterized by making trouble, involvement in acts of industrial sabotage, or by trying to substitute another more acceptable form of organization for the existing one – moves toward unionism or union militancy.

Signs of Job Dissatisfaction

There are a number of strong indicators of job dissatisfaction including high absenteeism rates, high turn-over rates, high accident rates, movement toward a union shop or the strengthening of union demands, and increased physical or imagined illnesses resulting in large numbers of employees on sick leave or long-term disability leave. Other signs include irritability, lack of interest and commitment, poor motivation, setting low goals, avoidance of difficult tasks, inferior or deteriorating quality of work, loss of concentration, and self-depreciation.

personal
matters

We must be careful not to immediately assume that the presence of any one of a few of the above-noted signs means job dissatisfaction. Personal life matters may be the root cause.

stimulaate
and reward

There are a number of specific administrator initiated activities which stimulate and reward able teachers. Doll (p. 264) elaborated upon seventeen specific suggestions.

1. Increase the overall involvement of able teachers in decision-making.

2. Arrange for the involvement of able teachers in unaccustomed ways and situations (budgeting, represent the school . . .)

3. Work closely with able teachers.

4. Put able teachers in compatible situations (personally fits work situation).

5. Redesign able teachers' jobs.

6. Observe able teachers closely to develop ideas for their improvement.

7. Use video tape recordings for feedback.

8. Place able teachers in small work groups. (Smaller groups with constant and unwavering purposes do best).

9. Organize able teachers into teams of specialists.

10. Push able teachers to their limits (satisfaction of their ego and self-actualization needs).

11. Permit able teachers to spend time trying to do better in the tasks in which they are weak.

12. Promote able teachers.

13. Keep the school organization *flat*, not tall.

14. Pay attention to the morale of able teachers.

15. Give able teachers across-job exposure (provide new images and new labels).

16. Place able teachers in mutual exchange programs (foreign service, local and national teacher-exchange programs).

17. Place able teachers in positions and roles that give maximum opportunity for motivation (task identify, task significance).

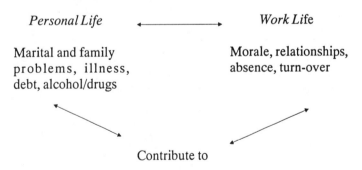

Exhibit 19-3
Interrelationship Between Personal and Work Life

Burnout

Burnout results from the subtle and progressive nature of job related stress. Teachers who suffer from burnout often become lethargic and lose interest in teaching. "I'm just worn out." The classic symptoms of burnout are physical, mental, and emotional exhaustion. Robert Coolembiewski and Robert Munzenrider (in Meggisen, Mosley & Pietri, 1992), noted that 40 percent of the more than 12 000 respondents from the 33 United States organizations included in their study suffered from advancing phases of burnout. Burnout is a problem, not for end-of-career workers, but for mid and earlier career workers. Disability insurance, available to most teachers for a premium, blunts the immediate financial impact of the condition, but recovery is a long process. Careful self assessment and preventative activities make sense.

Stress Management

Physical Strategies

Autogenetic training (self hypnosis)
Biofeedback (monitoring one's vital signs
Deep Breathing (focus on breathing itself
Diet
Exercise
Hot tubs, jacuzzi, sauna
Progressive relaxation
Massage
Sensory awareness
Visualization
Yoga

Social Strategies

Assertiveness training
Interpersonal skill training
Networking
Support groups

Spiritual Strategies

Faith/hope activities
Meditation
Prayer

Intellectual/Mental Strategies

Cognative restructuring
Covert sensitization
Paradoxical intention
Reframing (refining as man age-able)
Rehearsal (talk through with one-self)
Stress innoculation
Small wins strategy
Systemic desensitization
Thought stopping
Values clarification

Emotional Strategies

Catharsis
Covert assertion
Self awareness
Withdrawal

Environmental Strategies

Conflict resolution training
Decision making training
Goal setting activities
Lifestyle assessment programs
Problem solving techniques
Time management strategies

S T R E S S

S T R E S S

Exhibit 19-6
Stress Management

In summary, quality of the work life refers to the favorableness or unfavorableness of the job environment for teachers. Since teachers and the nature of schooling have changed over time, increased attention needs to be given to improving the teacher's life on the job. Jobs have to fit people as well as fit technology. Teachers should be given more control over essential task decisions. Pay attention to the morale of able teachers, and take responsibility for their achievement. More use should be made of *natural work teams*. Administration should give teachers more control over problem-solving and goal development. Decisions affecting teachers, their work, as well as instruction and student management procedure and policy changes should be discussed with teachers. A climate of partnership is essential. Administrators and central office staff need to become resource people, and evaluators of performance rather than controllers of teachers. But on the other hand, teachers must tolerate increased responsibility, must have strong growth and achievement drives, must have positive attitudes toward working with groups, must have a high tolerance of pressures level, must be able to deal with increased job complexity, and must feel secure in their own personal abilities and qualities.

Teacher Salary and Rewards

Payment for employee services is an economic transaction in which the
purchaser attempts to obtain the greatest quantity and the highest quality for
his/her money . . .

Castetter, 1986

```
Incentives

Non-monetary rewards

Monetary rewards

Salary Schedules

Bargaining Process

Pay Grids
```

Introduction

The purpose of the compensation process is to allocate organizational
resources for salaries, wages, benefits, and rewards in a manner which will
attract, retain and motivate teachers, administrators, and support personnel.

The range of rewards which can be employed by a school system are
extremely broad, but in general they include money, promotions, perquisites
(perks), and benefits such as: insurance and pensions, and special awards and
certificates.

range of
rewards

Obviously both employer and employee have a central and lasting interest
in *compensation* policies. Salaries, wages, and benefits constitute the single
largest expenditure for every school system; approximately 85 percent of the
costs of school operations are allocated to employee compensation. The level
of salaries and benefits is an important factor in attracting, retaining and
activating employees. For the employee, the level of compensation is directly
related to the satisfaction of personal needs since the level of salary is related
to status in society and to economic well-being. The distribution of compensation among the various levels of employees affects their performance since
monetary rewards are part of incentive systems. The nature of the compensation
demanded, the composition of the staff, and the rising expectations of workers
require that compensation packages be modified, regularly. In education this is
normally done on a yearly basis, or occasionally on a two-year cycle.

compensation
policies

The purpose of this chapter is to review some central issues in worker
compensation, the teacher salary bargaining process, and the structural features
of a teacher salary agreement.

Incentives

directed to
attainment of
objectives

The viability and productivity of any organization, from the most simply structured, single-purpose, local volunteer group to the most complex, diversified, industrial conglomerate, depends to a substantial degree upon its success in getting each member or employee to direct attention and energy toward the attainment of the objectives of the organization. How is the loyalty and commitment obtained, and once obtained, how is it maintained? Very simply, by the application of a system of incentives, that is, by applying rewards and in some instances, punishment.

All organizations are concerned about the most effective way to use rewards. Schools are no exception. Among administrators and employees disagreement exists about the best way to apply the types of rewards available. There are several bases upon which rewards can be made: performance, effort, seniority, and internal equity criteria.

performance
based

First, assessing teacher and administrator performance (student also) occupies numerous people and a considerable amount of effort. To the extent that the schools actually value good performance, performance can become a motivator.

effort based

Second, rewards for effort are frequently employed to encourage the new teacher (or the teacher assuming a new task) in order to keep that person from becoming discouraged and in the hopes that effort will soon be replaced by *actual performance*.

seniority
based

Third, in some institutions seniority (that is, sticking with the job) appears to be rewarded more than actual performance provided that the employee's performance is at an acceptable level. All too frequently seniority has become a substitute for performance. Finally, as it is hoped with the third basis noted above, internal *equity,* which can be used as a basis for rewarding employees, is not a compelling force with the school district's awards system. Equity is essential, but it should not be thought of as a motivator – if you work hard we will make you equal!

internal equity

intrinsic rewards

There are intrinsic rewards and extrinsic rewards. Intrinsic rewards are those rewards which teachers are able to give to themselves as their work unfolds. (See the section *quality of the work life.*) Extrinsic rewards are defined herein as those rewards which are administered by the educational system. They take place on the job but are external to doing the job itself.

extrinsic rewards

Extrinsic rewards may be further divided into indirect compensation and direct compensation (i.e., non-monetary and monetary rewards). Extrinsic rewards may also be related, not so much to tangible costs, but to good and bad administrative styles and actions and administrative cost.

basic
characteristics

Arnold & Feldman (1986) state there are five basic characteristics of rewards which can be used to analyze the strengths and weaknesses of the various types of rewards available.

1. A reward cannot influence what workers do on the job or how they feel if it is not important to them.

2. Rewards themselves must be flexible if they are to be tailored to the characteristics of individual members and be provided contingent upon an attainable level of performance.

3. The more frequently that a reward can be provided, the greater its potential for influencing employee performance.

4. When rewards are highly visible, the employee will perceive a relationship between performance level and reward.

5. Obviously, a reward system cannot be designed without careful consideration as to the costs involved.

In general terms, rewards do three things, they (1) encourage membership, (2) reward attendance, and (3) encourage effective performance.

Stroking Strategy

Many administrators have been able to improve employee morale and motivation through *stroking* which is usually conveyed by expressing verbal approval. The strategy of thanking and complementing teachers can lead to improvements. The literature sometimes refers to the systematic plan for stroking as behavior modification (Orwellion manipulation?), operant conditioning (salivating dog?) or the more euphemistic and more acceptable terminology, *performance improvement* or contingency management. The strategy is based upon the premise that future behavior is influenced by the outcomes of past behavior. If the outcomes are satisfying, the behavior will be repeated. Does this not sound like parts of an educational psychology course? There are some questions about how far the principal or department head, for example, can go with verbal stroking as a motivator. First, if used more-or-less continuously as one might do with a person learning a new skill or working on an unfamiliar task (continuous positive reinforcement), the process is time-consuming. Second, there is the problem of inflation. Just as the dollar loses its value when too many are in circulation, so do verbal approvals. Third, once continuous reinforcement becomes expected, its withdrawal may signal to the teacher that the behavior which was preciously stroked, is no longer appropriate. Most school administrators employ some form of random intermittent stroking. The value of this motivational device depends a great deal upon the personal need of the teacher – the strength of the need for praise.

[margin notes: thanking and complimenting; continuous use; random stroking]

Participation Strategy

Participation has become widely used by school administrators as a motivator. Certainly the strength, or accuracy, or correctness of group decision making exceeds that of individual decision making and this is the most positive of the attributes of participation, but the act of participation itself may also be a good motivator. Teachers often participate in the school decision making process in areas such as program planning, student supervision, and budgeting. This usually increases the level of achievement through sharing insights and resolving differences, increases the degree of commitment to the group decision, and reduces the resistance or hostility toward change. Teachers may become involved in MBO (management of objectives). In MBO the teacher and administrator (supervisor) jointly involve themselves in a performance or progress reviews which are *goal oriented.* New goals, changed goals, or new objectives are developed into action plans. Actions directed toward achieving the new goals or objectives are then undertaken. Those who participate in joint decision making and goal setting are believed to (and usually do) feel better about the organization. They feel rewarded. They are getting somewhere!

increasing
commitment

Rewarding the Wrong Thing

Despite the best intentions, many school administrators (perhaps teachers also) fall into the trap of rewarding the wrong thing. Usually this is done without thinking. People too often reward one kind of behavior while hoping to promote another, often divergent or opposite behavior. For example, how often have you offered a suggestion and then been asked to write the report? The reward for the suggestion is to do more work, and perhaps at the same time, inadvertently expose some personal weaknesses. When the report is written, and if the suggestions are accepted, then the work has only begun. Society hopes that teachers will teach well, but administration often rewards them more for involvement in the extra-curricular program. Teachers and coaches and players believe that team sports should foster body movement, cooperation, and sportsmanship, but which attributes get praised? Often, it is only the game-winning attributes which are noticed.

The organization (in this instance a school system and a school) operates in its essential features in very much the same way as the classroom teacher functions in the role of manager of human and physical resources within the classroom. Students are rewarded for behavior directed toward attainment of the objectives which have been set for the lesson and are not rewarded for other types of behavior which are extraneous or non-objective oriented. A system of incentives is being applied. Certainly, the nature of the rewards and punishments applied may vary: for example, we would not normally pay a student for attending school and devoting energies toward obtaining an education, nor would we fire the student for not learning the steps in deriving a square root. The types of rewards and punishments may vary for teacher and for student, but the consequences and their impact are no less pressing upon either person.

incentives

It is important at this time to insert a word of caution. There are factors other than *motives* and *needs* which determine the quality and efficiency of a worker's behavior. These include the ability of the worker, the level of experience, the physical conditions under which the work is done, and the social milieu within which the worker works. The worker has little direct and immediate control over these factors. Basically, there are three motives for working. Work may be done as an end in itself – work for work's sake. Work may be carried out

other factors

willingly for motives directly associated with the work situation, i.e. for comradeship, status, power, or escape from other less desirable circumstances or surroundings. Work may be done for genuinely extrinsic motives – money which may then be applied to various other purposes in order to fulfill the physiological, safety, love, esteem, or self-actualization needs of the employee. However, within the confines of the school system, and in a general sense, there are two reward systems which are operative for the teacher.

work for work's sake

two reward systems

Reward Systems

Non-Monetary Rewards

The non-monetary reward system operates through a number of mechanisms. The recognition/prestige payoff to the teacher may come through:

a. a lighter teaching load in the form of fewer classes to be taught, thus effectively reducing the amount of work required by the teacher or permitting him/her to engage in other activities, instructional or non-instructional, which are within themselves more interesting or satisfying than the usual assignment;

b. having fewer students to teach or consult, either within a specific class or in total throughout the school day. This has the effect of reducing the strain upon the teacher. Incidentally, it may have desirable outcomes as well for the purposes of the institution;

c. having fewer different courses to teach. This type of reward does at least two things. It says to the teacher, "You are a specialist. We have confidence in your abilities in this area." Further, it usually provides the teacher with a lighter work load;

d. being permitted the maximum allowable time for lesson preparation during the school day;

e. restricting a teacher's course load to those subjects in which the teacher has a special interest or special competencies; or

f. assigning the teacher the most desirable classes to teach. The payoff for the teacher usually comes through less effort being required to motivate or control students, and probably by providing a more stimulating classroom climate in which to work.

Other types of non-monetary rewards include consulting superior teachers on curricular matters, allowing time off to attend conferences, providing desirable classroom locations, providing preferred parking spaces, freeing the teacher from the extra mundane chores which are part of every school's operation, or providing business cards, impressive titles, and personal office or workspace. *Teacher of the Year* and other similar forms of community or school system recognition, although less frequently applied, are further illustrations of the non-monetary reward system that operates within our schools.

other non-monetary

Monetary Rewards

In the private sector and at some levels of the public sector, a discussion of extrinsic rewards would, of course, include merit compensation, but because of the way in which teacher salary scales are structured, and the nature of a school as an organization, many features of direct compensation package and almost all of the indirect compensation rewards are not available to be used by administrators. In the private sector, and at the teacher's approximate level of training, the *direct compensation package* may be supplemented by performance bonuses, overtime and holiday premiums, and other provisions such as stock options and profit sharing. At the *indirect compensation* level, certain private sector employees also have available *pay for time not worked*, flex time, services such as financial counselling, company cars, favorable loan interest rates, and perquisites such as fitness and social club memberships, publication subscriptions, and theatre and sporting event tickets.

direct compensation

indirect compensation

For teachers, almost all of the items enumerated above as additional direct or indirect compensation, if not found in the salary contract (salary schedule, collective agreement) will not be made available. School districts, in part because they are public institutions funded by public taxes, seldom have budgeted amounts for these types of expenditures. Thus, it is essential that teachers study the salary contract clause by clause. Make no assumptions. The exact wording of the contract will be applied.

Discussing teachers' salaries may be distasteful to some. One gets the impression that somehow teachers should live on satisfaction; the idea that the desire to serve should be more important than financial rewards is not an uncommon notion in the minds of many. Obviously non-monetary rewards like those suggested above contribute to our *good feeling* about our job and our performance in it, but for any teacher to refuse to recognize that money is basic to our system of rewards is to deny a central part of our social fabric.

money

With the exception of a few under-developed societies, and these are rapidly disappearing, money is a universally accepted method of bartering our talents for those things which satisfy our needs. The teacher has talents, skills, a *service*, which are supplied to the community in return for a pay cheque which, in its turn, is applied to the purchase of the talents, skills, and services of others. Elementary, yes, but somehow this is forgotten by some and therefore must be restated from time to time. No, the beginning teacher should not hesitate to consider the matter of salary level. To do otherwise would be foolish.

Teacher Salary Schedules

Teacher salary schedules (collective agreements) are arrived at through the bargaining process. Provincial legislation (frequently the Labor Act) provides the framework and rules under which the process will take place.

bargaining agents

The salary contract is a *contract* which specifies the parties to the contract, the bargaining agents who represent the parties, the application (which employees are covered and which are excluded), the term (time period) covered by the agreement, the methods and time lines for re-opening the contract, and the procedures for interpretation and grievance hearings, including who is entitled to be present, and how petitions for change are to be handled.

For most school jurisdictions, the teacher salary contract will be one of several salary contracts which the employer has entered into with its employees. Other bargaining units would include caretakers, building trades persons, clerical personnel (inside workers). Management or administrative personnel are excluded from the above agreements, because *they are* management and must thus be independent from the union (association). The employer (the school boards) frequently act upon their own (single-employer) behalf although using bargaining units (groups of employers) has become common. Bargaining units reduce the time and costs involved in lengthy direct contract negotiations with separate groups of employees, and also present a more solid front to the employees – there is solidarity in numbers, so to speak. The bottom line, the actual purpose of regional bargaining, is probably also to standardize salaries over a larger geographic area, and to prevent *whip sawing* wherein an employee bargaining unit gains a specific advantage which is (in the following round of negotiations) demanded by adjacent bargaining units. For example, if one unit obtains a more favorable level of employer contribution to health care premiums, all other units will demand the same concession. In some provinces the provincial government acts as the employer in negotiations on at least the basic salary scale. Often local employers are permitted to negotiate fringe items and perhaps working condition clauses, but the level of the salary package is negotiated provincially.

bargaining units

provincial bargaining

The bargaining agent for the teachers is normally the teachers' association, not the local employee unit. The reasons for this arrangement are bargaining strategy reasons: to plan a province-wide strategy; and to work toward satisfying major teacher-oriented goals such as increased levels of salary, cost-of-living adjustments, or student-to-teacher classroom ratios, dental plans, etcetera. Most, if not all of the local negotiations, however, are conducted between local teachers' representatives and trustees or trustee representatives. In larger centres the school jurisdiction's representatives are usually personnel department employees.

teacher bargaining agent

The bargaining process, as stated earlier, is directed toward a number of employer/employee goals, such as:

bargaining process

a. to attract and retain competent teachers;

b. to motivate teachers through incentives;

c. to get maximum return on public expenditures;

d. to create employee equity through internal consistency in compensation;

e. to relate level of compensation to the importance and the difficulty of the work undertaken, and the kinds of personnel the school organization requires;

f. to exercise control over expenditure levels – different from (c) above;

g. to develop a compensation package conducive to economic, social and psychological satisfaction of teachers; and

h. to minimize individual compensation-related grievances.

The school system agrees to provide equitable compensation, certain rights and privileges, security (job tenure), assistance in employee improvement, proper placement, equitable treatment, and opportunities for advancement. On the other hand, the teacher, for example, agrees to join, stay, meet or exceed role expectations of the school system, work with a minimum of direct supervision, strive to improve, be cooperative, and adhere to the policies and expectations of the school board and of senior administration.

Most writers in personnel administration observe that the exchange between the employer and employee involves not only economic, but also psychological, social, political, and ethical transactions. Payment for services is an economic transaction. The teacher sells a service in order to obtain income. The teacher holds out for the highest price that he/she can command. A psychological transaction is a contract between employees and the organization. The individual exchanges *employer-desired* behavior for pay and job satisfaction. Compensation also becomes a sociological transaction since organizations are, in fact, associations of people and employment is, in part, a social relationship between individual and group. Compensation agreements are political transactions involving the use of power and influence in the struggle between public good and personal gain. Compensation agreements involve ethical transactions in terms of fairness to both parties.

psychological transaction

economic value

The economic value of a teacher is influenced by his/her position in the school hierarchy; compensation and bargaining legislation; prevailing salaries and employment practices; the strength of unionization; supply and demand situation; community ability to pay; the standard and cost of living; and the strength or weakness of the reform forces respecting such matters as working conditions, disparity in pay, entry-level training needed, the position of teachers within society, and often *equal pay for unequal performance* criteria.

Prior to actual salary negotiations, both employee and employer groups will have established their respective benefit package goals. Obviously the positions will be modified as the negotiating process proceeds if a final agreement is to be reached, and it *must* be reached. Besides the basic salary package (for teachers based upon years of training, experience, and level of responsibility) a number of collateral or fringe benefits will be included in the terms (clauses) of the final contract. Some collateral benefits are legally required (for example, provincial teacher retirement plans and statutory sick leave benefits while others are privately offered and accepted negotiated).

collateral benefits

other collateral benefits

Other collateral benefits usually fall under three broad headings: *income replacement* (pensions, long and short-term disability insurance, death benefits, severance pay, professional liability insurance); *personal security* (provincial health care, extended health care to cover prescriptions, private hospital rooms, dental care, vision care insurance, ambulance service, extended sick leave beyond the statutory requirements, personal and family emergency leaves with pay; and *employee services* (vacation leaves, sabbatical leaves, leave to observe religious holidays, emergency and bereavement leaves, jury duty leave, leaves to attend professional meetings, to do exchange teaching, tuition reimbursement clauses, personal counselling service provisions for such matters as relief of school-induced stress, substance abuse, and legal and financial counselling, payment for convention expenses, transportation allowances, physical examinations, subsidized food services, and social and recreational programs). The list of benefits under all three categories could probably be expanded. Teacher negotiators are inventive in hunting for additional benefits!

Those who are required to administer the compensation package, usually a personnel superintendent or secretary treasurer, are faced with a number of problems. When not included in school jurisdiction policies, these matters may become part of the list of items under negotiation. Procedures must be established to govern matters such as:

administering compensation package

a. placement of new personnel at appropriate levels;

b. promotion increases;

c. demotion pay adjustments;

d. upgrading of positions, or clusters of positions;

e. downgrading of a cluster of salary positions;

f. re-evaluation of pay and benefits because of changes in the work of the position-holder;

g. inequity adjustments (changes designed to achieve salary or placement equity);

h. bases and frequency of pay increases;

i. promotions within grades or scales; and

j. special situations such as red-circling (where employees are being paid more than the agreed upon maximum so increases in the future are held to nil until the scale, in a sense, catches up), or to give another example, green-circling where the normal progression is modified to permit rapid catch up, or, on the other hand, what is sometimes called silver-circling wherein long-service employees who do not deserve pay increases based upon their current level of performance are held to the current level, and not reduced.

Salary schedules in education have been based upon merit, position, role performed, rank, grade level and sometimes gender or subject field taught. The most frequently utilized plan today is referred to as the *single salary schedule* in which equivalent salaries are paid for equivalent university preparation and years of teaching experience. Often teacher salary schedules make provision for indexing, usually to reflect the cost of living adjustments, however, most often cost-of-living arguments are involved in the bargaining process which

bases of salary schedules
single salary schedule

determines the base salary scale. Usually movement through the salary position range is automatic and definable, but sometimes teacher salary contracts will make provision for withholding increments due to marginal performance, or provide for additional salary (merit pay/performance pay) for exceptional service. In Canada these modifications are very uncommon.

The Bargaining Process

The bargaining power of the school board (where not restricted or interfered with by legislation) is based upon a balancing of the costs to the teachers of *not agreeing* with the proposals of the school board with the costs to the teachers of *agreeing* with the proposals of the board. Conversely, the power of the teachers rests upon the cost to the school board of *disagreeing* with the terms proposed by the teachers over the board's cost of *agreeing* to the teachers' demands. Political pressure, supply and demand, negotiating skills, and psychological tactics are the main sources of bargaining power. Almost always the overall advantages of *agreement* outweigh the advantages of *disagreement.* The formula for success is elusive; however, since bargaining is an art, not a science, teacher and trustee teams usually rely upon a repetition of previously successful tactics which in the final analysis are often designed to determine where the other side is willing to settle. What is their *final* position? At what point will they balk?

[margin note: balance between agreeing and not agreeing]

Impasse Resolution

Where persistent disagreement continues after normal negotiations procedures have been utilized, the bargaining teams will move toward impasse resolution processes through a series of steps endorsed by law and detailed in the statutes. Normally the first step is *mediation* whereby the teachers' bargaining team, or bargaining agent meets the school board's team with the help of an agreed-upon third party. The role of the mediator is advisory; however, the mediator *will* hear the representations of the parties, mediate between the positions held by the parties, and attempt to encourage a settlement of the items under dispute. Sometimes mediators will meet with each party separately to determine what concessions each party would be willing to make. Sometimes joint meetings will be helpful in clarifying areas of agreement and disagreement, and clarifying the degree of importance assigned to specific clauses or proposals.

[margin note: mediation]

After these fact-finding steps, the mediator begins shuttling proposals and counter-proposals between the parties. Mediators usually refrain from recommending a settlement (in the form of a mediator's report) until they are sure their recommendations will be accepted by both parties. When the mediator is unable to achieve a settlement, the parties will be notified and a *cooling off* period is normally required. In view of the intensity of the process, bargaining normally moves to the *arbitration* stage. Where one party to the disagreement accepts the recommendations of the mediator, the statutes normally permit each

[margin note: arbitration]

party to request a vote of acceptance or rejection on the part of the other party as the next step.

Arbitration is a process whereby the parties submit their dispute to an impartial third person or panel of persons appointed under the authority of the appropriate provincial statute. Sometimes arbitration is compulsory, sometimes it is voluntary. Sometimes the results of the arbitration award are binding, but usually they are not. The teacher's bargaining agent, of course, will be thoroughly conversant with all legal requirements and restrictions and may, as the employer may, use the provisions of the legislation to their own bargaining advantage. Some provinces have established *disputes inquiry boards* as an intermediate step between mediation and arbitration. The disputes inquiry board reports to the appropriate minister (usually the Minister of Labor), rather than to the parties. In many respects these boards serve the purpose of *enhanced mediation*. In general, the processes employed are the same as for mediation.

disputes inquiry board

Work Stoppage

Nothing is more destructive to a school district than a teachers' strike. Teachers understand this and have successfully used this fact as a *weapon* in negotiations. Provincial and local politicians know this also and have successfully lobbied in some provinces for anti-strike legislation. The point must also be made that strikes are a divisive matter among the rank-and-file of the teaching force. Employers know this. On balance, Canadian teachers are not prone to strike and probably because of the centralized strength found in teachers' associations, the *wild cat* teacher strike (walkout) is virtually unheard of as well. Sometimes the bargaining process is protracted, with plenty of *name calling* but almost always a settlement is finally reached.

strikes

Basic Salary Schedule

The major part of the salary schedule sets forward the provisions for direct compensation.

A teacher's basic pay is determined by his/her placement on a negotiated salary grid. The grid makes provision for two criteria:

a. years of education (university and teacher preparation); and

b. years of teaching experience (steps).

A schedule such as the one illustrated in Figure 20-1 would provide a salary figure for teachers who, because of their unique combination of experience and training, would find themselves described by one of the seventy-two salary grid boxes. Few new teachers would have less than three years of university, so for them the left side of the grid would be meaningless; however several older staff members (trained in an earlier era) may be at the maximum step of levels two, or three or even level one. For them, the right hand side of the grid is of little immediate personal interest.

experience and training

Other types of salary grids could be based upon level of certificate (also based upon training level) held, and upon the number of years of previous teaching or related experience. Teachers should determine early (for their province of employment) how training and experience are to be verified, and what documents are required by the employer. The salary grid provides the first and most important number in the compensation package, but there are other important clauses which the employee must consider. These are listed later.

Years of University Education

		1	2	3	4	5	6
	0				A		
	1					B	
Years of	2						
Experience	3						C
	4						
	5						
	6						
	7						
	8						
	9						
	10						
	11						

Exhibit 20-1
Prototype Salary Grid

Salary box A on the Salary Grid would indicate the dollar value of the salary of a teacher with no previous teaching experience and a four year degree (including teacher preparation). Salary box B would provide the amount of salary payable to a teacher with five years of university and one year of teaching experience. Grid position C would indicate the salary due a teacher with three years of teaching experience and a Master's degree, or equivalent.

initial placement clause

special placement

Some salary schedules restrict the number of years of previous experience which will be credited toward current salary. These are called *restricted initial placement* clauses. Sometimes special salary provisions are made for specific types of teachers, such as vocational education teachers, special class teachers, student counsellors, and substitute teachers.

Contracts frequently make special provisions (sometimes supplementary salary grids) for administrative and supervisory personal allowances. This holds true only where school administrators and supervisors are part of the bargaining unit (parties to the contract).

Salary agreements usually have a number of clauses related to general leave, leave for further study, illness, attendance at funerals (compassionate leave), attendance to sick children or spouse, maternity leave, paternity leave, adoption leave, temporary leave of absences without pay, and personal leave in extraordinary situations. All of these are important clauses; be sure to read the contract fully and carefully in order to understand the extent of the benefits available. If doubt arises, administrators and members of the teachers' association are helpful sources in providing clarification.

Another grouping of teacher benefits centres around group life insurance, health care, extended health care and hospitalization plans, and dental care plans. New employees will be given the opportunity to "sign up." (Sometimes participation in a plan is a condition of employment; sometimes it is optional.) The new employee should study the costs and benefits attached to the various options available, but as a general rule the premium costs are small because teacher negotiators in the past have been successful in passing the major portion of the financial burden for premiums along to the employer, and because larger groups of insured persons are normally able to obtain more favorable premium rates than are individual policy holders.

Many teacher contracts now include a number of clauses often appearing under the general heading "working conditions." Only after considerable effort have teacher associations been able to convince their employers that the number of hours or work, the number of hours of teaching duties, the number of students per class, the amount of preparation and marking time, and the number of extra-curricular duties, for example, are concerns which belong at the bargaining table and so are not strictly *management's perogatives* as had been argued by the school trustee employers and their administrative staffs.

working conditions

right to manage

Finally, the salary agreement will usually make provision for teacher secondment to the Department of Education, or for the purposes of involvement in teacher education, or teacher association business, or teaching overseas. Standard practice is for the current employer of the seconded teacher to keep that person on the employment roll in order for them to enjoy the benefits of the current salary and *benefits* packages as well as keep their seniority of administrative or supervisory designation. The *second* employer makes an equivalent payment or cash transfer to the permanent employer to cover the attendant costs.

secondment

Conclusion

The purpose of compensation packages (salaries and benefits) is to attract, retain, and motivate a competent staff. This is accomplished by providing incentives—working conditions, motivational devices, monetary and non-monetary rewards. Monetary benefits flow from a *collective* agreement negotiated under controlled conditions. Many of the collateral (fringe) benefits due the teacher are also determined by the process of negotiation. Teachers, because they are entering into a personal contract for professional services, have a responsibility to study and understand the consequences of each clause in the contract – as they would for the many other contracts which they, as individuals, enter into. It is truly a case of *buyer beware*. Teacher, know your contract. Do not rely on others, and if in doubt, seek advice.

Appendix A
Canadian Charter of Rights and Freedoms

Whereas Canada is founded upon principles that recognize the supremacy of God and the rule of law:

Guarantee of Rights and Freedoms

1. *The Canadian Charter of Rights and Freedoms* guarantees the rights and freedoms set out in its subject only to such reasonable limits prescribed by law as can be demonstrably justified in a free and democratic society.

Fundamental Freedoms

2. Everyone has the following fundamental freedoms:

a. freedom of conscience and religion;

b. freedom of thought, belief, opinion and expression, including freedom of the press and other media of communication;

c. freedom of peaceful assembly; and

d. freedom of association.

Democratic rights

3. Every citizen of Canada has the right to vote in an election of members of the House of Commons or of a legislative assembly and to be qualified for membership therein.

4.(1) No House of Commons and no legislative assembly shall continue for longer than five years from the date fixed for the return of the writs at a general election of its members.

(2) In time of real or apprehended war, invasion or insurrection, a House of Commons may be continued by Parliament and a legislative assembly may be continued by the legislature beyond five years if such continuation is not opposed by the votes of more than one-third of the members of the House of Commons or the legislative assembly, as the case may be.

5. There shall be a sitting of Parliament and of each legislature at least once every twelve months.

Mobility Rights

6.(1) Every citizen of Canada has the right to enter, remain in and leave Canada.

(2) Every citizen of Canada and every person who has the status of permanent resident of Canada has the right

a. to move to and take up residence in any province; and

b. to pursue the gaining of a livelihood in any province.

(3) The rights specified in subsection (2) are subject to

a. any laws or practices of general application in force in a province other than those that discriminate among persons primarily on the basis of province of present or previous residence; and

b. any laws providing for reasonable residency requirements as qualification for the receipt of publicly provided social services.

(4) Subsections (2) and (3) do not preclude any law, program or activity that has as its object the amelioration in a province of conditions of individuals in that province who are socially or economically disadvantaged if the rate of employment in that province is below the rate of employment in Canada.

Legal Rights

7. Everyone has the right to life, liberty and security of the person and the right not to be deprived thereof except in accordance with the principles of fundamental justice.

8. Everyone has the right to be secure against unreasonable search or seizure.

9. Everyone has the right not to be arbitrarily detained or imprisoned.

10. Everyone has the right on arrest or detention

a. to be informed promptly of the reasons therefor;

b. to retain and instruct counsel without delay and to be informed of that right; and

c. to have the validity of the detention determined by way of habeas corpus and to be released if the detention is not lawful.

11. Any person charged with an offence has the right

a. to be informed without unreasonable delay of the specific offence;

b. to be tried within a reasonable time;

c. not to be compelled to be a witness in proceedings against that person in respect of the offence;

d. to be presumed innocent until proven guilty according to law in a fair and public hearing by an independent and impartial tribunal;

e. not to be denied reasonable bail without just cause;

f. except in the case of an offence under military law tried before a military tribunal, to the benefit of trial by jury where the maximum punishment for the offence is imprisonment for five years or a more severe punishment;

g. not to be found guilty on account of any act or omission unless, at the time of the act or omission, it constituted an offence under Canadian or international law or was criminal according to the general principles of law recognized by the community of nations;

h. if finally acquitted of the offence, not to be tried for it again and, if finally found guilty and punished for the offence, not to be tried or punished for it again; and

i. if found guilty of the offence and if the punishment for the offence has been varied between the time of commission and the time of sentencing, to the benefit of the lesser punishment.

12. Everyone has the right not to be subjected to any cruel and unusual treatment or punishment.

13. A witness who testifies in any proceedings has the right not to have any incriminating evidence so given used to incriminate that witness in any other proceedings, except in a prosecution for perjury or for the giving of contradictory evidence.

14. A party or witness in any proceedings who does not understand or speak the language in which the proceedings are conducted or who is deaf has the right to the assistance of an interpreter.

Equality Rights

15.(1) Every individual is equal before and under the law and has the right to the equal protection and equal benefit of the law without discrimination and, in particular, without discrimination based on race, national or ethnic origin, colour, religion, sex, age or mental or physical disability.

(2) Subsection (1) does not preclude any law, program or activity that has as its object the amelioration of conditions of disadvantaged individuals or groups including those that are disadvantaged because of race, national or ethnic origin, colour, religion, sex, age or mental or physical disability.

16.(1) English and French are the official languages of Canada and have equality of status and equal rights and privileges as to their use in all institutions of the Parliament and government of Canada.

(2) English and French are the official languages of New Brunswick and have equality and equal rights and privileges as to their use in all institutions of the legislature and government of New Brunswick.

(3) Nothing in this charter limits the authority of Parliament or a legislature to advance the equality of status or use of English and French.

17.(1) Everyone has the right to use English or French in any debates and other proceedings of Parliament.

(2) Everyone has the right to use English or French in any debates and other proceedings of the legislature of New Brunswick.

18.(1) The statutes, records and journals of Parliament shall be printed and published in English and French and both language versions are equally authoritative.

19.(1) Either English or French may be used by any person in, or in any pleading in or process issuing from, any court established by Parliament.

(2) Either English or French may be used by any person in, or in any pleading in or process issuing from, any court of New Brunswick.

20.(1) Any member of the public in Canada has the right to communicate with, and to receive available service from, any head or central office of an institution of the Parliament or government of Canada in English or French, and has the same right with respect to any other office of any such institution where

a. there is a significant demand for communications with and services from that office in such language; or

b. due to the nature of the office, it is reasonable that communications with and services from that office be available in both English and French.

(2) Any member of the public in New Brunswick has the right to communicate with, and to receive available services from, any office of an institution of the legislature or government of New Brunswick in English or French.

21. Nothing in sections 16 to 20 abrogates or derogates from any right, privilege or obligation with respect to the English and French language, or either of them, that exists or is continued by virtue of any other provision of the Constitution of Canada.

22. Nothing in sections 16 to 20 abrogates or derogates from any legal or customary right or privilege acquired or enjoyed either before or after the coming into force of this Charter with respect to any language that is not English or French.

Minority Language Educational Rights

23.(1) Citizens of Canada

a. whose first language learned and still understood is that of the English or French linguistic minority population of the province in which they reside, or

b. who have received their primary school instruction in Canada in English or French and reside in a province where the language in which they received that instruction is the language of the English or French linguistic minority population of the province;

   have the right to have their children receive primary and secondary school instruction in that language in that province.

(2) Citizens of Canada of whom any child has received or is receiving primary or secondary school instruction in English or French in Canada, have the right to have all their children receive primary and secondary school instruction in the same language.

(3) The right of citizens of Canada under subsections (1) and (2) to have their children receive primary and secondary school instruction in the language of the English or French linguistic minority population of a province

a. applies wherever in the province the number of children of citizens who have such a right is sufficient to warrant that provision to them out of public funds of minority language instruction; and

b. includes, where the number of those children so warrants, the right to have them receive that instruction in minority language educational facilities provided out of public funds.

Enforcement

24.(1) anyone whose rights or freedoms, as guaranteed by this Charter, have been infringed or denied may apply to a court of competent jurisdiction to obtain such remedy as the court considers appropriate and just in the circumstances.

(2) Where, in proceedings under subsection (1), a court concludes that evidence was obtained in a manner that infringed or denied any rights or freedoms guaranteed by this Charter, the evidence shall be excluded if it is established that, having regard to all the circumstances, the admission of it in the proceedings would bring the administration of justice into disrepute.

General

25. The guarantee in this Charter of certain rights and freedoms shall not be construed so as to abrogate or derogate from any aboriginal, treaty or other rights or freedoms that pertain to the aboriginal people of Canada including

a. any rights or freedoms that have been recognized by the royal Proclamation of October 7, 1963; and

b. any rights or freedoms that may be acquired by the aboriginal peoples of Canada by way of land claims settlement.

26. The guarantee in this Charter of certain rights and freedoms shall not be construed as denying the existence of any other rights or freedoms that exist in Canada.

27. This Charter shall be interpreted in a manner consistent with the preservation and enhancement of the multicultural heritage of Canadians.

28. Notwithstanding anything in this charter, the rights and freedoms referred to in it are guaranteed equally to male and female persons.

29. Nothing in this Charter abrogates or derogates from any rights or privileges guaranteed by or under the Constitution of Canada in respect of denominational, separate or dissentient schools.

30. A reference in this Charter to a province or to the legislative assembly or legislature of a province shall be deemed to include a reference to the Yukon Territory and the Northwest Territories, or to the appropriate legislative authority thereof, as the case may be.

31. Nothing in this charter extends the legislative powers of any body or authority.

Application of Charter

32.(1) This charter applies

a. to the Parliament and government of Canada in respect of all matters within the authority of Parliament including all matters relating to the Yukon Territory and Northwest Territories; and

b. to the legislature and government of each province in respect of all matters within the authority of the legislature of each province.

(2) Notwithstanding subsection (1), section 15 shall not have effect until three years after this section comes into force.

33.(1) Parliament or the legislature of a province may expressly declare in an Act of Parliament or of the legislature, as the case may be, that the Act or a provision thereof shall operate notwithstanding a provision included in section 2 or sections 7 to 15 of this Charter.

(2) An Act or a provision of an Act in respect of which a declaration made under this section is in effect shall have such operation as it would have but for the provision of this Charter referred to in the declaration.

(3) A declaration made under subsection (1) shall cease to have effect five years after it comes into force or on such earlier date as may be specified in the declaration.

(4) Parliament or a legislature of a province may re-enact a declaration made under subsection (1).

(5) Subsection (3) applied in respect of a re-enactment made under subsection (4).

Citation

34. This Part may be cited as the *Canadian Charter of Rights and Freedoms.*

Cases Cited

1. *Barrett v. The city of Winnipeg* (1891) S.C.R. 19. p. 27.

2. *Beauparlant et al. v. The Appleby Separate School Trustees et al.* [1955] O.W.N. 286. p. 150.

3. *Brophy v. Attorney General at Manitoba* (1894) in Olmstead (1954) 1:316-343. p. 29.

4. *Brost v. Board of School Trustees of Eastern Irrigation School Division No. 44* [1955] 3 D.L.R. 159. p. 147.

5. *Butterworth et al. v. Collegiate Institute Board of Ottawa* [1940] 3 D.L.R. 466. p. 138, 147.

6. *Carmarthenshire County Council v. Lewis* [1955] A.C. 549. p. 143.

7. *Chabot v. School Commissioners oofLamorandière* (1957) Que. Q.B. 707 (C.A.) p. 33.

8. *Christian Brothers Canadian Supreme Court Cases* (1875-1906). p. 33.

9. *Donald v. Hamilton Board of Education* [1944] 4 D.L.R. 227; [1945] 3 D.L.R. 424. p. 123.

10. *Dunbar v. British Columbia School District No. 71* (1989) Doc. V. CA008589(B.C.C.A.).

11. *Dziwenka et al. v. The Queen in Right of Alberta et al.* (1971) 25 D.L.R. (3d) 12. p. 148.

12. *Earnest v. College of Physicians and Surgeons of Saskatchewan* (1954) C.C.P. 538. p. 294.

13. *Edmondson v. Board of Trustees for the Moose Jaw School District No. 1* (1920) 55 D.L.R. 563. p. 145.

14. *G.H. et al. v. Board of Education of Shamrock School Division No. 38 of Saskatchewan* [1987] 3 W.W.R. 270. p. 127.

15. *Gard v. Board of School Trustees of Duncan* [1946] 2 D.L.R. 441. p. 138.

16. *Gray et al. v. McGonegal and Trustees of Leeds and Lansdowne Front Township School Area* (1949) 4 D.L.R. 344; O.R. 749; O.W.N. 127; (1950) 4 D.L.R. 395; O.R. 512; O.W.N. 475; (1952) 2 D.L.R. 161; 2 S.C.R. 274. p. 147.

17. *Hutt et al. v. Governors of Haileybury College et al.* (1988) 4 T.L.R. 623. p. 124.

18. *James v. River East School Division No. 9* (1976) 64 D.L.R. (3d) 338. p. 142.

19. *Johnson v. Ryall* (1989) 76 Newfoundland and P.E.I.R. p. 121.

20. *Lamphier v. Phipos* (1838) 8 C. & P. 475. p. 284.

21. *Lavoie v. Nova Scotia* (1989) 47 D.L.R. (4th). p. 586.

22. *LeBlanc v. Board of Education of the City of Hamilton* (1962) 35 D.L.R. (2d) 548. p. 35.

23. *Mahe v. Alberta* (1990) 3 W.W.R. p. 97.

24. *Maher v. Town of Portland* (1974) In Wheeler (1896) 338-367. p. 25.

25. *Mainville v. Ottawa (City) Board of Education* (1990) 75 O.R. (2d). p. 315.

26. *Mallet v. Clarke* (1968) 70 D.L.R. (2d) 67. p. 294.

27. *Marchand v. Simcoe (County) Board of Education* (1986) 61 O.R. (2d). p. 651.

28. *McCarthy v. City of Regina and Regina Board of Public School Trustees* (1917) D.L.R. 32:741. p. 34.

29. *McKay v. Board of Govan School Unit No. 29* (1967) 62 D.L.R. (2d) 503 rev'd (1968) 68 D.L.R. (2d) 519, [1968] S.C.R. 589. p. 148.

30. *Moodejonge et al. v. Huron County Board of Education et al.* (1972) 25 D.L.R. (3d) 661, p. 142.

31. *Moorhouse v. University of New South Wales* (1974) 23 F.L.R. 112. p. 177.

32. *Myers et al v. Peel County Board of Education et al.* (1981) 123 D.L.R. (3d) 1. p. 148.

33. *Ottawa Separate School Trustees v. City of Ottawa* (1917) A.C. 76. 32 D.L.R. 10. 30 D.L.R. 770 (1916) 24 D.L.R. 497. p. 36.

34. *Pander v. Town of Melville* (1922) W.W.R. (1923) 3. 53. p. 37.

35. *Pook et al. v. Ernesttown Public School Trustees* [1944] 4 D.L.R. 268. p. 145.

36. *Poulton et al. v. Notre Dame College et al.* (1957) 60 D.L.R. (3d) 501. p. 153.

37. *R. v. Burko* [1968] 3 D.L.R. (3d) 330. p. 126.

38. *R. v. Cook* (1983) 37 R.F.L. (2d) 93. p. 163.

39. *R. v. Hildebrand* (1919) 3 W.W.R. 286. p. 33.

40. *R. v. Elmer Wiebe* (1978) 36-62. p. 33.

41. *Re Blainey and Ontario Hockey Association* (1986) O.R. (2d) 54. p. 513.

42. *Re Zylberberg et al. and Director of Education of Sudbury Board of Education* (1986) 25 C.R.R. 193. p. 123.

43. *Ramsden v. Hamilton Board of Education* [1942] 1 D.L.R. 770. p. 147.

44. *Renaud v. Board of Trustees of R.C. Separate School Section 11 in the Township of Tilbury North* (1934) O.W.N. 218 (1933) 3 D.L.R. 172 (1933) R.R. 565. p. 34.

45. *Renaud and others* (1873) 14:273-300. p. 34.

46. *Schade et al. v. Winnipeg School District No. 1 et al.* (1959) 28 W.W.R. 577. p. 150.

47. *Schmidt v. Calgary Board of Education and Alberta Human Rights Commission* (1975) 6 W.W.R. 279 (1975) 57 D.L.R. (3d) 746 (1976) 6 W.W.R. 717. p. 35.

48. *Sleeman v. Foothills School Division* (1946) 1 W.W.R. 145. p. 139.

49. *Storms v. School District of Winnipeg No. 1* (1963) 41 D.L.R. (2d) 216. p. 144.

50. *Thornton, Tanner et al. v. Board of School Trustees of School District No. 57 (Prince George) et al.* 5 W.W.R. 240. p. 132.

51. *Tuli v. The Board of Trustees of the St. Albert Protestant Separate School District No. 6* (1987) 8 C.H.R.R. D/3906. p. 125.

52. *Walton v. Vancouver Board of School Trustees* [1924] 2 D.L.R. 387. p. 150.

53. *Ward v. Board of Blaine Lake* [1971] 4 W.W.R. 161. p. 124.

References

One

References Cited

Department of Justice, Canada. (1986). *The constitution acts 1867 to 1982*. Ottawa: Minister of Supply and Services.

Henchey, Norman, & Burgess, Donald A. (1987). *Between past and future: Quebec education in transition*. Calgary: Detselig.

Mifflen, Frank J. & Mifflen, Sydney C. (1982). *The sociology of education: Canada and beyond*. Calgary: Detselig.

Prentice, Alison (1977). *The school promoters*. Toronto: McClelland & Stewart.

Titley, E. Brian, & Miller, Peter J. (1982). *Education in Canada: An interpretation*. Calgary: Detselig.

Other Sources

Gillette, M. (1969). *Readings in the history of education*. Toronto: McGraw-Hill.

Gue, Leslie R. (1985). *An introduction to educational administration in Canada*. Toronto: McGraw-Hill Ryerson.

Johnson, F.H. (1968). *A brief history of Canadian education*. Toronto: McGraw-Hill.

Munroe, D. (1974). *The organization and administration of education in Canada*. Ottawa: Secretary of State.

Phillips, C.E. (1957). *The development of education in Canada*. Toronto: W.J. Gage.

Prentice, A.L., & Houston, S.E. (1975). *Family, school, and society in nineteenth century Canada*. Toronto: Oxford University Press.

Wilson, J.D., Stamp, R.M., & Audet, L.P. (1970). *Canadian education: A history*. Scarborough: Prentice-Hall.

Two

References Cited

Alberta Act. (1905). Acts of the parliament of the Dominion of Canada. Ottawa: King's Printer.

Department of Justice, Canada. (1986). *The constitution acts 1867 to 1982*. Ottawa: Minister of Supply and Services.

Manley-Casimir, Michael E., & Sussel, Terri A. (1986). *Courts in the classroom*. Calgary: Detselig.

Note: Case citations are complete within the body of the text. See also List of Cases Cited.

Other Sources

Bargen, P.F. (1961). *The legal status of the Canadian public school pupil*. Toronto: Macmillan.

Bezeau, Lawrence M. (1989). *Educational administration for Canadian teachers*. Mississauga: Copp Clark Pitman.

Cameron, David M. (1972). *Schools of Ontario.* Toronto: University of Toronto Press.

Clark, Lovel (ed.). (1968). *The Manitoba school question: Majority rule or minority rights?* Toronto: Copp Clark.

Johnson, F.H. (1968). *A brief history of Canadian education.* Toronto: McGraw-Hill.

Olmstead, Richard A. (1954). *Decisions of the judicial committee of the Privy Council relating to the British North America Act, 1867 and the Canadian Constitution 1867-1954.* (3 volumes) Ottawa: Department of Justice.

Titley, E. Brian, & Miller, Peter J. (1982). *Education in Canada: An interpretation.* Calgary: Detselig.

Three

References Cited

Alberta School Act. (1988). Chapter S-3.1 Statutes of Alberta. Edmonton: Queen's Printer.

Ontario Education Act. (1988). Chapter 129, revised statutes of Ontario. Toronto: Queen's Printer.

Other Sources

Bezeau, Lawrence M. (1989). *Educational administration for Canadian teachers.* Toronto: Copp Clark Pitman.

Chalmers, J.W. (1967). *Schools of the foothills province.* Edmonton: The Alberta Teachers' Association.

Johnson, F.H. (1968). *A brief history of Canadian education.* Toronto: McGraw-Hill.

Lam, Y.L. Jack. (Ed.). (1990). *Canadian public education system.* Calgary: Detselig.

Mifflen, Frank J., & Mifflen, Sydney C. (1982). *The sociology of education: Canada and beyond.* Calgary: Detselig.

Munroe, D. (1974). *The organization and administration of education in Canada.* Otttawa: Secretary of State.

Phillips, C.E. (1957). *The development of education in Canada.* Toronto: Gage.

Four

References Cited

Alberta. (1978). *Goals of education.* Alberta Department of Education.

Alberta. (1978). *Goals of schooling.* Alberta Department of Education.

Canadian Teachers' Federation. (1986). *Canadian teachers' federation: Its objectives, its policy.* Ottawa: The Federation.

Downey, Lorne W. (1988). *Policy analysis in education.* Calgary: Detselig.

Ontario Education Act. (1988). Chapter 129, revised statutes of Ontario. Toronto: Queen's Printer.

Other Sources

Brown, A. (1968). *Changing districts in Canada.* Toronto: Ontario Institute for Studies in Education.

Chalmers, J.W. (1967). *Schools of the foothills province.* Edmonton: Alberta Teachers' Association.

Enns, F. (1963). *The legal status of the Canadian school board.* Toronto: Macmillan.

Lam, Y.L. Jack. (Ed.). (1990). *Canadian Public Education System.* Calgary: Detselig.

Monroe, David. (1974). *The organization and administration of education in Canada.* Information Canada.

Five

References Cited

Alberta, Department of Education. (1993). *Meeting the challenge: An education round table workbook.* Edmonton: Queen's Printer.

Ovsiew, Leon, & Castetter, William B. (1960). *Budgeting for better schools.* Englewood Cliffs: Prentice-Hall.

Thom, Douglas J. (1993). *Educational management and leadership.* Calgary: Detselig.

Other Sources

Annual reports and documents on the school support program for the province of employment.

Alexandruk, Fred. (1985). School budgeting in the Edmonton public school district. Unpublished master's thesis, University of Alberta. Edmonton.

Council of Ministers of Education. (1988). *The financing of elementary and secondary education in Canada.* Ottawa: Information Canada.

Candoli, I. Carol, Hack, Walter G., Ray, John R., & Strollar, Dewey H. (1984). *School business administration: A planning approach.* Boston: Allyn and Bacon.

Duncan, D.J., & Peach, J.W. (1977, Fall). School-based budgetting: Implications for the principal. *Education Canada.*

Statistics Canada (most recent available). *Survey of education finance.* Ottawa: Information Canada.

Six

References Cited

Government of Canada, Department of Indian and Northern Affairs, Indian and Inuit Branch, Northern District, Edmonton.

Wilson, J.D., Stamp, R.M., & Audet, L.P. (1970). *Canadian education: A history.* Scarborough: Prentice-Hall.

Other Sources

Bezeau, Lawrence M. (1989). *Educational administration for Canadian teachers.* Toronto: Copp Clark Pitman.

Brown, W.J. (1975). *The impact of federal financial support on elementary and secondary education in Canada.* Ottawa: The Canadian Teachers' Federation.

Daniels, E.R. (1973). The legal context of Indian education in Canada. Unpublished doctoral dissertation, University of Alberta, Edmonton.

Hodgson, Ernest D. (1976). *Federal involvement in public education.* Toronto: Canadian Education Association.

Hodgson, Ernest D. (1988). *Federal involvement in public education.* Toronto: Canadian Education Association.

Tombs, W.N. (1964). An analysis of parliamentary debates on federal financial participation in education in Canada 1867-1960. Unpublished master's thesis, University of Alberta, Edmonton.

Seven

References Cited

Alberta School Act. (1988). Chapter S-3.1 Statutes of Alberta. Edmonton: Queen's Printer.

Department of Justice, Canada. (1986). *The constitutional acts 1867 to 1982.* Ottawa: Minister of Supply & Services.

Ontario Education Act. (1988). Chapter 129, Revised Statutes of Ontario. Toronto: Queen's Printer.

Thom, Douglas J. (1993) *Educational management and leadership.* Calgary: Detselig.*Young Offenders Act.* SC 1980-81-82-83 c110. Ottawa: RSC.

Note: Case citations are complete within the body of the text. See also List of Cases Cited.

Other Sources

Alberta Individual Rights Protection Act, Board of Inquiry. (1987) 8CHRRD3736.

Balderson, J., & Kolmes, J. (eds.) (1983). *Legal issues on Canadian education: Proceedings of the 1982 Canadian school executives conference.* Edmonton: Xancor Canada.

Bala, N., Lilles & Thompson, G.M. (1982). *Canadian children's law.* Kingston: Queen's University.

Bargen, P.F. (1961). *The legal status of the Canadian public school pupil.* Toronto: MacMillan.

Bezeau, Lawrence M. (1989). *Educational administration for Canadian teachers.* Toronto: Copp Clark Pitman.

Canadian Education Association. (1986). *Education and the law.* Toronto: Canadian Education Association.

Enns, F. (1963). *The legal status of the Canadian school board.* Toronto: Macmillan.

Manley-Casimir, Michael E., & Sussel, Terri A. (1986). *Courts in the classroom: Education and the Charter of Rights and Freedoms.* Calgary: Detselig.

McKay, A.W. (1984). *Education law in Canada.* Toronto: Edmond Montgomery.

McCurdy, S. (1968). *The legal status of the Canadian school teacher.* Toronto: Macmillan.

Nicholls, A.C. (1984). *An introduction to school case law.* Vancouver: British Columbia Trustees' Association.

Proudfoot, Alex J., & Hutchings, Lawrence. (1988). *Teacher beware: A legal primer for the classroom teacher.* Calgary: Detselig.

Statutes of the Province of Ontario. (1981). *Human rights code.* Toronto: Queen's Printer.

Wilson, J., & Tomlinson, N. (1986). *Children and the law* (2nd ed.). Toronto: Butterworth.

Eight

References Cited

Anderson, Judith in (1991) *Canadian School Executive.*

Anderson, Judith in (1992) *Canadian School Executive.*

Bargen, P.F. (1961). *The legal status of the Canadian public school pupil.* Toronto: Macmillan.

Prosser, W.L. (1955). *Handbook of the law of torts.* (2nd ed.). St. Paul: West Publishing.

Prosser, W.L. (1971). *Law of torts.* (4th ed.). St. Paul: West Publishing.

Note: Case citations are complete within the body of the text. See also List of Cases Cited.

Other Sources

Dahlen, H.H. (1977). *The doctrine of in loco parentis. Education and the law: Emergence of legal issues.* Saskatoon: University of Saskatchewan.

Klar, Lewis (ed.). (1977). *Studies in Canadian tort law.* Toronto: Butterworths.

LaMorte, Michael. (1986). *School law: Cases and concepts.* Athens: University of Georgia.

Proudfoot, Alex J., & Hutchings, Lawrence. (1988). *Teacher beware: A legal primer for the classroom teacher.* Calgary: Detselig.

Nine

References Cited

Alberta Child Welfare Act. (1984). Chapter C-81 Statutes of Alberta. Edmonton: Queen's Printer.

Alberta Education. (1987). *Child welfare act: Information package.* Edmonton: Alberta Department of Education.

Child and Family Services Act. (1984). Chapter 55. Statutes of Ontario. Toronto: Queen's Printer.

Greenspan, Edward L. (1988). *Martin's annual criminal code.* Aurora, Ontario: Canadian Law Book.

Note: Case citations are complete within the body of the text. See also List of Cases Cited.

Other Sources

Bezeau, Lawrence M. (1989). *Educational administration for Canadian teachers.* Toronto: Copp Clark Pitman.

MacKay, A. Wayne. (1984). *Education law in Canada.* Toronto: Emand-Montgomery.

Manley-Casimir, Michael E., & Newman, B. (1976). Child abuse and the school. 52 *Canadian Welfare* (17).

Proudfoot, Alex J., & Hutchings, Lawrence (1988). *Teacher beware: A legal primer for the classroom teacher.* Calgary: Detselig.

Van Stolk, M. (1978). *The battered child in Canada.* (rev. ed.). Toronto: McClelland & Stewart.

Ten

References Cited

Copyright Act (Bill C-60) (Bill S-8). Ottawa: House of Commons of Canada.

Other Sources

Canadian Bookseller Association. (1986). *Copyright compliance.* Toronto: The Association.

Flint, M.F. (1979). *A user's guide to copyright.* London: Butterworth.

Fox, H.G. (1967). *The Canadian law of copyright and industrial design.* Toronto: Carswell.

Herbert, F. (1987). *Photocopying in Canadian libraries.* Ottawa: Canadian Library Association.

Hopkins, R. (1987, Oct.). Copyright: Complexities and concerns. *Canadian Library journal.*

Proudfoot, Alex J., & Hutchings, Lawrence. (1988). *Teacher beware: A legal primer for the classroom teacher.* Calgary: Detselig.

Torno, Barry. (1981). *Ownership of copyright in Canada.* Ottawa: Consumer and Corporate Affairs, Canada.

Eleven

References Cited

Alfonso, Robert J., Firth, Gerald R., & Neville, Richard F. (1981). *Instructional supervision.* Boston: Allyn and Bacon.

Blau, Peter, & Scott, W. Richard (1962). *Formal organizations.* San Francisco: Chandler.

Carlson, Richard O. (1964). Environmental constraints and organizational consequences: The public schools and its clients. In Daniel E. Griffiths (ed.) *Behavioral science and educational administration.* Chicago: University of Chicago Press.

Davis, Keith. (1967). *Human relations at work.* New York: McGraw-Hill.

Etzioni, Amitai. (1961). *A comparative analysis of complex organizations.* New York: Free Press.

Hills, Jean R. (1968). *Toward a science of organization.* New York: Free Press.

Hall, Richard H. (1962). The concept of bureaucracy: An empirical assessment. *American Sociological Review 27.*

Hoy, Wayne K., & Forsyth, Patrick B. (1986). *Effective supervision.* New York: Random House.

Hoy, Wayne K., & Miskel, Cecil G. (1987). *Educational adminstration: Theory research and practice* (3rd ed.). New York: Random House.

Jay, Anthony. (1967). *Management and Machiavelli.* New York: Holt, Rinehart & Winston.

Rutter, Michael, Maughan, Barbara, Mortimer, Peter, & Ouston, Janet (1979). *Fifteen thousand hours: Secondary schools and their effects on children.* London: Open Books.

Nevi, C. (1988). The future of staff development. *Journal of staff development.* 9(4).

Parsons, Talcott. (1960). *Structure and process in modern society.* New York: Free Press.

Peters, Thomas J., & Waterman, Robert H. (1982). *In search of excellence: Lessons from America's best run companies.* New York: Harper & Row.

Sergiovanni, Thomas, & Corbally, John E. (eds.). (1984). *Leadership and organizational culture.* Urbana: University of Illinois Press.

Timm, Paul R., & Peterson, Brent D. (1985). *People at work.* (2nd ed.). St. Paul: West Publishing.

Weick, Karl E. (1976). Educational organizations as loosely-coupled systems. *Administrative Science Quarterly.* 21.

Other Sources

Costley, Don L,. & Todd, Ralph. (1987). *Human relations in organizations.* (3rd ed.).. St. Paul: West Publishing.

Kanter, R. (1977). *Men and women of the corporation.* New York: Basic Books.

Newton, Earl, & Knight, Doug. (1993). *Understanding Change in Education.* Calgary: Detselig.

Pugh, D.S., Hickson, D.J., & Hinings, C.R. (1987). *Writers in organization.* Beverly Hills: Sage Publications.

Riecken, Ted, & Court, Deborah. (1993). *Dilemmas in Educationall Change.* Calgary: Detselig.

Twelve
References Cited

Bennis, W., & Nanus, B. (1985). *Leaders: The strategies for taking charge.* New York: Harper & Row.

Blake, R.R., & Mouton, J.J. (1964). *The management grid.* Houston: Gulf Publishing.

Giammattoe, Michael, & Giammattoe, Dolores. (1981). *Forces in leadership.* National Association of Secondary School Principals, Reston VA.

Hersey, Paul, & Blanchard, Kenneth H. (1988). *Management of organizational behavior: Utilizing human resources.* New Jersey: Prentice-Hall.

Hunter, Madeline. (1982). *Master teaching.* El Segundo, CA: Tip Publications.

Lovel, John T., & Wiles, Kimball. (1983). *Supervision for better schools* (5th ed.). Englewood Cliffs: Prentice-Hall.

Kanter, R.M. (1983). *The change masters: Innovation and entrepreneurship in the American corporation.* New York: Simon & Schuster.

McGregor, Douglas. (1960). *The human side of enterprise.* New York: McGraw-Hill.

Olivero, J. (1982, Feb.). *Principals and their inservice needs.* Educational Leadership 39.

Ouchi, William. (1981). *Theory Z.* New York: Avon Books.

Sergiovani, Thomas J. (1987). *The principalship: A reflective practice perspective.* Boston: Allyn and Bacon.

Other Sources

Hunsaker, Phillip, & Alessandra, Anthony J. (1980). *The art of managing people.* Englewood Cliffs: Prentice-Hall.

Glathorn, A., & Newberg N. (1984, Feb.). A team approach to instructional leadership. *Educational Leadership, 41.*

Joyce, B., Hersh, R., & McKibbon, M. (1983). *The structure of school improvement.* New York: Longman.

Martin, Yvonne M., & MacPherson, R.J.S. (1993). *Restructuring Administrative Policy.* Calgary: Detselig.

Newton, Earl, & Knight, Doug. (1993). *Understanding Change in Education.* Calgary: Detselig.

Thom, Douglas J. (1993). *Education management and leadership.* Calgary: Detselig.

Peters, T., & Austin, N. (1985). *A passion for excellance: The leadership difference.* New York: Warner.

Trump, J. (1987, Oct.). Instructional leadership: What do principals say prevents their effectiveness in this role? *National Association of Secondary School Principals.* 71.

Thirteen

References Cited

Costley, Don L., & Todd, Ralph (1987). *Human relations in organizations* (3rd ed.). St. Paul: West Publishing.

Glatthorn, A. (1984). *Differentiated supervision.* Alexandra, VA: Association of Supervision and Curriculum Development.

Hoy, Wayne K., & Miskel, Cecil G. (1987). *Educational administration: Theory, research and practice* (3rd ed.). New York: Random House.

Iaccoca, Lee. (1984). *Iacocca: An autobiography.* Toronto: Bantom.

Martin, Yvonne M., & MacPherson, R.J.S. (1993). *Restructuring Administrative Policy.* Calgary: Detselig.

Peters, Thomas, & Austin, N. (1985). *A passion for excellence: The leadership difference.* New York: Warner.

Peters, Thomas J., & Waterman, Robert H. (1982). *In search of excellence: Lessons from America's best run companies..* New York: Harper & Row.

Peters, Thomas J. (1987). *Thriving on chaos.* New York: Alfred A. Knopf.

Timm, Paul R., & Peterson, Brent D. (1986). *People at work: Human relations in organizations* (2nd ed.). St. Paul: West Publishing.

Rutter, Michael, Maugham, Barbara, Mortimer, Peter, & Ouston, Janet (1979). *Fifteen thousand hours: Secondary schools and their effects on children.* London: Open Books.

Selznick, Philip. (1957). *Leadership in administration.* New York: Harper & Row.

Sergiovanni, Thomas J. (1987). *The principalship: A reflective practice perspective.* Boston: Allyn & Bacon.

Vroom, Victor H. & Yetton, P.W. (1973). *Leadership and decision making.* Pittsburgh: University of Pittsburg Press.

Other Sources

Arnold, Hugh J., & Feldman, Daniel C. (1986). *Organizational behavior.* New York: McGraw-Hill.

Hellriegel, Don, Slocum, John W., Jr., & Woodman, Richard W. (1992). *Organizational behavior* (6th ed.). St. Paul: West Publishing.

Hoy, Wayne K., & Forsyth, Patrick B. (1986). *Effective supervision: Theory into practice.* New York: Random House.

Meggison, Leon C., Mosley, Donald C., & Pietri, Paul H., Jr. (1992). *Management concepts and applications.* New York: Harper Collins.

Myers, Gail E., & Myers, Michele Tolela. (1990). *The dynamics of human communication.* New York: McGraw-Hill.

Robbins, Stephen P. (1991). *Organizational behavior: Concepts, controversies and applications.* Englewood Cliffs: Prentice-Hall.

Schein, Edgar H. (1985). *Organizational culture and leadership.* San Francisco: Jossey-Bass.

Schermerhorn, John R., Jr., Hunt, James C., & Osborn, Richard N. (1991). *Managing organizational behavior* (4th ed.). New York: John Wiley.

Thom, Douglas J. (1993). *Educational Management and Leadership.* Calgary: Detselig.

White, Donald D., & Bednar, David A. (1991). *Organizational behavior: Understanding and managing people at work.* Boston: Allyn & Bacon.

Fourteen

References Cited

Albrecht, J. (1988, Oct.). Educational leadership: A focus on teacher-student interaction. *National Association of Secondary School Principals Bulletin, 72.*

Beach, D.M., & Reinhartz, J. (1989). *Supervision: Focus on instruction.* New York: Harper & Row.

Caldwell, S., & Marshall, J. (1982, Feb.). Staff development – Four approaches described, assessed for practitioner, theoretician. *National Association of Secondary School Principals Bulletin, 66.*

Castetter, William B. (1981). *The personnel function in educational administration* (3rd ed.). New York: Macmillan.

Davis, Keith, & Newstrom, John W. (1989). *Human behavior at work: Organizational behavior* (8th ed.). New York: McGraw-Hill.

Doggett, M. (1987, Mar.). Staff development: Eight leadership behaviors for principals. *National Association of Secondary School Principals Bulletin, 71.*

Doll, Ronald C. (1983). *Supervision for staff development: Ideas and application.* Boston: Allyn and Bacon.

Gleave, D. (1983). Staff development propositions. *Education Canada, 23.*

Goldhammer, Robert, Anderson, R.H., & Krajewski, R. (1980). *Clinical supervision: Special methods for the suupervision of teachers* (2nd ed.). New York: Holt, Rinehart and Winston.

Hoy, Wayne K., & Forsyth, Patrick B. (1986). *Effecctive supervision: Theory into practice.* New York: Random House.

Hunter, Madeline. (1976). *Improved instruction*. El Segundo, California: Tip Publications.

Joyce, B., Hersh, R., & McKibbin, M. (1983). *Effective staff training for school improvement*. The Structure of School Improvement. New York: Longman.

Joyce, B., Showers, B. (1982, Oct.). The coaching of teaching. *Educational Leadership, 40*.

Killioon, J. Huddelston, & Claspell, M. (1989, Winter). People developer: A new role for principals. *Journal of Staff Development, 10*.

Krupp, Judy-Arin. (1987). Mentoring: A means by which teachers become staff developers. *Journal of Staff Development. 8(1)*.

Lovell, John T., & Wiles, Kimball. (1983). *Supervision for better schools* (5th ed.). Englewood Cliffs: Prentice-Hall.

McEvoy, B. (1987, Feb.). Everyday acts: How principals influence development of their staffs. *Educational Leadership, 44*.

Neagley, R.L., & Evans, N.D. (1980). *Handbook for effectivve supervsion of instruction* (3rd ed.). Englewood Cliffs: Prentice-Hall.

Oliva, Peter F. (1989). *Supervision for today's schools*. New York: Longman.

Pfieffer, I.L., & Dunlop, J.B. (1982). *Supervision of teachers: A guide to improving instruction*. Phoenix: Oryx Press.

Rallis, S. & Highsmith, M. (1987, Spring). The myth of the "great principal." *American Educator*.

Sergiovanni, Thomas J., & Carver, Fred D. (1980). *The new school executive: A theory of administration* (2nd ed.). New York: Harper & Row.

Thompson, J. & Cooley, V. (1986, Winter). A national study of outstanding staff development. *Educational Horizons*.

Wiles, Kimball. (1950). *Supervision for better schools*. Englewood Cliffs: Prentice-Hall.

Wood, F., McQuarrie, F., & Thompson, S. (1982, Oct.). Practititoners and professors agree on effective development practices. *Educational Leadership, 40*.

Other Sources

Czarmston, R. (1988, Aug.). A call for collegial coaching. *The Developer*.

Glatthorn, A. (1984). *Differentiated supervision*. Alexandria, VA. Association for Supervision and Curriculum development.

Knowles, M. (1984). *The adult learner: A neglected species* (3rd ed.). Houston: Gulf Publishing.

Martin, Yvonne M., & MacPherson, R.J.S. (1993). *Restructuring Administrative Policy*. Calgary: Detselig.

Whetten, David A., & Cameron, Kim S. (1991). *Developing management skills*. New York: Harper Collins.

Fifteen

Other Sources

Beggs, D.W., & Buffie, E.G. (1967). *Nongraded schools in action: Bold new venture.* Bloomington, IN: Indiana University Press.

Buffie, E.G., & Jenkins, J.M. (1971). *Curriculum development in nongraded schools.* Bloomington, Indiana: Indiana University Press, 1971.

Goodlad, J.I., & Anderson, R.H. (1963). *The nongraded elementary school.* New York: Harcourt, Brace & World.

Glogau, L., & Fessel, M. (1967). *The nongraded primary school.* West Nyack, NY: Parker Publishing.

Hillson, M., & Bongo, J. (1971). *Continuous progress education.* Palo Alto: Science Research Associates, 1971.

Hillson, M., & Hyman, R. (1971). *Change and innovation in elementary and secondary organization.* New York: Holt, Rinehart.

McCarthy, R.J. (1967). *How to organize and operate an ungraded middle school.* Englewood Cliffs: Prentice-Hall.

Miller, R.I. (ed.) (1967). *The nongraded school: Analysis and review.* New York: Harper and Row.

Rogers, E.J. (1976). *Meeting student needs through the levels program and grade weighting.* The Clearing House.

Smith, L.L. (1968). *A practical approach to the nongraded elementary school.* West Nyack, NY: Parker Publishing.

Smith, L.L. (1970). *Teaching in an ungraded school.* West Nyack, NY: Parker Publishing.

Thelan, H.A. (1967). *Classroom grouping for teachability.* New York: John Wiley & Sons.

York, L.J. (1971). *Evaluation of team teaching and children's continuous progress.* Dallas: The Leslie Press.

York, L.J. (1971). *Team teaching as a facilitator of the nongraded school.* Dallas: The Leslie Press.

Sixteen

Other Sources

Barker, Lunn J.C. (1970). *Streaming in the pprimary school.* Slough, Bucks, England: National Foundation for Educational Research in England and Wales.

Borg, W.R. (1966). *Ability grouping in the public schools.* Madison, Wisconsin: Dembar Educational Research Services.

Bouri, J., & Lunn, J.B. (1969). *Too small to stream.* Bucks, England: National Foundation for Educational Research in England and Wales.

Dahllof, U.S. (1971). *Abiltiy grouping, content validity and curriculum process analysis.* New York: Teachers College Press.

Findley, W.G., & Bryan, M.M. (1971). *Ability grouping 1970: Status, impact and alternatives.* Athens, GA: University of Georgia, Center for Educational Improvement.

Findley, W., & Bryan, M. (1975). *The pros and cons of ability grouping.* Bloomington, IN: The Phi Delta Kappa Educational Foundation.

Glogau, L., & Fessel M. (1967). *The nongraded primary school.* West Nyack, NY: Parker Publishing.

Goldberg, M.L., Passow, A.H. & Justman, J. (1966). *The effects of ability grouping.* New York: Teachers College Press, Columbia University.

Hillson, M., & Hyman, R. (1971). *Change and innovation in elementary and secondary organization.* New York: Holt, Rinehart and Winston.

Kelly, D.H. (1975). Traching and its impact upon self-esteem: A neglected dimension. *Education.*

Taxey, P.J. (1975). Heterogeneous subgroups within a classroom. *American Biology Teacher.*

Seventeen

References Cited

Alberta School Act. (1988). Chapter S-31 Statutes of Alberta. Edmonton: Queen's Printer.

Alberta Teachers Association. (1989). Teachers' rights, responsibilities and legal liabilities. *Problems in Education Series, 1-7.*

Calgary Board of Education. (1986). *Policy handbook.* Calgary: The Board.

Knoll, Marcia Kolb. (1987). *Supervision for better schools.* Englewood Cliffs: Prentice-Hall.

Proudfoot, Alex J., & Hutchings, Lawrence. (1988). *Teacher beware: A legal primer for the classroom teacher* Calgary: Detselig.

Schön, Donald. (1983). *The reflective practitioner: How professionals think in action.* New York: Basic Books.

Other Sources

Alberta Teachers Association. (1989-90). *Teacher orientation kit.* Edmonton: The Association.

Carter, Barbara, & Dapper, Gloria. (1974). *Organizing school volunteer programs.* New York: Citation Press.

Hoover, Kenneth H. (1976). *The professional teacher's handbook: A guide for improving instruction in today's middle and secondary schools.* Boston: Allyn and Bacon.

Martin, Jack, & Sugarman, Jeff. (1993). *Models of Classroom Management* (2nd ed.). Calgary: Detselig.

Martin, Ralph E., Wood, George H., & Stevens, Edward W. (1988). *An introduction to teaching: A question of commitment*. Boston: Allyn and Bacon.

Eighteen
References Cited

Alberta Teachers' Association. (1967, 1989). *Member's handbook*. Edmonton: The Association.

Carver, F.D., & Sergiovanni, T.J. (1969). *Organizations and human behavior*. New York: McGraw-Hill.

Corwin, Ronald G. (1965). *A sociology of education: Emerging patterns of class status*. New York: Appleton-Century-Croft.

Flexner, A. (1915). *Is social work a profession? Proceedings of the national conference of charities and correction*. Chicago: Hildmann.

Giusti, Joseph P., & Hogg, H. (1973, Nov.). Teacher status: Practitioner or professional? *Clearinghouse, 48*.

Phi Delta Kappa (1983-84). Evaluation of teaching: The formative process. Bloomington: The Association.

Ryan, K., & Cooper, J. (1980). *Those who can, teach* (3rd ed.). Boston: Houghton Mifflin.

Other Sources

Note: Most provincial associations of teachers have a written history of teaching in their province. Contact the teachers' association in the province of employment for a suggested reading list.

Lieberman, M. (1956). *Education as a profession*. Englewood Cliffs, Prentice-Hall.

Nineteen
References Cited

Doll, Ronald C. (1983). *Supervision for staff development: Ideas and application* Boston: Allyn and Bacon.

Carver, F., & Sergiovanni, Thomas. (1969). Notes on the O.C.D.Q. *Journal of Educational Administration, 1*.

Guest, Robert. (1979 July-Aug.). Quality of work life: Learning from Tarrytown. *Harvard Business Review*.

Hackman J. Richard, & Oldman, Greg R. (1975). Development of the job diagnosis survey. *Journal of Applied Psychology, 60*.

Hertzberg, F., Mausner, B., & Synderman, B. (1959). *The motivation to work* (2nd ed.) New York: Wiley.

Kratzman, A. (1981). *A system on conflict*. Alberta Department of Labor.

Maslow, A. (1954). *Motivation and personality*. New York: Harper & Row.

Ouchi, William. (1981). *Theory Z*. Avon Books.

Raymond, H. Allan. (1916). *Management in the third wave*. Glenview, IL: Scott Foresman.

Rutter, Michael, Maughan, Barbara, Mortimer, Peter, & Ouston, Janet. (1979). *Fifteen thousand hours: Secondary schools and their effects on children*. London: Open Books.

Sparks, D.N., & Hammond, A. (1981). *Managing teacher stress and burnout*. Washington: ERIC Clearinghouse.

Truch, Stephen. (1980). *Teacher burnout, and what to do about it*. Novato, CA: Academic Therapy Publications.

Other Sources

Cedoline, Anthony J. (1982). *Job burnout in public education: Symptoms, causes, and survival skills*. New York: Teachers College Press.

Costley, Don L., & Todd, Ralph. (1982). *Human relations in organizations* (3rd ed.). St. Paul: West Publishing.

Dailey, Robert C. (1988). *Understanding people in organizations*. St. Paul: West Publishing.

Hellrigel, Don, Slocum, John W., Jr., & Woodman, Richard W. (1992). *Organizational behavior* (6th ed.). St. Paul: West Publishing.

Megginson, Leon C., Mosley, Donald C., & Pietri, Paul H., Jr. (1992). *Management: concepts and application* (4th ed.). New York: Harper Collins.

Robbins, Stephen. (1991). *Organizational behavior: Concepts, controversies and applications*. Englewood Cliffs: Prentice-Hall.

White, Donald D., & Bednar, David A. (1991). *Organizational behavior: Understanding and managing people at work*. Boston: Allyn and Bacon.

Twenty

Other Sources

Arnold, Hugh, & Feldman, Daniel C. (1986). *Organizational behavior*. New York: McGraw-Hill.

Castetter, William B. (1986). *The personnel function in educational administration* (4th ed.). New York: Macmillan.

Rebore, Ronald W. (1987). *Personnel administration: A management approach*. Englewood Cliffs: Prentice-Hall.

Weber, L. Dan, Greer, John T., Montello, Paul A., & Norton, M. Scott. (1987). *Personnel administration in education: New issues and new management in human resource management*. Toronto: Merrill.

Index

PRINTED IN CANADA